# Sexual Politics and Narrative Film

*Film and Culture*

*John Belton, General Editor*

# FILM AND CULTURE
*A Series of Columbia University Press*
*Edited by John Belton*

**Sexual Politics and Narrative Film**

# Hollywood
# and
# Beyond

## Robin Wood

COLUMBIA UNIVERSITY PRESS

*New York*

Columbia University Press

Publishers Since 1893

New York   Chichester, West Sussex

Copyright © 1998 by Columbia University Press

Library of Congress Cataloging-in-Publication Data

Wood, Robin

Sexual Politics and narrative film :

Hollywood and beyond  /  Robin Wood

p.   cm.—(Film and Culture)

Includes index.

ISBN  0–231–07604–5 (cloth : alk. paper).

—ISBN  0–231–07605–3 (paper : alk. paper)

1. Motion pictures—Political aspects.

2. Sex roles in motion pictures.  I. Title.  II. Series

PN1995.9.P6W66      1998

791.43'658—dc21      98–3413


∞

Casebound editions of Columbia University Press books are printed on permanent and
durable acid-free paper.

Printed in the United States of America

c 10 9 8 7 6 5 4 3 2 1

p 10 9 8 7 6 5 4 3 2 1

This book is dedicated to the memory of Andrew Britton, student, friend, mentor; the best writer on film in the English language and a major influence on my own work since the mid-1970s. His miscellaneous writings, critical and theoretical, scattered among various and often obscure periodicals, would, collected, amount to a book of incomparable distinction that would be indispensable to any university film course.

Andrew died of AIDS on April 3, 1994. His death was a great personal loss to his many friends, and an incalculable loss to the future of our film culture.

# Contents

# Acknowledgments

Roy Thomas, of Columbia University Press, has been my ideal editor. Nothing in my text has been changed against my wishes; his suggested changes (always to clarify, never to alter, my meaning) have frequently been most helpful, and I have adopted them gratefully; he has shown a perfect understanding of my arguments, my aims, and my politics.

Many of my friends and fellow critics have read sections of the book and discussed them with me, and often this has resulted in minor modifications and corrections. John Belton read the entire manuscript and was most helpful in several instances; Victor Perkins identified the piece of music being played at the concert in *Late Spring* (I had it firmly stuck in my head that it was by Schubert, on what grounds I know not); Brad Stevens noticed more (if very minor) instances of touch in *Tokyo Story* than I had been aware of. Florence Jacobowitz read the chapter on Renoir and caused me to modify my reading of Christine's expressed desire for motherhood; Tony French, in Australia, engaged me in a lengthy correspondence about *Letter from an Unknown Woman* which did nothing to alter my view of that film but a great deal to help me clarify and elaborate my argument. I tried out my ideas on *Mandingo* before an audience of my peers at a seminar in New York's Museum of Modern Art; Robert K. Lightning acted as my respondent and initiated a stimulating and far-ranging discussion. Bill MacGillivray and Rick Linklater have been very supportive, and supplied stills for (respectively) *Life Classes* and *Before Sunrise*.

As has usually been the case with my work, the essays in this book have evolved over a long period from lectures given during university film courses. It always embarrasses me to think how many ideas I may have taken from students in discussion which it is now impossible for me to identify and properly acknowledge; I know it was a student who, at least ten years ago, pointed out to me the detail of the spilled wine in the shot I analyze from *Rules of the Game*. Otherwise, I can only say that talking with students, answering their questions, debating our differences, has always been very important to me.

Certain chapters have appeared in journals (though in every case they have been revised and in some cases extensively). The essay on *Céline and Julie Go Boating* appeared long ago in *Film Quarterly* and is reprinted here with permission; others have appeared in *CineAction*, of which I am a contributing editor, and I have given myself permission to use them in this book (for which in any case they were from the outset intended). The Cinémathèque of Ontario provided a few of the stills (the great majority were purchased by me in stores), and *CineAction*'s admirable designer Bob Wilcox transferred these to disk for me.

By the time this book is published Richard Lippe and I will have celebrated the twentieth anniversary of our life together. He reads everything I write with a keenly critical mind and is never slow to tell me when I go wrong, though overall he is very supportive of my work. But, quite aside from such matters, the sum I owe over the years to our relationship—to his intelligence, patience, sweetness, and generosity—is beyond calculation.

I want to acknowledge the supportiveness, friendship, and generosity of my son Simon and his wife Jan, and their complete and unhesitating acceptance of a gay parent and his lover. The pattern we established of alternating Sunday dinner parties (culminating, usually, in the viewing of a movie) has become an important feature of my life, and I feel very fortunate to have a son who is also one of my best friends.

Finally, I want to acknowledge Max, who died of kidney failure in the late summer of 1997. Max made no direct contributions to the writing of this book—he was, as some would say, "just a cat." But his unfailing affection and companionship over fifteen years has been of great importance to me, and is sorely missed.

# A Note on "Political Correctness"

I fully accept the basic principles of the concept of "political correctness"—antisexism, antiracism, antihomophobia, support of environmentalism, a general commitment to the Left. In fact, I had already accepted them long before I was aware of the term's existence.

I cannot, however, accept what appear to me to be its excesses, especially its attitude to the past, which in its totally dismissive extremes strikes me as both foolish and very dangerous. I have had students in recent classes who reject out of hand (for example) *Gaslight* and *Letter from an Unknown Woman*, on the grounds of "Isn't it terrible that they used to make such films, presenting women as complicit victims?" The suggestion that the films may also present the most stringent analysis and critique of the social/ideological structures that have frequently *made* women complicit victims is never answered, merely ignored.

Political correctness is absolutely necessary today up to the point where it hardens into dogma and produces closed minds; beyond that point it is pernicious.

**Sexual Politics and Narrative Film**

*Film and Culture*

*John Belton, General Editor*

# PART I

## INTRODUCTORY

# CHAPTER I

# Introduction

**I**

This is to be my last book of film criticism. Although I may continue to produce occasional articles, I intend to devote my energies henceforward to writing fiction, my novels representing by no means a break with, but a continuation of, my critical work: they are single-mindedly concerned with sexual politics.

It has been a peculiarly difficult book to write. Some of the reasons for this are inherent in its ambitions (I have never before attempted anything of such scope) and the structural problems that evolved—questions of content, of what to include and what not, of how to organize the complex and heterogeneous material. But the fundamental reason has been quite simply a loss of faith.

I discarded any orthodox religious belief, including belief in a "personal god," in my late adolescence, but I always retained a belief in humanity, its enormous potential, its capacity to evolve and to learn; hence a belief in a possible future. During the past two decades such a faith has become increasingly difficult to sustain. The dominant movement of the civilization of which I'm a reluctant member seems currently to have acquired the overwhelming and irresistible power of a juggernaut, so that attacking it (the only possible creative and life-sustaining response) comes to appear about as effective as pouring a bucket of water into an erupting volcano.

The relentless, seemingly inevitable "progress" of capitalism in its "advanced" stage—the connotations of those words taking on a hideous irony—is destroying on all levels of society every possibility of a creative response to life, sweeping ineluctably on toward the physical destruction

of life itself through the devastation of the planet. The heads of corpora-
tions, the executives, the businessmen, the factory owners, who hold and
manipulate power because they hold and manipulate wealth, hence effectively control the media, care nothing apparently for the future of life on the
planet on which they live, even though it's the future of their own children
and grandchildren, so long as they can continue to amass capital during their
own lifetimes. The right-wing politicians, lacking all true moral sense under
cover of a repressive and discredited traditional "morality," fulfill the function
of sustaining and fostering the perpetuation and growth of that government
by the rich and for the rich which they hypocritically call "democracy." The
collapse of communism in Eastern Europe (initially hailed in the West, quite
understandably and to some extent justifiably, as unambiguously positive)
has brought in its wake a spiritually devastating consequence: the much
vaunted "victory of capitalism" (Gorbachev's vision of "socialism with a
human face" having been swept aside as contemptuously in his own country
as in the West, where the grotesque ideological equation of socialism with
Stalinism remains indelibly imprinted in the popular consciousness).

It has become transparently obvious that capitalism is unreformable.
Despite all the "liberal" dismay and warnings, the rich have got richer, the
poor poorer, the environment more polluted, the ozone layer more
depleted. "Global warming" and "the greenhouse effect" are now phrases in
common currency, but by most not taken very seriously: people trot them
out on a hot day, with an uneasy laugh. Telling the powerful wealthy to
behave more decently will have no *effective* result—a small, cheap concession
here and there, a few trees planted in your neighborhood streets to console
you for the devastation of another rain forest somewhere far away. They
don't care; they figure it won't all end in their lifetime, so what the hell, they
can buy bigger properties, bigger meals, bigger vacations, build themselves
bigger and bigger symbolic phalluses, screen themselves off from the hatred
and contempt of general humanity, from the even greater contempt of history (if the race has one to look forward to). The "liberal" position—that
capitalism is capable of reform—has become merely derisory, a mask of illusion and self-deceit with which people shield themselves from their own
despair.

What does it mean, within such a context, to produce yet another book
of film criticism? The undertaking, which I used to find so satisfying, now
appears, at least in my darkest moments (and they have become increasingly
frequent), merely frivolous. But to withdraw from active participation,
although a constant temptation, is no solution either: it starves and frus-
trates one's creative instincts, the source of life whose attempted fulfillment
is the motivation for living.

While carefully resisting the lure of false hope, we cannot simply give up: there is always, as a last refuge, one's self-respect, and to give up is to lose it. The "dominant movement" may appear overwhelming, but struggle still exists and in some ways it is stronger than ever, because better informed, more fully aware of the issues. Even as I write (in March 1997, following my usual practice of saving the introduction for last, when I know what I am introducing), there are daily reports of the growth of protest and revolt, both at home and from all corners of the world. If we can be patient, we may still see a rebirth of the forces for life, as anger and frustration intensify and spread.

If this is to happen, there is one essential prerequisite—the decisive coming together of the various progressive movements (feminism, antiracism, lesbian and gay rights, environmentalism) and their acknowledgment of a common enemy and a common goal. Such a unification will only come about with the rise of a new Left that has this as its central and explicit agenda, combined with a determined effort to reach and galvanize the increasingly oppressed poor, the homeless, the unemployed, and the disaffected and alienated youth. It seems doubtful whether any existing political party in the West is equipped to construct such an agenda and put it into effect: the project involves convincing people that radical change—and not mere piecemeal reform—is necessary, which in turn involves convincing them that it is possible. What is at issue is nothing less than the restructuring, from the base upward, of the entire social structure. The surviving Leftist parties (such as they are) would have to be dismantled and reconstructed from the ground upwards, or an entire new movement arise. The extreme urgency of such a project should be (but apparently isn't) obvious to anyone who opens his or her morning newspaper and can read between, as well as along, the lines.

It is not the job of an arts critic to work out the practicalities of how such a development might come about; that is the task of the political scientist, and of those whose work is in politics. What the arts critic (drawing upon the experience of art past and present as much as upon direct revulsion and rage at what is happening all around us) can do is to define what is necessary, and to produce today a book of responsible criticism is precisely to undertake such a task.

**II**

This book may appear initially to resemble in structure my earlier one, *Hollywood from Vietnam to Reagan*: an assemblage of essays written over a long period, some previously published, whose unity is guaranteed primarily by the fact that they were all written by the same person, hence share a common attitude or viewpoint; beyond which they happened, in the earlier book, to cohere into a partial and selective overview of Hollywood cinema from the mid-sixties through the 1970s and into the early 1980s. Up to a point this is an accurate description. Again, the work contained here should be read as a potentially endless series of probes rather than a wholly coherent thesis.

This is a form (or, if you prefer, a lack of one) that I greatly prefer. I have often heard students remark casually, "European Cinema? I've done that," or "Film and Society? I've done that." I don't want anyone to close this book and think, "Sexual Politics and Narrative Film? I've done that." All I offer is a beginning, or a series of beginnings. Each chapter (or "essay") is in one sense self-contained; they could be read in any order, and it would be possible to read the book in the way in which one "programs" a compact disc, constructing one's own arrangement of the contents. (I should say here that I like the term *essay* for its derivation from the French *essayer*, to attempt: each chapter is, precisely, an "attempt," and, as we know from T. S. Eliot, "Every attempt is a new beginning/And a different kind of failure.")

The new book, however, differs from its predecessor in that it was planned as a whole from the outset, rather than growing into one as I became aware of the interrelatedness of its sections. The chapters that have already appeared in print (mainly in *CineAction*) were written quite knowingly as part of a larger project. That project, however, has taken almost two decades to mature, and has inevitably passed through a considerable evolution—so much so that the original structure that I proposed to myself is almost unrecognizable in the finished work. The original project was for a book exclusively on European filmmakers which would attempt to trace a "progressive tradition" (my provisional title); it was to begin with *Sunrise* and end with *Céline and Julie Go Boating (Céline et Julie Vont en Bateau)*, and that framework is still just detectable (the final chapters being on recent films which seemed to me to demand inclusion). Its structure might now be defined as the movement from the sexual triangle of Murnau's film to that of *The Doom Generation*, or the shift in notions of "romantic love" from *Letter from an Unknown Woman* to *Before Sunrise*.

Various dissatisfactions grew over the years. First, the notion of a progressive *tradition* came to appear artificial: I discovered that the issues I was dealing with were very much more, no less than the traces of a striving toward liberation—toward "life"—in the human race. With this realization came the awareness that there was no reason to limit the book to Europe. Ozu and Mizoguchi were demanding admittance, and I finally found it merely perverse to exclude Hollywood (which I had decided to do for no better reason than that most of my attention as a critic had been concentrated there already). I became particularly worried lest the book fall into the trap of the old outmoded and pernicious opposition: foreign films *equal* art/Hollywood *equals* entertainment. With this, the original intention of preserving a chronological sequence became at once impractical and superfluous, an arbitrary form imposed upon material that constantly pushed against its confines. A radically different form of organization had to be found.

Casting a mental eye over my material—both what was already written and what was still to come—I found that these studies of a wildly heterogeneous, seemingly arbitrary, selection of films from different cultures and different periods had one common thread. One might define this in abstract terms as resistance (taking many forms, working on both conscious and unconscious levels) to the dominant ideological norms, and the very different degrees to which that resistance is successfully defined and worked through. But those ideological norms find their concrete embodiment (and social recognition) in the actualities of their culture: its institutions, its social/sexual arrangements, its methods of containment and repression— the monogamous heterosexual couple, legal marriage, the family, the ideal of sexual fidelity, romantic love, the strict organization of gender and gender roles, homophobia, racism, the horror of miscegenation . . .

The necessary new form became clear: chronology and national division must be abandoned, and the films regrouped in terms of their relation to this or that or the other of various interlocking components of this social/ideological complex. Immediately, the films all fell into place. The groupings remain to this extent arbitrary: a film about the couple may also be a film about the family, a film about romantic love may also be a film about marriage, and so on. But this proves simply what is already obvious, that the categories can never be discrete, they are indeed components of a single more-or-less-unified ideological system. In most cases the dominant concern of the film seemed clear enough, and its attribution followed from that. Certain of the resulting juxtapositions, across time and space, may seem at first jarring, but I hope an inner logic will always become discernible.

Over the past few decades we have gone through a great deal of more or less abstruse theorizing to the effect that narrative itself is somehow inherently conservative, to the point where it seemed that the human race should stop telling itself stories. Hollywood, of course, suffered especially from this, because it had evolved a very particular system of narration which was to varying degrees adopted all over the world. There was one attempt—instigated by feminist critics—to recuperate Hollywood into a progressive ideology, at a price: its products could perhaps be read "against the grain." The attempt deserves credit, at least, for the impulse that motivated it, but the attitude remains insufferably condescending. It is the contention of this book that the great films of mainstream narrative cinema, Hollywood or otherwise, do not have to be "read against the grain"; they simply have to be *read*. Read carefully (and collectively) they point in a single direction toward a single goal, the urgent need for social revolution—a revolution not only in society's material structures but in the structures of our thinking and feeling; in Marxist terms, in both the economic base and the ideological superstructure.

That said, the choice of films for this book remains somewhat arbitrary. I have chosen, overall, to write about films I love, films that on some level or in some way I can identify with. The book could easily have been twice the length, and a number of works I had initially intended for it had to be abandoned: chapters on Buñuel and Pasolini, a chapter on gay cinema, a chapter on *I Walked with a Zombie* to accompany that on *Mandingo*, a chapter on screwball comedy. But there comes a point when one must say, "Enough!"— and if one doesn't, your editor will say it for you. It is my hope that the book's open-endedness will invite readers to add their own examples to its various sections.

**III**

I have referred a number of times over the years to Norman O. Brown's *Life Against Death*. It is twenty years now since I read it, and I feel little impulse to reopen it: it is something of an ordeal to get through, its tortuous and verbose exposition of Freudian theory frequently impenetrable to the uninitiated, its style—clumsy, jargon-ridden, congested—alienating. Yet its premise—the premise implicit in its title, and in which the entire argument is in turn implicit—immediately struck a chord, suddenly crystallizing for me so much of what I had been feeling and (however incoherently) thinking, and its resonance sounds, today, more strongly than ever.

Restated in my own terms, that premise can be summarized as follows: that the human race (for whatever obscure reasons of evolution—economic, social, psychological) has been the battleground for a continuously developing and shifting struggle between the forces for Life (creativity, freedom, spontaneous impulse, joy, love unconstrained by rules or limits) and Death (repression, denial, punishment, prohibition, authoritarianism, mechanization, possessiveness, greed, money values); that this struggle is fought out on every level—the global level of international politics, the local level of the individual national culture, the personal level of the individual psyche, the level of consciousness and the level (above all, perhaps) of the unconscious; that, in our age, with its invention and proliferation of the means of universal destruction (the ultimate strategies of the "Death"-drive), that conflict is swiftly reaching its crisis, the point of decision where the human race must choose whether it is to transform itself or perish, perhaps taking everything else with it. I believe all this to be the case, and find confirmation in the current state of things. I am sometimes terrified and appalled that the choice has already been made. To throw away so much! And for what? For the petty satisfactions of power, domination, possession? Step, even if just for a moment, outside the confines of the dominant ideological system, and the full horror of this becomes apparent. It is not only the human race as it has so far evolved that will be lost, but the incalculable, unpredictable vastness of human potential—for my belief in the reality of human creativity, as the one foundation for what we think of as religious experience, remains as strong as ever.

The Death forces are easier to identify than the Life because they have crystallized into organizations and institutions: religion, at the point where it hardens into dogma; nationalism, at the point where it becomes imperialism; government, at the point where it becomes authoritarian or privileges one group above others—in short, everything that sets nation against nation, class against class, person against person, promoting hostility and competition instead of cooperation. "Religious experience" should never be defined or codified; forms of nationalism are necessary to oppressed or emergent peoples or groups (but to no others); the forms of government that are dominant are the product of religion, nationalism, and class structures, thus are invariably authoritarian, hence oppressive. In the utopia that, even if it proves unattainable, should be our goal, organized religion and nationalism would be superfluous, there would be no more race or class divisions, and the only government would be self-government.

The above will, I hope, forestall the obvious objection to the book's structure: that I have lifted these films out of their specific cultural contexts and have given scant attention to their precise "conditions of production." The struggle with which I'm concerned goes far beyond any local or temporal specificity, and seems to me to render such concerns relatively trivial. It is enough that all the films I deal with were produced within a very wide range of cultures which have in common that they are all both patriarchal and capitalist. Nor is the struggle limited to the twentieth century. It seemed important to extend it backward, although questions of space have precluded many ventures into a past before cinema existed. The fact that I have devoted part of a chapter to the analysis of a Mozart opera will hopefully indicate the possibilities.

✦ ✦ ✦

Finally, what claims do I wish to make, in relation to the above, for this book and for the films with which it deals? As far as the former is concerned, the claims must obviously be very modest. (I speak merely of the book's aims, not of the degree to which they are realized, which is for the reader to judge.) My area of expertise (such as it is) being film, and my experience (intellectual and emotional) being tied to the arts, I can neither engage responsibly with the wider problems that confront us nor provide solutions to them. My concern is with the ways in which the films relate to what we call sexual politics: the organization within our culture of gender and sexuality. My premise is that those "wider problems"—and especially the problem of power and domination—are implicit in the ways in which we relate to each other.

Less modest claims can be made for the films. Whether consciously or inadvertently (and the question of intention will always remain ambiguous), those discussed in the main body of the book expose for analysis all the social/ideological mechanisms which determine our oppression, thereby implicitly establishing the need for their overthrow. In the final section I discuss a few more recent films that go beyond that, suggesting, however tentatively, some of the paths that lead toward liberation.

# CHAPTER 2

# Fascism/Cinema

In a world generally under threat from the human race, the most obvious and immediate danger is the possibility (looking at times dismayingly like a probability) of a resurgence of fascism. The current proliferation of neo-Nazi groups is merely the external symptom; even the more benevolent forms of right-wing ideology are charged with fascist potential, in ways both obvious and subtle, often disguised in terms of "morality" or "family values." If it is misleading to describe the U.S. Republican party (for example) as fascist *tout court*, it is far more dangerous to ignore the possibility of a new fascism developing out of its policies and its mindset. It is the purpose of this chapter to examine, through film, the ways in which the fascist potential is a pervasive presence in Western culture. In fact, the right-wing positions on the topics with which this book is concerned—human sexuality, and the ways it can be restricted, molded, and organized by social institutions such as marriage and family, whose function is the definition of gender roles, the subordination of women, the elimination of sexual diversity—have nowhere been so eloquently (if implicitly) presented as in *Triumph of the Will*. Or, to put it another way: Riefenstahl's film offers an incomparably complete definition of the "death forces" which, if there is to be a human future, the "life forces" must most strenuously oppose.

The juxtaposition of *Triumph of the Will*, Leni Riefenstahl's record of the 1934 Nuremberg rally, and *Night and Fog*, Alain Resnais's documentary on the concentration camps, made twenty years later, offers an appropriate starting point: the "before" and "after" of Nazism vividly commemorated. Whatever one may think of the two films artistically, they are invaluable social documents, in more ways than—in either case—their makers can have intended; their value is greatly enhanced when they are placed side by side. The respective kinds of "art" they represent form an inseparable part of their social/ideological significance—an obvious enough point, but one that tends to get blunted by critics who believe that "art" can somehow be divorced from politics.

I shall not enter into the question of intentionality in Riefenstahl's film on a personal level, the question of whether or not she knew what she was doing: it has been definitively dealt with in Susan Sontag's brilliant essay "Fascinating Fascism." Hitler collaborated by staging the rally partly for Riefenstahl's cameras (and of course by financing the film); it is the product, not of one woman, but of a historical moment, of a specific movement within Western culture. It is not just a film "about" fascism but a fascist film: it celebrates a leader and a party that sought total domination, and it seeks totally to dominate its audience. Every technical and stylistic device is chosen to impose a single, simple, and unquestioned view on the spectator. The opening establishes Hitler as a god descending from heaven through the clouds, bringing "revelation" to Nuremberg and thence to the world; the film culminates in *(a)* Hitler's declaration that God has predetermined the rise and triumph of the Nazi party, and *(b)* the statement that "Hitler is Germany and Germany Hitler." No complexity or freedom of response is permitted at any point: one can only accept or reject the film in toto, as it allows no space for the critical-exploratory movement of thought and imagination. Music (Wagner and nationalist songs) is used purely emotively, as reinforcement; camera angles are ubiquitously dictatorial (low, personally to ennoble some very undistinguished-looking individuals; high, to display the spectacle of the Nazi military machine); the editing is elaborately and insistently rhythmic, reproducing on the formal level the notion of intricate mechanization.

A word must be said about the common "liberal" view of the film as ideologically monstrous but aesthetically irresistible. The following is typical:

> Difficult though it may be for almost any contemporary spectator to divorce himself altogether from attitudes towards the materials out of which the film is made, even such committedly left-wing, dedicatedly anti-Nazi writers as Paul Rotha have had to admit that there is little or nothing Leni Riefenstahl did not know about film-making, that her mastery of editing was comparable with Eisenstein's, and that the film, whatever one's attitude towards its content, does transcend that content and compel one to judge it absolutely as a film.
>
> —JOHN RUSSELL TAYLOR (in *Cinema: A Critical Dictionary*, ed. Richard Roud; Secker and Warburg, 1980)

Faced with such contemptible drivel as this, one hardly knows where to begin: with Taylor's quaint, antiquated notion of what constitutes a "committedly left-wing" writer; with his apparent sense of the *desirability* of the contemporary spectator's divorcing him / herself "altogether" (or to any degree at all?) from "attitudes towards the materials" (in the name of some mystical aestheticism?); with his apparent desire to separate himself from "dedicatedly anti-Nazi writers"; with the notion that Riefenstahl's mechanical textbook editing shows "a mastery . . . comparable to Eisenstein's"; or with the question of how exactly one judges something "absolutely as a film"—or indeed what that might *mean*, in terms of simple sense. Of course, *Triumph of the Will* is a "well-made film": that is, like, for example, *Raiders of the Lost Ark* or *True Lies*, it displays a high level of professional competence (it is possible to think of a number of far more admirable films that don't). In fact, Riefenstahl's camera rhetoric is extremely limited and monotonous: comparison with Eisenstein's emotionally and intellectually complex montage can only be to her great disadvantage, as the most elementary analysis of representative sequences would quickly demonstrate. What is fundamentally objectionable about Taylor's position, however, is its implicit notion of some kind of "absolute" beauty divorced from meaning. The notion of beauty is, on the contrary, always culturally determined: if we develop even the most rudimentary political awareness, it becomes necessary to *choose* the kinds of beauty we support, the kinds of pleasure that we enjoy. The alleged beauty of *Triumph of the Will* is a fascist beauty, centered on dehumanization, mechanization, the drive to domination, militarism. If one does not succumb to the fascist lure, one can only find the film uniformly boring and repellent.

*Night and Fog* (1955) quotes briefly from Riefenstahl's film, and the connection intensifies one's sense of Resnais's film as antidote—obviously enough in terms of content, but also in terms of style. The emotional impact of the material can scarcely not be overwhelming; but Resnais and his writer Jean Cayrol do everything possible to allow the spectator distance and analytical freedom. The film attempts to make it possible to contemplate the unendurable. The achieved distance has the effect, paradoxically, of *increasing* awareness of the appalling nature of what we are shown: instead of being numbed by horrors, the spectator's capacity for thought, imagination, and empathy is given scope and freedom. One is struck here (especially in comparison with Riefenstahl) by the complexity of means and effects within a half-hour documentary. Music is used as counterpoint rather than reinforcement; similarly, the cool, concise narration continuously counterpoints (without undercutting) the emotional impact of the images. The entire film is built on a complex pattern of formal alternations that foreground the medium, so that the sense of actuality is constantly paralleled by an awareness of filmic discourse: present / past, color / black-and-white, moving film / stills, stylized camera movement / authentic newsreel. We are encouraged—up to a certain point—to *think* about what we see. Like fascism itself, *Triumph of the Will* depends upon passivity, upon the readiness to accept, be led, be manipulated, be indoctrinated; *Night and Fog* presupposes and encourages the viewer's active intelligence.

It is easy to surrender to the film in admiration of its achievement, especially when it is seen in Riefenstahl's ominous shadow. Yet the more times I see it (influenced, certainly, by Peter Harcourt's excellent article on Resnais's documentaries in *Film Comment*, Nov./Dec. 1973), the more I am aware of that "certain point," the more I am left at the end with dissatisfaction, even anger. One cannot clearly separate the film's "poetry" from its attempts to create distance; but as it progresses one has a disturbing sense that poetry is being substituted for analysis, that, as much as it is a means of defining a sensitive and civilized attitude to the ultimately appalling, it is also a means of evasion and concealment. It is surely impossible not to be deeply affected by the ending, in which the camp authorities, on trial, from high to low, from commandant to *kapo*, disclaim responsibility, and the film leaves us with the question, "Who, then, *is* responsible?" Yet, unsupported by any effort to analyze the roots and sources of fascism in Western culture (which liberals, perhaps, cannot afford to do beyond "a certain point"—it would bring to consciousness the need for change that goes far beyond the "liberal" mentality), the film is able to avoid suggesting what the answer might be, and indeed suggests (far more dangerously) that there may not be one. In fact, "*Who* is responsible?" is the wrong question; the right one is "*What* is responsible?" What we are so tempted to surrender to may be not so much the film's intelligence and sensitivity as its seductive despair; and despair, while understandable enough as a response to the enormities we have been made to contemplate, is never a very helpful emotion. What the ending leaves us with is liberalism's familiar hands-in-the-air gesture of appalled helplessness: these things have happened before; they will happen (and today are happening) again; they are a part of nature or "the human condition"; there is nothing we can do except try to remember, and memory always fails. The film's position strongly reminds one of Freud's "compulsion to repeat," which he elevated from an accurate clinical observation into a very dubious eternal/metaphysical principle. Michael Schneider comments (in *Neurosis and Civilization*): "like decadent bourgeois philosophers he [Freud] mistook the 'death instinct' of a murderous and suicidal class, the imperialist bourgeoisie, for the 'instinctive nature of man *as such*.' " Resnais and Cayrol repeat the error. It is my purpose here (with these two films as guides or "markers') to suggest the lines along which an analysis of the sources of fascism, and an adequate theoretical opposition to it, might be developed.

✦ ✦ ✦

A dictionary definition offers:

> *Fascism*: Principles and organization of the patriotic and anti-communist movement in Italy started during the 1914–18 war, culminating in the dictatorship of Mussolini, and imitated by fascist or blackshirt associations in other countries.
>
> —*Concise OED*

The dictionary goes on to refer us to the Latin *fasces*:

> Bundles of rods with axe in the middle carried by lictors before high magistrates; ensigns of authority.

The definition (besides establishing that fascism is both theory and practice, "principles and organization') gives us three of its essential components: the emphasis on "patriotism" (which, however its defenders may describe it, always has a habit of slipping over into imperialism); the opposition to communism (which underlines the grotesqueness and opportunism of the phrase "National Socialism")—this at a time long before Soviet communism had hardened into Stalinism under the pressure of the forces of reaction, when the Russian Revolution (whatever its imperfections) might still have been legitimately regarded as inaugurating a movement toward a new, international society based on true liberation and equality; the logical progression toward the enthronement of a supreme authority-figure (Duce, Führer, God). The Latin derivation suggests that, even if the term fascism should *strictly* be applied only to a highly specific twentieth-century movement, product of a certain "advanced" phase of capitalism, its basic impulses and tendencies go right back through human history and are readily apparent around us today; in calling *Triumph of the Will* and *Night and Fog* "invaluable social documents," I had in mind less their illumination of events in another time and another place than the light they can throw on our contemporary cultural situation. "Authority" is clearly the key word: fascism, built on the notion of the right to dominate and exert power over others, backed whenever necessary by force and coercion, simply carries the authority principle to its logical culmination.

Against (or beside) the image of a fascist society, let us place our own. It bears the label "democracy," and is nourished by certain sustaining myths of freedom and equality. Rationally regarded, it can be seen to be built on interlocking structures of power/domination/oppression:

| | |
|---|---|
| rich | poor |
| employers | employees |

| | |
|---|---|
| men | women |
| whites | nonwhites |
| straights | gays |
| adults | children |

In short, there are *potentially* fascist tendencies all around us and within us, in the way we think and feel, in the ways our culture is constructed, ineradicable at the level of the individual because inscribed in the social conditions that largely determine our lives (whatever our personal choices), informing our relationships, both public and private, in our offices, our classrooms, our sitting-rooms, our bedrooms, in our streets and at all levels of government. If we add up the items in the above list, we arrive at the privileged figure of our culture, the white upper- or middle-class adult heterosexual male. Given the conditions of our culture, from its economic base to its ideological superstructure, such a figure is inherently fascist. I speak here, of course, of an ideological construct: it is not impossible for *individuals* to partly transcend it or negate its components (though they can do so only at the risk of a damaging degree of self-consciousness and self-discipline). It is perhaps surprising how many succeed: I can honestly say that some of my best friends are white middle-class adult heterosexual males.

Where did this begin? At that "moment" (or century) in prehistory when the two major foundations of our culture were laid: the institution of private property, and the institution of patriarchy. The two apparently coincided—not, of course, a "coincidence" in the popular sense of the term. The right to private ownership substituting competition for cooperation, and setting human beings against each other in the struggle for possession, seems immediately to have gone beyond the right to own land and objects to include the right to own people: the victor's ownership of captives, the imperialist's ownership of colonies, the master's ownership of slaves, the man's ownership of women (which will continue to be with us until men recognize a woman's right to have other sexual partners, if she wants to). Private ownership brings with it the institutions of marriage, monogamy, the patriarchal family. Have things changed that much? We still talk familiarly of employees as "wage-slaves" and of women as "domestic slaves"; the so-called sexual perversion of sadomasochism simply acts out the implications of the power relations basic to all our cultural institutions.

The fascist society, then, which *Triumph of the Will* gives us a privileged opportunity to examine in detail, simply carries to their logical conclusion many of the tendencies present in the society in which we live and by which we cannot fail to be contaminated. What can one set against it? Clearly, the notion of the "liberated" society. And if we are not yet—and hopefully may not become—a fascist society, we are even further from becoming a liberated one. ("Liberation" must never be confused with "permissiveness," the very name of which implies authority—what is permitted can also be forbidden.) The "liberated society" exists only as a notion, a concept (whereas the fascist society has already achieved various manifestations). It can best be defined in negative terms, as the elimination of all those instances of oppression itemized above. (The still somewhat primitive, but necessary, notion of "political correctness" represents an important step toward this.)

We can learn a lot more about fascism from *Triumph of the Will* than we can from *Night and Fog*: in this way, and in no other, it is a more valuable document. How much of Nazism is actually reflected in Riefenstahl's film?

**The Speeches.** They *say* remarkably little, consisting largely (like the visual "art" of the film) of empty, inflated, vaguely inspirational rhetoric: the Nazi party is "saving" Germany (primarily economically, but also morally and spiritually); patriotism is urged to the point of delirium; "racial purity" (the concept of which *Night and Fog* records the logical conclusion) is essential.

**Dehumanization.** The conversion of instinctual energies into mechanism: the parades, the marches, the goose-step. The film's famous "spectacle" is the spectacle of human beings objectified, mechanized, turned into tiny cogs in a vast machine. The equally celebrated spectacle of the production numbers in Busby Berkeley musicals provides a fascinating parallel/inversion: in Riefenstahl the spectacle is male and active, in Berkeley female and passive (and arguably tongue-in-cheek), but there is the same emphasis on the reduction of human individuals into virtually indistinguishable pieces of a giant mechanism.

**Maleness as Power.** Berkeley gives us women objectified as spectacle for the male gaze. *Triumph of the Will* reduces women to bystanders, whose function is to admire the assertion of phallic power (they are also permitted to appear, as a subordinate part of the spectacle, in peasant costumes exemplifying national tradition). The film insists on its phallic imagery ad nauseam (and, significantly, its defenders as "art" appear to be overwhelmingly male—I have yet to meet a woman who finds it other than loathsome): erect spades, erect weapons, erect flags, stiff legs thrust forward in the goose-step. Throughout this film directed by a woman at Hitler's demand, the phallus is celebrated as the supreme symbol of male dominance, the power of the phallus perversely equated with the power of the machine. (For an alternative role permitted women under Nazism, see the female concentration camp guards of *Night and Fog*—monstrous figures, stereotypically de-feminized.)

**The Indoctrination of Children.** The importance of the conscription of children (especially, of course, *male* children) for the glorious Nazi future is underlined repeatedly in Hitler's speeches and Riefenstahl's imagery. We may compare the indoctrination of children within our culture (we prefer to call it "socialization," a word that should always be profoundly mistrusted): the transmission of the dominant ideology (patriarchy, capitalism) as unquestionable fact and truth. The form this indoctrination takes is of course much less blatant and explicit (arguably, therefore, more dishonest) than the conditioning of the German young as future Nazis: our educational system is dedicated to "teaching children to think for themselves"—within carefully regulated limits. The two great seminal figures of twentieth-century thought, Marx and Freud, have no place within our pre-university curricula, except perhaps as bogeymen.

**Cleanliness/Work.** In *Night and Fog* the slogans inscribed above the concentration camp gates are not "Abandon hope, all ye who enter here," but "Cleanliness is Health" (a phrase our mothers might have taught us) and "Work is Freedom"—values insisted upon, both explicitly and in the visual rhetoric, in Riefenstahl. I shall consider each in turn.

In relation to the camps, the implications of "Cleanliness is Health" are sinister indeed, the cleanliness in question being the purity of the Aryan blood (promoted as different from and superior to any other blood, without the least rational or scientific justification). *Night and Fog* underlines the slogan's hideous irony: what the camps produced was the ultimate filth of rotting human corpses. Cleanliness is established early as a value in Riefenstahl's film: the all-boys-together washing scene with the hoses, our jolly Nazi lads romping around. Subsequently, the ideal of cleanliness aligns itself with militarism and mechanism, the cleanliness of the well-oiled machine. Freud saw the obsession with cleanliness as a mark of sexual repression (for a brilliant cinematic treatment of this, see Ophuls' *The Reckless Moment*), and surely all of us, at some point in our lives, have encountered the notion that "sex is dirty." (In any case it pervades our culture: how else could the word *fuck* be our ultimate "dirty word"?) The real "triumph of the will" is the conversion of sexual energies into the power drive (the subject, treated tragically, of Eisenstein's *Ivan the Terrible*). For an alternative image of health, one might oppose a character from a film made in France the same year as Riefenstahl's: le Père Jules in *L'Atalante*, who lives amid "filth" (the continuously multiplying cats) without a vestige of bourgeois squeamishness, who is totally unrepressed and triumphantly healthy.

As for "Work is Freedom," the vacuousness of the slogan is immediately apparent when we reflect that, under fascism as under democratic capitalism, "work" can only be, for the great majority of the population, alienated labor: the performance of nonpleasurable activities that allow the individual no creative satisfaction, for a motive that has no direct connection with the activities themselves (whether the motive be the acquisition of money or the fulfilment of patriotic duty scarcely matters). It is the necessity of alienated labor under capitalism that demands the high degree of "surplus repression": the degree that Freud saw as already imposing increasingly intolerable burdens on the individual. One must distinguish carefully here between two Freudian concepts that are often popularly confused—*repression* and *sublimation*. Libido (erotic energy) can be successfully and satisfyingly "sublimated" into pleasurable creative activity (which is why the great cultural achievements are always seen, psychoanalytically, as rooted in sexuality). Alienated labor, however, requires *repression* of libido: as the activity is by definition unpleasurable, unfulfilling, and (from any personal viewpoint) noncreative, there is no way in which its performance is accessible through sublimation. The emphasis on work in Hitler's speeches (grounded of course in the long-established and familiar "Protestant work ethic," with its assumption of the moral excellence of work and self-denial—"The devil finds work for idle hands") again underlines the conversion of sexuality into the power drive: the logical slogan would be "Work is Domination."

***The Popularity of Nazism.*** More frightening, perhaps, in their implications than the goose-stepping Nazis are the crowds that cheer them on, the involvement in and endorsement of fascism by "ordinary people": one cannot but relate them to the well-meaning majorities throughout the Western world who currently vote for right-wing governments. "Who is responsible?": on one level, all those honest citizens who "innocently" line the streets to cheer the jackbooted processions, and whose (culpable?) innocence made the concentration camps possible. *What* is responsible is on one level precisely this terrible innocence that has been taught to think no further than next week—the state of ignorance and mystification in which people are kept by our social institutions—politics, the media, the educational system, the nuclear family.

Other components of Nazism are not rendered explicit in Riefenstahl's film but can be "read" through it:

1. *Emphasis on the family*, as the means of perpetuating the race and containing sexuality, through the rigid definition of gender roles. Hence,

**2.** *The subordination of women within the family*: their role as reproducers, their sexual fidelity to their Aryan husbands guaranteeing racial purity.

**3.** *Strict traditional sexual morality*: sex for procreation, hence the channeling of surplus sexual energies into work/cleanliness/militarism.

**4.** *The persecution of gays*, which, throughout history, has always gone hand in hand with the oppression of women ('witches" and "faggots" were burned together at the stake). On the personal level, one can invariably deduce from the way a man treats women what will be his attitude to gays, and vice versa.

Doesn't all this sound frighteningly familiar, and very close to home?

In retrospect from the present, the persecution of gays—alluded to neither by the fascist Riefenstahl in 1934 nor by the liberal Resnais in 1955—assumes a particular significance. It appears to have been, in intention, as systematic as that of the Jews, except that gays—especially at that period of their history, necessarily closeted and with no official stamp on their passports—were much harder to track down (it's remarkable that the Nazis found 300,000, as one estimate has it, though, as they were lumped together with other "social deviants," estimates are inevitably approximate).

The repression of bisexuality (through "socialization") and the oppression of gays are necessary for the perpetuation of heterosexual male dominance, the rule of the symbolic Father, which entails among other things the rigid definition of what is "masculine" and what is "feminine" so that what is designated "feminine" can be subordinated as dependent and inferior, and what is "masculine" celebrated and nurtured. It is through the repression of bisexuality that the heterosexual male is constructed as potential fascist. The social acceptance of bisexuality, gayness, and other forms of what the Nazis termed "social deviancy," would seriously undermine the central unit of our society and the breeding ground of its inherent tendency to fascism, the patriarchal nuclear family. It would also be a crucial step in resolving the current crisis in heterosexual relations, in which women continue to be oppressed but (very inconveniently) *know* it. It is what the fascist mentality supremely cannot tolerate.

We cannot (except as polemical hyperbole) call our current right-wing governments fascist; one can, however, see very plainly the various components of fascism building all over the Western world: the "Moral Majority"; "revivalist" religious groups; the growing strength of overtly fascist organizations (the KKK, Aryan Nation, the National Front); the obsessive emphasis on the Family, and on the need to preserve/defend the traditional morality that supports it; the revival of "the good old values"; the backlash against feminism; the continuing oppression of gays. The concentration camps (though doubtless given other names—"Rehabilitation Centers," perhaps) may not be far away. (You see no clear or conclusive evidence for this? Neither did the German people in 1934.) The question "Who—or what—is responsible?" could be felt to have immediate personal relevance. The world's most powerful nation (and, since the demise of the USSR, its "Evil Empire") is the United States, a "democracy" that currently offers its voters merely a choice between more or less extreme right-wing governments.

As Western culture is pervaded—on all levels, in all its social relations—by fascist tendencies, it is inevitable that these should be reflected throughout its mainstream cinema. The camera rhetoric of *Triumph of the Will*—the concrete expression of a fascist aesthetic—is by no means unique to that film, to Riefenstahl, or to Nazi filmmaking, and it cannot be neatly packaged and put to one side. All the technical devices Riefenstahl employed are common currency in American and European cinema (if seldom concentrated in so rigidified, systematic, and exclusive a form), and they cannot be purged of their connotations of domination and manipulation.

This may sound like the preface to yet another of those blanket denunciations of Hollywood and mainstream narrative cinema; I intend it as exactly the reverse. While patriarchal capitalism continues (and I don't see it ending within my lifetime), the fascist potential will continue with it. Given that fact, it is difficult, perhaps impossible, for us to imagine what a cinema entirely purged of fascist connotations would be like; it could only be a cinema of deprivation. Perhaps domination and manipulation are inherent, to some degree, in *any* concept of "form" or "structure." The reader might like to consider whether, and to what extent, the present book escapes this. I have tried, by developing a structure that is loose and in some ways arbitrary, to leave plenty of spaces for the active play of intelligence, argument, dissent, but I cannot but be aware that I am also trying to enforce (an ugly, but I'm afraid accurate, word) agreement, to *convince* people. I see this as a tension, or contradiction, within the book, inherent in its project. The cinema that I am interested in is not one that attempts to transcend or eliminate the basic structures and conflicts of our culture, but one in which they are dramatized, made visible: to dramatize something inevitably involves reproducing it, but not inertly. Many films *merely* reproduce, and thereby reinforce, but there are also many—the interesting ones, the complex ones, the distinguished ones—that, in reproducing the social and psychic structures of our culture, also subject them to criticism. I shall glance briefly at the ways in which fascist impulses are dramatized in the work of two of the great Hollywood masters, Ford and Hitchcock.

John Ford's "historical" westerns are explicitly concerned with domination: the subjugation of the "Indian," the elimination of the "lawless," the chaining of the erotic, the subordination of women—in brief, with the multileveled imperialism upon which the history of America was, and continues to be, founded. A frequent characteristic of his work is the "ennobling" low-angle shot so common in *Triumph of the Will*, and, as in Riefenstahl, it is used to give stature to the figure of the charismatic leader, and to dignify and poeticize militarism (those famous images of the cavalry against the skyline). The militarism that is a prominent, at times dominant, thread of the cavalry films actually echoes, thematically, certain moments in Hitler's speeches: the notion that the individual achieves meaning and worth only through the self-abnegation of service, discipline, assimilation into the military group, the patriotic mission. There can be no doubt that such features answer to a powerful impulse in Ford's work, and no one who wishes to defend it should ignore or minimize this. Yet no one familiar with that work will be satisfied with such a description without qualification. The features I have isolated never exist in isolation in the films. They are everywhere qualified by a pervasive sense of defeat and loss, by intimations of resignation and disillusionment, by the emphasis (consistently conflicting with the notion of dignity-through-assimilation) on personal drama, personal sacrifice, personal tragedy; above all, by the continual play of paradox, the seeming commitment to America's "manifest destiny" ironically counterpointed by an awareness of the actual destiny that becomes manifest, of the loss entailed in converting the wilderness into a garden, the sense of desolation and disenchantment which is the final note of *The Man Who Shot Liberty Valance*. Fascist tendencies, that is, are at once inscribed and celebrated in the films (often quite explicitly, in jingoistic speech, the rhetoric associated with the cavalry) and repudiated by them.

The case of Alfred Hitchcock is even more extreme, even more fascinating. His celebrated technique is explicitly dedicated to power and manipulation ("putting the audience through it," "giving the audience emotions"); it is also, because invariably so transparent, the easiest of all cinematic techniques to deconstruct—it seems to *invite* the spectator to be aware of how he/she is being manipulated. His obsession with domination is evident at every level of his films, methodological, stylistic, thematic. The narratives are centered on power struggles, and Hitchcock seems to have seen all human relations in terms of the desire to dominate. One has only to qualify this as "all human relations *under patriarchal capitalism*" to grasp that in this he merely pushes to its logical excess the culture's dominant tendency. At the same time, the films continuously foreground the perverseness, the monstrousness, the destructiveness of the power drive (above all, in their pervasive sense of the *impossibility* of heterosexual relations that are not perverted and sadomasochistic). Characteristically, there comes a moment in the films where spectator identification (the mainstay of Hitchcock's domination of his audiences) is abruptly broken and everything is called into question: the moment in *Rear Window* when the audience sees what the protagonist doesn't; the "premature" revelation in *Vertigo*; the shower murder in *Psycho*. The Hitchcock villain (Uncle Charlie in *Shadow of a Doubt*, the U-boat commander in *Lifeboat*, the Nietzschean murderer of *Rope*, Bruno Anthony in *Strangers on a Train*) characteristically dramatizes fascist tendencies and is presented as at once fascinating, perverted, monstrous, and ultimately self-destructive, his seductive "potency" revealed as, at another level, impotence. So, while the domination impulse pervades Hitchcock's work at every level, the films are not fascist films: rather, they are films in which fascism is presented, dramatized, exposed, and dismantled. This is one of the major sources of their value.

## Three Addenda

### War Crimes

The popular notion of how to deal with the legacy of Nazism appears to be the tracking down, prosecution, and punishment of war criminals. While I sympathize strongly with, and respect, the impulse behind this, I remain somewhat skeptical about its efficacy. Certainly it satisfies the desire for revenge and punishment (who doesn't want to "beat the shit" out of those responsible?); beyond that, it is supposed to stand as a deterrent (the argument put forward also in favor of capital punishment), and to keep the memory of the camps alive—claims that I find somewhat dubious. There are two reasons for my skepticism. (I should make clear, however, that I certainly believe that war criminals should be exposed, their crimes made public, their responsibility known to the world, their families, their friends, their next-door neighbors.)

First, I am troubled by the fact that war criminals always seem to be on the "other" (losing) side. Do we have none on "ours"? When the atomic bomb was dropped on Hiroshima, it must have been clear to everyone concerned that most of the able-bodied young men were away in the armed forces, and that the city was populated largely by women, children, and the elderly. To my doubtless simple mind this appears to be a "war crime" of great magnitude, of an unsurpassable inhumanity and horror. Should not all those concerned, from the highest to the lowest, have been prosecuted and punished according to their place in the hierarchy and degree of responsibility? But this has not happened, nor, as far as I know, has it even been suggested.

But the fundamental reason for my skepticism is that I think the punishment of war criminals may work primarily as giving a sense of satisfaction ("Well, we've dealt with that") which may actually be counterproductive. I believe in personal responsibility only up to a certain point: that is why I think the question should be, not who, but *what* is responsible. The punishment of war criminals may have the effect of distracting us from the fundamental factors that make fascism possible—which, as I have tried to argue, I see as endemic to all patriarchal capitalist cultures. It is the *structures* (economic, social, ideological, psychological) of our society that have to be changed (which is what this entire book is about), and, while the task is dismayingly daunting, we have to confront it and allow nothing to distract us from it.

## In Praise of Stuart Marshall

The analysis I find lacking in *Night and Fog* is attempted, at least partially, by Stuart Marshall in a far lesser known and little celebrated documentary, *Desire*. There are perhaps two reasons for this neglect. Marshall's film does not have the self-consciousness of itself as a work of art that Resnais's has, frequently employing the conventional documentary method of "talking heads" (which *Night and Fog* scrupulously avoids)—though it is scarcely lacking in "art," notably in the rhythms of camera movement and editing, and in its use of music. And it is centrally concerned with the Nazi persecution of gays, often regarded as, at best, of secondary importance (it only is if one thinks in terms of numbers, not implications). Although a feature-length film widely available on video, it is listed neither in Leonard Maltin's *Movie and Video Guide* nor in its chief rival, the Martin and Porter *Video Movie Guide*. Its neglect might be felt to send a clear message: "Gays are not important."

Subtitled "Sexuality in Germany, 1906–1945," the film is of enormous interest seen in relation to *Triumph of the Will*. Without at any time pretending to be comprehensive, it traces one of the major sources of fascism from its gestation to its full development and consequences: the cult of nature (with its roots much earlier in German Romanticism) leading to the emphasis on health, exercise, a highly specific form of physical beauty; the rural health camps, where patriotic feeling was nourished along with the development of the perfect Aryan body, and where the sexes were segregated; the constant stimulation of same-sex attraction through the physical proximity of bodies and the encouragement of mutual admiration, accompanied always by the assumption that homosexual love was unnatural; the rigorous control over gender roles (while women were encouraged to be strong, healthy, and physically active, their destiny as future mothers was never in doubt). No one could have foreseen that all this "nature," all this health, all this beauty, all this celebration of nationalism, innocently perceived as the noblest of ideals, would lead eventually and logically to the concentration camps.

Clearly, through its explications by academics interspersed with surviving archival footage, the film presents a thesis, but it is far more than a tract. Above all, Marshall's intelligent and sensitive use of music raises it to the level of a deeply disturbing and moving elegy: the music of Schubert (who was gay) and Mahler (who was Jewish)—both, therefore, artists who, had they lived in the Nazi era, might well have become its victims. The use of the slow movement of Schubert's C Major String Quintet is particularly apposite: when he composed it he knew he was dying of syphilis, a rough nineteenth-century equivalent for AIDS as it was transmitted sexually and then incurable. Marshall himself died of AIDS after making the film.

At the end, Mahler's song "Ich bin der Welt abhanden gekommen" ("I have lost touch with the world . . .") accompanies, without further commentary, a series of shots of the various memorials to concentration camp victims in various countries, culminating in the only memorial to gays, in Amsterdam.

## In Praise of Yo-Yo Ma

I want to end this chapter (which completes the groundwork upon which the remainder of the book rests) by rectifying an elementary but common error arising from the word *liberation*. All too often (especially when used in conjunction with the word *repression*) it is assumed to mean something like "doing whatever you want to do whenever you feel like it." It is not the intention of this book to promote so foolish an idea.

Liberation, as I understand it, is necessary for our culture on every level, at the bottom of which is the level of the individual. An individual who seeks personal liberation within a repressive culture is most likely to end up alcoholic, drug-addicted, obsessed with the pursuit of sex for its own sake, or (as is all too often the case) all three, these being the most obvious and accessible forms of rebellion. "Liberation" implies the overthrow of authoritarianism and the right to make one's own choices, create one's own destiny. It does not imply the negation of self-control and self-discipline.

I propose the cellist Yo-Yo Ma as an exemplary figure. I listen frequently to his two recordings of Bach's suites for unaccompanied cello—works that require for their mastery the utmost in discipline and concentration in which any simple and egoistic notions of selfhood are transcended.

I have returned repeatedly to the earlier recording (1983) over the years, taking it on holidays to listen to in hotel rooms or parks; the new one (1997) arguably improves on it. Ma's technical mastery is now absolute, all of Bach's challenges met with consummate ease. Perhaps more than any other cellist he has discovered the full emotional range of these extraordinary works. Most performers, in my experience, forgivably somewhat in awe of them, make them too uniformly "serious"; Ma rises fully to the solemn and, in some cases, tragic feeling of their slow movements (the sarabandes), but finds elsewhere, at the other end of the spectrum, a captivating playfulness and lightness of spirit. Like certain of the finest works of Stravinsky's maturity (the Wind Octet, the Capriccio, the "Dumbarton Oaks" Concerto), the suites make clear the logical connection between two almost identical terms with very different connotations: the English "spiritual" and the French "spirituel." In Ma's performances this emotional range is contained within an overall mature and *earned* serenity which is perhaps the essential meaning of Bach's music, the quality that makes appropriate the term "religious" without restricting it to the merely denominational.

I also own a copy of the video *Yo-Yo Ma at Tanglewood*, in which he performs with other musicians, mingles with music students, holds master classes, and in which his openness and generosity of spirit, his rich enjoyment of music, of others, of life, shines continuously. Let him stand as a perfect paradigm of the human being in his/her fully creative flowering, from which all taint of the fascist mindset is totally absent.

# PART II

# MARRIAGE
# AND THE COUPLE

# CHAPTER 3

# The Couple and the Other

**I**

## *Sunrise:* A False Dawn

F. W. Murnau's *Sunrise* (1927–28) offers itself as a particularly useful starting point for an investigation into the functioning of sexual politics within narrative cinema, not because it has much to do with liberation (rather the contrary) but because it establishes with great clarity the basic principles of the sexual ideology that has been dominant in Western culture for at least the past century and at the same time unwittingly manifests the tremendous strain involved in their enforcement. A hybrid of German Expressionism and Hollywood convention, it is a reminder that the narrative structures and the ideological assumptions that underpin them belong essentially to the whole of Western culture, whatever their "local" variations and inflections. It is above all as a *synthetic* work that I want to discuss *Sunrise*; though its appropriateness as starting point has the further sanction of its having emerged in first place from a poll of the critics of *Cahiers du Cinéma* to choose the ten greatest films ever made, at that magazine's peak of prestige and influence (1960).

In what ways "synthetic"? I intend the word in its strict sense, but have no objection if its popular connotations creep in. What first strikes one about *Sunrise* is the vast discrepancy between the simple, "archetypal" subject matter and the elaborate art—the conscious and obtrusive artifice—with which it is presented; it is certainly paradoxical that a film so insistently dedicated to concepts of "nature" should be so determinedly (at times one might say laboriously) artificial. The sense of strain, however—the disproportionate labor of the "doing" in relation to what is actually done—is itself inadvertently expressive, an aspect of what the film, as total text not entirely under the control of its makers, wants to say: the strain becomes a commentary on the thematic/ideological project.

Though I want to concentrate on the cinematic aspects of the synthesis *Sunrise* represents, it should also be acknowledged that, in the range and wealth of its artifice, the film approaches (perhaps more closely than any other) that synthesis of the arts envisaged by Wagner. While remaining rooted in theater (actors within a decor, frequently of constructed sets) and the novel (freedom of movement in time and space, privileged access to inner states of mind and emotion), the film has more in common with poetry than with either: its figures are closer to archetypes than to psychologically rounded characters, and it is structured as much on the recurrence, development, and transformation of imagery as on "character development." At the same time, Murnau's background in art and music enriches the film's expressive means with important nonliterary affinities. Murnau's compositions evoke not only Expressionist painting but, somewhat eclectically, much of the European post-Renaissance tradition—the portrait, the still life, the genre painting. And the sensitivity to movement which is perhaps the film's greatest distinction—to the whole complex of filmic potentialities, movements of the actors, movement of the camera, movement of vehicles, the rhythms of editing—continually suggest analogies with music; indeed, the film is subtitled "A *Song* of Two Humans."

The simplest way of demonstrating *Sunrise*'s synthesis of the major potentialities of film that had developed outside the Soviet cinema is to invoke the familiar textbook opposition of Lumière and Méliès: the former's use of film to record an *apparently* authentic (but always highly selective, and never ideologically neutral) "reality," juxtaposed with the latter's emphasis on the "magic" of cinema, the possibilities opened up by technical tricks of editing and superimposition. The copresence in *Sunrise* of tendencies traditionally regarded as opposites is very striking, if not always harmonious. On the one hand, there are the cinematic tricks that testify most obviously to the film's Expressionist heritage, previously exploited by Murnau in *Faust*; on the other, moments of the purest technical simplicity where the camera is set down to record an action from a static position (one of the film's most moving climactic moments, the couple's exit from the church after their symbolic remarriage, with the spectators who are awaiting the real bride and groom automatically forming lines for them to pass between, is a perfect example). One must not, of course, be duped by technical simplicity into any simplistic opposition between artifice and "truth": the scene of the exit from the church is as stylized as anything in the film, with plausibility thoroughly subordinated to poetic symbolism (no one awaiting a bridegroom would mistake for him this unshaven peasant-farmer).

Following André Bazin, it has become customary to play down the Expressionist influence in Murnau's films; this seems the place to reinstate it, as it constitutes an important aspect of the aesthetic/ideological synthesis of *Sunrise*. Bazin's treatment of Murnau (in his seminal and generally indispensable essay "The Evolution of Film Language") is a glaring instance of parti pris: he wishes to enroll him in a Realist tradition that must be systematically opposed to both Eisensteinian montage on the one hand and the "deformations" of Expressionism on the other. We learn that "in neither *Nosferatu* nor *Sunrise* does editing play a decisive part," and are immediately warned against supposing "that the plasticity of Murnau's images has an affinity with a certain kind of expressionism," which would be "a superficial view" (Peter Graham's admirable translation in *The New Wave*). The passage continues:

> The way Murnau composes his images is not at all pictorial, it adds nothing to reality, it does not deform it; rather it strives to bring out the deeper structure of reality, to reveal pre-existent relationships which become the constituents of the drama. Thus, in *Tabu*, the entry of a ship into the left of the screen makes the spectator see it as a metaphor of fate, without Murnau in any way distorting the strict realism of the film, shot entirely on location.

The whole passage is built upon (and collapses over) Bazin's inveterate confusion between Realism as a style (i.e., a choice of one set of cinematic codes over others) and as a means of direct access to "reality." What is this "deeper structure of reality" that Murnau's (alleged) rejection of Expressionism here reveals? Presumably "fate." But "fate" is a philosophical/ideological concept whose claim to explain the nature of existence has scarcely gone unchallenged. Even stylistically, Murnau's decision to frame the shot so that the ship enters the frame from the left is—even while it eschews "special effects," painted sets, superimpositions, etc.—markedly Expressionist in impulse, notions of fate (or doom) being fundamental to the Expressionist ethos and aesthetic. So, in *Sunrise*, is the decision to weight George O'Brien's shoes with twenty pounds of lead, to impose upon him a way of walking that becomes a physical expression of an emotional state. As for the *obtrusively* Expressionist devices in both *Nosferatu* (1922) and *Sunrise*, Bazin simply ignores them, apparently choosing to regard those aspects of the films that don't support his argument as insignificant.

Grounding his aesthetic in the preservation of spatial/temporal reality, Bazin lays great emphasis on the long take and camera movement (the development of which Murnau was closely associated with). But even here, Murnau's achievements often reveal a very marked affinity with the funda-mental principles of Expressionism. Take the justly celebrated shot, totally free of cutting, in which the Man walks into the marshes for his tryst with the City Woman. It begins with the man, back to camera, crossing a bridge (a motif that, like so much else, links the film to *Nosferatu*), with the moon in the top left corner of the frame, a clump of trees in the right foreground, the ground covered in fog. The camera at first tracks with him, then allows him to move away as he circumvents the trees; he then turns and moves for-ward into close-up (the moon disappearing from the image). As he approaches the camera it turns from him and tracks toward some bushes; we assume that the shot has become subjective, that we are now occupying the man's position. We pass through the bushes and find the City Woman waiting, the moon to her right. But instead of looking into the camera she looks off left, expectantly, and begins to adjust her makeup. The rest of the shot is static, the man eventually reentering the frame from the left. According to Lotte Eisner, Murnau had two artificial moons constructed for this one shot. It takes great concentration to figure out consciously that the second moon is in a subtly wrong position, but the subliminal effect may be felt to contribute to the unease and disorientation the shot induces. Far from using the continuous take and moving camera to preserve a strict sense of spatial reality, Murnau is here concerned directly to communicate a state of mind in which all sense of spatial reality dissolves: we lose all sense of ori-entation in relation to the protagonist and the decor, and the shot (supported by the connotations of marshes, darkness, and fog) becomes a metaphorical expression of the man's moral and emotional confusion (as the caption in *Nosferatu* so aptly puts it, "And when he had crossed the bridge the phantoms came forth to meet him").

As for editing, the essential meaning of *Nosferatu* is crucially dependent upon montage (the intercutting of the parallel journeys by sea and land of the vampire and Jonathan, both with each other and with shots of Nina ambiguously awaiting the arrival of her "husband"). The role of editing never achieves quite that level of dominance in *Sunrise* (the level where it becomes indispensable to the film's symbolic structure), but there are sequences where it is decisive to the achieved effect. Take, for example, the scene of the couple's departure for their trip to the city (in the course of which the husband intends to drown his wife), and the use Murnau makes of the family dog. An elaborate buildup establishes the dog as (*a*) intimately connected to the wife and (*b*) the arouser of guilt feelings in the husband; hence, for the audience, the dog is linked to the notion of the woman's safety. Murnau then establishes a series of obstacles separating dog from

*Sunrise:* the Marsh scene (George O'Brien, Margaret Livingston).

woman: the dog is tied to its kennel; the high gate is closed; the husband casts off and rows the boat out into the lake. There then follows a minisequence of three shots that abruptly transforms the scene's rhythm, a sudden accelerando after a gloomy adagio: (1) the dog breaks the rope, (2) the dog leaps over the gate, (3) the dog leaps from the jetty and swims toward the boat. The emotional effect of the scene is created through the pattern of slowly built tension and abrupt release, in which the rhythms of editing are at least as important as action within the frame.

The *kind* of editing (the kind of effect) employed here has, of course, as little to do with Eisenstein as it has with Expressionism (one could adduce parallel examples from the work of Griffith). Although his emphases are seriously misleading and his theoretical basis often confused and mystificatory, Bazin drew attention to important aspects of film in general and Murnau in particular that previous film theory had offered little possibility of dealing with adequately. The third shot cited above is a case in point. Its effect depends on Murnau's decision *not* to cut between dog and boat: both are kept in the frame together, boat in foreground, jetty in background, dog struggling through the water from the latter to the former, so that the precise distance is a visible reality. Further, Bazin's sense that film is ontologically inimical to Expressionism has some arguable theoretical justification. With certain obvious qualifications, we may assume that the camera records the physical reality in front of it. It continues to do so whether that "reality" is an actual location or a painted set. The photographing of Expressionist sets is clearly not a genuine cinematic equivalent for Expressionist painting. The actual equivalents that film offers (focal distortion, special lenses, "special effects") are very limited and mechanical, in contrast to the painter with his brush, paints, and canvas. The reasons why, within mainstream cinema, Expressionism in anything like its pure form has become restricted to occasional subjective, fantasy, or dream sequences may not be *exclusively* ideological. Both Murnau and Fritz Lang moved swiftly away from pure Expressionism, while retaining many traces of its influence, more thematic than stylistic.

*Sunrise*, then, can be seen as synthesizing many of the major, though disparate, tendencies of the cinema as developed in Western culture, those tendencies deriving ultimately from a tradition that far antedates the invention of film. But it is not primarily in terms of an *aesthetic* synthesis that I wish to discuss the film: its usefulness for my purposes lies in its synthesis of ideological assumptions, of cultural myths, that partly transcend both national and class boundaries. Crucial here is another aspect of its hybrid nature: the relationship within it (not entirely harmonious, but impossible without basic compatibilities) between German cinema and Hollywood.

Originally, William Fox (of the studio eventually to evolve into Twentieth Century Fox) invited Murnau to Hollywood in order to bring into the American cinema those stylistic and technical innovations with the development of which his name was associated (the elaborate trick-work of *Faust*, the mobile camera of *The Last Laugh*), and the project was viewed in terms of cultural prestige, bringing "art" to the masses. But Fox seems to have decided at some point that European "culture" required some dilution if "the masses" were to find it palatable. Different versions of the "facts" have been reported, but studio pressure is often regarded as responsible for two modifications in the original concept—the substitution of a happy ending for the tragic-ironic one planned, wherein the husband was to die saving the wife he had intended to murder (although Murnau may already have abandoned this prior to his departure for the United States), and the lightening of tone in the central sections of the film through the addition of "comic relief" (the drunken pig, amongst other items). As a result, the film can be seen as an uneasy marriage, not only of German and American influences but, cutting across this, of "high" and "popular" culture. One might argue that here, at least, artistic failure correlates directly with sociological inter-

After the murder attempt, the husband pleads, the wife cowers
(George O'Brien, Janet Gaynor).

est: the evident strain of integrating the various ideological elements actually foregrounds rather than conceals them.

The alternative endings of *Sunrise* (proposed and actual) appear at first to be diametrically opposite, and not merely in terms of "happy" versus "sad": they imply contradictory metaphysical statements—that "Fate" *can't* be overcome, and that it can, Expressionist doom versus American optimism. In fact, they must be seen as representing national inflections of an all-embracing ideology. Both equally affirm traditional marriage/family as a supreme and unquestionable value. European national cinemas have always been readier to acknowledge the possibility of tragedy—the notion of irreparable loss—within that basic value structure, and in German Expressionist cinema this was strongly compounded by the emphasis on Fate (always adverse and implacable). The insistence on optimism in American culture (the assumption that everyone has the right to the pursuit of happiness hardening into a moral demand that everyone—provided he/she lives within the value system—*must* be happy, that to be otherwise is an insult to the American Way of Life) necessitated the "happy ending" of the classical Hollywood film, a final ideological straitjacket that many directors (especially European émigrés) devoted so much energy and ingenuity to circumventing. The unambiguously pessimistic ending is almost unknown in classical Hollywood: Lang's *Scarlet Street*, perhaps the most startling exception, is predominantly European in conception (French source, German director) and barely survived the strictures of the Production Code. Directors like von Sternberg, Sirk, and Ophuls used various strategies of style and emphasis to produce irony: finding the happy ending a prison for the artist, they manage to suggest that it is also a prison for the characters (see, for example, their treatments of absolutely traditional "family reunion" endings in, respectively, *Blonde Venus*, *There's Always Tomorrow*, and *The Reckless Moment*—all of which have in common the use of bars to signify entrapment). Such strategies produced genuinely subversive texts, in which the ideology is presented critically and ironically (for anyone prepared to view it that way). One must not, however, mistake pessimism for subversion: the proposed tragic ending of *Sunrise* would have left the value system unscathed, and the actual happy ending carries no hint of irony (though the film is inadvertently eloquent about the cost at which it is purchased).

The ideological overlap that makes possible the uneasy union of Germanic and Hollywood elements can be seen most obviously in the two female characters, Wife and City Woman. Although they play such prominent roles (even, in certain scenes, dominant roles, determining the actions of a largely passive male protagonist), neither has any real autonomy: both function exclusively in relation to the Man, the City Woman being there to tempt him, the Wife to save him. It is significant that they never appear together in the same scene: they are not permitted the closeness even of a hostile confrontation. An introductory caption neatly underlines the concept of the marriage-relation: the film is a "Song of *the* man and *his* wife." The Wife, at least, is in traditional terms psychologically comprehensible: she is devoted to her husband and to the preservation of the family. The City Woman, on the other hand, is on that level totally inexplicable: the film sees no need at any point to make her attraction to the hero psychologically plausible (I am thinking here, not in terms of "real life," where anything is possible, but in terms of generic conventions, where the possibilities are rigorously circumscribed).

The two women are to be seen as archetypes rather than "characters" (no major character in the film has a name), and what is fascinating is the way these archetypes cross all boundaries of nationality and high/popular culture. Although in most of Murnau's films the figure who threatens the heterosexual couple is male (*Nosferatu, Tartuffe, Faust, City Girl, Tabu*), the particular female opposition of *Sunrise* has a long history in Expressionist cinema (e.g., the two Marias of Lang's *Metropolis*) and in

European culture generally; it also represents one of the major recurrent structures of the American popular film, appearing within every genre. One can see the opposition in terms of good girl/bad girl, wife/seductress, respectable woman/gun moll, rancher's daughter/saloon entertainer. They all reduce basically to the Mother and the Whore, and the function of the Wife in *Sunrise* is consistently presented in terms of a mother figure, nurturer, comforter, forgiver of sins, culminating in the final "madonna" image, hair spread out over the pillow like the "glory" of a religious icon. The film testifies to the "universality" (within Western culture) of the archetypes, while presenting them, through the extreme stylization, in a particularly stark and clarified form: the women of *Sunrise* embody the two fundamental myths of women within patriarchal society, myths that are the product of the *male* needs that society creates and continuously reinforces.

The film's overall thematic/ideological project (in itself utterly banal, shared with a thousand other films)—the triumphant affirmation of marriage and family through the elimination of the threat embodied by the Other Woman—is to a large extent impressively realized: it is difficult not to be moved by its two climactic moments (the symbolic remarriage, the final domestic reunion). But it is also difficult not to feel that, as a coherent statement, the film is very seriously flawed, its project weakened by a number of demonstrable failures, confusions, and compromises. The most serious problem is its structural eccentricity. The major conflict is resolved about a third of the way through. From the scene of the symbolic remarriage, it is difficult to feel that the City Woman poses any real threat to the couple; by the point where Murnau cuts in a shot of her circling an advertisement in a newspaper (for farmers to sell their land and move to the city), we have virtually forgotten her existence. The constraints of symmetry and closure that characterize classical narrative may be felt to demand a "balancing" return journey, a confrontation with the City Woman, a conclusion in the home (all of which the last part of the film gives us); but dramatically the film feels complete from the moment of the exit from the church.

The result of this is that throughout the long central section—and especially the sequences in the amusement park—the viewer loses all clear sense of where the film is heading and attention is dissipated. The texture noticeably thins: there is little here of the dense poetic imagery that distinguishes the first and third parts. The comic incidents (drunken waiter, drunken pig, slipping dress-strap—the last presumably an *hommage* to Chaplin) might be amusing in another film but in this context produce mainly impatience; they have only the loosest relevance to the thematic structure (they relate vaguely to the country/city opposition, but conspicuously lack artistic necessity). In fact, the artistic failure here is ideologically very interesting. The film is insis-

tently dedicated to an idealization of marriage, but it can affirm that idealization convincingly only in a series of climactic romantic images. The central section demands that we be shown the marriage in its minute-by-minute
operation, and what we get amounts to an admission of defeat.
"Remarried," husband and wife slip instantly into incompatible, ideologically determined, male/female roles (he wants to bowl for the pig, she wants
to dance romantically); Murnau seems able to conceive their supposedly
perfected union only in terms of triviality. Two strategies are employed to
conceal this: (1) *distraction*, in the form of the sudden proliferation of extra-
neous incidents, comic relief, minor characters, etc., and (2) *romantic stylization*, in the form of subjective fantasy-shots (the flowery meadow, the circling cherubs) that are surely the film's worst moments, banal, falsely naive,
and (if taken as representing the visions of "simple countryfolk") condescending. The film can convincingly affirm the value of marriage, in fact,
only when the marriage is in jeopardy, whether from internal threat (the
husband's obsession with the City Woman) or external (the storm); it unwittingly supplies its own commentary on the idealization that is inextricable
from its artistic intensity and distinction. The city/country opposition is one
of the major sources of confusion. The opening caption informs us that
"wherever the sun rises and sets, in country or in city, life is much the same
. . ." and the film proceeds to demonstrate the exact opposite. There is a vast,
unexplained discrepancy between the vision of the city conjured up by the
City Woman in the marshes and the life of the actual city the couple subsequently visit: the former (in keeping with the erotic connotations of the
woman herself) is overwhelming and orgiastic, characterized by a stunning
montage of superimpositions and rapid tracking-shots, and by the violently
sexual movements of the jazz players; the latter could scarcely be accused of
anything worse than triviality. Murnau makes some attempts to connect the
two (imagery of whirling lights and wheels, the manicurist who strikingly
resembles the City Woman), but the overall purpose of the city/country
opposition becomes blurred. Doubtless the paradoxical relationship of the
film to the audience for whom it was made contributes to this. Common
sense tells us that an expensive Hollywood film completed in 1928 was
aimed primarily at an urban audience, and many details confirm this: a lot
of the jokes, such as the business with the Venus de Milo statuette in the
photographer's, or the wife's response to the barbershop manager's farewell
("And *you* must come and visit *us* sometime"), obviously presuppose a "superior" sophistication in the spectator. The tone is not, however, consistently
condescending. Throughout the serious and potentially tragic sections we
are invited to relate to the characters very directly, as "everyman" figures
whose emotional states we can understand and share. At the same time, the

Before reconciliation: the arrival in the city.

film offers its city audience a general sense that country life is somehow better—truer, purer, closer to nature, more authentic—than the city life (trivializing and hectic) which they are, of course, unlikely to forsake. The position the film defines for its spectator is not so much complex as bewildering: the characters represent ourselves, *but* we are superior to them, *but* they are better than us . . .

The central confusion, however, lies in the presentation of the City Woman herself. On the surface, she is the American Vamp (a figure that has, however, strong European affiliations; indeed, the City Woman bears some resemblance to the Louise Brooks of *Pandora's Box*, though without Brooks's innocence). Her clothes, hairstyle, makeup, high-heeled shoes, inconsiderate behavior (disturbing her landlady during dinner with a demand to have her shoes polished), all signify the type of the urban sophisticate of the jazz era. The imagery Murnau associates with her, however, pulls in quite another direction. Very insistently, she is a creature of the night: she appears in only one daytime shot and that is when she is being driven away from the village at the end of the film, vanquished by the sunrise. She is also linked with animals: sleek and dark, her appearance and movements are catlike; she attracts the attention of her mate by whistling for him; subsequently, after the wrecking of the boat in the storm, she is shown crawling out along the branch of a tree overhanging the pathway. She is associated in several shots with the moon, and (since we are certainly forbidden to think here of chastity) the obvious connotations are of witchcraft. She leads the man into the marshes, and is thereby linked to images of fog, mud, darkness, with notions of sinking and contamination. She represents an unbridled eroticism quite unlike the trivial love-play we later see in the city: her wild dance in the marshes contrasts markedly with the ballroom dancing in which the Wife longs to participate. She is sexually overwhelming: at the climax of the love scene in the swamp it is she who lies on top of the man, an image that (in the context of classical Hollywood conventions) carries strong overtones of the perverse, an implication emphasized by the earlier intercutting of the couple's guilty lovemaking with the archetypal innocence of the Wife at home on the bed with the baby. We may recall that the term *vamp* derives from *vampire*.

The City Woman provides the strongest link in *Sunrise* to *Nosferatu*: once the connection is made, the close structural parallels become obvious. Murnau's Dracula, also, is associated with night, animals, contamination, and the erotic; he, too, poses a threat to an "innocent" heterosexual couple; he, too, is vanquished by the rising sun. Like Dracula, the City Woman of the first part of the film becomes a figure of vaguely defined but irresistible power, before whom the male protagonist can only prostrate himself helplessly. Within the Expressionist context, Murnau's films inflect the notion of Fate very differently from Lang's. For Lang, Fate is a complex mechanism whose workings can be analyzed, understood, and defeated (though always at a cost); for Murnau, it is some terrible, implacable, and finally incomprehensible dark force. The helplessness of the hero is one of the most prominent motifs in the overall structure of his work. Its basis becomes clear if we look, by way of contrast, at the most striking exception—his last film, *Tabu* (1931). There, the central recurring structure of Murnau's films is at once repeated and transformed. We find again the couple and the threat to the couple, but the lovers are now completely eroticized, sexuality and innocence no longer seen as irreconcilable, and the threat—here clearly defined in social terms—is the embodiment of the Superego. Matahi is by far Murnau's most active hero, his unsuccessful struggle against the forces of repression giving the final half hour of *Tabu* a tragic urgency and drive unique in Murnau's work. In *Sunrise*—as in *Nosferatu* before it—the destructive forces are those of the Id, and the film becomes itself an enactment of repression, through the process of idealization. That the City Woman is a thoroughly inadequate substitute for Murnau's terrifying vampire—that so

slight a figure cannot possibly sustain the great weight of imagery and symbolic significance with which she is burdened—is but one more of the film's
problems.

The ultimate—and ultimately distasteful—paradox of *Sunrise* is that this
eloquent hymn to home and hearth, heterosexual marriage and family, was
the work of a homosexual. In making this point one is not laying a charge of
hypocrisy, exactly, nor would one wish to place personal blame on Murnau.
When the film was made there was no gay liberation movement, no "gay
consciousness," no public and accessible gay culture, and the male homosexual's central drives were (if acted upon) punishable by law, a situation
powerfully supported by the dominant social myths of homosexuality as
vice or sickness or both. To be homosexual then was to feel oneself to be living in a barren desert gazing longingly at the unattainable mirage of
home/marriage/family. And *Sunrise*, with its idealization and its artifice, has
something of the nature—even the *appearance*—of a mirage. Ostensibly a
hymn to health (as societally conceived), it in fact testifies to the essential
sickness of Western culture.

An act of self-oppression never stops there: it always transforms itself into
the oppression of others. In *Sunrise* evil is defined, not in terms of homosexuality (though that was doubtless for Murnau the root of it), but in terms
of sexuality itself: the erotic is associated with darkness, fog, mud, and "sin,"
and must be forcibly repressed in order that the idealized "holy family" (the
final image is eloquent about the holiness) can be (re-)constructed. That construction further demands the subordination of women and their relegation
to archetypal roles: the asexually "pure" wife/mother who is finally sancti-
fied, the sexually active "evil" woman who must be eliminated from the narrative altogether. Behind the realization of this project is not just Murnau
(though his presence lends it its wish-fulfilling intensity, its artistic distinction, and its ultimate perversity) but the whole tendency of Western culture
(European and American) toward repression and idealization (the two being
aspects of the same process).

*Sunrise* provides marvelous material for studying the process whereby
ideology is universalized, idealized, and naturalized. Universality is insisted
upon from the beginning ("This Song of the Man and his Wife is of no place
and every place . . ."); horse and dog (supported by the cultural myths they
have accumulated) are enlisted as defenders of the nuclear family; the rushes
gathered as an expedient in the plot to murder the wife become the means
of saving her, showing how good is brought forth out of evil with nature as
intermediary. Home, marriage, and family (together with the repression and
role-construction they demand) become emblematic of the law of nature
and the decree of God, cultural assumptions converted into universal and

eternal Truth. It is a question whether the essentially simple ideological structure of *Sunrise* is supported by the massive elaboration of "Art" or collapses under its weight. To whatever degree we may feel that its project is undermined by discernible strains and confusions, it remains after almost seventy years a formidable statement of assumptions central to the development of our culture.

**II**

## *L'Atalante:* **The Limits of Liberation**

To pass from *Sunrise* to *L'Atalante* (1934) is like emerging from a hothouse into fresh air. The two films may at first glance seem too remote from each other in background, atmosphere, ethos, aesthetic for there to be a point in juxtaposing and comparing them. In terms of fundamental narrative concerns, however, they have a surprising amount in common. Both start (admittedly like thousands of other films) from what is arguably the central, if generally unrecognized, problematic of Western culture—the problem of the heterosexual couple. The development of each is precipitated by a threat to the couple (in *Sunrise* the City Woman, in *L'Atalante* Père Jules and subsequently the peddler). Both move toward the elimination or defusing of the threat and the triumphant restoration of the marriage union. Both are structured on similar oppositions: country/city (*Sunrise*), barge life/city (*L'Atalante*). The definition of the couple, the nature of the threat, the process of resolution, all these are markedly different. Behind the differences are not only two strongly contrasted artistic personalities but the cultural traditions of Germany and France respectively and the modernist art movements that developed therein: specifically, we are concerned with the differences between Expressionism and Surrealism.

*L'Atalante* is no more (but no less) a Surrealist film than *Sunrise* is Expressionist, but its relationship to the Surrealist impulse is very strong. There is the evidence of Jean Vigo's own personal commitment to Surrealist art and principles (he wrote a brief but eloquent eulogy of Buñuel's *Un Chien Andalou*). More important is the internal evidence of the film itself. Admittedly, its juxtapositions are always circumscribed by the dictates of "Realism" and its demand for the plausible, yet in image after image, sequence after sequence, the juxtapositions startle the viewer into a new, heightened consciousness: the boy bearing the great tangled mass of creeper with which he intends to greet the bride, looking like a subproletarian nature-god; Juliette on the barge in her bride's dress; the isolated house the barge passes, in which the lights suddenly go on; the astonishing sequence of erotic longing in which the lovers, separated, express their yearning for each other by caressing their own bodies; Jean's hallucination of Juliette, in her bride's dress, under water; all testify to the potent presence of the Surrealist movement as an impulse crucial to the film's energies. Above all, there is Père Jules's cabin, in itself a little domain of the surreal, the marvelous—refuge from an outside world governed by rationalism and the utilitarian.

More generally, the film everywhere expresses the Surrealist commitment to impulse and spontaneity. There are obvious problems with the notion of "spontaneity" in relation to filmmaking (shots have to be set up, the movement of actors rehearsed in relation to the camera, etc.). Yet in terms of degree and effect, *L'Atalante* on all levels manifests a spontaneity of invention that contrasts markedly with the deliberate artifice of *Sunrise*: dramatic incident and incidental "business"; acting and characterization; framing (compositions that seldom look "composed," unself-consciously asymmetrical); camera position and actors' movements (witness, for example, the shot in which Jean crawls along the deck of the barge toward Juliette, first *into* and then *over* the camera); editing (the use of the kinds of jump-cut Godard "invented" nearly thirty years later: it is easy to see why the film was such a favorite with the New Wave, or how it found its high place in the "ten best" list of 1960 topped by *Sunrise*). Many of the cinematic devices and effects are very difficult to justify or explain in terms of academic-traditional "style expresses content" aesthetics: they relate less to the specific "meaning" of the action than to the general fidelity to freedom and impulse. This readiness to surrender to the "spontaneous" is as true to the spirit of Surrealism (with its interest in dreams and automatic writing) as the applied art of *Sunrise* is to that of Expressionism. One should qualify this by noting that such a *degree* of spontaneity became possible only with the advent of sound. The silent cinema's reliance on gesture and facial expression for the communication of meaning (an art that reached its peak in *Sunrise*) demanded acting that was carefully worked out and worked over, with camera positions chosen to serve it.

Expressionism and Surrealism have been too often lumped together as the two great manifestations of the avant-garde in the twentieth century. George Lukacs attacked, and Ernst Bloch defended, both, more or less indiscriminately, as the alternative to Realism. But spiritually, the two are worlds apart. I see little reason to take exception to Lukacs's observation that "the Fascists were not without justification in discerning in Expressionism a heritage they could use"—provided it is taken *as* an observation, not in itself a value judgment. Neither individuals nor movements are necessarily to be blamed for the uses to which posterity puts them. Christ is not to be blamed for the Inquisition, nor Marx for Stalin, and Wagner's *Ring* cycle has quite other, even contradictory, uses than to stand as an apologia for Nazism. The emotions that Expressionism most characteristically expresses—despair, anguish, terror, breakdown, helplessness—are predominantly negative. The Expressionist ethos might help pave the way for Fascism, but it cannot be held responsible for actively producing it; the most one can say is that their sources can be traced to the same set of economic/ideological factors.

One must beware equally, however, of simplistically opposing Expressionism and Surrealism in relation to their potential for Fascist appropriation. Indeed, for all the Surrealists' commitment to notions of liberation and lip service (at least in the early manifestos) to Marx, there are obvious aspects of the Surrealist ethos that might lend themselves *positively* to the right of the privileged individual (indubitably male) to pursue his urges at any price (Buñuel's description of *Un Chien Andalou* as "only a desperate and passionate appeal to murder" should not be taken lightly), combining with the insistent celebration of *masculine* passion and the contemptuous rejection of homosexuality that led to Cocteau's ostracism by the "official" Surrealist group.

The essential difference between the two movements (as manifested in both their writings and their art) lies in their attitudes to the unconscious. Both were heavily indebted to Freud (a much more decisive presence here than Marx): neither movement is conceivable without the theory of repression and the unconscious as a major determinant. But the ways in which "the repressed" is envisaged differ markedly. In Expressionist art the repressed is, characteristically—there are of course exceptions—a terrible dark force (easily assimilable into notions of Fate) whose eruption is irresistible but which, once released, is destructive and uncontrollable: the figure of the vampire in *Nosferatu* can stand as its definitive embodiment. The Surrealists, on the contrary, explicitly welcomed the eruption of the repressed as the undeniable prerequisite to liberation: its very dangers were conceived positively, as the necessary means to the overthrow of bourgeois concepts of "reality," hence of access to the authentic reality they deny. Surrealism, for all its flaws, belongs very clearly to the long and honorable revolutionary tradition in French culture, of which the French Revolution itself, the Paris Commune, the New Wave, and the events of May 1968 are other varied manifestations.

The differences between the characteristic techniques developed within Expressionist and Surrealist painting point to interesting conclusions in relation to the cinema. I argued earlier that film may be to a certain degree inimical to the principles of Expressionism, based on the distortion of appearances. The same is patently not true of Surrealism, which creates its disturbing effects through the incongruous juxtaposition of objects painted with trompe l'oeil exactitude. Yet the incorporation of Surrealism into mainstream cinema has been even more restricted than is the case with Expressionism, which at least proved a fruitful source of subjective effects (see, for example, Hitchcock's *Marnie*) and dream sequences, as well as more generally influencing the styles of certain genres (film noir, the horror film). The incongruous juxtapositions that delighted the Surrealists in Hollywood movies have been either inadvertent or restricted to slapstick comedy (witness their love of Laurel and Hardy); Dali's designs for Gregory Peck's dream in *Spellbound* were modified by the studio and the sequence drastically abridged. If the cinema has relegated Surrealism to the margins of the avant-garde, this has nothing to do with ontological incompatibility and everything to do with ideological threat: mainstream cinema has been dedicated—in its overall assumptions and surface forms—to reinforcing the bourgeois "reality" that the Surrealists committed themselves explicitly to smashing, a project from which their techniques can scarcely be detached for other, less openly subversive, uses.

The treatment of eroticism—hence the definition of the couple—in *Sunrise* and *L'Atalante* relates closely to the conflict between the Expressionist and Surrealist attitudes to the unconscious and, beyond that, to still-warring tendencies within Western culture. Marriage in *Sunrise* is built upon the repression of the erotic. The film makes a few attempts to re-eroticize the couple's relationship after the symbolic remarriage (the secret kiss at the photographer's, the peasant dance), but they remain half-hearted, nullified by their association with a thoroughly sentimental notion of "child-like" innocence which totally misconceives the innocence of children and adults alike. In *L'Atalante*, on the contrary, the marriage itself is founded upon the strong and marvelously communicated charge of eroticism between the couple—the corollary being that Père Jules and the peddler, unlike the City Woman, do not represent exclusively, or even primarily, *erotic* threats. The contrast becomes most vivid if one compares the scene in the marshes in *Sunrise* with the scene in *L'Atalante* already cited, where the couple express their longing for each other when separated. Murnau's imagery associates eroticism with night, fog, mud, and murder; Vigo's (the bodies covered in little shadow-spots like a mesh, a hallucinatory suggestion of an unendurable "itch" which could be purged only by sexual union) triumphantly vindicates the erotic as the source of life, energy, and fulfilment.

The opposition must be qualified by a striking plot dissimilarity: the marsh scene in *Sunrise* is a scene of adulterous lovemaking, whereas in the scene of erotic longing in *L'Atalante* the separated lovers are husband and wife. This serves on one level to strengthen my point: there is no husband/wife scene in *Sunrise* that has anything approaching a strong erotic

*L'Atlante:* honeymoon on the barge (Jean Dasté, Dita Parlo).

charge. On another level, the fact that in *L'Atalante* the eroticism is validated by marriage does produce certain problems, or point to limitations, inherent in the film's project and its realization. In terms of structure, the scene in *L'Atalante* that parallels the marsh scene is not the sequence of erotic long-ing but that between Juliette and Père Jules in the latter's cabin—a compari-son more complex than the one dealt with above, and one to which I shall return.

It is necessary at this point to introduce a digression, but one that will lead, eventually, right back to the heart of *L'Atalante.* Since Christian Metz (in *Film Language*), much work has been devoted to developing the idea of film as *discourse*—the (wholly admirable) aim being resistance to the ideo-logical impositions of "Realism." If a film is a "discourse" (i.e., emanating from a specific and identifiable source), it can no longer be a "window on the world," giving access to a universal/eternal "truth" or "reality." The ques-tion instantly arises, then, *"Whose* discourse?"—to which *auteur* theory (sup-ported by traditional aesthetics) had prematurely proposed a simple answer. No one, I take it, would today attribute a filmic text to a single authorial "voice" existing in a vacuum (although it seems to be undeniable that the individual presence is often—and in distinguished art always—crucial to defining its specificity). The individual discourse is necessarily contained within and complexly determined and constrained by (even while it may subvert) a wider discourse, the discourse of the culture. In *our* culture, the dominant discourse can only be that of patriarchal bourgeois capitalism. This does not mean that all texts are interchangeable, that they all merely reiterate the same discourse. A culture has many voices clamoring for attention, frequently speaking in opposition to each other, arguing both within and against the dominant discourse. One can imagine two poles: to the left, films whose relation to the dominant discourse is purely oppositional and which have totally purged themselves of all contamination by it; to the right, films that limply reiterate it, without producing any disturbances or contradictions whatever. Both poles must be understood as more "Platonic" than real: I don't know of any films that would fully correspond to either, and don't believe such films can exist. The concept, however, allows us to envisage all actual films existing on a continuum between the poles.

I want to focus here on the word *patriarchal*. The cinema has been from the first, and is still, like all our other institutions, overwhelmingly male-dominated. Its dominant discourse is consequently still a male discourse; more precisely, a patriarchal discourse, the discourse of the symbolic Father. Its mechanisms can be analyzed in the general movement of "classical" narrative. The text begins by establishing an order; the order is then disturbed, threatened, even destroyed—the disturbance (dramatized as specific character or relationship conflicts) generally constituting the major part of the fiction; finally, the order is restored—the initial order, or the order improved and strengthened, or (much less frequently) a new order. The order is of course patriarchal, organized in relation to the dominance of the heterosexual male, and typically embodied in marriage and family (think how many films culminate in variations on lines such as "I'll take you home now," "We can go home now," "Let's go home," . . .).

Both *Sunrise* and *L'Atalante* exemplify this structure very clearly. The essential difference is that in *Sunrise* the narrative movement and its resolution are presented—with great show of conviction and weight of art, to be sure—as entirely unproblematic, the enacted values never questioned. When the film opens, the initial order has already been disturbed, but we are given its essence in a brief, one-shot flashback (the plowing scene), when the elderly neighbor/nurse/mother figure talks of the couple's past ("They were like children . . ."). The City Woman (or the return of repressed libido) creates the disturbance and is finally eliminated from the narrative. Though in certain ways that I have indicated the structure of *Sunrise* is extremely problematic, one can argue for the *ideological* necessity of the last part.

Throughout, the husband has been presented as weak and helpless. The wife, on the other hand, is endowed with great *spiritual* strength (in her role as savior—a common strategy of male dominance that at once "ennobles" her, denies her sexuality, and places her in the service of the man). The final section of the film emphasizes the wife's *physical* helplessness: the female savior needs male protection. Her life is saved by her husband's presence of mind in binding her to the rushes as well as by the wise village elder who "knows the tides" and raises her unconscious body into his arms and boat just as she is about to drown. Meanwhile, the husband almost strangles the City Woman, to express his repudiation of everything that cannot be contained within marriage and family. His physical strength (supported by despair and outrage) compensates for his earlier moral weakness. The order restored at the end depends upon the City Woman's withdrawal, both from the village and from the narrative. If we ask what the future holds for the husband—besides plowing his field and tossing his baby in the air—the film overwhelms the question with its fusion of Nature and Religion (the sunrise, the Holy Family). As to what the future holds for the wife, we don't need to ask: she is perfectly content within her prescribed role and function.

The question I wish to raise is of the possibility of a woman's discourse asserting itself—to whatever degree—within the male discourse of mainstream cinema, wherein the overall project has traditionally been one of "placing," of subordination. It is a question that will recur (by implication if not explicitly) in many of the subsequent chapters of this book, and the answer will not always be negative.

In *Sunrise* the women are entirely subordinate to the man, in the sense that they exist only in relation to him. But Juliette is the center of *L'Atalante*. While the film's narrative has so much in common with that of *Sunrise*, in one crucial aspect it inverts it: here, the transgressor is the wife. Relative to the women in *Sunrise*, Juliette is allowed considerable autonomy. During the rare moments in Murnau's film where either woman is shown without the man, she is exclusively preoccupied with him: the wife, abandoned, grieves over the soup; the City Woman, awaiting the man's return from the supposedly murderous excursion, busies herself marking newspaper advertisements for farmers to move to the city. Juliette, on the contrary, is shown repeatedly alone or in the company of outsiders to the marriage, beginning with her moments of solitude on the barge in her bridal dress, already filled with doubts, questioning the marriage. She is allowed interests of her own (albeit stereotypically "feminine" ones—Paris fashions, etc.) and a lively curiosity about and delight in things (the cabin scene). Her desires are not bound by the marriage—at least, not until about two-thirds through the film.

Central to all Vigo's work is the impulse toward liberation. His first short, *Á Propos de Nice*, already combined Marxist, Freudian, and Surrealist thrusts in its attack on the complacent bourgeoisie; *Zéro de Conduite* (*Zero for Conduct*) culminates in a successful (if fantastic) revolution. The subject of *L'Atalante* was not chosen freely; it was a substitute for projects he couldn't get financed. Far from diminishing the film's interest, this in some respects enhances it, though it may also account for its ultimate unsatisfactoriness: the partial recalcitrance of the material foregrounds problems (of narrative, and beyond that of human relationships) that are central to our culture. Vigo's Surrealist derivation and commitment to liberation are here brought to bear on the theme of marriage—the social institution through which the oppression of women has been legalized, ratified, and reinforced. The film tries to achieve an equal balance of interest between the husband and wife. If Juliette moves to its center, that is because she constitutes its problem.

The "order" tentatively presented at the beginning of *L'Atalante* is immediately established in an ambiguous relationship to the dominant orthodoxy. It is important that we are introduced to Père Jules and his youthful sidekick *before* we see the bride and groom and the wedding procession: Vigo is more interested in celebrating the forces of disruption than in analyzing the forces of conformity. The opening images introduce *(a)* the barge, *(b)* industry/commerce (the smoke of a goods train that temporarily obliterates the barge), and *(c)* the church (pillar of the rural community from which Juliette comes). The greater part of the film is concerned with exploring life on the barge, its joys and tensions, seeing there the possibility of an alternative community, an existence relatively untrammeled by the constrictions of established society: a tentative, embryonic version, one might say, of Marcuse's non-surplus-repressive civilization, in which work and play, if not quite identical, move freely and easily into one another, and in which relationships are *potentially* released from the constraints of bourgeois morality, with its rigid roles and rules. But the film acknowledges, both implicitly and at moments explicitly, the barge's necessary ties to capitalist enterprise and to traditional values. If the barge is presented as an escape, not only from a paralyzing rural respectability but also from the horrors of a dehumanized urban proletariat—from both country and city—it is also shown to be dependent upon the commerce between the two.

The procession that follows Jean and Juliette from the church is presented (despite the jolly music from a group of village players) more in terms of a funeral than a wedding. On one level, the community is mourning the loss of Juliette, and her choice of a husband and a life that signally lack the approved signifiers of respectability. On another, the mise-en-scène connects marriage itself to mourning and the repression of impulse. The procession—with everyone dressed in black—consists almost exclusively of couples; the only exception, the man who makes a pass at the woman in front of him, is the only one who shows any spontaneity, and his levity is instantly rebuked. The film's point of departure establishes its central contradiction: it wants to celebrate the barge life as a freer alternative to established society without abandoning the marriage union that is the latter's pillar. To put it another way (with Vigo's commitment to Surrealism and the erotic always in mind), one might describe the film as an attempt to reconcile *l'amour fou* with domesticity.

As with *Sunrise*, the narrative premise of *L'Atalante* far transcends any boundaries of movement or nationality. Many films have established their essential problematic by opening with a wedding and the removal of the bride from the "safe" bounds of a known milieu: one might adduce Ford's splendid, underestimated *Drums Along the Mohawk* (1939), not only for its closely parallel action (secure society, grieving relatives, bride taken away to an altogether more primitive cultural situation to which she must learn to adapt), but because it evokes that peculiarly American genre the western, and a world and ethos as far removed as possible from French Surrealism. What the comparison points to is the strength and "universality" (again, within Western culture) of assumptions about male and female roles: man as adventurer/wanderer, woman as settler/domesticator. The specific cultural/generic context of *Drums* makes it possible for Ford to present Lana (Claudette Colbert) as largely unproblematic: after initial misgivings, she finds a vital role within a new, developing community, which she both enhances and is enhanced by. The sexual problematic of *L'Atalante* is closer, in fact, to that of many of Howard Hawks's adventure films—the introduction of a woman into a hitherto all-male "outsider" group which has already thrived without her and which seems to offer her no obvious or essential place. Yet Hawks continually evaded the problem of *marriage*: his films end with a heterosexual union whose permanency is never guaranteed, and the word "marriage" is never mentioned. The great interest of *L'Atalante* lies in its raising of problems that the cinema has usually side-stepped; one scarcely has the right to demand that it also solve them.

In the first half of the film, Père Jules is crucial to the (dramatic, thematic, ideological) testing of the marriage. Structurally, he corresponds to the City Woman in *Sunrise* (the external force that threatens the marriage by tempting one of the partners); the conception is as different as one can imagine, the final measure of the difference between the two films. Michel Simon's Jules relates clearly enough to his Boudu, in Renoir's admirable film of two years earlier (*Boudu Saved from Drowning*, 1932): both are associated with animals (Boudu with his dog, Jules with his fecundly proliferating cats); both resist bourgeois cleanliness, etiquette, and morality; both are associated with freedom (Boudu specifically with nature—especially in the film's closing minutes—and Jules with travel, the sea, foreign places); both intervene (temporarily) in a marriage. Yet not only the characterization but, more important, the *function* within the total text is subtly different in the two films, and the difference defines what separates Vigo from Renoir, for all their areas of compatibility. Boudu often (and Jules never) resembles an overgrown, rather cuddly child, presocialized and presexual (or at least prephallic): he has never kissed anyone but his dog, and when he suddenly becomes Mme Lestingois' enthusiastic and potent lover the audience is even more surprised than she is. Jules's sexuality, on the other hand, is never in the least ambiguous (at least as regards potency and experience). Boudu's intrusion into the Lestingois household never poses a serious threat to it. The affectionate/comic-satirical tone makes it possible for Renoir (and the viewer) not to take the constraints, repressions, and frustrations of the Lestingois marriage very seriously (indeed, the film's charm—not a word one would use of *L'Atalante*—very much depends on that). If there is little sense that Boudu might genuinely liberate the Lestingois couple, that is because Renoir cannot quite bring himself to believe that they really need it. The ending suggests that it is a pity Boudu can't be incorporated into the household, but that it will nevertheless continue without much harm done. Boudu, simultaneously, becomes translated to a symbolic level (the spirit of freedom, the spirit of nature): the implication seems to be that he represents something inextinguishable which (suitably tamed and modified) will somehow inform all human existence. The film is a prime example of that tendency in Renoir toward some kind of canceling out, a tendency derived from his attractive (and seductive) propensity for seeing good in all things (". . . everyone has his reasons"); a tendency, moreover, countered in his greatest films by more disturbing levels of awareness and perception (the quotation actually begins, "There's one thing in life that is terrible, and that's that . . ." etc.). Where Renoir's best work lends itself readily to radical appropriation, Vigo's *is* radical: Père Jules can be rendered harmless only at the cost of considerable violence to the narrative development.

The radical seriousness and complexity of the threat Jules poses reaches its fullest statement in the cabin scene, which occurs almost exactly halfway through and from which the film never recovers. I suggested earlier that—given the basic narrative patterns available within Western culture—the scene is the structural equivalent of the marsh scene in *Sunrise*, the scene in which one of the marriage partners is tempted toward the realization of desires that would destroy the union. In *Sunrise* the nature of the temptation is very simple—the man's erotic desire for a voluptuous, *vampire* woman.

*L'Atalante* never presents Jules as a possible alternative lover for Juliette (or anybody), though their relationship is not devoid of directly erotic overtones (before Jean's ultimate eruption into destructive fury, Jules is lying prone over her on the bunk, laughing lasciviously, without apparent protest on her side). But the temptation Jules represents is of an altogether different order—more complex and ideologically far more dangerous. The City Woman is a direct threat to the wife (murder her, live with me); Jules implicitly threatens the entire structure of patriarchal capitalism.

What, then, does Jules actually represent? With the cabin scene specifically in mind, one can specify the major components:

*Living at ease with "dirt."* Juliette's initial attempt to establish a role for herself on the barge takes the form of playing the good bourgeois housewife and doing the washing, with Jules reluctantly relinquishing his underwear. The film offers no sense that this accomplishes anything very beneficial. Jules is presented as perfectly robust, healthy, and happy. The "dirt" amid which he lives suggests his ability to embrace without squeamishness the basic physical conditions of existence: he can't understand Juliette's disgust that one of his cats has given birth to kittens in her bed (his reaction being

Père Jules in his cabin (Michel Simon).

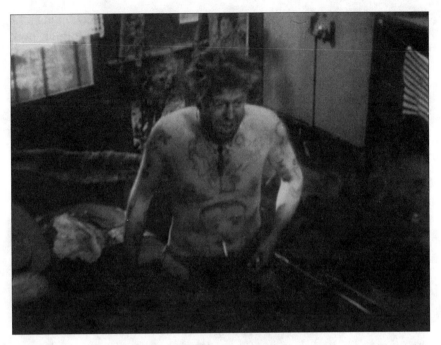

Jules displays his tattoos.

to deny paternity). Freud links the obsession with cleanliness (especially among bourgeois housewives) to sexual repression, both of oneself and of others (a perception marvelously developed by Ophuls in *The Reckless Moment*). Jules's ease with "dirt" represents a direct slap in the face to Protestant bourgeois values, where "cleanliness is next to godliness." ('Godliness" is summarily dealt with at the film's outset, in the wonderful moment when Jules, as an afterthought, dashes back into the church, splashes himself with holy water, and pronounces the couple man and wife). In fact, Jules never appears unsanitary; when he removes his clothes to show Juliette his tattoos, his body looks firm, clean, and healthy.

**Blood and pain.** In order to demonstrate to Juliette the use of a native knife, Jules casually slices across his open palm and licks the blood, showing no response to Juliette's exclamations that he has hurt himself or to her offer to get bandages. There is nothing remotely masochistic about the action, nor does it reflect any animus against the human body: quite the reverse. Jules's ease with physicality can embrace the realities of blood and pain without flinching: what's a cut here or there? Similarly with the jar of pickled hands: there is no trace of morbidity in Jules's attitude to this souvenir of his dead friend. On the contrary, it implies a thoroughly healthy, accepting attitude to death. The film at no point suggests that Jules lingers morbidly over this memento, or uses it as some kind of fetish: the friend was part of his life, and now that he's dead his hands are part of the decor.

*Playing with patriarchy.* Have you heard of Jane Glover? Or of Sian Edwards? I have the former's recordings of Haydn's "Paris" symphonies on CD and find them greatly superior to the much-praised recordings by Leonard Bernstein (no need to ask if you've heard of *him*). And I have the latter's two Tchaikovsky CDs, among the finest performances available within a flooded market. Neither Ms. Glover nor Ms. Edwards is likely to join the jet-setters or be invited to conduct the Berlin or Vienna Philharmonic orchestras. The point of this not-quite-irrelevant observation is to establish the fact that the orchestral conductor remains one of the most jealously guarded of all patriarchal roles: women may sing or play *under* a conductor, but if they embarrassingly insist on conducting (and conducting *men*!), their careers are likely to remain severely restricted. In the cabin, Jules produces a battered and shabby conductor-puppet and, hiding behind it, has it wave its arms; Juliette responds by "performing" on a mechanical toy. The charm of the scene lies in its reduction of an archetypal image of patriarchal dominance to play and parody, to a decrepit toy whose arms have to be waved for it; it is the moment where Juliette begins to relax and enjoy Jules's company, and where the two begin to communicate warmly, in a spirit of fun.

*Property.* Jean, seeing how attracted Juliette is to the values that Jules represents, denounces his collection as "junk" and proceeds to smash everything in sight. Jules, returning, shorn, from his visit to the dog-barber, finds one intact plate and smashes it on the floor, remarking "He missed that one." The incident makes clear that Jules doesn't depend on "things" for his identity: his "junk," though obviously treasured, is also readily expendable— he can lose it and remain himself. He is an affront to the whole capitalist emphasis on ownership and private property.

*Free sexuality and unattachment.* Juliette looks at a photograph of Jules with two women. "There's a story behind that," he tells her. We never get to hear it, but our imagination is left free to speculate. Jules's commitment to people and to relationships (his friend with the hands, Jean, the young boy, Juliette) is obvious, but it is never exclusive. The film presents him consistently as a happily unmarried man, able to respond to people freely and generously. Because he is not possessed, he is not possessive. His openness and generosity contrast markedly with the mean-minded anger of Jean, whose insecurity (characteristic of the heterosexual male under patriarchy) expresses itself in his fear of losing control over the woman when he sees her responding to anything outside his sphere of authority. Any suggestion that Jules exploits women is countered by the later delightful scene with the fortune-teller, where it is the woman who takes the sexual initiative, Jules enthusiastically following her lead. There are also possible overtones of bisexuality: whether Jules's commitment to his dead friend (not to mention the boy who shares his cabin) has sexual connotations is something the cinema in 1934 couldn't tell us (though Vigo's film doesn't say a word against it).

How are we to take Jean's brutal intervention? John Smith (in his Movie Paperback *Jean Vigo*) is quite clear on the subject: "Jean's intervention and his angry destructiveness are seen to be necessary." But not, certainly, by me; only, I think, from the viewpoint of the very value system Vigo's work in general dismisses (and even from *that* viewpoint it seems excessive). My feelings of disgust and outrage may be seen by some as just as subjective as Smith's endorsement, but they continue to seem to me precisely what the film, at that point, asks for. It is clear that what Jules offers Juliette is not some sordid (and ideologically recuperable) adultery, but liberation: he embodies quite a catalogue of challenges to patriarchal capitalism, not the least of which is his total rejection of the crucial principle of the right to possession (whether of objects or of persons). It is precisely this right that Jean's anger seeks to assert—specifically, the husband's right to possess his wife, to contain her within his own system of values. Seen in retrospect, the film raises vividly the increasingly vital issue of the incompatibility of women's liberation with marriage (at least as that institution has generally been understood and practiced). It is not an issue the film can deal with, nor should we expect it to. It is not only Jean who can't cope with Père Jules without recourse to violence—neither can the film.

Very few people (perhaps only John Smith) find the second half of *L'Atalante* satisfying; most feel cheated by it. It seems, however, irrelevant to blame Vigo for this. My own impulse, on the contrary, is to celebrate him for producing problems and tensions that can't be encompassed (without cheating) within the constraints of the forms of classical narrative. The liberation that Juliette glimpses and is attracted by, and that so appalls Jean, has to be denied in the interests of closure and the restoration of order.

The film adopts two strategies to bring this about: the substitution of the peddler for Jules, and the corresponding reduction and recuperation of Jules himself.

Concerning the first, the scene in the tavern (the "Four Nations") makes the act of substitution abundantly clear, for it recapitulates the entire pattern of the cabin scene: the arousal of Juliette's curiosity, her openness to experience and desire for things beyond the barge and marriage; the possibility of freedom, including sexual freedom; temptation and transgression, followed by the husband's angry reassertion of marital "rights'—his jealousy and possessiveness, his need to establish authority, are again presented as products of male insecurity. But the peddler is not Père Jules; or, more precisely, he offers what Jules offers, reduced to an easily recuperable form. He is a trickster (his conjuring tricks); he actually describes himself as the "peddler of dreams"; the liberation he represents is only pseudo-liberation, a matter of fantasy and deceit, trivial, easily exposed and repudiated. He promises Juliette the delights of the city, and the city proves to be (at least for an isolated woman) a kind of hell.

As for the second strategy, after the cabin scene Jules dwindles, both as a subversive force and as a leading character (classical narrative has its place for Jules, after all: "comic relief"). What is far more distressing, however, is his transformation into an agent of repression: "Le Père" Jules becomes the symbolic Father. Two images (both passed over in silence by John Smith) seem particularly significant: (a) Jules, finding the wandering Juliette in a music store, slings her over his shoulder and carries her out, without so much as a "by-your-leave" (anticipating Robert Mitchum's treatment of Marilyn Monroe at the end of River of No Return—one of Hollywood's archetypal sexist resolutions); and (b) having delivered her home (to the barge), Jules deposits her in Jean's cabin and closes the hatch over her—the woman finally shut away in her husband- and "father"-created prison. Of course, Juliette "wants" this (just as Monroe "wants" Mitchum to come and carry her home): that is what the narrative has reduced her to. And what else could it possibly say? This is followed by the famous last shot: the celebratory image of the phallic barge pushing on down the canal. Somehow, since the reawakening of the women's movement in the 1960s and 1970s, celebration seems less in order.

Nevertheless, the second half of L'Atalante contains several crucial scenes (one cannot simply write it off): Juliette in the city discovering the ignominious reality of the position of women in capitalist society (the all-male employment lines which she realizes there is no point in her joining); the ugliness of capitalist victimization and oppression (the thief who steals Juliette's purse and becomes the pathetic scapegoat of the dissatisfied mob); the revelation (when Jules visits the company boss to cover up Jean's failures) that the apparently carefree barge life depends upon capitalist enterprise and control. What is most interesting of all is the evidence that, while Juliette is beaten down by external, material circumstances (the ugliness of capitalist "reality"), Jean is beaten down simply by the humiliating (to the male ego) loss of "his" woman.

Behind the failure of *L'Atalante* lies the failure of Surrealism: its failure to grapple with social issues (the class struggle), its failure—for all its commitment to liberation—to acknowledge the oppression of women and develop a feminist theory. What remains remarkable about the film is how close it comes to transcending the boundaries both of the Surrealist movement and the traditional "realist" aesthetic it opposed.

# CHAPTER 4

# Renoir and Mozart

**I**

## Renoir at the Bullfight: *The Rules of the Game*

I was wrong to go to a bullfight without knowing the rules of the game. One must always know the rules of the game.

—JEAN RENOIR

Of course nothing is ever fixed or absolute.

—JEAN RENOIR

There appears to be a general consensus that *The Rules of the Game* (*La Règle du Jeu*, 1939) is one of the supreme achievements in cinema to date, yet (owing no doubt to the film's bewildering complexities) there is an equally general tendency to avoid too direct a confrontation. André Bazin, who wrote so often and so lovingly about Renoir, and who considered this film (as who does not?) his masterpiece, never tackled it in an article, though references to it abound throughout his work. There can be no such thing as a *definitive* account of a great film (unless one means "definitive" for a specific writer in a specific time and place), but I have never read a *satisfying* account, an account that gives one the sense (though it may in the long run prove illusory) that the writer has probed to its heart. There are two possible explanations for this: either (as most would have it) the film is so complex and multifaceted that, like life itself, it repels all attempts at definition; or, despite the almost universal (and I think justified) acclamation, it is itself on some deep level unsatisfactory, confused, evasive. It has always seemed to me a question whether it is a film about people who go too far or a film about people who can't quite go far enough, and I think Renoir himself may have shared this uncertainty. The dilemma to which it points is succinctly (if inadvertently) formulated by Robert, Marquis de la Chesnaye, when he informs his game-keeper that he doesn't want fences but he doesn't want rabbits.

The present account makes no pretensions to being definitive or even sat-isfying; it examines only one of the film's many aspects—its sexual politics (a formidable enough undertaking in itself). Two important issues that, in an account with any ambitions to completeness, would be discussed at length are barely touched on: class, and the film's relation to the social/polit-ical situation in France in 1939. (For a very different, but certainly valid and intelligent, account, see Christopher Faulkner's excellent book *The Social Cinema of Jean Renoir*, which approaches the film from an entirely different perspective.)

## The Film's System

Beneath its seemingly innocuous appearance the film attacks the very struc-ture of our society.

—RENOIR, *My life and my films*

People said I was attacking society but that is not true. I love those people. I would love to have lived in that society.

—RENOIR (in an interview)

Some might wish to argue that the above quotations are not necessarily con-tradictory—that one may wish to attack the *structure* of one's society whilst loving its inhabitants and enjoying life within it. They do, however, require some such rationalization, their compatibility not being immediately obvi-ous, and they seem to me to imply an uncertainty in Renoir on quite a deep level about what he was actually doing: Did he himself really know the "rules of the game" here any more securely than he did at the bullfight? Taking a cue from these quotations, I want this "essay" (and the term here is especially appropriate) to examine the film in light of its uncertainties, which may be argued to be also its greatest strength and distinction, accounting at once for both its complexity and the sense of dissatisfaction or confusion it leaves behind. Traditionally, the primary demand on an author has been that he must know what he wishes to say—in other words, that his work be "coherent," as that term is commonly understood. There seems to be another consensus, that *The Rules of the Game* was "ahead of its time," that it is a very "modern" film. (It was made when Joyce, Picasso, Stravinsky, and Schoenberg—to name but a few—were scarcely novelties; but, aside from an always marginal avant-garde, the cinema, as a "popular" and "commercial" art form has never been permitted to be "modern" in the sense in which the term applies to those figures, its occasional, usually very self-conscious, "modernities" either decried or celebrated as "shocks.") Perhaps we are readier today to accept the possibility that a film might be coherently incoherent, though the genuine article may be difficult to distinguish from the merely confused. One must not deny the artist the right to orchestrate his own uncertainties and hesitations.

The admirable series of television interviews produced in 1966 under the collective title *Renoir, le patron* (and available in English in *Renoir on Renoir*) are extremely illuminating in regard to Renoir's relationship with his material and with the completed film. It is clear that for him *The Rules of the Game* was never really *completed*: it remained, nearly thirty years later, alive and volatile, a text still amenable to new discoveries on the part of its creator, a text whose precise emphases are still to a degree uncertain and fluid. In his conversations (with Jacques Rivette and others), Renoir reveals that while making the film he kept looking for a "center" to cling to, whether a pivotal scene (like the murder in *La Chienne*) or a central character around whom everything revolves; unable to find one, he decides that none exists. Minutes later, he abruptly discovers that the "center" is the moment when Christine sees, through her field glasses, her husband and Geneviève embracing. This should have led him to the further perception (it seems to me indisputable and obvious) that Christine (the defining consciousness of that scene) is also the central character of the film.

Thanks to Renoir's candor—his readiness to talk about himself and his work very freely and spontaneously, without self-consciousness or the need for pretence and concealment—we can piece together an unusually full account of the film's origins, and of his working methods, affinities, and influences. All of these flow into each other, but I shall list them (in no particular order of importance) in the interests of clarity. Taken together, and with the addition of certain structuring principles, they certainly help to define the *nature* of *Rules of the Game* and perhaps help to explain why it is so difficult to pin it down to any fixable "meaning" (let alone "message").

1. *French Impressionism*. The importance to Renoir of his own father is well known and can scarcely be overestimated: his beautiful, touching, tender tribute *Renoir, My Father* is an account of, among other things, an exceptionally happy and emotionally secure childhood. Renoir paid homage on a number of occasions, in specific images, to his father's paintings (*Une Partie de Campagne*) and to those of other Impressionists (Degas and Toulouse-Lautrec in *French Cancan*). But the influence is far deeper than this suggests, going beyond the level of the visual, for Renoir inherited much of the aim and impulse of Impressionism. Impressionism represented (at least in many

of its manifestations) one particular type of Realism (a term so protean in its possible definitions that it can be made to cover almost anything): the attempt to capture the reality of the moment even as it passes. Earlier painting tended to lift its objects out of nature and eternalize them. When we look at a characteristic Impressionist work we are aware of the time of day, the exact condition of the light, the exact state of the weather; hence we are aware that all of these things must change, perhaps within minutes, that time passes, light shifts and fades, weather changes. What the Impressionists ultimately attempted to capture in paint (and obviously what lies at the heart of their work is a paradox) was transience and flux. This aesthetic is equally at the heart of Renoir's best work (and lends itself more readily to realization in a motion picture), embodied in the continuous reframings and regroupings, the constantly moving camera, the entries into and exits from the frame, the habit of "composing" not in static images but in time and space. What he says of his father is equally true of himself: "He really subscribed to that text of Lavoisier . . . 'In nature nothing is created, nothing is lost, everything is transformed . . .' "

2. *French Theater*. Renoir has repeatedly named Alfred de Musset's *Les Caprices de Marianne* as a source for *Rules of the Game*, while denying that it was ever more than a starting point. The film opens with a quotation from Beaumarchais' *The Marriage of Figaro*, accompanied on the soundtrack by a piece by Mozart (the first of the "Three German Dances," K.605). The influence of *Figaro* on the film (whether the play or Mozart's opera) appears considerable. One can discern a clear (if not quite clearcut) four-act structure: Act 1—the prologue in Paris; Act 2—from the arrival at La Colinière to the end of the hunt; Act 3—the masquerade party; Act 4—the aftermath, beginning with the shot of frogs by a fountain announcing (to quote *Figaro*'s Act 4 stage direction) "[*A garden at night*]." There are obvious (if not always very close) parallels between the characters: Christine the Marquise/Rosina the Countess, Lisette and Susanna, the denouement in both cases depending upon an exchange of cloaks between mistress and maid. Schumacher is quite unlike Figaro in character, but both are the servants of aristocrats and each is prone to jealousy, pain, and rage, exacerbated when he believes the cloaked woman to be his wife.

3. *Mozart*. The affinity between Renoir and Mozart deserves detailed acknowledgment (which I give later in my treatment of *Così fan tutte* in relation to the thematics of *Rules of the Game*); here I shall simply assert it and offer brief illustration. During a famous rehearsal of the "Linz" symphony (preserved in a recording), Bruno Walter tells the orchestra, "The expression changes in every bar." Of Renoir one might say similarly that (especially in

*Rules*) the expression changes not only from shot to shot but frequently *within* the shot. One might single out, from many possible instances, an exceptionally complex shot during the "Danse Macabre" of the masquerade:

**The immediate context.** The piano previously played by Madame de la Plante is suddenly revealed to be mechanical, and starts the Saint-Saëns music. The makeshift curtain is lowered to the ground to reveal a completely black setting and three figures dressed as ghosts, goaded into activity by Death (in the form of a man in a skeleton costume). They descend upon the audience, waving lanterns which cast eerie shifting patterns of light and shadow over the darkened auditorium.

The shot (throughout which the dance continues). The movement of the camera, left to right, reveals four "stations," slowing for each of the first three and pausing briefly for the fourth: extreme left, an entrance at which Schumacher appears searching for Lisette; a sofa, on which Christine sits with St. Aubin; an alcove, with Lisette and Marceau standing among other spectators, flirting; the extreme right, where André stands against a wall glowering at Christine. At the beginning of the shot a server at a table (Schumacher in the background) is attempting to pour wine and watch the ghosts' antics at the same time, and notices it spilling. The motivation of the camera movement seems at first to be the movement of a waiter carrying a tray of drinks, but he soon disappears from the frame; it is Schumacher's movement that is being followed, although he passes out of sight behind the wall. The camera passes over one alcove (Schumacher glimpsed briefly), slows to show Christine and St. Aubin (CHRISTINE: "I've drunk too much . . ."), moves, slows again to show Lisette and Marceau—and Schumacher discovering them— then pauses on André (Schumacher still in frame left). It then returns, following the same trajectory in reverse, this time pausing on Lisette and Schumacher; Marceau slips away left, and Lisette makes to follow but is restrained by Schumacher (SCHUMACHER [*pleadingly*]: "Lisette!"). It slows again to show Christine rising, then turning to leave, left, with St. Aubin, the camera following them. Christine pauses to turn back and look at André, then shrugs (signifying perhaps "He's a hopeless case," or "What does anything matter anyway?"); as they pass the drinks table the server is mopping up the spilled wine; they exit through the entrance at which Schumacher appeared at the beginning of the shot.

One could dwell at length here on Renoir's virtuosity: the orchestration of complex movements of camera and actors within the "real time" of a single take, the attention to small details (the spilled wine), the continuous awareness of offscreen space. But what I want to stress, with Mozart in mind, is the extraordinary emotional complexity and range covered within a single quite brief shot: the paralleling of the master-class and servant-class intrigues, with Marceau the poacher poaching Schumacher's wife while St. Aubin poaches Christine from André, who in turn is trying to poach her from Robert; the seductive charm of the Marceau/Lisette flirtation, with the pain that lies behind Schumacher's hitherto comic jealousy beginning to make itself felt; the brief juxtaposition of Schumacher and André in the frame, the film's two most possessive characters, with André's pain also seeming more genuine than it has before; our sense of the dangers of Christine's position, her recklessness, her sense that "nothing matters now" expressed in her readiness to have a fling even with the trivial and opportunistic St. Aubin; the overall sense, not only of Christine's world falling apart, but of a whole society entering its "Dance of Death" phase; the spilled wine as a marvelously casual and unobtrusive symbolic expression of the way in which everything is getting out of control. Here comedy becomes inseparable from incipient tragedy, the laughter continuously disturbed and threatened.

4. *Script/Actors*. Renoir's interviews return repeatedly to his attitude to the written script and his relationship with the actors—the two being inseparable aspects of his working method. Unlike, for example, Godard, he always began filming with a fully written screenplay—which was then progressively discarded or radically modified during shooting. One motive for this was his own love of spontaneity, his belief in "the moment"; closely related was his love of actors and his readiness to change the scenario during shooting to give freer expression to an actor's personality and talent. It is unfortunate that Renoir's original, preshooting, screenplay for *Rules of the Game* has apparently not been preserved; it would be fascinating to examine its precise relationship to the finished film. We can, however, piece together various bits of information as to how the film progressed. Renoir had originally cast his elder brother Pierre (who appeared in a number of major roles in his films, notably as Inspector Maigret in *La Nuit du Carrefour* and as Louis XVI in *La Marseillaise*) as Octave. He then cast Nora Grégor as Christine and became completely fascinated by her (as he was by a large number of actresses throughout his career, from Catherine Hessling to Paulette Goddard to Anna Magnani and Ingrid Bergman). Exit brother Pierre (we have no information about his reaction!), enter Jean. As a result, Octave's role was developed far beyond the original intent of the scenario, especially his scenes with Christine. (This explains one of the film's anomalies: its denouement depends partly on the—supposedly self-evident—fact that Octave is too old for Christine, yet with Renoir himself in the role the age discrepancy is by no means apparent.) Renoir's own accounts suggest that the role of the Marquis de la Chesnaye was also appreciably developed,

altered, expanded, in response to his relationship with Marcel Dalio, with whom he had already worked in *La Grande Illusion* (1937) and with whom he also appears to have been (platonically) in love. The word *love* may be found misleading and exaggerated in this context, but it seems to me unavoidable in discussing Renoir; his capacity for loving is central to his personality, his aesthetic, the nature of his films. One may assume that many other modifications and elaborations grew out of Renoir's attachment to, and sensitivity to the abilities of, his other actors. The one exception—a supposedly "key" role that seems curiously underdeveloped and whose realization does not at all correspond to Renoir's expressed intentions—is that of André Jurieu (Roland Toutain), a point to which I shall return.

5. *The Camera*. Renoir has always been noted for the "freedom" of his camera movements, and this is carried to its extreme in *Rules of the Game*. What must be said, however, is that it signifies not only the personal freedom of the director, but the (of course relative) freedom of the characters and the actors. To make clear what exactly this means, one might compare his work with that of Max Ophuls, whose films are also celebrated for their camera mobility. The difference is fundamental to an understanding of the two directors. With Ophuls, the camera movements are always meticulously *planned*, partly for their grace and elegance but more for their relation to the Ophulsian thematic: they guide (rather than follow) the characters, leading them from *here* to *here* in a progress that can suggest predestination or fate (if one accepts a metaphysical reading) or entrapment (if one prefers a social). With Renoir, on the contrary, the camera movement is primarily at the service of the actors, determined by *their* movements. Again, with Ophuls the extensive camera movements are almost invariably tied to the movements of a single character, or occasionally a couple, while in Renoir the camera passes frequently from character to character, group to group. I am not of course suggesting that the freedom of the characters/actors is complete: obviously, in the last resort, it is Renoir who determines the mise-en-scène, which must have been as meticulously worked out as it is in Ophuls. My concern here as usual is with the relationship between style and theme. The comparison is supported by a recurrent motif in the work of each director: in Ophuls the *closing* of windows (there are particularly striking instances in the "Madame Tellier" episode of *Le Plaisir* and in *The Earrings of Madame de . . .* ), in Renoir the *opening* of windows (*Le Crime de Monsieur Lange*, *La Grande Illusion*). The window in both cases represents a boundary beyond which may lie freedom; in Ophuls the transgression of the boundary is always forbidden or blocked, in Renoir the attempt must always be made (even if the "freedom" proves illusory). It is impossible to imagine an Ophuls film ending—as do *Le Crime de Monsieur Lange*, *La Grande Illusion*,

and *Diary of a Chambermaid*—with the characters escaping (literally, in the first two, crossing a border). In *Rules* the motif is given a particularly ironic and touching twist when Octave moves out onto the balcony from the increasing claustrophobia of the masquerade party to conduct an imaginary orchestra, only to be confronted with his own impotence.

6. *One Woman, Three Men*. Renoir's highly idiosyncratic extension of the triangle into a sexually unbalanced quadrangle is remarkably consistent throughout his work. It is at least embryonically present in earlier films: *Nana* and *Madame Bovary*, where one might argue that it comes with the material; *Le Crime de Monsieur Lange*, where Batala, Lange, and the young worker Charles are all in different ways attracted to Estelle. But it is in *Rules of the Game* that the pattern is established definitively, with the woman offered a choice among three men of more or less equal prominence and potential. (There is of course a fourth, St. Aubin, but he is there only to illustrate Christine's bewilderment and reckless desperation, never taken seriously as a suitor.) In Renoir's subsequent films this element becomes obsessive: *Diary of a Chambermaid*, *The Golden Coach*, *Eléna et les Hommes* are all elaborations of it, and it is also there in *French Cancan*, although there the woman is not the film's structural center. Only in *The River* is the pattern reversed, with three women attracted to one man. I don't think this is a trivial point: indeed, a pattern so consistent throughout an artist's work is likely to be crucial to an understanding of it. The traditional triangle (the "eternal" triangle), of which *Sunrise* can stand, among thousands, as a classic instance, is habitually based upon a clear choice: not merely between two men, but between love and duty, passion and domesticity, romance and security. Renoir's quadrangle—at least in the films from *Rules of the Game* on—makes choice itself problematic, raises the question of whether choice is meaningful or necessary, or is merely forced upon the woman by the jealousy, possessiveness, and competitiveness of the males. Indeed, in most of these films the woman does *not* choose among the men: Christine scarcely knows *what* she is doing, and cannot be said to "choose," in the closing sequence, to remain with her husband; in the endings of *The Golden Coach* and *Eléna et les Hommes*, the woman chooses to withdraw from all of them.

7. *Three "Worlds"—and Male Achievement*. Three "worlds" are present in the film, either directly or by reference; one might describe them loosely (but *only* loosely) as present, past, and future. Thus we have, fully dramatized, the "present" of the contemporary (1939) French upper class, its artificiality and archaism epitomized in La Chesnaye's mechanical birds; the "past," of which Octave is a relic, left behind by the tide, established by the references to Christine's father, the great Viennese conductor, evoking (in opposition to the birds) a culture in which art (Mozart, for example) was still

a living reality; and the "future" (which is already present in the world beyond the château) of technology, represented by André's solo flight across the Atlantic, his aeroplane, and the radio that connects all this to the obsolete present. The three leading male characters—La Chesnaye, Octave, André—hence belong respectively to each "world," at once defining it and defined by it. Hence also Christine's "choice" is not only among three men but among three "worlds." She herself remains essentially passive, lacking any firm sense of her identity, a kind of beautiful Rorschach blot awaiting definition by the male, and she is treated as such by all three suitors. The men, however, rely for *their* sense of identity upon achievement, and each is given his moment of glory or (in Octave's case) failure: La Chesnaye's absurd, pathetic, funny pride in the public display of his latest "acquisition," André's transatlantic flight, Octave's attempt (with no spectators) to enjoy, if only for a moment, the fantasy of being a great conductor like Christine's father, his grandiose opening gesture answered by the tinkling of the mechanical piano. Of the three men, Octave (because he is symbolically impotent) is the only one who doesn't treat Christine as a possession, an "acquisition" that confirms their "achievement" (the achievement being treated ironically in both cases). One can see how this points ahead to the extremely stylized and schematic postwar films, in which the three men are reduced to mere *roles* (actor, governor, bullfighter in *The Golden Coach*, for example).

8. *Pairings*. Perhaps the film's most striking structural principle (whether it was planned or "just happened" is beside the point) is the way in which two characters are briefly paired and permitted a moment of intimacy. Many of these pairings are perfectly logical and obvious (Robert and Christine, husband and wife; Octave and André, close friends), others extremely incongruous (Robert and Marceau, Marceau and Shumacher). The following list is by no means exhaustive:

|     |                      |                     |
| --- | -------------------- | ------------------- |
| 1.  | André/Octave         | Airport             |
| 2.  | Christine/Lisette    | Christine's bedroom |
| 3.  | Christine/Robert     | His study           |
| 4.  | Robert/Geneviève     | Her apartment       |
| 5.  | Octave/André         | The countryside     |
| 6.  | Christine/Octave     | Her bedroom         |
| 7.  | Octave/Robert        | The drawing room    |
| 8.  | Robert/Marceau       | Open country        |
| 9.  | Robert/Christine     | Bedroom doorway     |
| 10. | Christine/Lisette    | Christine's bedroom |
| 11. | Octave/André         | Their bedroom       |

| | |
|---|---|
| 12. André/Octave | During the hunt |
| 13. André/Jackie | During the hunt |
| 14. Robert/Geneviève | (The "farewell") |
| 15. Geneviève/Christine | Geneviève's room |
| 16. Schumacher/Lisette | The château's exterior |
| 17. Lisette/Marceau | The kitchen |
| 18. Marceau/Robert | The corridor |
| 19. André/Christine | (Her declaration) |
| 20. Christine/Octave | The balcony |
| 21. Robert/André | The dining room |
| 22. Octave/Christine | The château's exterior |
| 23. Marceau/Schumacher | The grounds |
| 24. Octave/Christine | The bridge |
| 25. Octave/Christine | The greenhouse |
| 26. Octave/Lisette | The hall |
| 27. Octave/Marceau | Outside the château (leaving) |

Many of these pairings lend themselves to organization into intricate patterns of correspondence and cross-reference which, if not perhaps consciously planned, cannot be dismissed as merely random or accidental: the structures that result are of the creative kind that will "naturally" develop when a great artist is working at full pressure. Take, as merely one example, the moment (no. 15) shared by Christine and Geneviève, La Chesnaye's wife and mistress, in which (now that Christine knows, or thinks she knows, "the truth") the women come to an amicable arrangement. The most obvious correspondence is with no. 21, shared by La Chesnaye and André, Christine's husband and would-be lover, when they reach their own arrangement. But one might equally align it with no. 2, the Christine/Lisette duologue, as one of the few moments in the film where two women share a significant intimacy, and that in turn might be related to no. 18 (La Chesnaye/Marceau), as one of the only significant moments of intimacy between members of the "master" and "servant" classes. I shall return to this last instance subsequently, merely remarking here that the construction of a diagram adequately charting the film's network of correspondences would tax the ingenuity (and the patience) of even the most dedicated semiotician.

This structure of continuously shifting couplings must be seen in relation to the fluidity of Renoir's style, in which the movements of the actors and the movements of the camera create continuously shifting patterns: groupings, regroupings, reframings. Taking in combination the structural and the stylistic, it seems apt to describe the film in terms of a kaleidoscope: the

Jean Renoir.

components remain the same but the patterns, the juxtapositions, constantly change in apparently infinite permutations. And the structure of pairings produces one striking irony. Among the main characters, André and Geneviève are almost the only two who never share one of these intimate moments; their "pairing" is proposed by Octave (in his conversation with Robert, no.7) as the ideal solution to everyone's problems.

Every film (every work of art) has a "system," and to grasp the system is to discover how all the various aspects (narrative, style, theme, structure) relate to one another. In the majority of films the system is simple, transparent: in the most primitive cinematic organisms it may amount to little more than the construction of a cause-and-effect linear narrative. *The Rules of the Game* has one of the most complex systems of any film ever made, to the extent that it is impossible to define in a single sentence. All of the above components feed into it and help to define it.

## What Is the Game and What Are the Rules?

Indeed, these are questions no one seems to bother to ask, presumably because the answers are obvious to everyone but myself. One may postulate with some confidence that the "game" is the game of love (or sex) in sophisticated social circles, and, with somewhat less sureness, that the chief "rule" is the one that Anna Karenina learned at such great cost: that liaisons and amorous intrigues, even if adulterous, are acceptable on condition that they don't become "serious." Yet each character seems to have his/her own set of rules, overlapping but not identical. The two sets that are (a) the most clearly defined and (b) the most extreme opposites belong, rather interestingly, to characters who happen to be husband and wife, Schumacher (strict traditional monogamy) and Lisette (casual "cheating" without commitment); and the film's three victims, André, Christine, and above all Octave, are caught in a pincer movement when the two conflicting sets converge. Lisette's rules correspond to that suggested above but add important codicils: that, if people really must get "serious," there should be no significant age difference between the partners, and the man must be in a position to keep the woman in the luxury to which she is accustomed. Hence, she is directly responsible for Octave's decision to send André out to the greenhouse in his place. Schumacher's rules are the simple and clearcut ones of patriarchy at its most dominating and oppressive: the wife is the man's possession, and he has the right to resort to any lengths, including murder, to defend himself against "poachers."

For Schumacher, such "traditional" rules are a fixed principle, an aspect of a general moral rigidity the film clearly relates to fascism: he is the film's anti-Renoir, and Renoir's ability to allow him, nonetheless, a certain circumscribed humanity testifies eloquently to the breadth of his own. For Christine, who appears to share these traditional rules (during the first half of the film), they are simply what she has grown up with in a more stable cultural situation, and can be discarded abruptly in favor of others when she discovers that they are not absolute. André (who is, according to Renoir, the one who doesn't understand the rules) in fact has strict rules of his own: the great romantic lover, whom Christine expects to sweep her up onto his white charger and carry her off to bliss, turns out to be an exemplary young bourgeois who wishes her to spend a month with his mother while he settles things with her husband. If one considers all the characters, the "rules of the game" seem as complicated as those of chess, or better still bridge, where different partners may be employing different conventions.

The roles of Christine and André, as the two characters most at sea amid the fluctuating "rules," invite more detailed examination here. I have already indicated that where I part company with Renoir most completely is in our attitudes to, or estimates of, André Jurieu. For Renoir, André is the one "pure" character in an "impure" society, and he dies as a result of his purity. Nowhere in his interviews does Renoir acknowledge that the viewer's reaction might differ markedly from this. For me, André is the one wholly unsympathetic character in the film, hence his death cannot carry the weight of significance Renoir intends. He behaves throughout with the petulance of the spoiled child, and appears totally self-centered and self-absorbed—characteristics I have difficulty reconciling with "purity," whatever definition of that term one adopts. If he loves Christine it is with that self-serving male possessiveness that too often passes for love in our culture, the "love" summed up by William Blake's "pebble of the brook":

> "Love seeketh only self to please,
> To bind another to its delight,
> Joys in another's loss of ease,
> And builds a Hell in Heaven's despite."

There is no point in the film where André shows the least concern for Christine or consideration for her feelings; he can conceive her happiness in no terms save the satisfaction of his own ego. Even more than Schumacher, who has the partial excuse of his entrapment in an inherited tradition of very long standing, André is the film's supreme egoist, and of all the men available to Christine the one with whom she is least likely to be happy. The film seems to me to say this very clearly, whatever Renoir may have intended; I have a strong impression that he really wasn't very interested in André (or perhaps in the actor, which with Renoir amounts to the same thing), though he may have convinced himself that he was. Of all the leading characters André remains the least rounded, the least complex, the most predictable: he never surprises us. La Chesnaye, Christine, Octave, Schumacher, Lisette, Marceau are all possessors of an inner life that André totally lacks. It is impossible to perceive his death as a tragedy, and difficult even to be touched by it. What we are moved by, at the film's conclusion, is the effect of his death on the other characters. (Interestingly, this view of the character seems confirmed—doubtless inadvertently—by a curious and consistent feature of the published screenplay: the translators throughout give La Chesnaye as "Robert," while André remains, intractably, "Jurieu").

Renoir's remarks also seem to imply that he sees André as the film's central character (despite his denial elsewhere that it has one), the one it is "about," and this is also misleading. Stylistically, the camera, passing from

André arrives at La Colinière (Jean Renoir, Roland Toutain, Nora Grégor).

person to person, group to group, constantly including, excluding, reframing, frequently recording simultaneous actions in foreground and background, may seem to privilege no one, but structurally the central character of *Rules of the Game* is certainly Christine because the three main male characters are all (in their different ways) in love with her and all offer her different lifestyles, sets of values, identities. Christine is the center of the film's problematic—precisely, its highly idiosyncratic treatment of sexual politics—and everything revolves around her and around the choices and decisions that she is quite incapable of making.

To a lesser extent, it is also misleading to imply that André is the outsider attempting membership of a coherent and unified group. *All* the main characters, with the partial exceptions of Geneviève and Lisette, are outsiders, in different ways and to differing degrees, in relation to the milieu depicted. La Chesnaye is Jewish, Christine is from Vienna, Octave is a hanger-on ("un parasite," as he himself acknowledges); Schumacher is from Alsace, Marceau is a poacher masquerading (with notable lack of success) as an accomplished servant. It is partly this sense that no one really belongs to, or fully represents, the society that makes it so fluid and volatile. (The one character who appears—superficially—to "represent" the society in a stable and coherent manner, the old General, is in fact a relic of the past, his obsoleteness repeatedly foregrounded).

Renoir's unconscious animus seems further motivated by the fact that André (whose function is quite complex, beyond what the two-dimensional characterization can sustain) is the film's representative of the modern world, the world of technology, mass communication, and celebrity worship, which for Renoir (as expressed through the mouth of Octave) is also the world of "lies," pervasively corrupting, and the world that threatens with obsolescence the society Renoir depicts and for which he feels an affection amply realized within the film, without recourse to his own explicit confession. If one is fully to appreciate his distinction, it is important to realize that he was in some respects a deeply conservative artist, so long as one does not reduce his work to that, or permit it to eclipse his paradoxical radicalism. The conservatism can be traced, I think, to the nostalgia for the lost world of his childhood that produced *Renoir, My Father*. It was seriously threatened, almost eradicated, by his commitment to radical movements and positions in the 1930s that produced *Le Crime de Monsieur Lange* and his participation in *La Vie Est à Nous*, a direct product and expression of the Front Populaire (though the commitment was never free of ambiguities). In his final phase (after the fascinating uncertainties and various "essays" of the American period), he seems to me to have retreated into it thoroughly—retreated from social engagement into a hermetic world of nostalgia and "art." Many critics (notably those of *Cahiers du Cinéma*) have championed the late films as Renoir's most "modern," most "progressive," most "radical," but this can only be argued on a formal level, and the kind of formal play the films exemplify, while often very engaging, is perfectly compatible with a reactionary position, a retreat into the world of the "aesthetic."

What ensures Christine's centrality and distinguishes her from all the other characters, male or female, master or servant class, is that she is the only one who lacks a clear sense of identity. The sense of identity by which the others are defined rests upon a dual basis: social position, and the identity of the stereotype. This is clear in the minor characters: the old General, "the homosexual," Madame la Bruyère, Corneille . . . They are and remain simple stereotypes, vivid and animated enough (stereotypes, while necessarily two-dimensional, don't have to be lifeless), who fulfill their functions but are left undeveloped. Yet it should also be clear that the "rounded" characters are equally based on easily identifiable stereotypes taken over by Renoir from a complex tradition in which French theater is perhaps the most important element, transformed into what we call "characters" by a complex process in which the crucial factor is their incarnation as actors. The supreme instance is La Chesnaye, and the casting of Renoir's friend Marcel Dalio. Renoir said that he chose Dalio because he was "exactly the opposite of the 'cliché' of a marquis," yet our sense of the character's complexity depends finally on the existence of the "cliché"—the stereotype—as point of departure. Renoir said approvingly of his father, "He thought that the artist's proper function was to absorb material, to digest it and pass it on," and his own greatness is a consequence of the richness and complexity of the tradition he absorbed and his capacity for digesting it fully.

Renoir discusses Christine's lack of a sense of identity (her unfamiliarity with "the rules of the game") purely in terms of her foreignness, and this is clearly what distinguishes her from the other women in the film, notably Geneviève and Lisette. But there is another, more fundamental source, perhaps undiscussable before the evolution of a feminist consciousness in the 1960s and 1970s: the simple fact that she is not only foreign but a woman. Central to the initial impetus of modern feminism was the perception that, if there *is* such a thing as an authentic "feminine," we don't know what it is, because "femininity" has always been defined by men for their own convenience; that women's identities are constructed not by themselves but by the "rules" of patriarchy and its assumptions. (One of our civilization's most dedicated researchers into human needs and desires, Sigmund Freud, confessed himself baffled by the question, What does a woman *want*?) This seems to me to provide an admirable example of the way in which a supposedly known and catalogued work of art can suddenly be reopened and reanimated by social change. It offers an approach to *Rules of the Game* that Renoir could not have formulated in the 1930s and that his interviewers (all male) were still unable to formulate in the 1960s, even though it is the one direct entry to the very heart of the film.

There have been innumerable films in which an essentially passive, or confused, or "torn" woman learns to accept the identity imposed upon her by men: it is the very basis of the "happy ending," succinctly exemplified in recent years by *Die Hard* and *The Abyss*, both of which required an elaborate action narrative, a riot of special effects, all the technology of modern Hollywood, and many millions of dollars to induce a woman to accept her husband's surname. What distinguishes *Rules* is not so much the absence of a happy ending as the way in which it foregrounds and dramatizes Christine's bewilderment, making it the film's central crux. Renoir gives us only minimal information about Christine's (and indeed anyone else's) background, but it is sufficient for us to read her behavior and make the necessary deductions. It is she, not André, who is the film's one authentically "pure" character. Daughter of a famous Viennese conductor, she is the product of a sheltered upbringing within a stable environment presided over by the benevolent figure of her illustrious father—hence completely unequipped to cope within the conspicuously *un*stable milieu into which she has married, populated by sophisticates with fragile identities. She has translated the security she experienced with her father (so complete that she never felt the need to develop any independent personal identity) into an assumption of security where it doesn't exist. This includes translating her allegiance to (dependence on) her father into a fidelity to her husband, the inevitability of which she has never questioned, any more than she has ever questioned his to her (she is certainly telling the truth when she says that what she felt for André was "friendship"). This false security has been bolstered by the presence of Octave, the one-time student and trusted family friend who is a direct link back to her father and Vienna, and who is for Christine more brother figure than father substitute (as he entirely lacks any vestige of patriarchal authority). Her sense of security, though without foundation, is so strong that she can romp on a bed with Octave and believe sincerely in the possibility of "amitié avec un homme," within a milieu in which every male-female relationship is instantly sexualized. (Everyone, including, the film hints, her husband, automatically believes that she *did* sleep with André.) Renoir has embodied in Christine the best that can be said for a benevolent patriarchal past, and dramatized its inappropriateness to—and vulnerability within—a present where the finer standards and secure values of that past are in a state of advanced disintegration. Until the revelation of her husband's infidelity, Christine's sense of identity is built precisely upon the traditional "needs" a woman is supposed to have: she gives her husband all that he appears to want of her, and (as testified by her dialogue with Lisette the first night of the gathering at La Colinière), she longs for motherhood.

Why is the La Chesnaye marriage childless? For Christine's commitment to motherhood ("I think of nothing else any more"), although it is never referred to in the film again, seems more than one of her passing whims. (Compare the conviction with which she states it, and the closeness of the camera at this point, with, for example, the moment during the masquerade party when she tells André she loves him—in the isolation of long shot, and with a visible stiffness.) With no other information provided, I think we must assume that it is essentially her husband's decision (temporarily, at least—they have been married only three years). There is no indication anywhere in the film that he is romantically in love with Christine. They have separate apartments, their manner toward each other is more courteous than amorous, there is no suggestion of a sexual passion. It is tempting to say that Christine is just another of his "acquisitions," but that would be unfair: his behavior makes it clear that he is fond of her and that he respects her, both for herself and for what she represents. If he is proud of his ownership of her, he is also proud of her in a more legitimate sense—because he genuinely appreciates her qualities. Until Christine's declaration of absolute faith in him he has clearly had no qualms about having Geneviève as his mistress: the relationship began before he met Christine, everyone except Christine knows about it, for a man (especially an aristocrat) it is a socially accepted, even *expected*, arrangement.

Geneviève, Christine's rival in the narrative, is her perfect foil in the film's complex structure of characters. If Christine has no support beyond the taken-for-granted traditional identity of a woman in patriarchy, Geneviève has constructed her own identity within the parameters that patriarchy constructs: the independent society hostess. This means of course that she is ultimately as powerless as Christine to effect her own destiny. Of all the characters, it is perhaps Geneviève who understands the "rules of the game" most thoroughly and is most at home within them, yet this involves a coarsening of sensibility and an acceptance of the ignominious role of mistress, in which she has no real rights. Renoir—and I think the audience—finds Christine much the more sympathetic of the two. Is this an insidiously male preference for the more "feminine" (i.e., passive, vulnerable, helpless, "soft") woman over the seemingly tougher, independent, "hard" one (who nevertheless collapses in hysterics under stress)? I think it goes deeper than that: Geneviève is a "closed" character, Christine an "open" one; Christine is still capable of "becoming," whereas Geneviève has already become. If Christine embodies the "feminine," it is precisely a "feminine" which remains undefined, hence suggestive of a potential that Geneviève lacks.

## The Ideology of the Couple

What follows will be familiar (though perhaps in a less detailed form) to readers of my previous books; its repetition here is necessary to my argument, but anyone who gets that "We've been here before" feeling will of course be able to skim or even skip this section.

We cannot remind ourselves too often that what we call "the dominant ideology"—the system of assumptions, beliefs, values dominant in a given culture at a given time—is never monolithic. The more complex the culture, the more protean it must be if it is to continue to maintain its hegemony. There are two main points to be made about the dominant ideology of our own culture. First, it must be able to encompass contradiction and struggle. It is still correct to see feminism as an oppositional ideology which resists assimilation so long as it adheres to its basic rigorous principles, yet even this the dominant ideology must appear to tolerate because of its commitment to the "democratic process" and "freedom of speech"; it therefore assimilates whatever it can by transforming it into something unthreatening, and marginalizes or ridicules the rest. Yet when one focuses on specific issues, one sees that the task of the ideology is far from simple. Take, for instance, the abortion issue at the present time. It would I think be impossible to say whether the "pro-choice" or "pro-life" position is dominant. Consequently, both of two diametrically opposed and irreconcilable positions must be acknowledged, a feat achieved in the media via notions of "fair play," each side, by and large, receiving favorable or unfavorable coverage according to its "good" or "bad" behavior. Implicitly, the dominant ideology has already shown its readiness to assimilate abortion rights. It is a two-way process: every time the dominant ideology assimilates something potentially threatening it finds a way to defuse the threat, but at the same time it is modified and partially transformed by what it is has assimilated. Hence it is not fixed or stable, though the transformation may be so gradual as to pass unnoticed. The legal victory of the pro-choice movement would certainly be a victory for feminism (despite the fact that many who support abortion rights do not call themselves feminists), although it would probably not be hailed as such in the media. The "dominant ideology," which it has been customary to think of as centered in traditional patriarchal "family values," would never be the same. We cannot even assert confidently today that the belief in traditional "family values" *is* still dominant in the culture: certainly its hold has become very seriously weakened.

The second point is that the dominant ideology is always multilayered. The uppermost layers, at once the most obvious and the most transient, are those explicitly reinforced (and perhaps sometimes constructed) by the media: the latest "trends" (in politics, movements, the arts, fashion . . . ). Some of these remain remarkably persistent (we are still solemnly invited, against all sense and reason, to interest ourselves in the doings of the British royal family), but on the whole these layers appear and disappear, shift, change, reverse themselves. The deeper you dig, the more permanent the layers appear, and the ideology is underpinned by those most resistant to change, the least questioned, the most completely "naturalized." But they are not unchallengeable: one of the most fundamental—patriarchy, the "law of the Father," male dominance—has been and continues (with setbacks) to be vociferously and to varying degrees effectively challenged during our own lifetimes.

One of the deepest and most resistant layers—perhaps because it is "evidently" grounded in "nature"—deeper than the ideology of patriarchy, deeper than the ideology of sexual difference, the ideology of heterosexism—is the ideology of the couple. We may ask what exactly *is* the grounding in nature, or in biology? No more than the need (if the human race is to perpetuate itself) for a man and a woman to come together in order that the woman may conceive, and with recent scientific developments (artificial insemination, "test-tube babies") even that "necessity" is thrown into doubt. Beyond it, surely, we must see that the entire superstructure that has been erected upon this dubious foundation is a matter, not of "nature," but of ideology. There is no necessity whatever for the man and woman to get married, to live together, to be monogamous, or even to know each other in any but the "biblical" sense. Neither is there any necessity for children to be reared by their biological parents, or even to know who they were. (That adopted children seem often to experience a desire to trace their biological parents testifies, not to the "naturalness" of such a desire, but to the power of the ideology: they grow up in a culture where the *norm* is to be raised by one's biological parents.) Yet the ideology of the couple has proved amazingly tenacious: most would deny, probably with indignation, that it *is* an ideological assumption, the indignation being a response to any threat to its emotional hold. The assumption that the "right," "natural" way to live is as a heterosexual couple continues to hold sway, though it too has not escaped erosion. Many now reject legal marriage (the only practical function of which appears to be to make it more difficult to separate if you're miserable); a smaller, but still significant, number, while wishing to remain in "couple" relationships, resist the demands of monogamy and exclusivity (openly, as opposed to the time-dishonored practice of "cheating"). Even gays and lesbians, who live of necessity outside the hegemony of heterosexism, tend to subscribe (or succumb) to the ideology of the couple. I agree, of course, that gays and lesbians should like everyone else have the right to legal marriage (without it they are being discriminated against); but I can't see why they should *want* it, except as a political gesture, any more than I can see why they should *want* to enter the military.

Out of the cultural commitment to living in couples grows the ideology of romantic love and the ideology of the family, both of which function as major instruments of oppression, as future chapters will illustrate. The operations of romantic love have received definitive analyses within the Hollywood cinema alone: the female version, with great tenderness, by Ophuls (*Letter from an Unknown Woman*), the male version, with consummate brutality, by Hitchcock (*Vertigo*). As for the family, even films ostensibly committed to it cannot fail (with whatever degree of conscious intention) to expose its oppressive mechanisms: *Shadow of a Doubt* and *Meet Me in St. Louis* can be read as (respectively) "affectionate" or "nostalgic" paeans to family life only by those who refuse to be aware of their detail. Mainstream cinema has also reflected consistently the impossible irreconcilability of these twin pillars of our sexual ideology: romantic love and marriage have been repeatedly dramatized as not merely incompatible but antagonistic, the latter destroying the illusions of the former. Films centered on the "romantic couple" traditionally *end* in marriage but are conspicuously silent about what happens next. The genre that has dealt with marriage most extensively is the melodrama, where the marriage is always under threat, internal, external, or, typically, both. Marriages in mainstream cinema are usually restored (unless a spouse, usually female, has transgressed the boundaries of legal and/or moral pardon)—as indeed is the marriage in *Rules of the Game*, though there it isn't offered even superficially as a "happy ending." But the restoration typically rests on the woman's remorse and "learning her true duty," or on the husband seeing the error of his errancy, discovering that the "other woman" isn't all she seemed, or grasping that he shouldn't ask too much from life: as in Renoir's film, the effect is of making the best of a bad job, resigning oneself. It all amounts to an overwhelming testimony to the falseness of the ideological imperative, and to our knowledge of its falseness even as we continue to obey it.

I am not of course suggesting that we abruptly pass a law saying "No more marriages, no more couples, no more families"—or even that we try to change, overnight, our whole pattern of thinking and feeling: we would succeed only in doing ourselves immense psychological damage. I am simply trying to look to the past, and to where it has brought us, and forward to possible futures: to suggest that there are enormous fundamental questions to be asked that never get asked, and that now—with the ideological grip of marriage and family demonstrably weakened, and the Right trying artificially to restore its strength—is a good time to begin asking them. When we have confronted—via all the work in the last decades on the oppression of women and the abuse of children within the traditional family—all the necessary questions about what is irredeemably wrong with the social/sexual organization within which we have grown up and which structures all our patterns of thinking and feeling, we shall have to confront the question that will inevitably develop out of this process: What would a civilization be like in which people did *not* live as couples unless they chose to do so in complete freedom, with no ideological pressures?

All of this may seem to have taken us a very long way from Renoir's film, but it is where the preceding analysis logically leads, and will not seem so far if one grasps the implications of the various components—methodological, conceptual, thematic, stylistic—that I have enumerated. I shall now attempt to spell out those implications, and in doing so reveal my own solution to what one might call the *Rules of the Game* quandary: almost everyone seems to agree that it is one of the most important films ever made, but no one seems prepared to say *why*.

# In Defense of "Promiscuity"

*Promiscuity* is a dirty word, and once a word has accumulated so much dirt through the centuries it is difficult to cleanse. Anyone bothered by it can substitute the phrase "relating freely." In some ways that is preferable, because "promiscuity" has come to be used in an exclusively sexual sense, and I use it here in a much wider one: a sense that *includes* sexuality but is not restricted to it.

The word has acquired its negative connotations from its association with sexual practices that, as side effects, are the direct product of our culture's ideology and its dominant social/sexual arrangements. Within the heterosexual moral system (centered on monogamy and family) it implies the exploitation of women (wife, mistresses, casual encounters, prostitutes) by the male (at once accepted as "normal" and denounced as "immoral"), or, for a woman, a sexual deviancy categorized by such labels as *nymphomaniac, whore, tramp*. In gay sexual practice it implies a fondness for casual, often anonymous, sex—pickups in gay bars, encounters in bathhouses, parks, backrooms, or washrooms. Of these various forms of "promiscuity," only that of the heterosexual male appears to me morally reprehensible, as it is *necessarily* (given the position of the heterosexual male as the ideologically privileged figure of the culture) built upon exploitation; it is also the form that society at large continues to regard as the *least* objectionable. But simply because all these forms are products of the dominant system that officially disowns them, hence colored and defined in relation to it, they all contribute to giving "promiscuity" a bad name.

People often lament that sex has assumed such disproportionate importance in our culture, that it pervades everything, there is no escape or respite: it permeates our movies, our fiction, our television, it is used to sell beers, shampoos, deodorants, even detergents . . . In one sense this is all quite true, as exhaustively analyzed by Stephen Heath in his brilliant and accessible book *The Sexual Fix*, a book that richly deserves bestseller status and yet has unaccountably slipped from sight, conveniently ignored in a culture in which sex and consumerism continuously bolster each other. But in another sense, sex has become far *less* important in our century than it was for the Victorians and before them. For the Victorians (who never talked about it openly) it assumed such importance that it seems at times that they wished they could dispense with it altogether, especially in women, where it was peculiarly inconvenient, threatening the certitude of the patriarchal lineage. The immense importance attributed to sex in the past (and still, largely, in the present, although perhaps this is weakening along with all the other "good old values" of patriarchy) can be gauged if one ponders the meaning our culture has assigned to the word *fidelity*. Like *promiscuity* (its extreme opposite) it is commonly used in an exclusively sexual sense. A married woman may fall in love with another man, spend all her days fantasizing about him, lose all sexual interest in her husband, but so long as she doesn't have sexual intercourse with her potential lover (which might swiftly put an end to most of the fantasies) she has not been "unfaithful." Our culture will remain obsessed with the sexual act, in one way or another, while it continues to place such ridiculous and irrational importance on it. One may ask (and will probably receive no answer to so inconvenient a question) why sexual attraction is regarded as a reason for people to live together. There are dozens of more cogent motives, such as sharing the same interests or even simply liking the same food, though the most important (and least recognized) would logically be a mutual respect for each other's freedom and independence, sexual and otherwise. One (entirely positive) consequence of such an arrangement is that it would become completely irrelevant whether those choosing to live together were of the same or different gender, and whether there were two of them or more than two. The "friendship" between men and women—the very notion of which Lisette finds so hilarious—would become a practical reality, and sex could take its rightful place as a natural, unremarkable, part of daily life, like eating and drinking. Such an arrangement, far from dissociating sex and love, would surely foster the human potential to love more freely, more generously. As for "fidelity," should one not be faithful to *all* those whom one loves?

To return, then, to the film. Aside from the solitary minor instance of Jackie and her parents, there are no families in *The Rules of the Game* (it is not only the La Chesnayes who are childless), and romantic love is exposed, through André, as mere blatant male egoism. This leaves Renoir free to explore, from the woman's viewpoint, the ideology of the couple (though he himself would not have used such a term). The stylistic and thematic components I have outlined are by no means disparate, unconnected "happenings": they do indeed form a "system," a very specific and very rare psychological complex, perhaps unique in the cinema, which Renoir came closest to realizing fully in *Rules of the Game*. Of all filmmakers, Renoir is the one psychologically most attuned to the acceptance of "promiscuity" in its widest sense: even his attitude to ideas and theories is promiscuous. He remarked (in the interview with Louis Marcorelles, most accessible in Andrew Sarris's compilation *Interviews with Film Directors*):

> You know, I can't believe in the general ideas, really I can't believe in them at all. I try too hard to respect human personality not to feel that, at bottom,

there must be grain of truth in every idea. I can even believe that all the ideas are true in themselves, and that it's the application of them which gives them value or not in particular circumstances. . . . No, I don't believe there are such things as absolute truths; but I do believe in absolute human qualities—generosity, for instance, which is one of the basic ones . . .

Renoir's openness (to theories, to methods, to influences, to interpretations, to characters, to relationships) is enacted in the film on all levels, as much in the style as in the content: a complex that, if it can be summed up in a single word, might equally be called "promiscuity" or "generosity," the "absolute human value" which he so significantly singles out, and one that our social and sexual arrangements tend strongly to discourage. The best phrase that comes to mind to define Renoir's style is "visual promiscuity," Renoir himself "relating freely" to his characters and actors, refusing to be tied to any one relationship. Hence the significance of the "one woman/three men" pattern, so different from the traditional triangle where the woman is confronted with a clearcut choice. Surely, if one opens oneself to the film's implications, the question inevitably arises, Why must Christine choose at all? Why may she not freely conduct relationships with all three (perhaps, but not necessarily, sexual, it shouldn't matter), as each offers her something different? The answer lies not merely in social convention (its demands unusually lax in the milieu depicted) but in the demands of men, especially the importunings of André, the film's explicit hero-figure and implicit villain, who wants Christine all to himself, for the satisfaction of his childish ego.

I said that I would return to the second pairing (no. 18) of La Chesnaye and Marceau, among the film's privileged moments. Of the twenty-seven pairings listed, only five cross the class barrier, two for La Chesnaye and Marceau, two for Christine and Lisette, one (the film's final pairing) for Marceau and Octave, immediately before they go their separate ways into the darkness with which it ends. Unlike the Christine/Lisette exchanges, the second Marceau/La Chesnaye encounter is arbitrary and accidental (Marceau could have asked *anyone* to look out for Schumacher); it is also the unique moment of intimacy between the "highest" and "lowest" characters in the class hierarchy, the titled aristocrat and the disreputable poacher whose role as servant is tenuous and peripheral. The incongruity underlines what is evidently the scene's raison d'être and one of the key dialogues in the film: La Chesnaye's "harem" speech (broken up by interjections from Marceau):

"The Moslems are the only ones who've shown the slightest sense in this notorious question of relationships between men and women . . . There's always one woman they like best . . . But they don't think that just because of that they have to throw the others out . . ."

Obviously, in the mouth of La Chesnaye, a thoroughly sexist statement, reeking of the "double standard." Yet its resonance in the film seems to me far to transcend its literal and immediate meaning. One may note that it is not particularly apposite to La Chesnaye's situation: nowhere in the film does he show any sign of wanting a "harem." He has a wife for whom he at least has a deep and solidly grounded respect and affection, and a mistress from before his marriage of whom he is tired but whom he doesn't wish to hurt. One may therefore postulate here a displacement: Renoir is putting into the mouth of one character an idea he wishes (unconsciously) to apply to another. And there is one (and *only* one) character in the film to whom the speech applies perfectly: Christine. She even begins to put it into practice; after the revelation of her husband's "infidelity," her spontaneous choice of St. Aubin (who clearly offers her no more than a "fling"), "hysterical" as it is, can also be read as her signal (especially to André) that she will no longer be "chosen," that she rejects the male imperative. When one grasps this, the sexism of the "harem" speech disappears—or, more precisely, becomes merely the sexism of La Chesnaye, not of Renoir—and the superficial frivo-

La Chesnaye and Marceau: the "harem" speech (Marcel Dalio, Julien Carette).

lousness disappears with it. The profoundly subversive question of why Christine should be forced to choose lurks only just below the film's surface and might be taken for its animating principle.

I am not suggesting that *Rules of the Game* (or any film) provides any answers to the problems (which most people prefer not to confront as such) of our social/sexual arrangements: that is the province of social theorists. But Renoir's film at the very least suggests that they have not been doing their job, as it raises all the questions, throws all existing arrangements into jeopardy, and no one so far appears to have taken up its challenge. And it needs to be reiterated once more that the film's achievement does not by any means consist in delivering a "message" or even a coherent statement (some might argue that it leaves us with no more than the quandary: "I don't want fences and I don't want rabbits"). Its achievement lies in its unity of style, theme, and structure, and its "meaning" arises, not from conscious intention, but from its creator's whole being, and its expression (possible only because he was a great artist) in every aspect of the creation.

## II

## Mozart's "Immorality": The Couples of *Così fan tutte*

> Rompasi omai quel laccio, segno di servitu.
> —DESPINA in *Così fan tutte* (ACT 2, SCENE 3)

For those fortunate enough—because they have in store so wonderful a discovery—to be unfamiliar with Mozart's opera, I offer the following very brief plot synopsis, though it should not be taken as a substitute (what I want to say being dependent on Mozart's music, which transforms a seemingly frivolous and arguably sexist farce into something very different):

> *Guglielmo and Ferrando, two young officers, are betrothed to two well-bred sisters, respectively Fiordiligi and Dorabella. When they extol the idealized virtues of their fiancées to their cynical older friend Don Alfonso, he challenges them to a wager: he will prove to them within twenty-four hours that the women are not the faithful goddesses of which the two young men boast, if they will simply follow his instructions.*
>
> *Accordingly, Guglielmo and Ferrando pretend to leave immediately for an unspecified war. Alfonso enlists the aid of the ladies' maid Despina, without letting her in on the plot. The lovers return, disguised as wealthy Albanian merchants, and lay siege to the women, who, with Despina's enthusiastic encouragement, after many protestations of shock, surrender; but they choose the "wrong" partners. A double marriage is arranged, with Despina masquerading as the officiating lawyer, but just as it is about to take place the sounds of the returning army are heard. The men pretend to hide,*

*then return as themselves. Don Alfonso tells them that they have all learned a valuable lesson and can now be more rational about human relationships. The original pairings are restored.*

I cannot think of another film that comes as close to loosening the ideological grip of the couple as *The Rules of the Game*, but a parallel exists in music. Both Beethoven and Wagner regarded *Così fan tutte* as "immoral," but I wonder whether either of them grasped the full profundity of its "immorality" (I would prefer "undermining of the moral norm")? The parallels I noted between Renoir's film and *The Marriage of Figaro*, though clear, are relatively superficial. Although there is little resemblance on the level of character and narrative structure, there seems to me a much deeper affinity between *Rules* and *Così*. The one clear instance of character resemblance is, however, worth noting: Lisette, although her structural position and relationship with her mistress (as much confidante as servant) recall Susanna's, in attitude and behavior bears a far closer resemblance to Despina, who, referring to *her* mistresses' by then wavering commitment to monogamy, advises them to "break this knot, symbol of servitude."

Of the four operas that are generally recognized as Mozart's greatest achievements, together constituting one of the peaks of Western culture, *The Marriage of Figaro* is the only one that can reasonably lay claim to coherence (doubtless in large part a legacy from Beaumarchais): the characters are clearly defined and consistently motivated, the plot scrupulously worked out and logically and satisfyingly resolved. (I am not of course suggesting that this makes it superior to the other three; it is not a valid criterion of great art that it leaves us feeling satisfied.) The other three, *Don Giovanni*, *Così fan tutte* and *The Magic Flute*, are each incoherent in quite different ways. It is quite impossible, I think, to state confidently what exactly it is that they *are* saying (taking into account, necessarily, not just the plot or the text but the music, and its precise relationship to the action, which can be as complex as that between script and mise-en-scène in any movie you care to think of). The problem of *Don Giovanni* can be summed up fairly simply in a question: What exactly are we to make of Giovanni himself? In other words, what exactly are the degrees of attraction and repulsion, admiration and contempt, and how are they defined through the interplay of characters and, crucially, the music by which Mozart defines them? The incoherence of *The Magic Flute*, on the other hand, is notorious (and much less interesting), existing on the simplest, most superficial level of plot, though it also manifests itself on a deeper level, in the relationship of music to action. The incoherence of *Così* is perhaps the most interesting of all: no two accounts of what it is about seem to agree. I am going to argue that its incoherence is very like that of *Rules of the Game*, and that it derives ultimately from very much the same source.

One "interpretation" (if it deserves that term—it takes into account so little of the detail) of *Così* can be quickly discounted: the notion that it is a simple expression of misogyny. True, Don Alfonso demonstrates his theorem that "all women are the same" in that they succumb to temptations even when they profess to be above them. But this demonstration has to be seen in context—or, indeed, a number of contexts. First and most obvious, the music: compare the music Mozart gives to Don Alfonso with the music he gives to the other characters—especially the women and *including* Despina. There are many resources in literature for "placing" a character for the reader; Mozart has his resources in music, which proves Don Alfonso's self-congratulatory cynicism to be considerably less than the final word. His music tells us, for example, that he is quite incapable of understanding the feelings that Fiordiligi expresses in "Per pietà . . ." It should be obvious that Mozart's music is on the women's side throughout, however one interprets the libretto.

Mozart's tendency to identify with the female characters is by no means exclusive to *Così* but a constant characteristic of the operas. It manifests itself most strikingly, perhaps, in *The Magic Flute*, where Mozart involved himself in a project shot through with sexism and racism in which misogyny runs rampant: the music given to the arch-villainess the Queen of the Night is simply so much more *interesting* than that given to the supposedly godlike father figure (and crashing old bore) Sarastro, and both her arias are through-composed, while Mozart gives Sarastro, in his major aria, musically identical stanzas. It is not a matter of the old cliché of Evil being more interesting than Good: Mozart was perfectly capable of vivifying "good" characters, especially if they were women (witness the noble and virtuous Constanze in *Die Entführung aus dem Serail* [*The Abduction from the Seraglio*], whose two "big" arias strikingly parallel the Queen of the Night's). It must also, I think, be generally agreed that the emotional core of that frustrating opera is the music given to Pamina. It is the Mozartian bias that finally disrupts the project, rendering the work (taken as an entity) quite unintelligible. What remains mysterious is how and why such a non-sense inspired some of the finest music ever composed.

It might be argued that the narrative, at least, of *Così* is quite explicitly a demonstration that all *women* are likely to be unfaithful, that there is no clear comparable exposure of male infidelity. The answer, I think, is clear: there doesn't need to be, it is taken for granted. The "double standard" has been familiar throughout our history: women's fidelity is necessary to guarantee the patriarchal lineage, but no such necessity applies to men, who merely pay lip service to the notion. This is so strongly entrenched in the traditions of our culture that we scarcely need Despina's first act aria ('In uomini, in soldati . . .") to expound it for us, but Mozart and da Ponte give it to us as an apt and shrewd reminder: "Do you expect fidelity in *men*? In *soldiers*??!" The opening of the opera clearly differentiates the men's world from the women's: the men out carousing in a cafe, the women mooning over their portraits in the house they will never leave throughout the opera. Both pairs sing of the transcendent wonderfulness of their prospective marriage partners, and in each case there is an element of competition, each man insisting on the perfection of his betrothed, each of the sisters (as they compare miniatures) extolling the particular merits of hers. But there is a significant difference: the women's concern is with their men's beauty and personal qualities; the men's is (even from the start, before the wager) exclusively with their women's fidelity. In other words, the women (however misguidedly) adore the men for their perceived or imagined personal attractions; the men adore the women as their *possessions*, to serve and bolster their egos (beauty being taken for granted as the guarantee of value).

Of the various other interpretations of *Così*, one cannot say that they are "wrong": they simply seem inadequate to encompass the work's complexities.

1. The opera is a simple expression of cynicism, exposing the illusoriness of such ideals as virtue, honor, fidelity; nothing positive is left intact at the end. It might be just possible to argue this from a reading of the libretto; no one sensitive to Mozart's music will find it worth more than a passing shrug.

2. Composed at the period of transition, the work is a satire on the "new" romanticism—specifically, the excesses of "romantic love"—from the standpoint of eighteenth-century rationalism. Such a reading might seem confirmed by the "moral" sung by the six characters collectively at the end ("Happy is he who . . . always lets reason be his guide"), and by the deliberately exaggerated emotions of much of the first act (the two great quintets, Fiordiligi's "Come scoglio," etc.). Yet the pointing of such a moral was a convention of the period (compare the end of *Don Giovanni*, and Stravinsky's appropriation of it for *The Rake's Progress*); its very triteness should make us wary of reducing the complexities of all that has gone before to a simple banal "message," the actual effect being rather of a knowingly conventional resolution of problems that can't be resolved. One might also suggest that the kind of "romantic love" dramatized in *Così*, with its idealization of the love-object, was scarcely an invention of the Romantic period: it goes right back through history to the troubadours, and was a commonplace of the eighteenth-century pastoral.

3. The opera (subtitled "The School for Lovers") is about the necessity of

learning to accept human weakness and live with it; in the future the lovers will not idealize each other, will have no exaggerated expectations, and will thereby achieve a livable degree of happiness. This is a variant on the "rationalism" reading. I find it reasonable enough, except that I have my doubts as to whether anyone, let alone Fiordiligi, is likely to be happy for very long with Guglielmo, or, for that matter, whether Ferrando will be content for long with a wife whose capacity for commitment is as precarious as Dorabella's. Such doubts have, in recent years, led to:

4. The notion that the opera should end with the two pairs of lovers being recoupled for the promised wedding, Fiordiligi with Ferrando, Dorabella with Guglielmo (at least one recent production, to my knowledge, has made this explicit, overriding the minor inconvenience of the text). In such a literal form I find this unacceptable (and in any case the furiously jealous and - possessive Guglielmo and the flighty Dorabella appear even more mismatched than they were with their original partners), but it points to elements that are clearly there. A common structure in Mozart's operas (and elsewhere—see, for example, certain Astaire/Rogers musicals) juxtaposes a pair of "serious" lovers with a pair of "comic" ones, the latter invariably occupying a lower position in the social hierarchy, usually that of servants: the clearest instances are *Die Entführung aus dem Serail* and *The Magic Flute*, but *Figaro* has essentially the same pattern. One might argue that certain of the poignance and disturbance of *Così* derives from the fact that the couples have got jumbled up, Guglielmo's comic vanity and bluster and Dorabella's barely suppressible flightiness marking them as the "inferior" couple (though not in this case socially). Clearly, Fiordiligi and Ferrando are characterized as capable of far greater depth and delicacy of feeling. I accept that they are far more suited to each other than to their respective partners; that in the course of the opera they recognize each other's qualities; and that they at least *begin* to fall genuinely in love. Certainly, this helps toward explaining the sense of dissonance and unease commonly experienced at the ending, but I don't think it should be resolved by recoupling the pairs. The point is surely that even after all the illusions have been shattered, the pull of social convention remains. The characters return, almost automatically, to their original lovers: if there is no such thing as authentic fidelity, there is still its social concept that must be respected. And, after all, the "happy ending" was not invented by Hollywood. Comedies have happy endings—which can then be inflected by their authors with various degrees of irony. In this case, Mozart withholds in the music any suggestion of the "bella calma" promised by the text, setting it as a boisterous *allegro* accompanied by a burbling, disruptive figure in the woodwind.

However, the real reason why I find this interpretation inadequate is that the opera has established long before the finale is reached that *no* pairing or re-pairing of the characters can constitute an uncompromised or convincing happy ending.

Mozart seems in general not to have regarded his operas as sacrosanct, as having necessarily achieved a final, definitive form: in both *Figaro* and *Don Giovanni* he was not above adding or substituting new arias (usually to satisfy the needs of particular singers). But *Così* strikes me as carrying this kind of fluidity much further. It is not only that Mozart composed a substitute aria for Guglielmo, and sanctioned various cuts in a work that can feel very long on stage; one has a pervasive sense (quite different from the effect of, especially, *Figaro*, with its very strong cause-and-effect narrative line and its clearly delineated characters) that many things could be added, subtracted, and transposed. Of all the Mozart operas *Così* is the most fluid in effect, the usual clearcut formal divisions (recitative, aria, ensemble . . .) almost breaking down, so that one flows into the other. There are more ensembles than ever before or after, and remarkably few "big" arias. Think the phrase "Mozart aria" and let examples come spontaneously into your mind: it is unlikely that any of the first six—or even twelve—will be from *Così*. Mozart here anticipates the breakdown of such formal divisions that occurred well into the nineteenth century, when the "opera" becomes the "music drama."

This sense of fluidity applies also to the four leading characters. Alfonso and Despina are sharply defined, but with the lovers we feel a pervasive uncertainty: for example, in the scene of farewells, are the men *merely* play-acting, or are they also imagining how they would feel were the situation genuine? Are the women behaving merely as they think women *ought* to behave, or is there a degree of authenticity in their protestations, and if so *what* degree? (Our uncertainty, it must be added, is entirely the product of Mozart's music, which both transforms and transcends the libretto's brittle comedy.) Do the men merely *feign* to fall in love with each other's partners, or is there a point where the feigning becomes reality? And if so, at *which* point? Is the newfound passion with which Ferrando eventually seduces Fiordiligi (in the great duet "Fra gli amplessi . . .") motivated by genuine feeling for her or by a desire to prove that she is no better than Dorabella (who has already succumbed) and, especially, by his hurt at his "friend" Guglielmo's brutal assertion of his innate superiority? Or all of these? We can never be sure, from the music, and a sensitive producer would leave us uncertain instead of (as usually happens) tipping the scales in favor of one "coherent" reading or another. The effect is to suggest that, as the opera progresses, the characters themselves no longer understand their own motivations and emotions, all certitude dissolving—precisely what happens to Christine in *Rules of the Game*, and for very similar reasons. This gradual erosion of certainties seems to me the key to the innermost meaning of both works.

The six characters of *Così* could be arranged on a grid according to their degrees of knowledge: at the top, Don Alfonso, who knows everything (including the outcome); below him, the two men, who know everything *except* the outcome; below them, Despina, who is let in on some of the secrets and assists in certain of the deceptions, but doesn't know until the end that the "Albanians" are the lovers in disguise; at the bottom, the two sisters, who know nothing of what is going on until the final "unmasking." Turn the grid upside down, and you have (with one partial exception) a grid of Mozart's (and the audience's) sympathies, in exactly inverse ratio to the degree of knowledge. The partial exception is that Ferrando is clearly differentiated (especially in his music) from Guglielmo: more sensitive, less vain, susceptible to hurt beyond the mere injury to his ego. It is as impossible (aside from the requirements of vocal range) to imagine Ferrando singing "Donne mie, le fate e tanti . . ." as it is to imagine Guglielmo singing "Una aura amorosa." Significantly, in the Act 2 finale, after Don Alfonso tells them to marry anyway, with illusions dispelled and in full knowledge of human "weakness," Ferrando sings with the women while Guglielmo continues to curse and grumble in counterpoint (Fiordiligi is clearly doomed to one hell of a life). Yet Ferrando, for all his superior sensibility, is equally complicit in a plot that exploits and manipulates the women, the purpose of which is essentially to reassure and bolster the male ego at their expense.

The opera makes it clear that the people who are most bound by the rules of this particular game are the women: the "rules" involving not only strict fidelity but also the willingness to accept subordination, restriction to the domestic sphere, and respectability. If Fiordiligi, in the course of the action, comes somewhat to resemble Christine, it is in her confusion, but a confusion precipitated by her discovery, not of her spouse's infidelity, but of her own. In her efforts to talk herself out of surrendering she runs the whole gamut from "What will the neighbors say?" through "Suppose our lovers find out?" to a genuine (if somewhat misguided) concern for her lover's potential hurt. Her surrender to Ferrando is quite different from Dorabella's to Guglielmo: one has only to compare the two marvelous duets in which the respective surrenders occur. "Il core vi dono . . ." (Dorabella / Guglielmo) is charming and lightweight, neither character deeply engaged, but (from very different motives) enjoying the "play." "Fra gli amplessi . . . ," on the contrary, which opens with Fiordiligi alone, about to flee temptation, intercepted by Ferrando, grows in intensity and culminates in the magnificent coda of (perhaps mutual) surrender, "Abbracciami . . ."

Mozart's setting of this moment brings me to what seems the crux: the way in which the music (especially the *women's* music) repeatedly expresses a longing in excess of the actual content of the text, a longing that perhaps resists definition in terms of an object—a longing for the "impossible," for *something beyond* what the rules of society permit, a utopian longing. This ineffable *something* is present in numbers signified in the text as both "happy" (the sisters' first duet, "Ah guarda, sorella . . . ," where, curiously, the longing reaches its peak at the words "Io sono felice," "I am happy") and "sad" (the opening of the Act 1 finale, "Ah se tutta . . ."). It pervades the entire first act scene of farewells (which should *never* be acted or sung as merely comic). The music consistently confers upon the action and the characters (the women, and sometimes Ferrando) an emotional authenticity that completely invalidates the notion that the opera is primarily satirical or only concerned with illusions and pretense: the emotion communicated is pervasively *in excess* of the apparent meaning of the action. It is of course a component of that extraordinary complex of (sometimes contradictory or ambivalent) emotional expression we call "Mozartian," but it pervades *Così* more than any of the other operas to the extent that it might be claimed as the work's dominant mode. And its full expression is almost exclusively reserved for the sisters, with Ferrando allowed to share it at privileged moments.

What, exactly, do the characters of *Così* learn (those who are capable of learning)? Not merely, I think, that they are mismatched and might more appropriately exchange partners (though this is true, in the case at least of Fiordiligi and Ferrando). Don't they rather come dangerously close (closer, perhaps, even than the characters of *Rules of the Game*) to the explosive perception that the concept of the "couple" is itself absurdly restrictive and oppressive? Isn't the pervasive yearning for something more than just a different partner? Isn't the real logic of the women's discovery that they can move quite swiftly from one commitment to another, that they should be able to enjoy the company (in or out of bed) of *both* men? Fiordiligi (surely the character one most trusts and respects?), when she at last allows herself to recognize her weakness, confesses, not that she has simply switched allegiance from one man to another (like the flibbertigibbet Dorabella), but that she is experiencing "feelings of love, and not *just* for Guglielmo." Like *Rules of the Game*, is this a work about people who go too far, or about people who can't quite go far enough? What exactly *do* we feel at that extraordinary, tantalizing, enigmatic "happy ending"?

And what of Despina, the opera's highly explicit spokesperson for promiscuity? She is crucial, I think, in defining what *Così* is about, but to say this is by no means to imply that her position is endorsed. The version of "promiscuity" she promotes with such conviction is not in the least revolutionary but simply the other side of the same coin: on the one side monogamous marriage and the ideal of exclusive romantic love, on the other the fun and excitement of breaking the rules surreptitiously—"cheating," deceit, endless flirtation and titillation, the exploitation of her sexuality as the woman's weapon in the "battle of the sexes": the "rules of the game" when it is controlled by men versus the rules when it is controlled by women, both versions coexisting within the dominant organization of sexuality, both having their source in the exercise of power. Mozart makes the Despina credo almost irresistibly attractive and seductive (as the sisters discover): after all, it does offer women an escape from the "servitude" of monogamy. What "places" it definitively, however, is an absence: Despina is the only character in the opera who is denied all access to the music of "yearning" (even Don Alfonso, who, one might argue, either is or ought to be gay, within a society that can't recognize such things, is allowed to participate in what is surely, from the viewpoint of sheer beauty, one of the opera's high points, the trio of prayer and longing as the lovers' boat disappears in the distance). If the "music of yearning" embodies the profound question of *Così fan tutte*, Despina clearly cannot provide an answer. "Promiscuity" within the rules must not be mistaken for the authentic sexual freedom— sexuality freed from all taint of jealousy, possessiveness, and domination— that would shatter them forever.

Belonging respectively to the end of the eighteenth century and the middle of the twentieth, these works raise issues—or better, *feelings*—that our culture is still afraid to confront. They would undermine its very foundations.

# CHAPTER 5

# Resistance to Definition: Ozu's "Noriko" Trilogy

> They don't understand—that's why they say it's Zen or something like that.
> —Ozu on foreign critics

## I

### Clearing the Ground

This "essay" has developed out of my great love for Ozu's work—his best films, for me, belong up there with the finest of Mizoguchi, Renoir, Ophuls, Hitchcock, and Hawks as representative of the peaks of cinematic achievement so far—and a general dissatisfaction with Western critical accounts of its significance. The first part will examine the reception (in all its variety and contradiction) of Ozu's work in the West, then outline my own general attitude to his films; the second will offer a reading of three films from his late (post-World War II) period, *Late Spring* (1949), *Early Summer* (1951), and *Tokyo Story* (1953). All three are now widely available on video in North America.

### Ozu's "Japaneseness"

It has become a commonplace in the West that Yasujiro Ozu is the most "Japanese" of directors; it seems to me a commonplace that, like many others, needs to be carefully examined and challenged. The reason usually given for Ozu's late recognition in the West is that the Japanese themselves considered his work "unexportable" because it belonged so peculiarly to its culture as to be virtually inaccessible beyond it. I have encountered this "fact" many times but have never seen a source cited: it may well be less fact than convenient myth. From the meager evidence it seems more likely that, by the mid-1950s, it never occurred to the Japanese to "export" Ozu, not because his work is inaccessible (which it obviously isn't), but because it was widely regarded in Japan as old-fashioned, conservative, and rather boring.

One should also take into account the alleged unexportability historically, within the context of what the Japanese *did* consider as exportable. We know that the (cinematic) gateway to the West was opened by Akira Kurosawa's *Rashomon* and its Grand Prix at Venice in 1951. It was followed by Teinosuke Kinugasa's *Gate of Hell* (1954), instantly hailed as a revelatory masterpiece, now seen to have been massively overrated, an academic piece with beautiful color and costumes; by other Kurosawa period films (notably *The Seven Samurai*); and by Kenji Mizoguchi's late period films, *Ugetsu Monogatari*, *Sansho Dayu* (*Sansho the Bailiff*), *The Life of Oharu*. The case of the Mizoguchi works is especially revealing because there is evidence that they were made partly *for* the West and designed to win prizes at European festivals. Though Kurosawa was at the time regarded in the West as the major figure in this newly discovered national cinema, the only one of his contemporary dramas to get any wide exposure or critical recognition was *Ikiru* (1952), a fact I would account for by reference to its very striking structural complexity and visual rhetoric (this was roughly the period when *Citizen Kane* began to emerge from critics' polls as "the greatest film ever made"). Minor (and to me not very interesting) works like *Tora No-O* and *The Hidden Fortress* (and subsequently *Yojimbo* and *Sanjuro*) circulated in the West long before the far superior films noirs *Drunken Angel*, *Stray Dog*, and above all *High and Low*. Similarly, the only contemporary film of Mizoguchi that received widespread distribution (at least in English-speaking countries) was his last, *Street of Shame*. It played in London at a theatre normally dedicated to soft-core pornography, with lurid posters of prostitutes leaning against lampposts in provocative poses and the slogan "Night Life of the Orient!!!" I don't think one can attribute its exposure to Mizoguchi's reputation as an artist.

In brief, what the Japanese assumed (by and large correctly) that the West was interested in was the "exotic": the Japanese past, with its feudal lords, civil wars, wandering samurai, strange attire, alien landscapes ("just like Japanese paintings"), elaborate ceremony and ritual, weird legends, folktales and ghost stories (*Onibaba* and *Kwaidan* were among the most commercially successful Japanese films in the West). And, conversely, if this assessment was correct, then why would we pay money to see a series of films with confusingly similar titles about "ordinary" middle-class people going about their daily lives in a contemporary setting, without even the benefit of "striking" camera angles?—films that deliberately eschewed Kurosawan visual rhetoric as an aesthetic principle?

I would argue that on the level of actual human emotional contact, Ozu is the *most* accessible to Western audiences of all the major figures of Japanese cinema. But we were supposed to want "otherness" and that is what we got: why send us films that, for all the "local" cultural variations, spoke to us very directly of problems inevitably faced by people living within a contemporary patriarchal-capitalist culture?

I am in a somewhat delicate position here. I don't wish to underestimate the importance of cultural difference, which gives Ozu's work something of its specificity. On the other hand, I feel strongly that his "Japaneseness" has been grossly overemphasized by Western critics. Claims for it have of course been made primarily (and correctly) on grounds of the peculiarities of his shooting/editing style, the aspect of his work that has received (understandably but disproportionately) the most serious critical attention. But, unless one is a theory-oriented critic dedicated to a search for alternatives to the classical Hollywood style, one does not go to Ozu's films to count the number of times the camera crosses the 180-degree line or to meditate on the deprivation (in the last six color films the absence) of camera movement. I am not suggesting that these things are unimportant: they crucially determine *how* we experience the films' narratives. But for most of us it is still the narrative that is our primary focus, the primary source of our emotional experience. We care, shall we say, whether or not Setsuko Hara is going to get married, and if so to whom, before we care about the height and distance at which Ozu has placed the camera, and I would dare hazard a guess that Ozu shared that priority. His films are not reducible to exercises in style.

I shall return to the question of style and its function later. I want first to consider briefly to what extent a study of Japanese culture is necessary for an understanding of Ozu's films. My contention—which will not be popular with scholars—is that, with certain qualifications, a sensitive and responsive viewer can deduce *from* the films all that is needed, by and large, for a general understanding of them. Such a viewer will not need to be told of the importance in Japanese culture of the figure of the father, the stress placed on filial duty, and the traditional (if archaic) belief in the impropriety of a widower or (more particularly) a widow remarrying. What she/he will of course miss is the significance of a number of details, but when this is grasped it generally (in my experience) confirms the correctness of one's perceptions rather than contradicting them.

Take a somewhat extreme example, from Ozu's late silent film *A Story of Floating Weeds* (1934; remade by Ozu in 1959 as *Floating Weeds*, aka *Drifting*

*Weeds*). It is certainly useful to know that the beautiful old but flourishing tree, surrounded by mysterious (to the uninitiated) little white markers stuck in the ground, the scene of the young lovers' nocturnal rendezvous, is a Shinto shrine, hence associated with fertility, nature, life-renewal, and that this contrasts with the figure of the Buddha repeatedly linked to the older characters within the theater, a symbol of resignation and acceptance. But does such knowledge do more than confirm what is already clear in the imagery, transculturally: the flourishing tree in its natural setting, the impassive stone figure in its gloomy interior? Nothing in the film suggests that we are to find deep religious meaning in these images, whose effect is more poetic than metaphysical.

There are difficult critical issues involved here. It seems to me that, unless one is born and raised in it, one will always view a foreign culture from the outside: even to spend ten years in Japan as an adult is not commensurate with being born Japanese. And Pope's familiar adage applies here: a little learning is indeed a dangerous thing if we trust it too far. One can become so impressed with one's assumed grasp of Japanese culture that one succumbs to the temptation to interpret Japanese films exclusively in relation to it (Japanese culture encourages such-and-such an attitude to life, *therefore* Ozu, who is known to be "typically" Japanese, must share that attitude), forgetting that much of what is important may be eccentric, individual, critical, or anomalous. A knowledge of the culture is important as a safeguard against demonstrable error, but in the last resort critics must trust their own perceptions, their own sense of relatedness to the works.

Further, the value of a work of art can never be objectively defined and fixed; its value will depend on its usefulness (when it ceases to be useful to us it can be abandoned to the scholars), and its usefulness will vary, both in degree and in kind, with the historical/cultural situation within which it is received. Even if we *could* experience Ozu's films exactly as a Japanese experiences them (and *which* Japanese?—it is the grossest of errors to suppose that all members of a foreign culture share the same perceptions), I am not convinced that this would be desirable: we can only use the films insofar as we can relate to them, and relate them to our own cultural situation (without, of course, demanding a perfect fit!) and its problems, tensions, contradictions.

It is relevant here to mention one Japanese film critic whose work has been extensively translated into English, Tadao Sato, because in some quarters it has been assumed to carry more weight than it deserves. Sato is essentially a journalist-critic whose writings have no firmer basis than a middle-of-the-road bourgeois humanism (if there are Japanese equivalents for, say, Andrew Britton, Stephen Heath, Richard Dyer, or Noel Burch, they remain inaccessible in the West). The resulting perceptions, though sometimes interesting, strike me as in the main casual and unsystematic, the value judgments largely conventional. The quite widespread sense that Sato must be "right" about Japanese films because he is Japanese has no firmer basis than a belief that, say, Judith Crist must be "right" about American films because she is American. I see Ozu as far more complex, difficult, and ambiguous than the conventional conservative figure presented by Sato (which appears to represent a Japanese consensus which the West has been all too ready to adopt without question). This is not of course to suggest that he is not worth reading: within the limitations of his ambitions he is sympathetic and intelligent, and we can learn a lot from him about how Japanese films have been received by the middle-to-highbrow sector of the Japanese bourgeoisie. I don't see that it follows that we must receive them in the same way.

Ozu is difficult not because of cultural difference but because he represents the finest type of artist: he is difficult in the sense in which Mozart is difficult, the difficulty arising from the complexities of the artist's apprehension of human life within a certain phase of cultural evolution and his openness to shifting cross-currents and conflicting impulses, and it is compounded by the deceptive simplicity and transparency of his style.

## Western Approaches to Ozu

It seems obligatory to begin with Donald Richie, whose pioneer work was instrumental in—if not quite introducing Japanese cinema to Western criticism—helping to make it accessible. Western critical discourse on Japanese cinema in general, and especially on Ozu and Kurosawa, stems from Richie even when it substantially departs from him, and his work established, for better or for worse, how most people still look at Ozu's films. Unlike much "pioneer" work his book on Ozu (published in 1974, but much of it had appeared in journals earlier) remains readable and stimulating, if open to disagreement.

We owe Richie an immense debt, and it seems ungrateful to go on to say that his influence has ultimately blocked as much as it opened. This is not his fault. We live in a culture that calls itself a democracy but does not encourage its inhabitants to think independently—a "democracy" built upon interlocking systems of authority, domination, and coercion which determine their very thought-patterns and attitudes. Within it the critic (because he speaks as he must from a position of knowledge and expertise) is all too readily accepted as a kind of oracle of "truth" in which the distinction between knowledge and opinion becomes blurred. This attribution of the wrong kind of "authority" is all too frequently buttressed by the glib clichés of reviewers. I am looking at a prime example quoted on the back cover of Richie's Ozu book ("Is and probably will remain the definitive in-English study of Ozu and his films"), the kind of remark that it is illegitimate to make about anyone and anything, and which one hopes Richie himself would have repudiated. In such a culture, the critic is not to blame if he/she is not read critically.

Richie established two basic assumptions about Ozu that have proved very hard to undermine or dislodge (they are plausible enough, and one cannot exactly say that they are "wrong"): his Japaneseness and his essentialism. Here they are, conveniently combined in two sentences almost at the beginning of the book: "In the feeling of transience, of the mutability and beauty of all life, Ozu joins the greatest Japanese artists. It is here that we taste, undiluted and authentic, the Japanese flavor." That strikes me, in fact, as a sentimentalization of Ozu that obliterates most of the tensions and complexities that underlie his work. It may seem curious that the films are conceived as at once quintessentially Japanese (i.e., culturally specific) and about "the human condition" (a phrase that recurs), conceived of as universal and eternal. But the apparent paradox rests upon a further assumption very common in the West (it seems to be shared by, for example, so different a critic as Noel Burch), the assumption that Eastern cultures are in some profound way superior, repositories of a deeper (or "higher") spiritual knowledge and "truth" to which we cannot expect to gain complete access. This turns up in the West repeatedly in the veneration for "Eastern philosophies," invariably detached from the cultural realities that gave rise to them. I was struck by this all over again when I visited the (very impressive) touring exhibition of Tibetan art: the very elaborate and learned program guide presented the works exclusively in terms of a transcendent "wisdom," offering no assistance whatever to anyone interested in learning something about the material realities (social, political, economic) of the culture within which the works were produced, a point recently reinforced by Scorsese's *Kundun*.

From these basic assumptions about Ozu others follow, becoming progressively misleading and restrictive. Richie opens his introductory chapter on "the subject and theme of Ozu's films" with the following: "Yasujiro Ozu, the man whom his kinsmen consider the most Japanese of all film directors, has but one major subject, the Japanese family, and but one major theme, its dissolution." Again, such an assertion gains weight (and a very long life) from its obvious plausibility: virtually all of Ozu's films are about families, and many (though by no means all) trace their dissolution or its consequences. Yet its dangers become clear in the immediate sequel: "the characters are family members rather than members of a society." This appears obvious nonsense (how can they possibly be one without also being the other?), but in reference to Ozu of all artists it becomes staggeringly obtuse. It's true that Richie applies it to "the later pictures," but presumably he includes *Tokyo Story* (to take but one obvious example) among them, and it's difficult to see how anyone could watch that film and fail to be aware of its complex analysis and critique of a society at a certain phase of its evolution.

The emphasis on Japaneseness and essentialism also established—greatly to Ozu's harm—the inevitable corollary, that the values the films enact and endorse are in a clearcut, unambiguous way very conservative, reactionary, and traditional. This view (sanctioned, after all, by the Japanese themselves, though they have tended in recent decades to deplore rather than sentimentalize it) still appears to remain substantially unchallenged, the alternative view of Ozu's work as "radical" being restricted exclusively to its formal strategies and stylistic devices to which the dramatic content is apparently irrelevant. The emphasis on the films' supposed embodiment of some form of transcendental contemplation also leads Richie into some very strange specific readings that seem quite at odds with the particular film's tone: one is pulled up short when one finds the conclusion of *Late Spring*—among the most disturbing and desolate in all Ozu's work—described in terms of "untroubled serenity."

Richie's book was followed in the later 1970s by two other works on Japanese cinema that represent diametrically opposed approaches; they might at first glance appear complementary but prove merely incompatible: Joan Mellen's *The Waves at Genji's Door* (1976), dedicated to Donald Richie, and Noel Burch's *To the Distant Observer* (1979). Traditional aesthetics has discussed works of art as a marriage of "form" and "content." In this case content analysis (Mellen) and formalism (Burch) signally fail to combine to produce a satisfying synthesis, both critics seeming serenely unaware of the deficiencies of their approaches.

Mellen offers a type of feminist-oriented sociology. It is only a slight exaggeration to describe her procedure thus: she gives us a plot synopsis, then tells us on the strength of it whether the film is conservative, liberal, radical, etc. Her intermittent (and always halfhearted) attempts to acknowledge the films' stylistic dimension manage to be both vague and irrelevant. We are told, for example, that in Mizoguchi's *Osaka Elegy* ("his most brilliant prewar film"—but one must assume that she had not seen *Sisters of the Gion* as it gets no mention), "the mature Mizoguchi style emerges for the first time." But what is this "mature Mizoguchi style"? The style of *Zangiku Monogatari* (*Story of the Last Chrysanthemums*) or that of the late works of the 1950s? The two are quite distinct. If Mellen is referring to Mizoguchi's predilection for long takes (the one feature that unites the various periods), *that* emerged long before *Osaka Elegy*. Or what is one to make of an unfortunately representative remark (it occurs in the discussion of *Sansho Dayu/Sansho the Bailiff*) such as, "In a very deep-focus shot, reflective of Mizoguchi's sense of ubiquitous evil, Zushio marches with his men on Sancho's (*sic*) manor"? I have been unable to identify the "very deep-focus shot" to which Mellen is referring, and am quite at a loss to see exactly how (if it in fact exists) it could reflect a "sense of ubiquitous evil."

The plot synopses might be held to have a certain limited usefulness: if they tell us nothing about intrinsic artistic value (which is not Mellen's concern, though she occasionally dabbles in it), they are likely to reveal the major themes of Japanese cinema in specific periods and the preoccupations of leading filmmakers. Mellen has researched her subject with formidable determination and energy, reporting on an immense number of films, many of which most of us may never get the chance to see. Unfortunately, even this limited usefulness proves seriously compromised when one happens upon the synopsis of a film with which one is familiar and finds it riddled with inaccuracies. The following, again from the account of *Sansho Dayu* (the spelling "Sancho" is consistent throughout, giving the impression that Mellen believes him to be Spanish) can stand as representative: "As loyal and cynical servant of the Bailiff, Zushio is assigned the most despicable chores. He must take an old woman, Namiji, into the woods where she will be left to die. Because she is too old to work, the Bailiff refuses to feed her. . . . Anju, unlike her brother, is pained by the cruelty, and wishes for Namiji that in her next life she will be born into a rich family." In fact, three female characters appear in the sequence in question and Mellen has confused them. Namiji is middle-aged and by no means "too old to work": she *is* severely ill, perhaps dying. There is indeed an "old woman" (who eventually helps Anju to escape), and it is she (not Anju, who would never say such a thing) who expresses the wish that Namiji be reincarnated in a wealthy family. The problem, of course, is not with specific instances: when one realizes just how sloppy these synopses are of films one has seen (my copy of Mellen's book has fifteen question marks penciled in the margins of the account of *Sansho Dayu* alone), how is one to trust the synopses of all those one hasn't? Mellen's project, a feminist overview of Japanese cinema, is admirable, but its execution is so slipshod and breathless that one ends up questioning the book's value.

Mellen's view of Ozu is perhaps predictable, given the book's general crudity, though rather surprisingly the sections on his films are among its better parts, relatively accurate and thoughtful, conveying an attempt at scrupulous fairness toward an artist whose position Mellen clearly finds antipathetic; although seen overall as enclosed within a conservative-traditional value system, Ozu is at least permitted a certain complexity and sense of disturbance. The enclosure, however, is established in the very first sentence of her first discussion of Ozu, and, significantly, it is given as received opinion and never challenged: "Ozu and Kurosawa are *said* [my italics] to be at opposite political poles." The implicit assumption determines Mellen's treatment of Ozu throughout the book, severely inhibiting any possibility of a free and open exploration of his films. To reduce the work of a great artist to the (alleged) political opinions of the person is as great an error with Ozu as it is with Ford. That said, I shall not examine Mellen's treatment of Ozu in detail, preferring to let her account of *Tokyo Story* stand beside my own and leave judgment to the reader.

Noel Burch's *To the Distant Observer* is a very different story: it is one of the very few books of film criticism to which I return repeatedly, and always with profit (if also with increasing dissatisfaction). Burch's analyses are invariably illuminating, and he pursues his argument with rigorous logic; his book performs to a high degree what is perhaps criticism's most important function—not the production of "truth" or of "definitive" readings, but the opening up of whole new aspects of an artist's work, or of cinema itself, rendering accessible what was previously closed (the same quality that makes Bazin a great critic, rather than any confidence in his theories). My problem with the book—and it is a huge one—is that I happen not to share most of the assumptions that form its premise.

It will here be necessary for me to outline what I take those assumptions (both explicit and implicit) to be, and I do so with some misgiving. The delicacy and subtlety of Burch's best work always makes my own seem, in comparison, ham-fisted, and I am afraid of falling into the common error of producing a parody rather than a fair assessment. It is important, then, that readers test my summary by reference to the original; it is in any case obligatory reading for anyone seriously interested in the cinema (and not only Japanese). The basic assumptions seem to me to be

- that the "great" or significant works of art are those which are *formally* innovative, exploring and extending the material properties of their medium, and that their greatness lies precisely in this.

- that the material properties of film are those that it inherited from photography and developed into cinematography—camera movement, framing, editing, etc.—combined, subsequently, with the material properties of sound recording; they are not those it inherited from the realist novel (which of course cannot be regarded as "material" in the same sense). Narrative patterns, the direction of actors and the actors themselves, plot and characterization, the thematic organization of the narrative material, the ideological/political position of the filmmaker(s) as realized in the narrative development—none of these is among the "material properties" of film, hence all are irrelevant to an aesthetics of film. (This, already, is where I begin to be afraid of lapsing into parody: can anyone *really* mean this? Yet it is what I understand from Burch's writings.)

- that mainstream American, and most other mainstream, cinema (aside from an occasional anomaly), from the point quite early on when its shooting and editing methods became organized into what have come to be called "the Hollywood codes," or "the Western codes," must be dismissed in toto. The Hollywood codes render innovation impossible because they subordinate the material properties to narrative, and they have come to dominate the development of cinema all over the world.

- that beyond this, however, there is something fundamentally wrong and misguided not only about mainstream *cinema* but with the entire Western tradition that produced it. The ultimate enemy is the Renaissance discovery (or invention) of the laws of perspective, which impose on the spectator a certain way of looking and a delusion that reality is unified. All the major developments in mainstream Western art since have their source in this disastrous historical moment by which all of us have subsequently been victimized. (Therefore all mainstream Western art from the Renaissance on until the evolution of Modernism is worse than worthless, is actively reprehensible??? I don't think anyone has actually *said* this, but it seems to follow logically).

- and that it follows, then, that the critic's task is to seek out alternatives to the mainstream: specifically, types of cinema that do not subordinate the "material properties" to narrative, do not impose a unified vision on the spectator, and (a related concern) are not "anthropocentric." (I may as well say at once that I don't believe that any of these alternatives can be found in the work of Ozu.) Such types should be the critic's only *positive* interest, his/her only duty beyond them being to explain as succinctly as possible why he/she rejects everything else.

Such assumptions have drastic consequences, the first of which is the logical, inevitable attraction to the avant-garde, or at least certain forms of it. As

we now understand the term, avant-garde art—works *deliberately* opposed
to the mainstream produced by and for a small alienated elite, with no
hope of or wish for incorporation or wider recognition, which would
instantly defeat their purpose—is a purely twentieth-century phenomenon.
Earlier, "difficult," "advanced," or "problematic" work (that of late
Beethoven or late Schubert, for example) was regarded as the product of personal eccentricity rather than as part of a deliberately oppositional, more
or less organized, movement, and eventually either would (Berlioz) or
wouldn't (the later works of William Blake) find its place in the mainstream,
which it would then in the former case profoundly influence and transform.
In fact, the richest periods in the history of art production (and I would
hazard a not entirely uneducated guess that this applies beyond Western culture) have always been characterized (like classical Hollywood) by the existence of a generally accepted set of conventions, forms, and idioms which
the great artists, far from simply rejecting, have *used*, often extending and
developing them to the point where they are transformed: Shakespeare,
Bach, Mozart, and Hitchcock will do as examples. From this viewpoint, an
aesthetic that would logically produce, say, Michael Snow's *Wave Length* as a
supreme achievement and dismiss *The Quiet Man*, *Rio Bravo*, and *North by
Northwest* as so negligible as to be unworthy of serious attention can only
appear ridiculous.

Burch does not of course attempt to enlist Ozu in an avant-garde. Perhaps
the most impressive and valuable aspect of his book (though—also
perhaps—it is the aspect about which one should be most cautious) is his
loving re-creation of elements of a peculiarly Japanese aesthetic tradition in
a kind of selective *collage*, to which the work of Ozu, Mizoguchi, and others
is then convincingly and illuminatingly related. The problem here is that
the "Japanese" elements selected (those most antipathetic to the traditions
of the West), and their transformation into filmic practice, are then erected
into an alternative to the Western modes, and it is clear that what Burch
has in mind is not an alternative in the usual sense (as one might say meat
is an alternative to fish, so that one might enjoy the one on Monday,
the other on Tuesday): the implication here is that you must choose one
and rigorously forswear the other forever. Personally, I experience not the
slightest difficulty in passing from, say, *A Story of Floating Weeds* to *The Scarlet
Empress* (they were made in the same year): both seem to me masterpieces,
and I see no reason to reject Sternberg's film because the eyelines match
(somewhat dubiously at times—witness the supposed exchange of
looks between Dietrich and John Lodge in the astonishing wedding
sequence, where his actual position has never been established) and it obeys
the 180-degree rule. At one point in his book Burch makes a disparaging

comment on Western critics who "make a fetish" of Hollywood genre movies. If one takes the term in its strict sense—the isolation of a part, which is then separated from and substituted for the whole, as a defense against full involvement—then the remark rebounds: Burch makes, precisely, a "fetish" out of the formal elements he isolates from the films' total "signifying practice."

All this has further drastic consequences not only for his attitude to Western cinema but for the films of Ozu and Mizoguchi themselves. Only a very small handful of films from their respective oeuvres can be permitted entrance into this strange and very exclusive new pantheon: to be precise, those made in the 1930s and early 1940s. Their post-World War II work is rejected virtually in toto: Ozu's because the alternative practice rigidified into academicism (translate: he was content to *use* the innovations he had already developed rather than continue to innovate), Mizoguchi's because he was guilty of the far more reprehensible act of capitulating to the Western modes (the fact that he developed them, beyond anything in Orson Welles or William Wyler, into a medium for the most delicate and complex expression is of no significance). Hence none of the films with which the present chapter is concerned is accorded a single reference in Burch's book. Let me repeat, this follows with perfect logic from the premises: it is the premises I find totally unacceptable. The effect of his work has been, for me, enormously to increase my understanding of, and admiration for, say, *A Story of Floating Weeds* and *Sisters of the Gion*, while leaving completely intact my love for *Late Spring* and *Tokyo Story*, or for *My Love Has Been Burning* and *Ugetsu Monogatari*.

I don't, however, wish to end on a note of absolute or clearcut opposition. Burch and I both present ourselves as radicals in relation to Western culture and its cinema; the difference is not the simple one between rejection and acceptance. It is perhaps rooted in a deeply personal difference: he has been able to locate himself, psychologically, outside mainstream Western culture and I have not. That is to say that my own sense of alienation, while extreme, is not complete. Hence he looks at mainstream Western cinema from outside, and dismisses it; I remain within, exploring its products, probing its cracks and fissures, its contradictions, the ideological ambiguities of its greatest works. It would be as impossible for me to reject Hawks, Hitchcock, Ford, McCarey, Ophuls, Sternberg . . . in favor of a handful of Japanese movies, as it would be to reject Mozart, Mahler, Stravinsky in favor of traditional Japanese music. Which would amount, in principle, to the same thing.

✦ ✦ ✦

I am reluctant to comment on the work of David Bordwell, rather as I was on that of Donald Richie: I owe his book (*Ozu and the Poetics of Cinema*) a considerable debt of gratitude. My reservations arise from fundamental differences both of aims and temperament.

Among serious writers on the arts one can broadly distinguish three categories which interact but also serve distinct functions: the theorist, the scholar, the critic. (A fourth category, the reviewer, is, in the great majority of cases, discrete from all three, though it pretends to the third.) The theorist develops theories, the scholar amasses information, the critic engages passionately with specific works and arrives at value judgments. If I see the critic as the highest of these functions, I am perfectly aware that this goes quite against the flow of the last few decades of serious work on the cinema (which have strongly favored theory, or an amalgam of theory and scholarship, attempting to exile the critic into the outer circles of journalism), and also that a strongly personal bias operates here: I aspire, however inadequately, to the almost lost status of the critic. In a sense, certainly, the critic is a parasite, depending upon the theorist for theories and the scholar for information: this is what distinguishes her/him from the reviewer, who is typically innocent of either theory or scholarship.

For me, Bordwell's value is that of the scholar, and his problem is that he seems to want to conflate scholarship with criticism. The point can be made by comparing him with Noel Burch, many of whose premises he shares. Burch's work has a strong basis in both theory and scholarship, but it is animated everywhere by the critic's passionate engagement—that is what makes it so exciting and challenging. Although I disagree with Bordwell on many issues, I never feel particularly challenged; beside Burch, his writings strike me as laborious and pedantic, with frequent lapses into obviousness (and he demonstrates yet again that one must never equate obviousness with truth): I have to confess that I find it very hard to get through them. I am sure that he, as a scholar, has even less patience with my work and finds far greater deficiencies there, my "scholarship," such as it is, being very much that of a magpie collecting the twigs it needs to build its particular nest (the nest, not the twigs, being the point). I have pillaged a fair number of twigs from his book, which I use frankly as a work of reference. Bordwell is clearly the outstanding Ozu scholar of our time: he is familiar with far more of the films than I am, and has systematically amassed a vast quantity of valuable information with a patience and discipline of which I am totally incapable.

But I don't find him a very stimulating or rewarding critic. As far as I am able to judge, his descriptions of films achieve a high level of accuracy, aside from the occasional careless slip of which we are all sometimes guilty (for example, the confusion of names on page 311, where, in the closing sequences of *Late Spring*, Somiya suddenly becomes Hattori, a character who makes no appearance in the later part of the film). But one tiny slip, in itself trivial, seems to me revealing. In the exegesis of *Late Spring* (I am restricting my comments to Bordwell's accounts of the films with which this chapter is concerned), he remarks of the "Noh" sequence: "The scene ends with a bold stroke. Ozu cuts to a leafless tree outside (fig. 200)." "Fig. 200," the frame reproduction of the shot in question that appears immediately beside this in the text, shows a tree covered with luxuriant foliage (it is even more striking in the film, where the leaves are stirred by a strong breeze). Presumably, the leaflessness crept in automatically, by a process of association: Noriko is distressed, "wounded by the sight of Mrs. Miwa," and the shot ". . . privileges the noh scene as the turning point of Noriko's emotional response." But, in my experience, Ozu *never* uses his transition shots in this directly anthropomorphic way, which evokes Ingmar Bergman rather than Ozu. A minuscule point, apparently, yet it epitomizes for me the general conventionality of Bordwell's responses as a critic.

Much more serious is Bordwell's failure (preoccupied as he is with formal elements on the one hand and the desire to relate the film directly to contemporary social developments on the other) to grasp that the whole progress of *Tokyo Story* is toward the formation of the embryonic relationship between Noriko and Kyoko, mentioned neither in his plot synopsis nor in his account of the film's conclusion (he refers earlier to their "stunning final dialogue," but only in relation to "explicit discussions of piety, kindness, and the nature of life").

The essence of scholarship ("pure" scholarship, as it is sometimes called, as if it were some kind of virgin birth uncontaminated by ideology) is its assumption of objectivity, its assumption that it has no political position, that it is "above all that." Which strikes me as the ultimate in arrogance. One definition of scholarship (of course a highly tendentious one) might be "the mystification of politics under the cover of perfect neutrality." I will highlight here just one further point, though I think it can stand for a lot more. Bordwell writes of *Equinox Flower* that it "revives the theme of the loss of masculinity, setting its hero's decline against the quiet but assured authority of the father in *Late Spring* and the husband in *Flavor of Green Tea Over Rice*." I would wish to substitute for the word "decline" the word "growth," and to point out that "the quiet but assured authority of the father" in *Late Spring* leads to tragedy and is implicitly discredited. But I have never aspired to the neutrality and objectivity of "scholarship."

## Ozu's Style

Critics who wish to offer Ozu's cinema as an alternative to Western cinema tend at some point to define the latter as "anthropocentric," with the implication that Ozu's is not. I have never seen this curious allegation justified—it is asserted as if its truth were self-evident. But if "anthropocentric" means "centered on human beings" (and I can't see what other meaning it could have), then it seems undeniable that Ozu's cinema is firmly anthropocentric: what are we to contemplate at its core if not human life? Ozu's films are centrally *about* social human relations—not vases or railway stations or trees (leafless or otherwise), and they are certainly not about mismatched eyelines. What we know of his own practice bears this out. Those long nights drinking sake with his resident screenwriter Kogo Noda were passed in the meticulous planning of the narrative development, the action, the dialogue, the characterization; and there is ample testimony to the care Ozu lavished on his actors, insisting upon endless retakes of the same simple gesture, movement, or expression until it was exactly "right." If one wants to get at the core of Ozu's art, that is where one must look. This is not to belittle either the importance of his style or its uniqueness (aside from the occasional imitator). But the purpose and function of the style is not to distract our attention from the characters and the narrative by displacing it on to something else: it is to guide our concentration firmly upon them and define a particular way of regarding them.

I shall not attempt here a comprehensive description of Ozu's style; it has been done before (notably in a characteristically thorough and groundbreaking article by Kristin Thompson and David Bordwell, published in *Screen* [Summer 1976], to which everyone with a serious interest in Ozu must be indebted), and my aim is to right the balance and redirect attention to what the films are *about* (of which my account will be somewhat at odds with the customary shamefaced apology for Ozu's "conservatism"). I shall simply note what seem to me its most *effective* features, commenting when necessary, then discuss the relationship it defines of spectator to action:

*The static camera*. This is the first thing Westerners notice about Ozu's cinema: the severe restrictions placed upon camera mobility. In *Tokyo Story*, the film most familiar in the West, there are only two autonomous camera movements, both very brief, the second so slight as often to pass unnoticed. One reason for this appears to be Ozu's preoccupation with the most meticulous composition within the frame, each object precisely placed, which camera movement would destroy. When he abruptly (and irrevocably) switched to color at the end of his career, the preoccupation became obsessional: there is not a single camera movement in the last six films.

This self-denial takes two forms. Ozu rigorously eschews all those simple, "lazy" reframings, purely functional to the narrative, that we are so used to from Hollywood movies—especially the panning shot: he will never follow a character across a room, and if an actor stands up he cuts to a more distant position, refusing the convenient and more economical tilt-up. But he also rejects those potentialities of camera movement that Mizoguchi, for example, developed into an aesthetic principle: what we might term *composition-in-movement*. In rare sequences where camera movement is used extensively and expressively (such as the bicycle ride in *Late Spring*), it is strictly incorporated in the rhythms of the editing, the shots brief, the movement unidirectional.

*The head-on camera:* squares and rectangles. The various components of Ozu's style, while they can be listed separately, are closely and logically interdependent. With the static camera goes the preference for shooting both decor and actors at angles of either 180 or 90 degrees, so that the actors are either full face or in profile, the walls behind them seen as squares or rectangles, with very few oblique angles. Again one may contrast Mizoguchi, whose compositions are typically constructed on intersecting diagonals. The characteristic Mizoguchi composition (in the late films) directs the gaze outward toward areas beyond the screen, an effect greatly intensified by the frequent and complex camera movements; the characteristic Ozu composition shuts off anything beyond the frame, directing our gaze inward, to the center of the static composition. Hence:

*The use of frames within the frame.* Ozu habitually uses the decor of Japanese homes—the *shoji* (movable screens and partitions) and doorways—as framing devices within the cinema screen, intensifying the general tendency of his style toward the still life or portrait. Hence:

*The preservation of the intactness of the cinema frame.* However, this rule is broken more frequently than the others—the first minutes of *Early Summer*, for example, are unusually free in this respect, perhaps because the characters who break the rule are the two naughty young boys. Characters enter from and exit behind the frame-within-the-frame, rather than be seen to pass the confines of the screen.

*The absence of dissolves.* An unbreakable rule, one guesses, since very early in Ozu's career. (Again, contrast Mizoguchi, who used dissolves with

increasing frequency and often very expressively, for example near the beginning of *Sansho Dayu*, where dissolves suggest that a memory-flashback is
shared by two characters.) The rationale is presumably the same as that for
the refusal to pan: a dissolve destroys the precision and clear lines of the
composition, producing a messy blur. Hence:

**The celebrated use of transition shots to replace the dissolve.** Ozu's style
evolved out of a desire to create a contemplative distance, not disruption or
disorientation, such as would be produced by replacing the dissolve with a
direct cut to the next sequence with no indication of time-lapse or place-
change. It would be interesting to know whether Ozu's development of this
highly idiosyncratic transition technique coincided with his rejection of the
dissolve, though probably too many of the early films are lost for this supposition to be confidently confirmed or denied. What one assumes origi-
nated as the solution to a simple technical problem rapidly evolved into an
artistic principle: far from remaining a mere convenient transition device,
each shot-series becomes, for the spectator, a point of repose and reflection.
These transition shots are never, in my experience, nondiegetic, though they
may sometimes appear so as we watch them; in retrospect, we shall find that
they relate to the locations where the action takes place. Yet this initial uncertainty distinguishes them sharply from the simple establishing shot to which
Hollywood has long accustomed us ("contemplation" must never be confused with an absence of mental activity, quite the contrary). The occasional
cutaways to objects seen by the audience but not by the characters have the
same function: the two oft-quoted shots of the vase, with its background of
bamboo stirring in the breeze beyond the window, in the Kyoto hotel of *Late
Spring* (which Donald Richie mistook for point-of-view shots—the vase is
clearly located behind Noriko's head, and it is not she but the spectator who
is invited to contemplate it) are a good example, providing a moment of distance during one of the film's most poignant, complex, and emotionally disturbing scenes.

**Camera height and distance.** Ozu habitually places his camera somewhere
around waist-to-chest level, and at a distance ranging between medium and
long shot. Again, the principle is essentially one of self-denial: the refusal of
extremes, the rejection of the kinds of camera rhetoric we associate with
Welles, Hitchcock, Kurosawa.

**"False" eyeline-matches and the use of 360-degree shooting space.** Perhaps
it is perverse overreaction that makes me leave to very late those features of
which formalist critics have made so much—for this is where Ozu can be

most clearly and *practically* presented as breaking the Hollywood rules. But I am concerned with how Ozu's style affects our relationship to the action, and from this viewpoint they seem the *least* important. My problem is perhaps that, discovering Ozu (like most Westerners) through the late films, where they are much less obtrusive, I never became conscious of them until I began reading Ozu criticism, and therefore experienced no thrill of dislocation, no difficulty in adjusting. Did they affect my experience of the films subconsciously, demanding more mental activity on that level? I cannot say, but would be happy to believe it. Doubtless my corruption, by long exposure to anthropocentric narrative from Sophocles to Scorsese via Chaucer, Shakespeare, Mozart/da Ponte, and Dickens, was too complete. Burch (page 159) tells us that, confronted with a practical lesson in "how to" and "how not to" by his film editor, Ozu remarked, "There's no difference," and characterizes the comment as "cryptic." Yet it is quite possible that, *within the context of his own style*, Ozu simply meant what he said. Most of the components I have described have the effect of presenting each character separately, as in a discrete still picture—separated both by the editing and by framing devices. In a Hollywood film Ozu's "wrong" eyeline-matches and the spatial dislocation of 360-degree shooting would be immediately jarring. But we need not go so far afield: they would be equally jarring in Mizoguchi (the Mizoguchi of any of his various "periods") because in his films characters habitually share the screen, look at each other and touch each other, and their exact positions and the direction of their looks in relation to each other are hence of prime importance.

*Touch.* The preceding connects to my final point, generally neglected by the formalists as it has nothing whatever to do with the "material properties" of film as they understand them, being as much a matter of "content" as of "style": Ozu's characters rarely touch each other. Like his static camera, transition shots, and false eyeline-matches, this is not in the least typical of Japanese cinema in general (as the most cursory glance at Mizoguchi or Kurosawa would confirm). It *is*, to an extent, a consequence of Ozu's particular, highly idiosyncratic, form of "realism," the rejection of dramatically (or melodramatically) charged subject matter in favor of the "typical" situations of family life; but before assuming that this is "typically" Japanese, we might ask ourselves how often *we*, in the course of an average day, touch other people. (The answer, I think, would be somewhat, but not much, more than seems customary with the Japanese middle class: we shake hands instead of bowing to each other, and Western tradition encourages the hugging, kissing, and patting on the back of friends and family members a little more than seems common in Japan.) Again, however, it seems clear that Ozu extends a simple "given" into an artistic principle: the formal separation of his characters is so extreme that the rare moments of touch become privileged.

What advantages does Ozu achieve with this elaborate complex of interdependent stylistic components? There seem to me to be three:

1. I have already suggested that Ozu's concern is to construct a spectator/action relationship of contemplative distance. This might at first seem to approach perilously close to "Zen or something like that" and, despite Ozu's stricture, I don't think that can be entirely avoided. I would, however, place the stress on what we are being invited to contemplate—not some ineffable eternal mystery but the concrete and often prosaic realities of life-in-society. The "contemplative distance" does indeed place these "realities" in a context one might loosely term metaphysical: the awareness of time, transience, death, and an inanimate universe. But that is scarcely something mystical or alien to Western culture (one finds such awareness in, for example, *Only Angels Have Wings* or *She Wore a Yellow Ribbon*).

Involved, sympathetic, and compassionate, yet always maintaining sufficient detachment to remain aware (of relations, of values, of issues both social and metaphysical)—that seems to me to define Ozu's attitude, and the attitude he wishes to communicate to the spectator. Like all great art, the films are *educational* in the best sense, while totally free of any bullying or didacticism, and one shouldn't be afraid of the word just because the educational system under which we have all suffered has thrown the very concept of "education" into disrepute: the films educate us in a way of looking, a way that strikes me as at once marvelously mature and extremely difficult to achieve. It also defines Noriko, and especially the Noriko of *Tokyo Story*, which suggests the absolutely central role the character plays in Ozu's evolving value system. One might say that the purpose of the films is to invite us (with characteristic Japanese courtesy and reticence) to become the Noriko of *Tokyo Story*.

2. To adopt (if it is already available) or construct (if it isn't) an art form of the most rigorous discipline and deprivation is to make available the possibility of *creative deviation* from the rules. In the former case one might think of Pope's use of the most rigid and convention-bound of poetic forms—the "heroic couplet"—where he achieves the subtlest effects and inflections simply by shifting the caesura (the midline pause) or allowing the sense to run on beyond the end of a line; in the latter case, of the electrifying effect of the solitary cymbal clash at the climax of Sibelius's *En Saga*, simply because it *is* the only one. I shall argue later that camera movement is one of the keys to *Late Spring* and touch one of the keys to *Tokyo Story*. The latter instance provides a particularly fine example of the principle involved: if the characters

touched one another all the time, what I take to be the film's climactic moment would go for nothing.

3. Ozu's camera is scrupulously *nonjudgmental*. Every character is filmed from the same angle, the same height, the same distance, and the lighting is uniform for all. Those sophisticated technical means of angle and lighting elaborated by Western cinema (and still taught to film students) to inform us whether we are to find the characters "good," "evil," admirable, heroic, monstrous, pathetic, etc. are rigorously refused. This does not of course mean that the films overall are "neutral"; no filmmaker in my experience communicates a surer, securer, more precise (if highly complex) sense of values. What it means is that we come to share Ozu's judgments by sharing his understanding. In *Tokyo Story*, for example, the camera makes no distinction whatever between Noriko and Shige: we arrive at our (and, we must assume, Ozu's) relative valuation of them strictly on the grounds of their respective behavior and its consequences, the most important criteria defined by the film's overall progress being emotional generosity and the level of awareness. If we are led to concur with Ozu's implicit valuations, that concurrence is never forced upon us and is reached by our own mental and emotional activity.

It should be said finally that the combination of contemplative distance and the nonjudgmental camera allows for considerable complexity and range of response. On the one hand it is very far from being the case that "anything goes," that we are free to feel as we choose; on the other, the distance makes it possible to contemplate the issues and the values they involve from many sides. This does not entirely preclude what we are accustomed to call "identification," but it strongly qualifies it: identification ("sympathy" or "empathy" might be better terms here) is arrived at gradually, so that it seems reasonable to claim that we identify with Noriko *by the end* of *Tokyo Story*. It is safe to assert that this complexity and openness is not fortuitous but corresponds to Ozu's own awareness that life is never simple. A related point is that there are no villains in his films, there are only social conditions: for example, the behavior of Shige in *Tokyo Story* may be hateful, but we are led fully to understand why she is like this (and when we hate her, aren't we perhaps hating something within ourselves, something typical of human existence under capitalism?). This does not exempt her (or us) from personal blame (we simply do not believe Noriko, and are not meant to believe her, when she tells Kyoko that she too may become like Shige), but it places that blame in a wider context of social relations.

It is this openness that makes it so hazardous to stick political labels on Ozu's work—which is not of course to deny that, like all art, it has a political dimension, or to claim for it some kind of impossible neutrality.

Neutrality is not the same as complexity. Is Ozu's cinema "conservative," "liberal," "radical"? I think it permits appropriation by any of those positions—or all of them—and if in this chapter I stress its radicalism I am merely righting a misleading and conventional imbalance.

**II**

## Noriko and Marriage

"Has she ever been in love?"
"Maybe not. She only collected pictures of Katharine Hepburn."
"Who is that?"
"An actress."
"A woman? Is she a lesbian?" (*Laughter*) "She's very strange, anyway."
—Conversation about Noriko in *Early Summer*

I must first explain why I claim *Late Spring*, *Early Summer*, and *Tokyo Story* as a (loose) trilogy.

Ozu made six films with Setsuko Hara, of which these are the first three. They are spaced symmetrically in his career, one every two years (1949, 1951, and 1953 respectively), alternating with two films in which Hara does not appear; the subsequent three films with Hara are not spaced in this way. In the three films of the trilogy, Hara's character is called Noriko, which is not the case in the three later ones. And in the trilogy, a leading thematic/narrative issue (the mainspring of the first two; of secondary but increasing importance in *Tokyo Story*) is the pressures put on Noriko to marry or (in *Tokyo Story*) to remarry, and her resistance to this. Further, I think it is possible to argue that *Equinox Flower* (1958), Ozu's first color film, relates to the trilogy thematically, and I shall discuss it briefly in a postscript. By that time, Hara was too old to play the character who in important respects resembles Noriko; but is it coincidence that she is now called "Setsuko" and has the surname "Hirayama" (Hara's married surname in *Tokyo Story*)?

It may be objected that *Tokyo Story* stands somewhat apart in that Hara's is not the central role, the film being "about" the old couple. Yet there is an important sense in which Noriko is (or gradually becomes) the film's central focus: she, not the parents, embodies most clearly the film's positive values, the values that are being affirmed. That those values are somewhat intangible, resisting precise definition, is inherent in the project itself (and in the Noriko character throughout the trilogy), and it is a strength, not a weakness, a mark of Ozu's intelligence and honesty: he is attempting to define values that are not yet practically accessible within the culture. Also, *Tokyo Story* is closely bound to *Early Summer* by links other than Noriko. In both, the surviving son of the family is a doctor; in both he is called Koichi and is the father of two young boys named Minoru (played in both by the same actor) and Isamu. In both narratives there is also a dead son, killed in the war (Noriko's brother and husband respectively), called Shoji. Finally, in both films grandmother and daughter-in-law (Koichi's wife) are played by the same two actresses.

Each film of the trilogy can be read as a variation on a theme. Noriko remains essentially the same character throughout, the variations arising from the different situations in which she is placed: increasing age, family connections, marital status, relation to the world of work and employment, geographical location (country, city). Finally, the trilogy is unified by its underlying *progressive* movement, a progression from the unqualified tragedy of *Late Spring* through the ambiguous "happy ending" of *Early Summer* to the authentic and fully earned note of bleak and tentative hope at the end of *Tokyo Story*. From a certain viewpoint the triumphant comedy of *Equinox Flower* completes this progress, though only by sidestepping the implications of *Tokyo Story*'s conclusion, a move facilitated by the shift into the comic mode.

What follows is not offered as a comprehensive, let alone "definitive," reading of the three films. My aim is to trace the development of the "Noriko" figure and the thematic complex of which she is the center. I believe this will take us to the heart of the films' intention. (I write "the films' intention" rather than "Ozu's," not by any means to suggest that it could somehow exist apart from him, but simply because to most people "the artist's intention" seems to imply a fully conscious design which preceded the act of creation. Anyone who has tried to produce works of fiction will know that the work's "intention" is something you discover gradually, both in the process of work and after completion, and sometimes it needs to be explained to you by other people.)

A word here about Setsuko Hara. Her place seems assured as one of the great movie stars, as surely as that of Katharine Hepburn and Ingrid Bergman, the two Hollywood stars with whom she can most appropriately be compared, and despite the fact that in the West we know her only from the Ozu films and Kurosawa's *No Regrets for Our Youth*. Like Hepburn (albeit less aggressively) she is constantly searching for the means to independence in a male-dominated world; and as with Bergman, her screen persona is characterized by the radiance of her smile and an essential, irreducible, "niceness." It is apparently customary in Japan to disparage her, and for precisely those qualities that are central to the meaning of the Ozu films: she is referred to popularly as "the eternal virgin," a typical male chauvinist response to a woman who resists being defined by her relations with men; and cynics who cannot believe in innate human goodness find her insufferable.

## *Late Spring*

*Late Spring* was made the same year as Mizoguchi's *My Love Has Been Burning*, with *Victory of Women* his most explicitly and militantly feminist film. Ozu would never—*could* never—have made such a film, with its overt rage and passion, its all-out assault on the emotions, its explicit parti pris; yet it seems that a new awareness of, and growing identification with, the cultural predicament of women develops in the Ozu films of this period also, climaxing with *Equinox Flower*, and it seems not entirely fortuitous that his professional relationship with Setsuko Hara begins here. Attribute this, if you will, to the American occupation and its demands for the "liberalization" of Japanese cinema. But in the case of Mizoguchi, it is striking that he seized upon this to go much further in terms of feminist statement than *any* Hollywood film has ventured in *any* period; and the roots of this development are plainly visible in the earlier work of both directors.

A common account of *Late Spring* is that it is about a young woman, traditionally Japanese and old-fashioned, who out of a sense of filial obligation determines to sacrifice her own happiness to look after her widowed father (Chishu Ryu) in his old age. The film is doubtless accessible to various interpretations, but this is not one of them. It is quite simply and demonstrably *wrong*, the kind of reading that derives from Western assumptions about Japanese culture rather than any close (or even perfunctory) attention to the film. Certainly it is about the sacrifice of Noriko's happiness in the interest of maintaining and continuing "tradition," but the sacrifice takes the form of her marriage, and everyone in the film—including the father and finally the defeated Noriko herself—is complicit in it.

We are left in no doubt that a strong mutual attachment exists between father and daughter (that we are never tempted to think of it as incestuous, even on an unconscious level, is doubtless due to cultural difference—it would be impossible to remake *Late Spring* in the West and avoid such a suspicion). The attachment is based on mutual respect and affection, and takes the form of a kind of transgenerational friendship; in their first scene together they parody the traditional patriarchal authoritarian/filial subservience ethic, treating it as play, with Noriko "bossing" her father as much as vice versa, and later, when Noriko's friend Aya visits, the father waits on them, bringing tea. Yet the film—if we look at it without prior assumptions—also leaves us in no doubt that Noriko's determination not to marry is motivated by her own personal wish, her sense of what is best for herself: if her father's potential loneliness is more than a pretext (they enjoy each other's company and the relationship is strikingly nonoppressive), concern about it is never offered us as Noriko's prime motivation. Ozu's analysis makes it clear that with her father, and only with him, can Noriko preserve a personal freedom which the other options the culture makes available to women would destroy; she can wander about the city at will, visit sake bars with male acquaintances, go for bicycle rides by the sea with unmarried men, enjoy a freedom of movement which is both physical and spiritual. The essence of this freedom, and what the society cannot tolerate (our own still has great problems with it), is that she remains undefined, except as herself—no identity in the form of social role is imposed on her.

The precise function of camera movement in Ozu varies considerably from film to film (though we may be sure it always has one). Sometimes, as in *Tokyo Story*, it is used simply as a *marker*, underlining a crucial moment in the narrative: the film's two brief tracking shots (one lateral, one following) around its midpoint mark the lowest ebb of the old couple's fortunes, when they become literally homeless, just before Tomi goes to Noriko's for the night and the film's upward movement begins. In *Late Spring*, on the other hand, camera movement has a clear expressive function, intimately bound up with the progress of the narrative. In the first half of the film there is (for late Ozu) an unusual amount of it, closely linked to the depiction of Noriko's freedom and in two sequences conveying an effect of release and exhilaration.

(Parenthetically, one should perhaps distinguish between shots in which the camera moves because it is inside a moving vehicle—car, bus, train—and *autonomous* camera movements when the camera moves because the cinematographer moves it. *Tokyo Story* contains a sequence employing shots of the former kind—the bus tour of Tokyo—and the sensation of movement there is clearly important, celebrating not the tour itself (the old couple experience mainly discomfort) but Noriko's generosity. A further subdistinction, in the former case, should be between shots looking out from a moving vehicle, which convey the *effect* of movement, and shots centered on the people inside, which do not.)

The train sequence (one of Ozu's "signatures"—I have not seen an Ozu film in which a train does not at some point appear) opens with a sudden burst of energy (and "upbeat" music): the film's first camera movement has the camera attached to the exterior of a train as it emerges from a tunnel, and the effect is repeated several times. The sense of liveliness is intensified by Ozu's disorienting play with the characters' positions inside the train: father and daughter exchange places (sitting, standing) in a series of shots that have almost the effect of jump-cuts. What is being celebrated is not so much the joint outing (the two will separate when they get to the city, going their own ways), but Noriko's personal autonomy: her time is her own, unsupervised, with no explanations demanded, and when she encounters one of her father's old friends by chance she does not hesitate to accompany him to a bar and invite him home without asking permission.

The bicycle ride is even stronger in its expressiveness, clearly among the film's most privileged sequences—a whole series of varied tracking shots (lateral, leading, following) among which, startlingly, occurs the only panning shot I have ever seen in an Ozu movie. The exceptional freedom of the camera involves us in Noriko's exhilaration as she cycles to the sea with her father's handsome young assistant Hattori—an exhilaration that has its sequel in their brief, humorous, innocent flirtation among the sand dunes. Innocent, at least, on *her* side; on his, we are less sure. It is one of a number of scenes in Ozu which we read slightly differently in retrospect; while it plays, it can be taken for the beginning of a mutual romantic interest, and we learn only later that Hattori was already engaged and that Noriko knew this all along (and, presumably, knew that he knew she knew). Her behavior was, in other words, based on the assumption that she was "safe," that no romantic involvement was possible, and this is confirmed by her uncontrollable laughter when her father questions her about Hattori as possible husband; as soon as Hattori *does* manifest a romantic interest in her (inviting her to accompany him to a concert for which he has already bought the tickets), she ends the relationship, and he is seen listening to Joachim Raff's *Cavatina* beside an empty seat. The sequence ends with Noriko walking slowly away from the concert hall (now with two *slow* tracking shots, one following, one leading) and looking regretful. Because the pleasant, easy friendship between them is no longer possible? But it is also conceivable that Hattori *did* constitute a temptation for her (the only one offered in the film) as a solution to the marriage dilemma: he is her father's assistant, almost a member of the family, and he would not want to dominate her.

In the course of the film—as the pressures on Noriko begin to wear down her resistance—camera movement becomes progressively depleted. It stops altogether about two-thirds of the way through: the last camera movement occurs during the scene in the park between father and aunt, the scene in which Noriko's marriage is finalized by her elders, where the trap closes, the aunt finding a dropped wallet and declaring it a good omen, the wedding will take place.

The film's progress toward camera stasis corresponds to the cumulative deprivation of Noriko's freedom of movement, her energy, her exuberance, a progress that culminates logically in her literal immobility, weighed down by the cumbersome traditional wedding headdress imposed upon Japanese brides. The film could scarcely be more eloquent, though the eloquence appears to have been lost on those intent on interpreting Ozu in terms of their own notions of "Japaneseness." Hara's spontaneous, open smile hardens into a fixed grimace, and through most of the scene we are prevented from seeing her eyes, the wide brim of the headdress concealing the upper half of her submissively lowered face; our last view of her has her reduced to a reflection in a mirror as she sadly surveys herself in her wedding finery. Then Ozu caps even this: after everyone has left the room for the wedding ceremony, he ends the sequence with a shot of the empty mirror. Noriko is no longer even a reflection, she has disappeared from the narrative, she is no longer "Noriko" but "wife." The effect is that of a death.

We never see the husband, and all Noriko (who is barely acquainted with him) says of him is that he looks like Gary Cooper; we also know that he works for Nitto Chemicals, and that by marrying him Noriko will enter a world remote from the academic life of her father. Ozu deliberately withholds any indication of how the marriage will turn out; we are not invited to assume that it will be any more unhappy than most. The point is far more radical—that the *institution of marriage itself*, as traditionally practiced (and I see no reason to qualify that with "in Japan"), functions as a means of subordinating and imprisoning the woman, her identity now socially inscribed as "wife." Freedom is a thing of the past.

If a "traditional" Japanese expectation operates in the film it is not filial obligation but the obligation of women to marry; for an exploration of the major traditional alternative—to become a geisha—we would have to turn to Mizoguchi. We should have no difficulty in adjusting to this in the West, where the same "obligation" functioned until not so long ago (and still does, in many areas of our culture), and where the Mother/Whore opposition is surely familiar enough: the only real difference is that in Japanese culture the opposition has been more explicit and systematized, given "official" recognition. As far as marriage is concerned, Ozu—at least in the more woman-aware postwar films—makes a clear distinction based on his precise and practical sense of the potentialities within any given cultural-historical situation: for women of an older generation and from a nonurban culture marriage was endurable and even, within strict limits, fulfilling (see the mothers played by Chieko Higashiyama in *Early Summer* and *Tokyo Story*) because they were raised within a cultural tradition that provided a strong framework and offered no other option to the imagination. Marriage works, in other words, provided the woman—like Tomi in *Tokyo Story*—has been taught not to think too much. Even this needs further qualification: when the father in *Late Spring*, during the heartbreaking Kyoto sequences, helps Noriko to resign herself to her fate (against his own as well as her inclination), he tells her how he and her mother had to work for years for their conjugal happiness, and adds that her mother cried through most of the early years of their marriage. (For critics to assume that Ozu *condones* this seems a peculiar insult to his intelligence and sensitivity.)

On the other hand, marriage (as traditionally practiced) for an intelligent, educated, and fully aware woman like Noriko is presented consistently as a tragic fate, a brutal curtailment of her growth. And a similar implicit verdict holds not only for a Noriko but for all women who have matured outside the rigorous indoctrination of feudal tradition; if there is a single marriage among the younger, urbanized generation in the postwar films that is depicted as happy and fulfilling for the woman, it has escaped my notice. (We do have some hopes for Noriko's marriage to Yabe in *Early Summer*, but, as I shall argue, that is a special case.)

Two facts from Ozu's biography seem relevant to his identification (or imaginative empathy) with the Noriko of the trilogy, and to his attitude to marriage. The first is widely known and is familiar from most critical commentaries on his work ("safe," because it fits securely into Western notions of Japanese propriety): he himself never married, and he lived with his mother until her death. Whether he "nobly devoted his life to her," as

*Late Spring:* the reluctant bride (Chishu Ryu, Setsuko Hara).

Westerners like to assume, or simply, like Noriko but with the privilege of the male's right of choice, followed his own preference, cannot be determined. The second fact has been scrupulously avoided by (as far as I know) every critic who has written on Ozu (I know of it only from a brief aside hidden away at the end of Richie's book, in the "Biographical Filmography," page 196, where it is instantly glossed over): Ozu was expelled from senior high school for writing a love letter (in Richie's "tasteful" words, "a letter apparently as indiscreet as it was sentimental") to a younger boy. Richie's comment, typically liberal-homophobic, is: "Such letters and such attachments among boys were [sic!] common in an educational system that so rigorously separated the sexes, and such sentiments are normal at a certain age"—the customary dismissal of the final healthy eruption of our constitutional bisexuality, before the process of repression is completed. Let me be clear about this: I am not suggesting that Ozu passed his entire life as a closet gay (we know that he had numerous liaisons with women, the equivalent of which would have been difficult, if not impossible, for a Noriko). What this incident indicates is that (indeed like many others, which makes the phenomenon more, not less, significant) Ozu was able to remain in touch with his innate bisexuality at least until the age of senior high school—prior, that is, to the final stage of what is euphemistically called "socialization" ("graduation" in more senses than one, entry into the work force, submission to the social demands for conformity to the heterosexual norms). He was able, being an artist of exceptional sensitivity and intelligence, to understand very well Noriko's reluctance to accept a socially imposed identity and definition.

Noriko is associated in the film frequently with tradition and the past (it opens with her attending a formal tea ceremony, given, appropriately, in honor of a new bride-to-be). Yet she habitually dresses in Western clothes (the only exception after the tea ceremony being when she is costumed for her own wedding), and her best friend is a young woman so thoroughly Westernized that her back gets stiff if she has to sit on *tatami* (when we subsequently see her apartment it is furnished entirely in Western style, with straight-backed chairs and sofa). Aya's function in the film is to embody the practical alternative to marriage for the modern Japanese woman: she is "emancipated," independent, earning her own living. It is clear that both Ozu and Noriko find her very attractive; she is bright and vivacious, warm-hearted, fundamentally well-meaning. But it is equally clear that what she represents is not, for Noriko, a serious temptation: incorporation in the world of alienated labor under capitalism, in one of the subordinate positions available to women (Aya is a stenographer), is not a viable alternative for a woman of Noriko's depth and awareness—although, in desperation, when she feels marriage being forced upon her, she consults Aya about the possibilities. (The incongruity of Noriko as office worker in a large company will be realized four years later in *Tokyo Story*.) And Ozu shows the alternative Aya represents as illusory anyway: she is working because a man has let her down (she is a divorcée), and the implication is that sooner or later she will have better luck. Hence the irony (marked by one of Ozu's rare close-ups, Aya moving forward into camera) of her final appearance, when she impulsively leans over to embrace Noriko's father in the sake bar on the evening after the wedding: he has just revealed that he only *pretended* that he was planning to remarry, and Aya is expressing her admiration for his participation in the conspiracy to entrap his daughter, characteristically with no thought for *his* future (we don't take her promise of frequent visits seriously). Ironically, Aya becomes one of the most aggressive participants in the conspiracy to force Noriko into marriage, despite her own thoroughly cynical and opportunistic view of it.

Of the three films, *Late Spring* is the only one that ends on a note of unqualified tragedy, the image of the empty mirror that stands for our last memory of Noriko answered by the desolate closing scene of her father's aloneness. The final shot of the empty sea is one of those moments that

After Noriko's wedding: Noriko's father with Aya in the sake bar.

Western critics fasten on to "say it is Zen or something like that" (i.e., don't worry about the misery of the characters, think about Eternity and the Infinite). For me it functions both as an image of desolation and a reminder of the sequence (the first shot of which it closely mirrors) of the bicycle ride with Hattori—the zenith of Noriko's freedom.

## Early Summer

Of the three films, *Early Summer* is the only one in which Noriko indisputably occupies the central position; one might argue that *Late Spring* is shared equally between Hara and Chishu Ryu, and that in *Tokyo Story* Ryu is the central figure (both films end by focusing on the father and his lonely future)—though for me Noriko is the *emotional* center of all three. As in *Late Spring*, the narrative is firmly centered on the pressures on Noriko to marry, and once again she succumbs. (Only in *Tokyo Story* is she able to withstand the pressures, and there only because she has a socially acceptable pretext, fidelity to the memory of her late husband, in the traditional—though by the 1950s largely archaic—manner of Japanese widows.) The tone, however, is somewhat different, the unqualified tragedy of *Late Spring* giving way to an emotional complexity one might justly call "Mozartian." One could apply to the film the description of Mozart by one of his most distinguished contemporary interpreters, the Japanese pianist Mitsuko Uchida: "You are never sure if you're in the shadow or in the sunshine. You are never in *direct* sunshine."

This is perhaps as good a place as any to comment on the dialogue quoted at the head of this second part of the chapter. The film is set in 1950, and Noriko is now twenty-eight. If she collected photographs of Hepburn as an adolescent, we may assume that the Hepburn with whom she identified was the pre-*Philadelphia Story* Hepburn of the 1930s, Hepburn at her most rebellious: the Hepburn of female activeness and self-assertion (*Christopher Strong*), of explicit rebellion against the male order (*A Woman Rebels*), of female bonding (*Stage Door, Little Women*)—"lesbianism" in the wider, more comprehensive sense sanctioned by the women's movement. What appears to be a casual, humorous "aside" is in fact immensely suggestive (and Ozu's immersion in and love of Hollywood cinema suggests that he knew what he was doing): all these aspects of Hepburn's 1930s persona (see Andrew Britton's *Katharine Hepburn: The Thirties and After*) are reflected in Noriko, and this is especially clear in *Early Summer*. One may even see the film as "correcting" the "happy endings" of most of the Hepburn movies, that have her capitulating to an appropriate male; here, Noriko chooses a husband because she knows she has to, and the film makes it clear that she chooses the least of the available evils: as a "happy ending" it is singularly qualified and relative.

I also find it interesting that the issue of lesbianism is raised here, if only as a joke (though we have all heard about "true words spoken in jest"). There is of course no suggestion anywhere in the films that Noriko is sexually attracted to women ("lesbian" in the narrow, purely sexual sense in which it is popularly understood and where patriarchy would plainly like to keep it, the wider sense being far more threatening). On the other hand, the films provide absolutely no evidence that she is sexually attracted to *men*; she tends to treat the men she likes—Hattori in *Late Spring*, the man she marries in *Early Summer*—as friends. What one *can* confidently assert is that this snatch of dialogue adds a further dimension, a further potentiality, to Noriko's "strangeness," our sense that, as a matter of choice, she eludes definition, society's habit of "fixing" people (and especially women) by applying labels to them ("wife," "mother," "career woman," "old maid," "lesbian," . . .).

The generally lighter tone and the more ambiguous ending are reflected in the camera movement, less systematic than in *Late Spring* but on the whole increasing rather than diminishing in the later part of the film, and at times positively playful. The film actually ends in mid-tracking-shot, a gesture as far as I know unique in Ozu and rare enough in *any* cinema (indeed, no other instances spring to mind, though *Ugetsu Monogatari* starts in midtrack). The film also contains the only crane shot I have ever seen in an Ozu movie (as Noriko and her sister-in-law mount the sand dunes). And there is what I take to be a Hitchcock joke: After Noriko has made her own choice of husband, a woman friend induces her to seize an opportunity for a peek at the rejected suitor (whom she has never met) chosen for her by her family and friends. The two women sneak up the stairs and start along a corridor, with suppressed nervous giggles. Suspense! Ozu cuts to a forward tracking shot from their point of view, moving along the corridor toward a doorway (like Joan Fontaine approaching the forbidden wing of Manderley). But then we suddenly realize that this is not only *not* the same corridor, it isn't even in the same building, and the two women whose point of view we have been tricked into believing we share are not present . . . We never do get to see the rejected suitor, and never learn whether Noriko did either.

I want to discuss three aspects of the narrative: the family, female bonding, and Noriko's choice. *Early Summer* is the only film of the trilogy in which Noriko is a member of a viable family. In *Late Spring* she has only a father (and an aunt, who lives elsewhere); in *Tokyo Story* she appears to have no blood relatives. In *Early Summer* she has a father and mother and a married elder brother (hence also a sister-in-law and two young nephews), and they all live together. It seems clear that, when he made *Tokyo Story* two years later, by constructing all the links I detailed earlier Ozu wished us to compare the two families and draw conclusions about the relative harmony of the family in *Early Summer* and the multiple discords of that in the later film. The basic contrast is between two models of "family": the extended family of the past, that survives today only in rural areas; the nuclear family of the urban and suburban present. Three factors are relevant:

Environment. The family of *Early Summer* lives outside Tokyo in a relatively spacious house in the country (Koichi and Noriko both commute to work), that of *Tokyo Story* in a cramped accommodation in a squalid outlying district of Tokyo itself. While based in elementary economics, the difference is not merely one of relative affluence/poverty: it makes possible the preservation of a *sense* of family, and of values beyond the crudely material. This is supported by:

The presence of the grandparents, who in many ways closely resemble the old couple in *Tokyo Story* (Chieko Higashiyama here is a Tomi mercifully spared the disappointments). It is a family still in touch with its roots, and with the finest of traditional values. Ozu certainly does not idealize this but he clearly acknowledges it.

The presence of Noriko. As David Bordwell points out, this has an economic function: in *Tokyo Story* Koichi is the sole breadwinner, whereas in *Early Summer* the family is also sustained by Noriko's income (she is personal secretary in a small firm, with a friendly and nonoppressive boss, a very different situation from her position as one-among-many in the large impersonal corporate office of *Tokyo Story*). But Ozu's emphasis is far more on her personal attributes: her radiance, generosity, awareness. It is Noriko's presence that both vivifies and harmonizes the family, making it possible for its potentially discordant elements to be contained or neutralized. Discord, here, has its source in the elder brother Koichi (Chishu Ryu in one of his very rare unsympathetic roles, looking twenty years younger than he did in *Late Spring* and thirty years younger than he will in *Tokyo Story*—it is impossible to guess the actor's real age from the films). Stiff, humorless, and essentially mean-spirited (see the "moral lesson" he tries to teach his children, by presenting them with a wrapped-up loaf of bread when he knows they are eagerly anticipating model railway tracks—a "moral lesson" that provokes their attempt to run away), he embodies "traditional" values at their worst—most inflexible and oppressive. One guesses that for Ozu his view that modern women (as represented by his wife and Noriko) have become "impudent" because they stand up to men is particularly odious. His presence within the family is made bearable only by Noriko's consistent refusal to take him seriously, which is all that prevents him from assuming the dominant role in the household, a role to which he clearly aspires. Most interesting of all is the difference in attitude toward Minoru and Isamu because, superficially at least, their behavior in the two films seems as identical as their names: lively, rebellious, habitually insolent to their elders. In *Early Summer* this is treated humorously, with great affection, by Ozu and by the adults (their father always excepted); we are clearly intended, taking our cue from Noriko, to side with them against Koichi. In *Tokyo Story* the insubordination becomes ugly, the boys expressing an impotent resentment of an adult world that treats them without respect, consideration, or even interest, as nonpersons: there is no Noriko to take their part.

Noriko's role vis-à-vis the family constitutes a variation on her role vis-à-vis her father in *Late Spring*: she is content, she has a sense of belonging, she feels useful. The major difference is that there is less emphasis on her freedom, her time being largely shared between work and family. When she marries, the family breaks up, the old couple moving to a remote country area, Koichi and his family also, we assume, moving from a house they can no longer afford and which is now too big for them. Do we assume they move into Tokyo, nearer his work? In retrospect, the ending looks very like preparation for the familial situation that forms the starting point of *Tokyo Story*; one sees, at any rate, how the germ of the later film is already present.

The use Noriko makes of her limited freedom permits Ozu to develop a theme barely sketched in *Late Spring* (Noriko's relationship with Aya), which will acquire particular resonance at the end of *Tokyo Story*, and will become the central theme of *Equinox Flower*—female bonding. It is introduced shortly after the presentation of the family and its dynamics, in the scene where Noriko and her brother and sister-in-law eat out in a restaurant prior to meeting the uncle from the country: the two women band together to criticize and tease Koichi, deflating his male ego and stiff, artificial dignity. It is Noriko who is able both to attack her brother and maintain throughout a humorous, bantering tone; we sense that his wife alone would either have preserved a resentful but submissive silence or provoked an ugly scene. The sequence adds a new dimension to the critique of traditional marriage (from the woman's viewpoint) initiated in *Late Spring*, and this is developed in a subsequent scene where Noriko (parents and uncle safely ensconced in a Kabuki theater) consorts with two of her female friends, one married, the other not. Their initial conviviality swiftly modulates into a conversation in which the married woman, very defensively aggressive, tries to assert the superiority of her position over the other two who have not so far been so fortunate as to acquire husbands, an attempt they greet with cheerful ridicule. The party swiftly breaks up, and we are left to reflect upon the destructive effect marriage has on women's friendships, Ozu (that diehard old fuddy-duddy advocate of the good old feudal values) here antic- ipating the theme of Claudia Weill's explicitly feminist *Girlfriends* by over a quarter of a century. I admire Weill's movie, which was important in its social context, but have to say that it does nothing that Ozu had not already done better.

As in *Late Spring*, the film analyzes the way in which the pressures build up: Noriko is twenty-eight—past "late spring" now and well on into "early summer"—and the duty of the Japanese woman to marry cannot be post- poned much longer. Her boss, always helpful and benevolent, provides a suitor who, although twelve years older than Noriko, has all the appropriate and desirable advantages ("handsome, a golfer"—what woman could resist?), and her family, after having him investigated in the approved Japanese manner and ascertaining that he is a respectable and extremely prosperous businessman, accept him gratefully: indeed, he is exactly the match of which a Koichi would approve. But Noriko is somewhat older than she was in *Late Spring*, more experienced and mature, her independence less vulnerable. She responds by choosing her own husband, without even the courtesy of a family consultation.

The man she chooses is anything but a "good match": far from rich, a wid- ower with two young children (interestingly, two girls, in contrast to Minoru and Isamu), not especially handsome and not even (as far as we know) a golfer—Koichi's assistant in his medical practice. Worse, he is about to leave for the wilds to start a new hospital; even Noriko's closest friend cannot understand how she can give up city sophistication for a life in the outer boondocks. He is, in fact, a variation on the Hattori of *Late Spring*, the man with whom Noriko took her bicycle ride, there the *father's* assistant (but father and brother are both Chishu Ryu). Here, he is unencumbered by any prior engagement: he seems, in fact, a confirmed bachelor (or more pre- cisely a confirmed widower) and, although when his mother informs him that Noriko has announced that she will marry him he acquiesces, he seems somewhat low on enthusiasm.

Why does Noriko choose him, and stick to her choice against all her fam- ily's hostility? Her friend tries to insist that she's "in love," but Noriko con- tinues to deny it (even when the friend threatens to hit her and chases her around a table trying to carry out the threat); the most she will concede is that "I know him well and can trust him"—a rejection, in other words, of the traditional arranged marriage which the Setsuko of *Equinox Flower* will carry further, though there in the name of love. Negatively, Noriko knows she is going to have to get married and opts for the least of the available evils. Yabe's lack of enthusiasm (it is clear that he likes Noriko and enjoys her company) could be due to his understanding of this, which is not exactly flattering—or simply to his sense that he is in a singularly unfavorable position to enter upon a new marriage (Ozu, characteristically, withholds any decisive explanation). There are, however, positive aspects, one being precisely that Noriko is *not* "in love," with all the emotional dependency that condition implies. She sees Yabe—as in *Late Spring* she saw Hattori—essentially as a friend to whom she can relate on terms of equality. This is underlined by the fact that she connects him to her dead brother Shoji, who was his close friend; if one *must* have a husband, a brother figure will be less oppressive than a father figure. There is also the sense that Yabe is a serious and responsible man whom Noriko respects and who will be engaged in valuable and perhaps arduous work, in a new enterprise: the Noriko with whom we are familiar would find that far more attractive than becoming the wife of an affluent businessman who needs her, if at all, simply as a social ornament.

Hence the Mozartian, shadow-and-sunshine, tone of the film's closing sequences. As marriage goes, Ozu seems to be suggesting, we can hold out some degree of hope for this one, in that it differs significantly from either the arranged marriage or the love-match: he doesn't encourage us to put it higher than that. Against this, there is the dissolution of the extended family (not only its physical dispersal but the removal of its source of precarious harmony), the isolation of the old couple, the depressing prognosis for Koichi's wife and kids, without Noriko as mediator; and the sense that Noriko has accepted a certain loss for an uncertain (though perhaps fulfilling) gain.

## Tokyo Story

I need here to make explicit certain concepts that underpin my reading of the entire trilogy but which become particularly suggestive in relation to *Tokyo Story*: the Marxist concepts of the "dominant," the "residual," and the "emergent," as formulated by Raymond Williams in *Marxism and Literature*. The terms—which can be applied, for analytical purposes, to any culture at any point in its history and, by extension, to any of its products—are perhaps self-explanatory, but, briefly, the *dominant* refers to the entire multilevel complex of material practices (economic, social, political), assumptions, beliefs, and values dominant in a culture at a given historical moment, the *residual* to those elements inherited from the past but still preserving a degree of potency. The *emergent* refers to those factors that point or move toward a possible future—by definition much harder to define than the other two categories because these factors haven't yet quite "emerged," and hence are not fully formulated. According to Williams, when the "dominant" becomes completely unacceptable it is possible for the "residual" and the "emergent" to form an uneasy and temporary alliance against it.

This can be applied to *Tokyo Story* with particular precision and clarity. The "dominant" is represented by the values of postwar, Americanized Tokyo, built upon a brutal capitalist economy and a crass materialism that debases all human relationships (it is also, by and large, the world with which all of us are familiar today). The "residual" is represented by the little, tranquil, obsolete world of Onomichi and the values of the old couple who live there. The "emergent" is represented by Noriko and, especially, by the tentative relationship that begins to develop between her and the old couple's youngest child, the schoolteacher Kyoko.

But this needs qualification: in fact, throughout the trilogy, the residual and the emergent meet and harmonize in Noriko (which is, among other things, a way of defining the complexity and richness of the characterization). Noriko is usually seen by critics simply as the embodiment of traditional values and of Ozu's "conservatism," but this is really *too* simple. She has managed to retain and develop the finest humane values which the modern capitalist world, fostering greed, competition, and materialism above everything, tramples underfoot—consideration, emotional generosity, the ability to care and empathize, and above all, awareness. But she habitually dresses in Western-style clothes, consistently resists the traditional destiny of a woman, and is able to acclimatize herself to life in the modern world, within which in *Tokyo Story* she successfully holds down a nine-to-five job as an office worker. The Noriko of *Tokyo Story* would feel just as trapped, would be just as much an anomaly, in Onomichi as she is in Tokyo.

The chief ground on which critics base their claim that Noriko represents "traditional values" is the character's attitude to remarriage, in both *Late Spring* and *Tokyo Story*. Curious, then, that in *Early Summer* she *chooses* to marry a widower; and both the other films strike me as, at most, ambiguous. In *Late Spring* her objection is specifically to *men* remarrying (she expresses no distaste or shock at the idea that Mrs. Miwa might be looking for a new husband); this is already somewhat eccentric, the traditional Japanese emphasis being on the impropriety of *women* remarrying. And her objection is expressed in so jarringly extreme a form (it is "filthy" and "unclean," according to the subtitles) that one is driven to look for a motive in her personal psychology—which, given her desire to continue as the central figure in her father's household, is scarcely difficult to find. In *Tokyo Story* Noriko at no point says or even hints that her motivation for not wanting to remarry (or, to put it more strongly, for wanting *not* to remarry) is allegiance to her dead husband. That is of course what the old couple *assume* to be the case (they adhere completely to "residual" values, and he was after all their son), and Noriko fully understands this and is reluctant to disillusion them: hence her ashamed and desperate confession to her father-in-law in their final duologue that she doesn't think about Shoji *all* the time. Indeed, aside from the fact that she still keeps his picture on display (it would be rather brutal to throw it in the garbage), there is no indication that she *ever* thinks of him, except when prompted. Her only memory of her marriage appears to be that (like his father before him!) Shoji went out drinking with his buddies almost every night, leaving her alone, and she often had to put him drunk to bed—which seems a pretty adequate motivation for resisting the pressures on her to fall into the same trap a second time. Whatever it is that Noriko can't help yearning for (and it is the capacity to yearn that distinguishes her from a Shige—the couple's older daughter), we can take it that it is not another husband.

As for Ozu the artist, it seems to me that, in both *Late Spring* and *Tokyo Story*, his empathy is divided between Chishu Ryu and Setsuko Hara, the traditional patriarch (at his best) and the woman who, however tentatively, is trying to extricate herself from the entrapments and constrictions of patriarchy. In both films, their mutual affection and respect for one another is central to the emotional (the "Mozartian") complexity of the total effect. In other words, in his rigorous and indefatigable search for positive values by which to live in a culture increasingly devoid of them, Ozu is drawn to both the residual and the emergent, and Noriko is as important to him as she obviously is because she enables him convincingly to harmonize the two.

*Tokyo Story* (like Leo McCarey's *Make Way for Tomorrow* before it) has been viewed too narrowly as a film about a dear old couple with ungrateful children. Its scope is enormous, encompassing a searching social analysis of which Noriko gradually becomes the focal point, and to which the question of marriage is central. We are shown three marriages in the film: two Tokyo marriages (contained within the "dominant"), one Onomichi marriage (contained within the "residual"). The Tokyo marriages are presented as at once representative and inverse images of each other. In that of the old couple's eldest son, the man (Koichi, the doctor) is the dominant partner, the woman reduced to status of housewife/mother, and there are two children; in that of the elder daughter, the woman (Shige, the "beautician") is dominant, the man nagged and submissive, and the marriage is childless. Both are indistinguishable from American models (and Shige's work might be defined as the Americanization of Japanese women), with dominance determined by the purely material issue of "Who makes the money." These represent the chief models available to Noriko if she decided to remarry, though we are permitted a glimpse of one other (Noriko's neighbor, who keeps her baby under what looks like a kind of cover to keep flies off meat) and the memory of Noriko's own.

Set against this distinctly unencouraging portrayal of the potentialities of marriage within the "dominant," it is hardly surprising that the Onomichi marriage of the old couple, Shukichi and Tomi Hirayama, acquires certain positive connotations, embodying the values of the "residual" which modern Tokyo has obliterated. As with the other marriages in the film, the prime focus is on the position of the woman. Joan Mellen offers a remarkable account of Tomi, seeing her as representing some kind of lost ideal (from Ozu's diehard feudal perspective, that is): "The old lady, shrewd and perceptive, is a living example of all that is beautiful and becoming in the manner and behavior of the past. In her person, woman at her most splendid and feudal values at their apogee are conjoined." (Though later we are told that "she is not so much expressive of her sex, being far beyond the age of sexuality. . . . The ideal *woman*"—Mellen's emphasis—"is the widowed Noriko." I thought the notion that women can be defined strictly in terms of their sexuality was now regarded as a form of male chauvinism.)

Ozu *never* sentimentalizes Tomi in that manner. True, he treats her with compassion and respect, wholly without condescension, because he understands her and her position so well; the attitude, once again, is dramatized in Noriko and communicated through her to the spectator. But what is stressed most obviously, I would have thought, is Tomi's *limitations*, the limitations imposed on her by her upbringing and by the traditional expectations of womanhood. She moves through the film—once cut adrift from her native environment—in a kind of daze, afraid to think too much, afraid to ask too many questions. Her life is lived in a state of self-delusion of which she is poignantly half-conscious: she clings, for example, to the belief that Shoji, "missing in action" for eight years, is still alive somewhere, but if she *really* believed this she could hardly urge Noriko to remarry. David Bordwell tells us that Kogo Noda, though not at that time Ozu, had seen *Make Way for Tomorrow*, and one can see strong parallels between Tomi and McCarey's Lucy Cooper, with her perpetual hesitation between "facing facts" and "pretending there *are* no facts to face." Shoji, of course, being dead, can linger on in memory as the one child who might not have disappointed her, a wish strong enough, apparently, to survive Noriko's account of their marriage. That marriage, in fact, echoes Tomi's: we learn that Hirayama, too, habitually went out drinking (closely paralleling Barc Cooper's nights out at the barbershop), leaving his wife to mind the kids and coming home drunk, behavior we see reactivated under stress in Tokyo, in his night out boozing with an old crony, showing that, as far as male/female relations are concerned, Tokyo mores and Onomichi mores are not entirely discrete. After

Tomi's death, Shukichi is left wishing—not that the relationship had been radically different—but that he'd been "kinder" to her. Noriko cannot possibly be seen as some kind of throwback to the values Tomi embodies, though an important relationship is established between them because of the human values they share—goodwill, emotional generosity, a capacity for caring. In all other ways, Noriko is presented in strong contrast to Tomi: she is in full possession of an awareness that the older woman can barely imagine and would never dare permit herself.

Of the three films, it is only in *Tokyo Story* that Noriko's resistance is successful. This does not of course leave her happy: in the postwar Tokyo that Ozu depicts there is no fulfilling role available to a woman, and Noriko could never return to the kind of uneasy, part-illusory, fragile fulfillment represented by Tomi. Yet, if the film moves inexorably to the famous formulation, "Life is disappointing, isn't it?" (taken, far too often, as its "message," as if Ozu were a delivery boy), it is important to see that it also moves beyond it. Indeed, it is out of the scene in which that formulation occurs— the sudden, unexpected but completely convincing development of intimacy between Noriko and Kyoko—that the qualified, tentative note of hope (the crystallization of the "emergent") on which the film ends, grows.

I suggested earlier that one of the keys to the film is touch. Aside from a few casual and insignificant moments, touching is all but banished from the film, and at one point at least this absence acquires expressive force: when Tomi collapses on the seawall at Atami (the film's strongest foreshadowing of her death), her husband does not even move to help her to her feet—not, we understand, out of callousness or indifference, but from a refusal to confront the serious implications (Tomi is not the only one reluctant to "face facts"). There are only two instances of significant touch prior to the final sequences, and their function is to underline the contrast between Shige and Noriko: during the parents' first night in Tokyo, Shige aggressively pushes her two little nephews into the room; when Tomi spends the night in her apartment, Noriko gently and tenderly massages the old woman's aching back and later presses money into her hands.

In both these instances touch is functional—that is to say it has a purpose beyond itself. There is I think only one moment in the whole film of *autonomous* touch, as a spontaneous gesture of tenderness and affection: as they say goodbye, Noriko first clasps Kyoko's hand in hers, then reaches up lightly to stroke her hair, then clasps the hand again and holds it until Kyoko moves away to leave for her work. The gesture roughly coincides with Noriko's invitation to Kyoko to visit her in Tokyo, and Kyoko's pleased acceptance. We cannot say confidently that the two women will ever meet again; on the other hand we cannot doubt their mutual sincerity.

*Tokyo Story:* the old couple at Atami (Chishu Ryu, Chieko Higashiyama).

Homelessness and comfort: Noriko welcomes her parents-in-law.

"Positive" touch: Noriko massages Tomi.

Between this and Noriko's departure for Tokyo comes the lengthy duologue between her and Shukichi, in the course of which he gives her Tomi's watch, telling her that Tomi said she had never met a nicer woman. Noriko reacts with the embarrassment which is (in my experience) a typical, even obligatory, Japanese response to explicit praise, but the embarrassment is intensified by her assumption (doubtless *partly* correct) that Tomi found her so "nice" because she has remained faithful to Shoji's memory. Hence her ashamed confession to Shukichi that sometimes goes for days without thinking of his son. The rising emotion takes her quickly to breakdown and the expression of despair—that sometimes she feels she "can't go on"—but she is unable to formulate any possible antidote: she yearns for something but she can't say what.

The gift of the watch may be taken as formulating for us what Noriko can't yet define. As passed down from woman to woman (via a sensitive and sympathetic male), it carries a particular charge: we have seen so many movies in which a watch is passed from father to son, to symbolize continuity of the male line (for suggestive variations on this—but still within the syndrome of male inheritance—see the Christmas gift of the watch in *Night of the Hunter* and the watch without hands in *Wild Strawberries*). In *Tokyo*

*Story* it serves as a link between three generations of women. Kyoko, in the classroom among her pupils (it is important that she is a teacher), looks at her watch, moves to the window overlooking the railway tracks, looks at the watch again, waits to see Noriko's train go by; Noriko, on the train, takes out Tomi's watch and looks at it, with an expression combining sorrow with a muted pleasure. Hence Ozu establishes a bond between women, across time and space, transcending death. One can read the sequence as, among other things, the redemption of Tomi's wasted life, given sudden and unexpected posthumous meaning in the solidarity of women.

If one takes the term *lesbian* in the more comprehensive sense legitimized by radical feminism—female bonding, for mutual support and strength within a male-dominated culture—then the term is perfectly appropriate here. Ozu could not of course define the precise nature of the "emergent" to which these indications (arrived at no doubt intuitively, with the intuitive freedom of the truly creative artist) point: it achieved definition only after his death, in the women's movement of the 1960s and 1970s.

## A Note on *Equinox Flower*

I should confess to a certain arbitrariness in annexing *Equinox Flower* as an addendum to the trilogy. Setsukos and Hirayamas weave in and out of Ozu's work, so one cannot make too much of the names (on the other hand, a search through the available credits reveals only one Noriko outside the trilogy, in *The End of Summer*). It is also stretching things to relate the Setsuko here to the Noriko of the trilogy: she is a far less potentially threatening and radical figure, and is far from reluctant to marry, her choice being based on a strong romantic attachment that, if Noriko ever experiences it, she never reveals. Yet, like Noriko, Setsuko fights for her right to independence and personal autonomy, resisting the encroachments of tradition. The film also takes up and develops, beyond any other late Ozu work, the theme of female bonding. Indeed, it strikes me as his most *overtly* feminist film: one might without inappropriateness borrow a title from Mizoguchi (in his most radical period) and rename it *Victory of Women*.

Ozu's title has its own resonance and beauty (the season of change, and the flowers that bloom out of it), and it refers us to a major aspect of the films that I have hitherto underplayed: Ozu's evident involvement with, and qualified emotional commitment to, the figure of the Father, the Japanese patriarch. One might describe *Equinox Flower* as a feminist film made from the viewpoint of the traditional patriarch: the seeming paradox marks its particular richness and distinction.

There is no question that the patriarch is the film's central figure, still named Hirayama but no longer played by Chishu Ryu, whose fathers are in general more permissive and open to change than the staunchly traditionalist and authoritarian figure enacted by Shin Saburi. Ryu here plays another father, whose daughter is living with her lover out of wedlock, one of the film's multiple ironies being that Saburi, the far more inflexible father within his own family, is instrumental in persuading Ryu to accept the situation. The film is about Saburi's education at the hands of the women, and Ozu's complexity of response is nowhere more vividly exemplified than in his ability simultaneously to empathize with the patriarch's sense of loss and to celebrate the women's victory.

This time, Ozu makes his concern with marriage almost schematically explicit. Never has a theme been more clearly stated in a film's opening moments: two railway workers sit together at a station between trains; one comments on the unusual number of newly married couples; the other remarks that stormy weather is forecast. The film's central tension is also established very early, in the sequence of the wedding banquet where Hirayama has been appointed to make the chief speech. This marriage, he tells the assembly, with some discomfort, is a love match (the bride and groom actually chose each other), and of course that is a Good Thing, we're adjusting nowadays to these new-fangled notions. But his own marriage (he feels compelled to add) was a traditional "arranged" marriage, and is a living testimony to the success of such arrangements. In the midst of this awkward and convoluted mélange of would-be liberal-conservative self-defensiveness, we are shown his wife (the great Kinuyo Tanaka, star of so many late Mizoguchi films but also in fact an Ozu "regular" in a far earlier period), looking extremely dubious and not a little embarrassed. Ozu's pervasive awareness that "arranged" marriages were always arranged at the women's expense is eloquently realized in her expression. Tanaka's performance throughout the film is extraordinary (and we should remember that Ozu never permitted a gesture or expression that he himself didn't "mean"): a woman saved from the misery of a life of hatred and resentment purely by her innate and irreducible good humor, too old-fashioned not to be subservient (to the letter rather than the spirit), and too aware not to view her own situation (and her lord-and-master) with quiet irony; losing the little battles (whether or not she is allowed to listen to "pop" music on the radio) while she gently and surreptitiously wins the war.

The film's main plot, thematically adumbrated here with masterly economy, concerns the daughter Setsuko's fixed and irreversible decision to marry "for love," and the father's obstinate recalcitrance in accepting her right to do so. But Ozu is far too intelligent to fall into the sentimental "modern is better" trap: the film denies us any guarantee whatever that the "love" marriages of the present will be any more successful than the "arranged" marriages of the past. That is not the issue. What *is* the issue is whether or not women have the right to make their own decisions, and here the film is entirely unambiguous.

The power of female bonding has never (as far as I am aware) been carried so far in any previous Ozu movie, and it will never be carried as far in the five subsequent ones. (I should say here, parenthetically, that I agree—tentatively, I am open to conversion—with Noel Burch, though for utterly different reasons, that Ozu finally declined into academicism. Only I set the date much later: the last color films strike me as tired, the creative impetus weakened, a retreat into a formal play with color that, at its worst, becomes almost a kind of painting-by-numbers. That the feminist thrust of *Equinox Flower* was not followed through seems to me infinitely more significant than any failure to mismatch eyelines. A parallel case in the West might be Hawks's retreat from the radical narrative experimentation of *Red Line 7000*: with both directors the retreat took the form of reworking earlier successes.) Ozu presents us with a veritable conspiracy of women to induce Hirayama to accept his daughter's right to decide her own destiny—to accept the marriage chosen by her and not himself.

*Equinox Flower:* the arranged marriage—acceptance and resignation
(Kinuyo Tanaka, Shin Saburi).

I shall not attempt to trace here the complicated process by which this is brought about; suffice it to say that every episode is relevant to it. I want simply to isolate two moments that seem to me to epitomize the Ozuesque complexity:

—The whole film moves toward Setsuko's wedding, yet (typically, of Ozu) we are denied the satisfaction of the ceremony, its preparation, or its aftermath (her father has refused to attend). In its place we have another ceremony: Hirayama's participation in an all-male "Old Boys' Reunion" in celebration of the Emperor's birthday, replete with patriotic recitations and songs. Ozu enters into this wholeheartedly, at the same time foregrounding its nostalgia, the irrevocable pastness of what is being commemorated. The patriotic poem recited (appropriately, by Chishu Ryu) is about failure, defeat, and loss.

—In this, his first color film, Ozu indulges to the limit his fondness for red: composition after composition is centered (or significantly de-centered) on bright red objects. Yet repeatedly, throughout, we are shown a red chair, out in the corridor where the telephone is located, in which nobody ever sits. The film's climax comes when Mrs. Hirayama, over the telephone, finally extracts from her husband (as the last move in all the pressures the women have exerted on him) the promise to visit their daughter and the man she has married. She replaces the receiver, and goes and sits, triumphant, in the red chair. It is so typical and beautiful of Ozu that so tiny and apparently trivial a gesture should signify so much: the "victory of women" could not be more appropriately celebrated.

The film ends with Hirayama, on the train en route to visit Setsuko and her chosen husband, humming to himself the patriotic song of defeat, and smiling contentedly.

*This essay is dedicated to Yuichi Takahashi, whom I shall describe once again, despite his contortions of agonized embarrassment, as one of the most wholly admirable human beings I have ever met.*

# PART III

# THE FAMILY

# CHAPTER 6

# Leo McCarey and "Family Values"

**I**

## The Family, Normal and Dysfunctional; Or, by all means, *Make Way for Tomorrow*

The work of Leo McCarey continues to be generally undervalued and misrepresented. The films seem so easy, so transparent, so heart-on-sleeve, but actually reading them is another matter altogether. One can begin by asking whether McCarey himself knew what he was really doing and saying—or what the films do and say despite him. I can think of no other major artist—and I believe him to be one—in whose work the disjuncture between discernible conscious intention and actual realized significance is so extreme. He has never been forgiven for the—indeed unforgivable—sin of "naming names" before the House Committee on Un-American Activities (HUAC). But can any of us confidently assert that we have not committed unforgivable acts at some point in our lives? And if we can't forgive the person (while declining to forgive the act), then who shall 'scape whipping? What interests me is that McCarey's act appears to have been motivated, not by the usual motive of political expediency or saving one's own skin (he really had nothing to fear, his films having generally been received as wholesome at best, harmless at worst), but by a genuine belief that he was "doing the right thing."

We may begin, then, with a brief glance at *My Son John* (1952), McCarey's "unforgivable" movie. The film has rarely been shown since the 1950s, and its recent occasional resurfacings on television (typically introduced with an apologetic chuckle signifying, "Nowadays, of course, we can laugh at this") seem to have done little to affect its reputation as a crude and insufferable anti-Communist tract. It is that, certainly—for its last forty-five minutes; few seem aware that well over an hour of a very different movie has passed before their eyes prior to the abrupt shift of tone and collapse of quality.

McCarey's occasional defenders sometimes try to blame the failure of the later parts exclusively on the fact that Robert Walker died before shooting was completed. Certainly, the clumsy patching-in of shots of Walker from other films (notably *Strangers on a Train*) is very jarring, but the trouble has begun long before that and can in fact be quite precisely pinpointed—the scene by the lake in Washington (the familiar government buildings on display across the water) where Van Heflin reveals to Helen Hayes "the awful truth" that her son John is indeed a Communist. Before that moment the film is not really about "my son John" but about his mother; Helen Hayes is not merely its emotional center, but receives all that intimate attention (details of inflection, expression, body language) that McCarey customarily lavishes on actors and characters he patently loves.

Its subject might be stated as follows: a mother is pushed to the very brink of insanity by the Oedipal conflicts between her husband and her son, in which she is necessarily but unwillingly implicated. And the chief culprit in this is clearly not John (arrogant as he often is) but his father (Dean Jagger), a blustering, insensitive, narrow-minded and fundamentally stupid bigot who is primarily responsible for the disruption of whatever family harmony might have existed, and who remains culpably unaware of the precariousness of his wife's mental state, despite her frequent signals. If these are "archetypal apple-pie parents" (the description offered in Leonard Maltin's *Movie and Video Guide*), the film can scarcely be taken as an advertisement for apple pies.

This theme, and its implications for the structures and values of the traditional nuclear family ("normal" and dysfunctional simultaneously), take us right to the vital animating core of McCarey's best work. The irony is, of course, that he might himself have been hauled before a committee on "un-American activities" if his films had been properly understood; and if he had permitted himself fully to understand them, he might well have felt compelled to make a full confession, then retreat into alcoholism long before he in fact did. What is really unforgivable about the last part of *My Son John* is not that it is anti-Communist in the most naive, propaganda-conditioned way, but that it brutally and blatantly negates everything the film has said and done up to the turning point: suddenly, we are indeed asked to accept this wretched family as not only typical but admirable, and to see the father as a stalwart and heroic pillar of "correct" American values. The transparency of the film's cheating is underlined by the sudden hysterical insistence, the riding roughshod over all complexity, the sheer embarrassing crudity of utterance: all one can salvage of the last forty-five minutes are a few brief moments of Helen Hayes.

Here one can put one's finger on the precise point where McCarey's consciously held beliefs (superficially "sincere" yet thoroughly spurious) have overridden the spontaneous-intuitive impulses that activate his best work, the victory (in Freudian terms) of superego over id. Certain important aspects of his early work illuminate the nature of those impulses and the influences that nurtured them.

Before *Ruggles of Red Gap* (1935), McCarey's most significant work was with the Hollywood "clowns." He directed Harold Lloyd, Eddie Cantor, Mae West, W. C. Fields, and Burns and Allen at various times, and he is credited with what is generally acknowledged as the Marx Brothers' best (most coherent, most disciplined, most consistently inventive) film, *Duck Soup*. In every case he brought out the best in the performers, and the films testify to the affinity he felt for the central, most obvious attraction common to these comedians—the tendency, in one way or another, to anarchic impulse. Above all, however, his work with Laurel and Hardy was clearly a formative experience that influenced all his subsequent films. He is credited with directing only three of their silent two-reelers (at least two of which, *Liberty* and *Wrong Again*, are among the masterpieces), but he was supervising manager on all their films prior to 1930. In that capacity he involved himself in all stages of production, including working with the couple on the scenarios. Memories of Hardy in particular—his mannerisms, facial expressions, "bits of business"—seem to have haunted him throughout his career, manifesting themselves especially when he worked with actors tending, like Hardy, to the chubby: Mary Boland in *Ruggles of Red Gap*, Walter Slezak in *Once Upon a Honeymoon*, Jack Carson in *Rally 'Round the Flag, Boys!*—all have moments of pure Hardy.

But the influence—or, if you prefer, the affinity—is both wider and deeper. The defining core of Laurel and Hardy's humor might be described thusly: they are two well-intentioned individuals who, on the conscious level, would like above all things to be good citizens, conforming to all the best bourgeois conventions, but who, because of their incorrigible proneness to anarchic impulse (whether in the form of spontaneous/deliberate acts or "accidents"), invariably end up causing disruption, disaster, and chaos. That is not a bad paradigm for the filmmaker who testified before HUAC and then, a few years later, cowrote, produced, and directed that un-American activity par excellence *Rally 'Round the Flag, Boys!* Throughout his career McCarey shows a particular attraction to characters who, outwardly respectable and conformist, surrender (often with remarkably minimal reluctance) to anarchic impulse. The line runs from Charles Laughton in *Ruggles* to Paul Newman in *Rally*, via Irene Dunne (the "masquerade" in *The Awful Truth*), Victor Moore (*Make Way for Tomorrow*), and, perhaps less obviously, Ingrid Bergman in *The Bells of St. Mary's* (see, for example, the magnificent sequences of the boxing lesson and the Christmas play). The definitive moment is the turning point of *Make Way for Tomorrow*: the moment when Victor Moore, with a sense of sudden revelation or awakening, echoes the friendly car salesman's "Why not?"—and a very good film abruptly becomes a great one.

One might amend Renoir's famous but problematic remark that McCarey was one of the great American directors because he "really understood people" to "because he really understood actors: actors as people." Like Renoir, and unlike, for example, Hitchcock or von Sternberg, McCarey was first and foremost an actors' director, and the beauty of his work arises from the manifold ways in which his actors interact with, lend themselves to, his recurring thematic concerns. No one is likely to celebrate McCarey for the beauty of his compositions or the skills of his editing (though both are manifestly there, as subordinate components of his art). One wonders whether the secret of his work with Laurel and Hardy was not so much that he understood how they should be directed, as that he knew how to prevent their being directed at all. One would not presume, surely, to direct Laurel and Hardy: one might enjoy their company, establish a rapport, encourage them, make a few modest suggestions, ask them if they did not want to push a scene even further, then set the camera down in front of them and refrain from moving it (unless to follow their movements), from cutting (until they finished what they were doing), and from surrendering to any temptation to indulge in the "Art of the Film," as it is commonly understood. It's a lesson McCarey never forgot, which is why his films will still be alive when innumerable "artistic" productions have become mere fossils.

The creative intercourse with actors-as-people, intimate and spontaneous, is the key not only to McCarey's method but to his thematic. There is a wonderfully funny and ironic moment in *Once Upon a Honeymoon* that might stand as a mini-testament. Walter Slezak is preparing Cary Grant for the broadcast he has agreed to give on behalf of the Nazis (which Grant, of course, intends to subvert). He tells him that he must above all sound "sincere," then goes on to say that he must also express "shpontanuity." On a simple level, the values of "sincerity" and "spontaneity" are clearly central to McCarey's work; the moment constitutes his acknowledgment that they can also be faked, while at the same time reaffirming them by putting their perversion in the mouth of a Nazi. "Sincerity" is always a problematic concept: McCarey was doubtless, on a certain level, "sincere" when he aligned himself with the McCarthy witch-hunts. But a far deeper and very different sincerity animates, say, the last half hour of *Make Way for Tomorrow*, the Christmas play sequence of *The Bells of St. Mary's*, the Thanksgiving Day pageant of *Rally 'Round the Flag, Boys!* The former type offers the "sincerity" of a consciously held, "respectable" belief; the latter type the sincerity of spontaneous impulse. "Sincerity" becomes authentic only when it is fused with spontaneity.

It was a friend, John Anderson, who in the early 1970s introduced me to *Make Way for Tomorrow* (which I previously hadn't even heard of) and who started me thinking about Leo McCarey with a remark, dropped in his quiet and casual way, to the effect that McCarey disliked families but loved couples. Such a formulation immediately suggests a paradox: after all, the whole point of the couple in our culture has traditionally been the formation of the family, the basis of the social structure. (Clearly, this is much less true today, when so many couples are refusing legal marriage and the obligation to produce children, single-parent families are becoming common, and same-sex couples are steadily gaining social acceptance.) The couples of McCarey's films, however, have certain idiosyncrasies that at least partially resolve this. Their most obvious characteristic is the movement toward equalization. Presumptions of male privilege are invariably chastised (*The Awful Truth*; Victor Moore's "I'm ashamed," during the drive to the Hotel Vogard in *Make Way for Tomorrow*; the "fatherly" authority of Bing Crosby, allowed no role participation in the Christmas play). Gender differences are progressively minimized, the partners both modifying and enriching each other's attitudes and behavior patterns in a process of exchange and reciprocal learning.

The other major characteristic is that the traditional function of procreation is not even raised, or if (as in *Make Way*, *Rally 'Round*, and the good part of *My Son John*) a family already exists it is treated in purely negative terms, as an obstacle, encumbrance, or source of tension and conflict. It is the traditional family, of course, that defines and reproduces the patriarchal gender roles and functions: its absence or negation is essential to the equalization of the couple (which in *Make Way for Tomorrow* cannot begin until the family have been rejected).

There is one final condition for the construction of the McCareyan ideal couple: it can exist only if *(a)* the partners have creative occupations that enable them to work side by side (*The Bells of St. Mary's*) or *(b)* they are so wealthy that they don't have to work at all (*The Awful Truth*) or *(c)* they are past retirement age (*Make Way for Tomorrow*). McCarey can't tell us what will become of Nicky and Terry (with their appropriately androgynous names), after the endings of *Love Affair* and *An Affair to Remember*; and the final scene of *Rally 'Round the Flag, Boys!* is clearly a bit of a cheat, a wish-fulfillment that will dissolve with the return to routine and its rude awakening.

Before examining *Make Way for Tomorrow* and *Rally 'Round the Flag, Boys!* in some detail, I want to touch briefly on five of McCarey's most famous and popular films (all of them also in my view among his major artistic successes).

1. *Ruggles of Red Gap* (1935). The revealing comparison here is with Ford, and especially *Drums Along the Mohawk*, made four years later (though one might equally adduce *My Darling Clementine*, with its symbolic depiction of an "ideal" America in the celebrated sequence of the unfinished church). Both *Ruggles* and *Drums* are single-mindedly concerned with defining an "ideal" America in terms of the coming together and harmonization of seemingly incompatible components that are equally valued and regarded as equally necessary: essentially, both films attempt to resolve, in positive terms, the familiar civilization/wilderness antinomy of the classical western. Both move toward the recitation or display of a "defining" text or emblem—the Gettysburg address in *Ruggles*, "My country, 'tis of thee" and the hoisting of the new flag in *Drums*. The figure of the "girl from the East" who reappears throughout Ford's westerns as the bearer of civilization who must also accept and be modified by the "natural" values of the wilderness has her counterpart in Ruggles (Charles Laughton), the archetypal British valet.

Ford's vision is centered firmly on the concept of Woman-as-Mother, and on the family; the almost schematic development of *Drums* follows a process of the integration of smaller units into larger: the couple, the family, the community, the nation. Its climactic moment is the reunion of husband, wife, and child, immediately following which the destructive forces (represented by John Carradine's Caldwell) can be shown to be destroyed, the Indian "threat" nullified, and the flag hoisted. *Ruggles*, on the other hand, produces no less than three major couples (two formed in the course of the film) but virtually no familial relationships: the one exception is Effie Floud (Mary Boland) and her mother, who barely tolerate each other (insofar, indeed, as they even *notice* each other!). Of the three couples, the Flouds are middle-aged and still significantly childless; Ruggles and Mrs. Judson (Zasu Pitts), who are also getting on in years, seem more interested in sharing recipes and perfecting their culinary activities than in raising a family; and the very odd (and all the more delightful for that) couple, the British aristocrat Lord Birnstead (Roland Young) and the "notorious" proprietress of an "establishment," Nell Kenner (Leila Hyams), look neither suited to nor desirous of parenthood.

The famous scene in which Leila Hyams teaches Roland Young to play the drums deserves special mention here because it epitomizes so much of McCarey's method and its thematic dimension. Reputedly, it began as an improvization, and it retains that quality of spontaneity: Young and Hyams were fooling around with the drums between takes, amusing themselves; McCarey saw them and promptly incorporated their "performance" into the scenario. One must assume that it replaced a (probably far more conventional) scripted scene because *something* is clearly demanded around that point to make credible the Birnstead/Kenner liaison. It stands in for, therefore, and in effect becomes, a McCarey love scene—two seemingly ill-matched people discovering a mutual delight in each other through play, their shared fun dissolving social and cultural barriers and equalizing them, as the British lord voluntarily submits to the good-humored musical authority of an American "woman of ill repute." One may add that this is another striking instance where McCarey's "ideal" notion of community differs from Ford's: the Fordian vision has no place for a Nell Kenner (unless, like Dallas [Claire Trevor] in *Stagecoach*, she discovers a yearning for motherhood). Chihuahua (Linda Darnell) in *My Darling Clementine* cannot be contained within the Fordian community where she has no role, and is accordingly treated with contempt while she is alive and hypocritically sentimentalized over when she dies. McCarey's far more inclusive and generous vision is achieved, admittedly, at the price of a certain equivocation: he cannot tell us what Nell actually *does*—whether she simply provides facilities for "beer-busts," or entertains her customers in more intimate ways.

2 and 3. *Love Affair* (1939) and *An Affair to Remember* (1957). The story is attributed to McCarey personally, and the fact that he filmed it twice (and con amore on both occasions) speaks eloquently of its personal nature. It is perhaps the most fully developed example of the process of equalization: the partners, in order to "earn" their relationship, must not only extricate themselves from other entanglements but prove (the woman as much as the man) their ability to stand on their own feet and earn their own livings. Terry (Irene Dunne/Deborah Kerr) is associated in both versions with children, but in her capacity as a singing teacher, after she is crippled. May one not, in the context of McCarey's work, read her accident as the director's (doubtless unconscious) guarantee that she will not be able to have children of her own?

4. *The Awful Truth* (1937). Here, in this comedy of remarriage, instead of a child, the couple have a dog. It has been suggested that, in the context of "screwball" comedy, this was merely a necessary convenience: the presence of a child would have introduced emotional complications quite incompatible with the genre. I think it equally arguable that McCarey understood that

the substitution of a dog would leave the couple free to renegotiate their relationship without external pressure; they reunite, not "for the sake of the children," but because that is what they both really want.

5. *The Bells of St. Mary's* (1945). Far from being the piece of sentimental kitsch it's usually represented as—sneered at by intellectuals, watched annually by millions as a wholesome 'family" Christmas entertainment, the two views equally misguided and perfectly complementary—*The Bells of St. Mary's* occupies a privileged position in the McCarey oeuvre as the one film that moves beyond the implicit rejection of the traditional patriarchal family to suggest (tentatively, sketchily) the possibility of an alternative model. Most people see it as some kind of love story (the "nicer" because all that nasty business of sex is sidestepped), and it is clear that Father O'Malley (Bing Crosby) and Sister Benedict (Ingrid Bergman) learn, by a gradual process of mutual acceptance, equalization, and the undermining of gender roles, to love each other. He helps a girl pupil write a sensitive English essay, she gives a boy pupil boxing lessons: the concepts of "masculine" and "feminine" become progressively blurred.

The film uses this basis to juxtapose two families: the archetypal broken family of capitalist society (disturbed daughter, father an irresponsible "wanderer," mother resorting to prostitution to make ends meet), and the "family" within the convent, presided over by "Father" O'Malley and "Mother" Sister Superior. The latter family has numerous distinguishing characteristics. First, it is not of course a family at all, in any sense our culture recognizes. Second, the "parents" can never marry or engage in domesticity together, as he is a priest, she a nun. Third, the children are not biologically related to them. The implications of this—pointing toward an entirely different and (potentially, if it were thought through) far more satisfactory concept of "family," in which parents and children no longer make inordinate and damaging emotional demands on each other in the name of "love" and "duty"—are covered by the "alibi" of Catholicism. (Again, I am not suggesting that this could have been McCarey's conscious intention—he was the least devious of artists. On a superficial level his commitment to Catholicism was as "sincere" as his animus against Communism, the two poles becoming, in his work, not merely opposites but, like so many opposites, complements. Both operate subconsciously as concealments for what the man could never dare to think but what the artist could "spontaneously" express.)

Here the privileged scene—equivalent to the drum scene in *Ruggles* as a McCareyan epitome (or epiphany)—is that of the Christmas play. It is an improvization both in method and content: within the diegesis Sister Superior admits that the text changes every time they rehearse it and she never knows what the children are going to say, and outside it it seems clear that McCarey exercised as little control as possible over its performance. The authority of the "Father" is immediately undermined; there is no room in the play for the rendering of "Silent Night" he has been assiduously preparing with the older children. O'Malley accepts this graciously enough, and "Father" and "Mother," on either side of the aisle but in exactly parallel positions, watch the performance as necessary adult figures, without in any way controlling it or interfering. The children are free (within the bounds of the Nativity story) to invent for themselves; the "parents" do not attempt to mold (or straitjacket) them into a prewritten text, allowing them a rare degree of self-determination. Given McCarey's official commitment to Catholicism, it is striking that the play that he and Sister Superior allow to happen is almost completely secularized. There is a token angel, but beyond that the children enact, very simply, the "birth" of a palpably human (and about eleven-month-old) baby, the play culminating in the singing, not of a Christmas carol, but of "Happy birthday to you." The entire sequence might stand as a model for parents: simply "being there" and letting their kids determine their own "texts," a phenomenon still all too rare in traditional families, in which the familiar teenage rebellion is a direct product of the seemingly ineradicable desire of parents to mold their children into replicas of what they are or (more frequently perhaps) of what they wish they had been.

But beyond this the sequence can surely be taken as implying that there are possible forms of social organization superior to the patriarchal nuclear family, and that there is no particularly cogent reason why children should be raised by their biological parents. In fact, when one moves outside this scene to the film's wider context one may (if one wishes) take away from it the sense that they *shouldn't*. The St. Mary's "family" is juxtaposed with a "real" family in the outside world and its supposedly happy reconstitution. Significantly, the nonbiological, non-nuclear family of the Christmas play is presided over by a woman, while the agent for reassembling the "normal" family is the man. (It is also obvious throughout the film that McCarey is far more interested in working with Ingrid Bergman—together they produce one of her finest performances—than with Bing Crosby.) The reunion of Patsy's father and mother is surely one of the most embarrassing scenes McCarey ever directed; one keeps wanting to avert one's eyes. I am not of course suggesting that this is the effect McCarey consciously intended: the embarrassment is due in part to the fact that on a certain level he obviously believed in it. Doubtless he was "sincerely" assured of the rightness of restoring the nuclear family in all its glory. What he cannot do—because he was, above all, an artist—is to convince us of the glory. Instead, we have two people making the best of a very bad job because there is really no alternative; within the patriarchal capitalist organization there is nowhere else for them to go, short of the self-destruction on which both have been bent. What will become of Patsy within such a family is clearly not something McCarey could safely contemplate.

The above account of McCarey's treatment of family requires two slight modifications. First, there is one form of biological relationship which the films clearly endorse: veneration for a parent figure provided she is *(a)* female, *(b)* very old, and that *(c)* one doesn't have to live with her. I see this essentially as further evidence of McCarey's bias toward women and his sensitivity to their predicament in a culture built upon male privilege (though his sympathies also encompass *redeemable* men, i.e., those capable of learning). I think here of Barry Fitzgerald's ancient mother in *Going My Way* (the climactic scene of their reunion standing out in what is in general one of McCarey's least interesting films) and Nicky's grandmother in both *Love Affair* and *An Affair to Remember*; above all, there is McCarey's own commitment to and empathy with the Beulah Bondi character in *Make Way for Tomorrow*. Second, there is the obvious problem of *Good Sam*, the one McCarey film that can be read as producing a positive (if confused) image of the nuclear family.

The film, made in the shadow of *It's a Wonderful Life*, is heavily in debt to Capra; its thoroughly botched second half, proceeding in a series of abrupt and contradictory jolts, is far more like failed Capra than failed McCarey. It has, however, an excellent first hour, exploring (in a way both funny and uncomfortable, a mode common to much of McCarey's work) the difficulties of being a saint in a culture characterized by competitiveness, greed, and exploitation. Throughout this, Lou (Ann Sheridan), the saint's increasingly desperate wife, unambiguously represents the voice of reason, of a realistic practicality. Then, abruptly, Sam (Gary Cooper) is thoroughly vindicated after all, Lou made to appear selfish and mean-minded: Capra-like, Sam's beneficiaries come up trumps, rescuing the couple from financial disaster. Then, equally abruptly, ruined again, Sam discovers that you can't trust people after all. Yet another volte-face: the bank manager who refused him a loan arbitrarily changes his mind, and simultaneously Sam has suddenly and inexplicably been promoted to vice president of the department store where he works. But he doesn't learn all this immediately: he is out getting drunk. A friendly bartender sings him "Home, Sweet Home," and the Salvation Army takes him back to it. The film's ups and downs become so arbitrary that it is impossible to discern any coherent position whatever.

McCarey is clearly unable to resolve the Sam/Lou dialectic: they are both right, they are both wrong. As for the family, for the purposes of my argument it is neither here nor there. In *It's a Wonderful Life* Capra movingly and richly realized the possible binding affection and solidarity of family life *and* the ways in which domesticity becomes a prison. McCarey in *Good Sam* realizes neither with much conviction. Characteristically, the emphasis is more on the couple than on the family group; the two kids are lovable enough but—as will later be the case in *Rally 'Round the Flag, Boys!* where it is more fully and abrasively developed—a constant impediment to their parents' sexual and amorous relationship.

The ending is, in the context of McCarey's work, quite striking, but insufficiently supported by what has preceded it to carry much weight. Sam, brought home by the Salvation Army, insists on singing one last song before he enters the house with Lou. But instead of the expected reprise of "Home, Sweet Home," he chooses "Let Me Call You Sweetheart," ending the film on a somewhat weak and arbitrary reminder of the "unmarrying" motif so powerful and logical at the close of *Make Way for Tomorrow*.

*Make Way for Tomorrow* was McCarey's personal project, and remained, throughout his life, his personal favorite among his own films. His difficulties in setting it up can be deduced from the film itself: not only is it one of the few Hollywood films about old age and its problems, it also rigorously refuses a happy, or even vaguely consoling, ending. The amazing thing is that it got made at all. Nor is it surprising that it was a box office disaster and almost became a lost film. Paramount, having with great reluctance (and after some hard bargaining) allowed McCarey to make it, threw it away. There is a lingering rumor that certain of the few people who saw it during its very brief public exposure committed suicide as a result, but I've never seen this substantiated and it seems extremely improbable: its characteristic generosity, humanity, and humor prevent it from being *that* demoralizing.

The credits tell us it was adapted from a novel and a play. I have been unable to trace copies of either so can only speculate. Most of the first hour *could* derive from a play (though one with an unusual number of scene changes, and one key scene—the bridge lesson—demanding an unusual number of "extras")—in which case it is a sensitive realization of congenial material. I suppose the magnificent last half hour *could* have been adapted from a novel; if so, McCarey has made it so completely his own that anyone familiar with his work would certainly assume that it belongs exclusively to him. It is the core of his entire oeuvre.

The film begins by asserting a perfectly respectable, socially acceptable, ideologically secure maxim, ratified by the Bible itself: "Honor thy father and thy mother." Presumably, McCarey really believed that this was his message. Not, of course, that the film says that one shouldn't, very much the contrary; rather, it demonstrates the impossibility of putting the maxim into practice within the living conditions of modern middle-class culture. About fourteen years later, Ozu made *Tokyo Story*, of which *Make Way for Tomorrow* was one of the sources. Comparison is fascinating—the work of an American "primitive" (for so indeed McCarey appears beside the Japanese master) juxtaposed with that of one of the most sophisticated and fully conscious figures of world cinema. Ultimately it must tell in Ozu's favor, highlighting the limitations of the ideological system within which McCarey worked: his film has no place for a Noriko, and his vision could not encompass any equivalent. Yet directness and unself-conscious spontaneity have their own rewards. I introduce the comparison here to discuss one of the most striking parallels—the move from country to city used by both directors to encapsulate fifty years of social change. Both the Hirayamas and the Coopers, left behind in the country, have also been left behind by the movement of capitalist civilization; in the cities both couples are lost, the move exposing the limitations and inadequacies of an insulated value system, but also suggesting its superiority to anything that has replaced it. Both films imply that the living conditions of the small-town "past" are preferable to those of the urban present (with which it continues, marginalized, to coexist). But neither Ozu nor McCarey idealizes or sentimentalizes the past.

The Coopers discover a nostalgia for the time before they were married (and proceed to relive it briefly before their final separation), but not for any specific environment or social order. Ozu endows life in Onomichi with certain positive values—tranquillity, stability, the possibility of contemplation so central to Japanese culture, so alien to American—totally lacking in the lives (Noriko's excepted) of the younger generation in the Americanized postwar Tokyo, but places the stress on its limitations: intimacy has degenerated into routine, the Hirayamas (just as much as the Coopers) have been quite unable to instill in their children a sense of values that might enable them to preserve some of the finer human qualities even amid the modern capitalist rat race where financial concerns determine everything. Notably, both husbands are brought to the point where they recognize the inadequacy of their attitude to wives who have thoroughly assimilated the doctrine that "a woman's place is in the home": Hirayama, after his wife's death, acknowledges that he "should have been kinder to her," and Barclay Cooper, during the drive that initiates their greatly foreshortened "second honeymoon," suddenly confronts the facts that this is the first time they've been away together since their first, and that in all the intervening years he left Lucy at home with (and later without) the kids, preferring the company of his barbershop cronies ("I'm ashamed").

The Coopers' country environment (presumably on the fringe of a small town, though it is neither named nor shown) lacks even the limited "positives" of Ozu's Onomichi: there is no stability (Barc and Lucy are about to lose their home to the bank), tranquillity has clearly become stagnation, and no one appears to contemplate anything (or even to wish to do so)—they simply wait for "something to turn up." The house itself has all the reality of a Christmas card illustration. For the opening "gathering of the clan," Pa, though ruined, sits in state in his "old armchair," while Lucy (who has clearly done all the work unaided) stands beside it. Four of the five "children" are present (the third daughter, Addie, lives in California). Of them, the two daughters, Cora and Nellie, come across as, respectively, unhelpful and mean-minded, while the younger son, Robert, good-natured but ineffectual, seems to be in training to follow in his father's footsteps as the "town clown." Only the elder son George strikes one as combining decency with a degree of awareness, an impression confirmed later in the film.

As for the parents, they are simply *there*, waiting, obviously taking for granted that the children will find them some way out of their predicament. Isn't that what children are for? Awareness (the awareness, for example, of a Noriko) is the necessary quality, as lacking here as it is in the parents and off-spring of *Tokyo Story*: on the one hand the stagnation of small-town life, on the other the constant urban preoccupation with "keeping up" or "making ends meet" that leaves neither the time, energy, nor inclination for anything beyond. Clearly, the family is presented throughout as typical—average Americans leading average American lives with average American spouses.

As in *Tokyo Story*, the implicit critique is directed not at individuals so much as at the conditions imposed on them, the stunted values fostered, by capitalist culture. There is one feeble attempt at recuperation, abruptly pre-tending the family is atypical: the film's brief penultimate scene that awk-wardly intrudes upon the sequences of Barc and Lucy's last minutes together. Nellie, realizing that their parents are not coming by for the token farewell dinner she and Cora have prepared, and that they don't have time to get to the station to see Barc off on his long and presumably final journey to California, exclaims, "They'll think we're terrible!" and George responds, "Aren't we?" followed by Robert's "You're telling us right, brother," delivered with his habitual complacent smirk. But the attempt to set them apart from other American families is canceled out by the context of the film as a whole. Indeed, their typicality has already been established at the outset, when Barc—told that living with the children will "work out"—appears to agree, then adds, "Except that . . . it never has for anyone else."

Despite the opening statement, McCarey is too intelligent to sentimen-talize the parents and put all the blame on the children, whose living condi-tions, determined by the "nuclear" model and the kinds of accommodation it requires, offer no space for an "extended" family. Neither the two-bedroom city apartment that house George, his wife Anita, and their teenage daughter Rhoda, nor the small-town bungalow where Cora and her husband live (and where Barc sleeps on a made-up couch) could possibly contain both parents, or even one as more than a stopgap. And neither Barc nor Lucy is easy to live with, especially in such cramped quarters where everyone is on top of everyone else most of the time. Under the circumstances, "Honor thy father and thy mother," for all its time-honored noble sentiment, has little practical applicability. Beyond the dubious ties of biology, the parents and children have nothing in common, and neither do the children with each other. The family is dispersed, separated either geographically (George in New York, Cora somewhere in the country, the remaining unseen daughter in California, with the feckless Robert's whereabouts unspecified as everyone recognizes his uselessness) or by social status (Nellie and her obnoxious husband Harvey, while they appear not to be living in any noticeable luxury, have the pretensions and single-mindedness of the determined social climber). Whatever McCarey may have thought he was saying, the film says that family unity in the modern world is an illusion and the "ties that bind" a pointless and empty social convention. If Lucy and Barc were permitted to enjoy a contented old age together, it would (and should) have nothing to do with their offspring (children don't ask to be born) and everything to do with a radically different form of social organization. Hence the film cannot (and cannot be expected to) provide any solution to the problems it raises. A solution would presuppose a kind of radical political awareness unavailable in the Hollywood cinema.

Two characters in the film appear to be enjoying precisely such an old age, however: Max Rubens, whose little general store provides him with financial independence and Barc with a refuge from Cora, and his wife Sarah. Mr. Rubens sums up certain of the conditions for their happiness succinctly, when he remarks of their equally dispersed family, "We leave them alone, and they leave us alone."

Under capitalism one must be useful, and one's usefulness is defined by one's ability to make money (if one is a man) or by one's ability to bear and raise children (if one is a woman).

The leading theme of the film's central movement is the social marginalization of the aged, who are no longer useful and consequently have no socially valued function. From the brutalized capitalist perspective, Barc and Lucy are not merely passively use-less, they are an active encumbrance, since they have outgrown their proper functions and have no money of their own hoarded away with which to support themselves. This is an inescapable fact of a culture that has made money into the supreme value, and no amount

*Make way for Tomorrow:* the opening scene—Barclay and Lucy greet George, her "favorite" child (Beulah Bondi, Victor Moore, Thomas Mitchell).

of expressions of goodwill or biblical references is going to change it. So much is made clear in the agonizingly painful scene in which Lucy discovers that George, the one genuinely caring and decent figure among the children, intends to exile her to the "Idlewyld Home for Aged Women" (which she has already been taken to visit, and which she has expressed a horror of in a letter to her husband), thereby cutting her off definitively from her one source of potential (if illusory) comfort, the expectation of eventual reunion with Barc. Tacitly acknowledging that she has seen the envelope from the "home" and understands its implications, she tells him that she *wants* to go there, then confesses that he's always been her favorite child. The confession is both a deserved tribute to her son and her means (perhaps unconscious) of intensifying his sense of guilt, while accepting the impossibility of her present situation. But what else could he reasonably be expected to do, short of abandoning his and Anita's aspirations to social status and their intention of sending Rhoda to college, and moving to a cheaper apartment (in which living conditions with Grandma would be even more intolerable)? Even aside from her uselessness, Lucy has consistently disrupted life in the apartment and been a perpetual source of embarrassment. She is at least speaking the truth when she admits to George that she has "not been happy here," though the Idlewyld Home (sexually segregated, presumably very cheap, and clearly an institution with no higher purpose than that of ridding society of the embarrassment and inconvenience of the useless) is obviously the worse of the two evils.

The marginalization of Barc and Lucy is underlined by their association with two "fringe" figures from diverse ethnic groups, respectively the Jewish Max Rubens and Mamie, George and Anita's black maid. Cora's antagonism to Max, taking the form of downright rudeness, seems so extreme as to suggest a source deeper than mere resentment at the unsolicited gift of chicken soup; the film hints that, aside from Max's usefulness as a storekeeper, he and Sarah live in isolation, that their source of satisfaction is each other's company rather than any sense of *belonging*.

McCarey's use of Mamie is even more interesting, although her role is small. The politically correct will no doubt wish to point out that she conforms, by and large, to the comic stereotype of the black female servant (and, like so many such characters, is played by Louise Beavers)—though it should be pointed out that she is the *producer* of humor (the ironic raised eyebrows as she intrudes upon Anita's bridge class with Lucy's rocking chair) rather than its object. In my view such an objection is no longer very interesting. The stereotype is there, we are all familiar with it, we all know what is the "correct" thing to say about it. What black female servant in the Hollywood cinema does *not* conform to it, more or less? (The only obvious exception I can think of is Francis Williams's Sybil in *The Reckless Moment*, who is certainly not comic and is treated by Ophuls with great sensitivity; but I have heard people object even to her.) What is still of interest is to recognize the moments when the stereotype is undermined and implicitly subjected to criticism, its nature and function exposed: the moment in *Duel in the Sun* when Vashti (Butterfly McQueen) reveals that her "stupidity" is the product of her training by her sweet, gentle, white mistress (Lillian Gish); or the recognition in *I Walked with a Zombie* that Alma's obsequiousness is simply the cover for the contempt and resentment she really feels. There is a parallel, though gentler, moment in *Make Way for Tomorrow*. Lucy, preparing to leave for her few final hours with Barc before her incarceration in the Idlewyld Home, presents Mamie with a quilt she has made for her, and the two outsiders, the black and the aged, share a privileged moment of intimacy. The parallel between them is made quite explicit in the dialogue: Mamie's "I'm going to meet my husband" gets its echo in Lucy's "So am I." But the real point is the sudden revelation (for the audience as much as for

Lucy) that Mamie *has* a husband, and an existence aside from her job; previously, her sole function—her "usefulness"—has appeared to be that she cleans the apartment of a white middle-class couple, decent well-meaning people who have shown no interest in her beyond that function. The "outsider" status of Max and Mamie adds a further dimension to that of Barc and Lucy: the "social problems" of white bourgeois culture—race, class, and age—are all pointedly present in the film.

Two other scenes from the film's middle movement demand mention—the sequence of the bridge lesson, and the exchange between Lucy and her granddaughter Rhoda about "facing facts." The latter is a crux of the film (and of McCarey's work in general), and I shall return to it later. The former—though arguably the finest, most sustained sequence of this part of the film—needs only acknowledgment here, since it encapsulates, painfully and poignantly, points already made: the marginalization of the aged; the impossibility for George and Anita of having Lucy as a permanent resident; the issue of class, underlined here by the opposition small-town simplicity/urban sophistication (pretension?). Lucy's disruption of her daughter-in-law's bridge lesson for the socially climbing affluent—clearly, on the conscious level, unintentional, yet readable as an expression of her resentment of exclusion and need for acknowledgment—is at once funny, sad, and acutely embarrassing for both the characters and the audience: archetypal McCarey.

I have suggested that the Coopers' encounter with the car salesman marks the point where a very good film becomes a great one, and I have speculated that this is the point where McCarey takes complete possession of his material, making it essentially his own. It is the moment where one senses that both the director and the actors are partly liberated from a predetermined text, where the spontaneity and readiness to accommodate fresh ideas that gave us the drum scene in *Ruggles of Red Gap* add a new dimension of aliveness (one sees again why Renoir felt such an affinity for McCarey). It seems appropriate that this turning point is marked by the appearance of McCarey's old friend Del Henderson, who played small roles in so many of McCarey's early films (most memorably, he was the millionaire owner of "Blue Boy" in *Wrong Again*, and the bartender of the Gettysburg address scene in *Ruggles*), as Mr. Weldon, the salesman.

The action of the film's last movement divides neatly into ten episodes linked by a simple trajectory: the (re)construction of the "McCarey couple" and its logical corollary, the systematic rejection of the family, culminating in the "unmarrying motif" (recapitulated twenty-one years later in *Rally 'Round the Flag, Boys!*).

Barc and Lucy accosted by Mr. Weldon (Del Henderson).

1. Mr. Weldon is the first in a series of four characters who treat the old couple with kindness, consideration, and respect (subsequently, at the Hotel Vogard, the hatcheck girl, the manager Mr. Norton, and the bandleader)—in marked contrast to the repeated humiliations to which they have been subjected by their children. The obvious, immediate reaction to this is at once valid and somewhat cynical: these people can afford to be kind because they don't have to live with them. A connected, but more thoughtful, reaction implicitly develops the McCareyan critique of the nuclear family—these strangers treat Barc and Lucy not as "parents" but as human beings, autonomous and independent individuals; their attitudes are therefore uncorrupted by that deadening sense of "duty" (and the resentment that goes with it) that children are supposed to feel in gratitude for having been born. Mr. Weldon is initially motivated by typical consumer-capitalist money interests; the Coopers strike him as the type who have "a heap of money salted away," and he will "pry some of it loose." The innocent Coopers misread his offer to try out his car as a genuine offer to be kind. McCarey leads us to expect another of his moments of acute embarrassment, but he is after something quite different now: we have entered the ter-

ritory of the anarchic, with Barc's 'Why not?" as he agrees to the drive despite his wife's anxious resistance ("Oh, we *couldn't*").

2. During the drive, Mr. Weldon overhears them reminiscing about their lives, culminating in Barc's realization of what Lucy already knows—that this is the first time they've been away together since their honeymoon. This initiates the impulse to reconstruct the relationship as it was before the children were born, and to revisit the Vogard, their honeymoon hotel. When the mutual misreadings become obvious, Mr. Weldon (who is not played by Del Henderson for nothing) is able to respond to Lucy's fear that they've wasted his time by telling them generously that they were "right the first time"—he "just wanted to show off [his] car."

3. The hatcheck girl welcomes them, then responds to their realization that the hotel has changed (and, as Barc says, "So have we") by showing them the painting of the original lobby. She tells them, very sweetly and without condescension, that they won't need a ticket stub because she'll remember them. She also, apparently, alerts the manager to their presence.

4. At the bar, Barc's newfound spirit of anarchy begins to spread to Lucy, who agrees to have a cocktail when he points out that "ladies are drinking here." (She refused a drink in the film's first scene because "that doesn't go with working over a hot stove"). There is a brief insert scene of the children, wondering what has happened to their parents, who are already late for the last family reunion ("The roast will be ruined").

The manager, Mr. Norton, joins them to welcome them briefly, and Barc and Lucy resume a friendly argument begun in Mr. Weldon's car as to which days they did what on their honeymoon. When he leaves, after signing their check, Barc suggests that Lucy is "a little tipsy," and tests her with tongue twisters learned during his nights at the barbershop and clearly never shared with her before. This precipitates the first major step in Barc's rejection of the family: he decides that "we're having fun," and that they will not attend the reunion dinner. Lucy protests, but is overruled.

It is always Barc who takes the initiative here; many today, since the great feminist awakening of the 1960s, would doubtless prefer it to be Lucy. However, in terms of social history and his characters' positions within it, McCarey's decision seems absolutely right. Barc and Lucy *are* old-fashioned (for their cocktails, taking a hint from the barman, Barc orders "two old-fashioned cocktails for two old-fashioned people") and belong to an era when women were conditioned from infancy to be wives and mothers and no more (many of course still are); it would be unthinkable for Lucy to repudiate the children to whom most of her younger life has been devoted. Barc's "male chauvinist" evenings outside the home, while reprehensible (as he himself comes to understand), have at least equipped him with something of an outsider's viewpoint, and it is logical that he should take the lead. It should also be said, however, that (the excellence of Victor Moore's performance notwithstanding) Beulah Bondi's extraordinary characterization (playing, at forty-five, a woman in her late seventies, without a single false moment) is at the very heart of the film. McCarey gravitates to her as he was later to gravitate to Helen Hayes in *My Son John.*

5. Barc, having assured Lucy that he can do it "in a nice way," phones the children to tell them they aren't coming to dinner ("We're enjoying ourselves"). We don't hear the last part of his speech, but Nellie's expression tells us that the promise of the "nice way," if it was ever genuine, has not withstood her uncomprehending insistence on all the trouble she has been to in preparing a roast. He tells Lucy, "She took it very nicely."

6. Mr. Norton joins them briefly again at their dinner table for drinks and a further conversation, agreeing tactfully to Barc's suggestion that he would never guess that Lucy was a grandmother. Norton comments that he must be very proud of his children. Barc's response, after a slight hesitation, is "I bet you don't have any children." Norton, mildly embarrassed, politely withdraws.

7. Alone again, Barc tells Lucy tenderly that she's "kept her looks," and that no other woman in the restaurant can hold a candle to her; the second honeymoon shows signs of becoming a second courtship. They lean toward each other across the table to kiss, and then, in one of the film's most extraordinary moments, Lucy turns aside and looks into the camera, as if meeting the gaze of the audience in the theater, shakes her head slightly, and moves back. It is we—society in general—who prohibit the "embarrassing" public display of intimacy between the elderly.

Barc then reminds her of a poem she loved, the place marked in the book (now gone with the rest of their belongings) with a pressed rosebud—a motif repeated more perfunctorily in *The Bells of St. Mary's.* Lucy then recites the entire poem for him, in an unbroken static take. I can't think of another Hollywood director who would dare to risk embarrassing and alienating his audience in this way. The poem, about a newly married couple's doubts about the uncertainties of the future, is heavy with what we now think of as "Victorian" sentimentality; in 1937 it must already have struck audiences as "corny" in the extreme. Yet there is not the slightest suspicion of condescension in McCarey's presentation; Bondi's delivery is poignant in its very simplicity, its combination of the hesitant with the nostalgic.

There are two stanzas. The first ends with the line, " 'Are you afraid?' said the man to the maid"; the second answers this: " 'With you,' said the maid, 'I'm not afraid' "—delivered by Bondi with a show of confidence that seems her means of concealing the trembling of her voice. At which point Lucy, who has held Barc's gaze throughout the recitation, turns her head aside toward the audience, and we see (though Barc cannot) a fleeting shadow of deep disturbance, despair, perhaps terror, pass over her face.

8. Lucy quickly recovers and says, "Shall we dance, Barc? It's a waltz"—the first time she has taken the initiative.

But the waltz ends the moment they reach the dance floor, and is replaced by something more "modern" and up-tempo. The old couple stand helplessly. The genial bandleader sees their discomfiture, stops the music, and launches into "Let Me Call You Sweetheart." But after just a few bars he speaks over the music: "It's nine o'clock. . . . The evening's fun is about to start,/And you can't go wrong with a song in your heart." Lucy and Barc stop dancing, exchange glances, and hastily depart. It is the last of three moments where our knowledge that they have only a very short time left together is brought to painful consciousness, counterpointing the couple's reawakened pleasure in each other. The other two were Lucy's look of fear at the end of the poem, and Mr. Norton's cheerful, well-intentioned exit line as he left the dinner table: "Next time, don't stay away so long."

9. Barc and Lucy ride to the train station in a taxi. The "song in your heart" with which "you can't go wrong"—even when you are speeding toward your final separation from the only person you wish to spend the rest of your life with—is, again, "Let Me Call You Sweetheart," now sung with perfect appropriateness by Barc to Lucy, and its precise significance at this point in the film becomes clear: "sweetheart," not "wife." At the line, "Let me hear you whisper that you love me too," Lucy leans across and murmurs in Barc's ear, "I love you too." It is another of those *echt*-McCarey moments of embarrassing intimacy; we feel that we are intruders on a moment so private and personal that we have no right to be present.

The underlying, unstressed irony of these last sequences is by now clear: it is *because of* the hopelessness of their situation that the couple are able to rediscover this intimacy from their premarital days, which clearly did not exist in their home life. (There follows the inserted scene with the children—"They'll think we're terrible"—discussed earlier.)

10. Beside the train, on the station platform, Barc and Lucy speak what they know to be their final farewells (whilst carefully denying the finality), and the film reaches in a single simple line the climactic moment of its trajectory. With the train about to depart, Barc, in what amounts to a concise and informal ceremony, "unmarries" them: "It's been very nice knowing you, Miss Breckinridge." And Lucy's response ("Barc, that's the loveliest speech you've ever made") eloquently expresses her acquiescence. The train leaves, Lucy stands watching, waves tentatively, turns, and walks away to her future in the Idlewyld Home. It must surely be numbered among the great-

est closing shots in the entire history of cinema, and it could never have been accomplished without the collaboration of McCarey and Beulah Bondi, whose hesitant movements and shifting expressions within the scope of a single take make this the crowning moment of her career.

Every class to whom I have shown *Make Way for Tomorrow* (and I have screened it almost every year of my teaching career) has expressed astonishment—at the whole film, but especially at the ending, the more so as a conventional "Hollywood happy ending" was readily available, the ending, in fact, that we surely anticipate. It would go something like this: The children, realizing that their parents have abandoned them, have a somewhat severer crisis of conscience, dash to the station at the last minute (suspense sequence, with inserts of clock-faces, speeding taxis, rapid editing, lively music . . . ), drag Barc off the train just as it is pulling out, and reunite him with a radiant Lucy, promising to club together and "somehow" raise the money to buy them a snug little home in the country where they can pass the rest of their days in blissful contentment, with the promise of periodic holiday visits from the chastened offspring.

Such an ending could have been prepared with minimal changes in the characterization of the children; it would fulfill the traditional function of reassuring the audience that everything can come right in the end, that there is nothing wrong with the social system that a little kindness can't cure; its optimism would be by no means incompatible with the general tendency of McCarey's other work or with the general tone of the film, which contains its share of humor, albeit of a somewhat uneasy, overclouded kind (McCarey, like Carl Nielsen composing his devastating Sixth Symphony, has "tried to keep the music as cheerful as possible"). It would not *entirely* destroy the film, though obviously it would compromise it very severely, undermining the logic of its trajectory and above all violating the ending.

It is also possible (just—for it would demand a far greater leap of the imagination) to fantasize a third ending, one quite impossible for Hollywood in general or for McCarey personally, and anyway not available in the America of the late 1930s: Barc and Lucy join a Marxist-feminist commune and become revolutionaries. The suggestion is not entirely frivolous: although it would of course demand a complete reworking of the screenplay, there is much in the film's inner movement that points to it as the only logical *happy* ending. McCarey, the rabid anti-Communist and Catholic apologist, would doubtless have been horrified to be told that his personal favorite among his own works offers itself readily, on certain levels, to a Marxist reading.

The ending we have is clearly the right one, the perfect one, for the film McCarey made. That it provides no solution to the social problems it raises is beside the point; it speaks most eloquently for the necessity of seeking one. Its seemingly inevitable artistic rightness is underlined by a theme that runs through McCarey's work but is particularly pervasive and insistent here: the theme neatly epitomized in the song in *Love Affair* ("Wishing will make it so"), the theme one might define as that of necessary self-delusion.

It receives its definitive (and heartrending) statement in the scene, around the midpoint of *Make Way for Tomorrow*, between Lucy and Rhoda, her granddaughter. Lucy tells Rhoda (her suppressed awareness that wishing never *can* "make it so," beautifully suggested in Bondi's performance) of her conviction that Barc will get a job and be able to support them. The subsequent dialogue must be quoted in full:

LUCY:     Well . . . I won't be picking on you much longer. You'll soon have your room to yourself again.

RHODA:     Have you got some kind of a plan, Grandma?

LUCY:     Well, *I* haven't. But your Grandpa has. His letter says he's negotiating a piece of business with some lawyer, and if it works out satisfactory, then everything's going to be all right.

RHODA:     (*disappointed*): Oh . . .

LUCY:     What's the matter? (*Rhoda kneels down beside Lucy's rocking chair*)

RHODA:     Why kid yourself, Grandma? You know he can't get a job, he's much too old.

LUCY:     Well, I have faith in your Grandpa's ability.

RHODA:     That's just fooling yourself. Why don't you face facts, Grandma?

LUCY:     Oh, Rhoda . . . When you're seventeen, and the world is beautiful, facing facts is just as slick fun as dancing or going to parties. But when you're seventy . . . well, you don't care about dancing, you don't think about parties any more. And about the only fun you have left is pretending that there aren't any facts to face. So would you mind if I just kind of went on pretending?

It is a scene, as played, of exquisite tenderness between two women of different generations, the tenderness confirmed in Rhoda's final inarticulate "Grandma . . . I didn't mean . . . ," and Lucy's "Yes, I know." And in retrospect it adds to the poignance of the last sequences, where Lucy initiates the dance and does, in a sense, have a "party." It is also the scene, before all else in his work, that encapsulates the essential McCarey quandary: Is life in our culture so inherently and irredeemably depressing that "pretending" is the only way to make it endurable, or is the escape into "pretending" precisely the obstacle to doing anything about it? The theme haunts the entire film, from the first sequence (Lucy's "Your father and I were hoping that something would turn up") to the last, where Barc tells Lucy that he is sure to find a job in California, and Lucy responds, "I don't doubt that, Barc. You'll get a job." It is the quandary of the artist who sees that everything is wrong but is prohibited (by both external and internal "censorship") from seeking any way to correct it—a quandary that, within the Hollywood cinema (and American culture at large), is by no means exclusive to one individual. *Make Way for Tomorrow* can be read both as an endorsement of the necessity to "pretend" and as a critique of it (where, after all, has it taken Barc and Lucy?). One might compare Ford, in the celebrated ending of *The Man Who Shot Liberty Valence*—the much-quoted line, "When the legend becomes fact, print the legend," offered as the culmination of a film that has systematically exposed the legend's falseness, yet cannot quite bring itself firmly to repudiate it. The spectator, however, in the cases of both McCarey and Ford, is free to draw her/his own conclusion.

**II**

### "Give It Back to the Indians"

*Rally 'Round the Flag, Boys!* is one of many films that seems stuck with the reputation it acquired on its first release: it is somehow mysteriously "known" to be a failure, so there can be no reason to reassess or even *see* it. Even Leland Poague, in one of the very few extended and sympathetic studies of McCarey (in *The Hollywood Professionals*, vol. 7), ignores it, neglecting to include it in his list of McCarey's "family" films (it seems to me, with *Make Way for Tomorrow*, one of the two "key" ones); but this may be because it consorts somewhat awkwardly (to put it mildly) with Poague's extremely conservative reading of McCarey.

The commonest line of attack is to regard the film as "disappointing" as an adaptation of Max Shulman's then very popular novel (does anyone still read it?). To me this verdict is not merely unacceptable but incomprehensible. The novel's satire is at once too "obvious" and too smugly self-congratulatory, and its attitude is thoroughly mean-minded, falling right into that common would-be-satirist's trap of having constantly to alert the reader to the author's superiority to his characters. McCarey's film manages to be simultaneously more radical and more generous, and all the best things in it (including, remarkably, the sequence of the Thanksgiving Day pageant, toward which the entire film moves) are not to be found in the novel.

I think there was another reason for the film's initial failure. It came out, in 1958, right on the cusp of drastic change: censorship was about to break down, yet the Hays code was still firmly in place, including its rigid stipulation that adultery was not a subject for comedy. Hence a certain awkwardness at certain climactic moments in the treatment of the film's sexual themes. The hilarious sequence of the Paul Newman/Joan Collins mutual seduction had to (but couldn't) end with them having sex, since alcohol has by then removed all restraint. When Newman abruptly and illogically puts on his coat and leaves, the audience (who certainly want them to "go all the way") must have felt a bit cheated; still constrained by the conventions of 1930s and 1940s screwball comedy, the film must have appeared a bit old-fashioned. Today, surely, we can understand and forgive.

*Rally 'Round the Flag Boys!*—the happy husband's night out
(Joan Collins, Paul Newman).

But if the film's logic is occasionally thwarted by censorship on one level, on another it evades it triumphantly. One can suggest a partial analogy (I am aware that it can't be pressed very far) between "entertainment" and dreams. According to Freud, dreams express unconscious desires—desires so socially unacceptable that our conscious minds cannot accept that we do indeed wish them. When we fall asleep the censor that stands guard over our unconscious dozes off too, and these shameful wishes, after donning disguises that may make them difficult for the dreamer to recognize, can slip by him (the censor, representing the "Law of the Father," is emphatically male). The notion of "entertainment" (by definition, that which is not to be taken seriously) functions as a kind of sleep, and the "censor" is lulled: "censor" here to be understood on various levels—the external censor (e.g., the Hays Office code), the precensor (in the form of producers, financiers, and studio heads), the internal censor within the filmmaker. It is important to stress this last: Hawks and McCarey, for example, habitually discussed their films on the level of plot, action, characters (the "entertainment" level) rather than on the level of thematic or ideological content, and there is no reason to suspect them of disingenuousness. It is unlikely that in making *Rally 'Round the Flag, Boys!* McCarey was aware that he was expressing a wish that America (not merely as a nation, but its social structures, values, and ideology) had never existed, and there seems to have been no one around to explain it to him. He saw himself as making a comedy about "people," and followed his "instinct" for what he found (and hoped audiences would find) funny.

Obviously, comedy occupies (at least potentially) a privileged position within this concept of entertainment: it is a truism that one of the functions of jokes is to say what one means in a way that suggests one doesn't really mean it, and which allows the joker to believe this. Here we have the "Catch-22" of entertainment—one can make the most radically disruptive statements provided one makes them in a form that ensures that no one (including perhaps oneself) takes them seriously.

I want here (as I did with *Ruggles of Red Gap*, though in a somewhat different way) to have *Drums Along the Mohawk* present as a point of reference. *Rally* is to *Drums* the ideal complement and contradiction—one of the greatest westerns answered by one of the greatest Hollywood comedies. I am following tradition in classifying *Drums* as a western (on the grounds of thematic content: settlers versus Indians), but it clearly isn't, in the geographical sense: the Mohawk valley is in New York State, which is also the location of *Rally*'s small town cum garden suburb. It is not far-fetched to suggest that the log cabin of *Drums* becomes inevitably (given the developing social structures—capitalism, private ownership, the nuclear family, monogamy, the division of labor, cultural concepts of "masculinity" and 'femininity") the suburban home of *Rally* a century and a half later. Both are emblems of white settling/imperialism, the Putnam's Landing of *Rally* associated explicitly, at the film's opening, with the arrival of the Pilgrim Fathers. Ford's celebration, in 1939, of the founding of America is answered, almost two decades later, by McCarey's wish-fulfillment of its *un*-founding.

In the interests of clarity, I shall discuss the four major components of *Rally 'Round the Flag, Boys!* (the family, sexuality, the Tuesday Weld subplot, the missile base) before considering the climax (the pageant, where all the threads come together) and anticlimax (the "happy ending," obligatory in a comedy, with its perfunctory restoration of an order the film has by then thoroughly discredited).

## The Family

If the film has nothing exactly new to say about the patriarchal nuclear family, it says it with remarkable force, economy, and clarity, and with a refusal of compromise made possible by the adoption of the comic mode. We are given:

*The home.* Putnam's Landing (where, in anticipation of the film's climax, Samuel Putnam was scalped as soon as he landed) has become the "ideal" garden suburb, seventy minutes from New York by commuter train, each house a neat, immaculate, well-appointed family prison.

*The division of labor.* If the home is a prison, the wife is its chief prisoner. Ford's convincing celebration of monogamy/family in *Drums Along the Mohawk* depended on the film's being set in a particular, and very early, phase of American history, specifically a phase when the family was self-supporting and (to a degree, backed by a strong sense of community) self-sufficient: husband and wife could work side by side in the fields in nonalienated labor that was directly productive, its fruits directly enjoyed. In *Rally*, Harry Bannerman (Paul Newman) commutes while his wife Grace (Joanne Woodward) manages the house and the children; the husband arrives home in a state of exhaustion and frustration, wanting nothing but alcohol, to confront a preoccupied wife and two alienated children. The gender-division of *Drums* (the man works to build civilization for the woman who embodies and perpetuates its finer values) has here reached its culmination; the civilization initiated by the building of the cabin and the subjugation of the Indians has developed to a point where it is characterized by overwhelming and continuous repression and frustration, the couple separated for most of

Disharmony in the Happy Marriage (Paul Newman, Joanne Woodward).

their lives as breadwinner and nurturer respectively, and engaged in uncreative and unfulfilling labor.

**Oedipus in the suburbs.** The children (both boys), as a direct result of this total division of labor, are consistently in their mother's charge, the father an intruder who drops in every evening just before bedtime. The film anticipates a perception now common in post-Freudian thinking: that the Oedipus complex is not some "natural" process every child in every culture must pass through, but a product of our specific social/sexual arrangements. The father's return from alienated labor (in one of its extreme forms—"public relations") is "greeted" by a series of unconscious/"accidental" responses: the two boys (a) completely ignore him in favor of television, (b) spill his drink (the last of the whiskey), (c) defy his authority. Indeed, all the marital/familial relationships in the film (aside from that of Comfort Goodpasture and her resignedly tolerant father) are characterized by tension, ambivalence, and mutual hostility: Harry's comment on his firstborn is "I love him as if he was human." Characteristically, McCarey manages through all this to communicate his affection for human beings (as distinct from the social institutions in which they are trapped) and to suggest, beneath the frustrations, the continuing mutual affection of the couple.

*Escape and sublimation.* Harry escapes, Grace sublimates. The film is clear that all that makes Harry's life tolerable is the combination of alcohol (the whiskey he is deprived of, first on the train, then in the home) and sexual fantasy (the exotic "movies" he projects on his eyelids simply by closing his eyes). Grace, on the other hand, sublimates her sexual energies into civic "duty," the efficaciousness of which the film thoroughly undercuts: her obsessive committee work (including the "Committee for the Preservation of Unknown Landmarks," a title that beautifully encapsulates the phantasmal nature of the benefits to society).

It will be noticed that so far I have not made the film sound particularly hilarious. This is intentional. On the level of thematic/ideological concerns, the raw material of *Rally* could easily be inflected toward melodrama (*There's Always Tomorrow*) or the horror film (*The Shining*). Suffice it to say here that the comedy of *Rally*'s exposition is built entirely upon the conformity/resistance tension, and that there are moments when the exchanges between the two stars irresistibly evoke Laurel and Hardy. As for auteurship, the key moment of this opening section eloquently repeats the "unmarrying" motif from *Make Way for Tomorrow*: "We had more home life *before* we were married, Grace Oglethorpe."

## Sexuality

A female friend who wishes not to be named remarked to me once in conversation, "There is nothing so desexualizing as monogamy": a pithy way of putting Freud's perception that the monogamous union on which the nuclear family is based (monogamy, at least for the wife, and in theory for the husband) requires the repression or sublimation of enormous quantities of "excess" sexual energy. In *Drums Along the Mohawk*, the degree of necessary repression is relatively low, and the possibility of successful (i.e., satisfying) sublimation strong: husband and wife live, work, play, and fight the enemy side by side, and are members of a close-knit and highly motivated community that at times (in the childbirth sequence, the Halloween dance, and especially in the person of Mrs. McClennan) takes on the character of an extended family. In *Rally*, all such potentialities have disappeared. It is particularly necessary (for the guarantee of the patriarchal lineage) that the women be desexualized. The unhappy consequence of this is that, if the process is really successful, the wife may no longer feel sexual desires for anyone, including her husband; hence the sexual frustration of Harry, a dutifully monogamous male whose wife prefers committees. The primary motivation of his fantasy movies is clearly the desire to resexualize Grace: she functions in them as an exotic Arabian seductress. The embodiment of unrepressed sexuality in the film is Angela Harper (Joan Collins) (unhappily married—consciously and explicitly so, in contrast to Harry's overinsistent protestations of his "happiness"—childless, and with no interest in committees). Angela's campaign to seduce Harry (who reveals repeatedly, if inadvertently, that he wants to be tempted) provides the main impetus of the film's first half, producing a series of magnificent comic setpieces: the car ride from the station; the scene in Angela's home where she gets him drunk, and a logical progress of derepression that links the film directly to the screwball comedies of the 1930s culminates in his swinging from a chandelier; the showdown in the New York hotel. This last—besides providing Newman with an elaborate Oliver Hardy routine involving his trousers—has as its climax the moment when Grace, turning up to surprise her husband, confronts Angela emerging from the bedroom performing an exotic (ambiguously Arabian/Indian) dance in a bedspread. The ambiguity of the dance's ethnicity allows us to connect it both to Grace's seductions in Harry's fantasies and to Angela's Indian dance in the pageant, the erotic (banished from the home) returning as the exotic. As usual with McCarey, all the performances in *Rally* are superb, every scene animated by continual inventions of mime and body language; but one senses that he was particularly drawn to Joan Collins, who realizes here a comic potential that one would hardly have guessed at and that was never repeated. It is striking that the character, against all generic expectations and requirements, is never put down or punished, and is actually permitted to intrude briefly into the final scene of marital reconciliation. (In Shulman's novel, she is meted out the worst punishment imaginable: she ends up married to Captain Hoxie.) As the embodiment (on the level of family/monogamy) of anarchy, she is in some respects the film's true center, a point well understood in France—the French title was *La Brune Brûlante*, inspired no doubt by Angela's pageant persona, Princess Flaming Teepee.

## Boys and "Boojums": The New Generation

The film's other potentially subversive figure is Comfort Goodpasture (Tuesday Weld). The conflicting connotations of her name (erotic/Puritan) sum up the ambiguity of her role. Insofar as she embodies teenage rebellion (in her spiritedness, her energy, her slangy vocabulary, her readiness to abandon an unwanted but persistent and presumptuous suitor in the middle of a lake), it is a rebellion that can easily be contained. I have not been able to ascertain whether the term "boojum" was in current usage in the 1950s or was invented for the film (perhaps by McCarey himself: the hilarious song, "Seein' As How You're My Boojum," is credited to him). In any case, it is Comfort's readiness to be somebody's "boojum" that defines her; the word, presumably a male construction amalgamating "boobs" and "yum-yum," on the one hand expresses her overt sexuality, on the other her consumability. Tuesday Weld's reactions (really indescribable in words—a marvelous manifestation of the McCareyan use of body language and facial expression) to the song as sung to her by the soldier from the South Opie (Tom Gilson) beautifully capture the combination of energy and subjugation.

It is fitting, then, that in the pageant Comfort is cast as Pocahontas, the betrayer of her race, her saving of Captain John Smith historically emblematic of the triumph of white imperialism.

## From the Nuclear Family to Nuclear Missiles

Although it provides one of the major narrative threads, the explicitly political issue of the film need not detain us long: McCarey's satirical treatment speaks for itself, his anarchic disrespect for the military mentality and the political authority that sustains it (and which it in turn sustains) going back at least to *Duck Soup*. Again one might note the transgeneric nature of basic thematic material: the type of accident that launches the (harmless) missile in *Rally* could, in a "serious" film, launch an atomic warhead. McCarey refuses to endorse any political position dramatized within the film, the confrontation of the military and the women of Putnam's Landing being treated as another comic setpiece in which both sides are absurd. On the one side is the gross stupidity of the military mind as represented by Captain Hoxie (Jack Carson, directed to play the role as a kind of malignant Oliver Hardy); on the other, the women are not protesting against nuclear energy (they don't know at this point that the army is building a missile base) but against the disruptive influence of soldiers on the (repressive) orderliness of the town. They are specifically motivated by concern for the safety of their daughters—who welcome the soldiers as liberators.

## The Pageant

It should be clear by this point that the film offers, through its complex juxtapositions, a fairly comprehensive and thoroughly negative portrayal of modern American capitalist society: the patriarchal nuclear family, alienated labor, the repression of sexuality (the root of anarchy), the repressiveness of the modern small town cum suburbia, the monstrous absurdity

Captain Hoxie in need of assistance (Jack Carson, Paul Newman, Joan Collins).

of military authority and technology-as-power (backed by the "democratic" political machinery). All this is linked from the outset (the opening commentary) to the founding of America, and it is that founding that becomes the subject of the Thanksgiving Day pageant, organized by Grace in the interests of peaceful coexistence. By casting Angela as Princess Flaming Teepee (taking up the time-honored association of subversive women with fire), the film makes explicit the connection between the Indians and sexuality—specifically, sexual threat, the potential disruption of monogamy/family—that haunts *Drums Along the Mohawk* as disturbing subtext. But the outcome of the pageant—planned by Grace, its narrator, to culminate in the smoking of the peace pipe, the establishment of order, hence by implication of modern America—is its collapse into ignominious chaos, a collapse that embodies the film's comedic wish-fulfillment that America had never existed. What was planned as a celebration of harmony becomes a celebration of anarchy, centered on the Indians, hence the culmination and reversal of a whole tradition of history/mythology: the progress of the film is from the unmarrying of the couple to the unmaking of America. Captain John Smith (Opie) is burned at the stake, the Indians massacre the Pilgrim Fathers, Governor John Carver (Captain Hoxie) falls off Plymouth Rock, the Mayflower sinks.

## The "Happy End"

The pageant is the film's true climax; the ensuing comic scene at the missile base (with Captain Hoxie launched into space instead of the experimental monkey), while funny enough in itself, is somewhat anticlimactic. One of its functions is to prepare the way toward the "happy ending" by facilitating the husband/wife reconciliation (anticipated by Grace's dive into the sea to rescue Harry at the pageant's end). The restoration of the norms is ideologically obligatory: it is unthinkable that a classical American comedy should end with the abolition of home/family/marriage, though the film's logic demands precisely that. Yet, given the McCareyan thematic, it is notable that the 'happy ending" is only made possible by the expedient of surreptitiously eliminating the family in order to confirm the couple. In the control room at the missile base, Harry and Grace join forces (inadvertently) to send the obnoxious Hoxie into space, and Harry repeats the act of "unmarrying." First, he reveals that he thought Grace (who can't swim) was attempting suicide when she plunged into the water. In response to his mild rebuke that she wasn't thinking of their motherless children, she replies that she was "thinking of their father." This clears the way for Harry's tender "Grace Oglethorpe, home we go." But in a strikingly perfunctory coda we see the couple, not at home, but enjoying a second honeymoon in the New York hotel where they spent their first (shades of *Make Way for Tomorrow!*)—the second honeymoon that Grace's familial and social commitments had earlier prevented. The "happy ending" is of course an illusion and a cheat; nothing in the couple's fictional situation has changed—home, family, and alienated labor are still there (if conveniently forgotten). The best one can say is that Angela's continuing presence is at least acknowledged: she telephones from her bathtub; Harry hangs up—for the time being?

# CHAPTER 7

# Family "Loyalties"

*Loyalties** is centered on the developing relationship between two seemingly quite incompatible women, who win through to friendship and solidarity simply because they *are* women, their growing insights into their situations (their own and each other's) gradually overcoming all the social barriers of class, race, and upbringing. The women are characterized through a system of oppositions (starting with their names, Lily and Roseanne) so complete as to appear on paper schematic, a danger avoided *(a)* because the acting is so detailed, the characterizations so intelligently thought through, that one never sees them as mere examples in a thesis, *(b)* because each woman is presented independently, in the context of an intricately described complex of personal relations involving male partners, children, and mothers, and *(c)* because the stages in the evolution of the relationship are realized so convincingly (in retrospect) and so unobtrusively (we don't grasp quite where the film is heading until at least halfway through). For purposes of analysis, however, it is useful to strip away the film's living flesh of acting and mise-en-scène in order to expose the schematic skeleton (as it might have appeared on paper, during the elaboration of the scenario)—though I shall try to restore some of the flesh in my annotations.

**Race**. Lily Sutton (Susan Wooldridge, best known for her role in the *Jewel in the Crown* television production) is white (*"very* white—lilywhite," as Roseanne caustically informs her mother in the early stage of the women's acquaintance): blonde, pale, slender, refined, and fragile-looking. Roseanne

---

*Loyalties* (1987), a Canadian film written by Sharon Riis asnd directed by Anne Wheeler, has received only limited distribution but is available on video in North America. In view of its limited accessibility, I have tried to make the narrative clear in the course of this analysis.

(the magnificent Tantoo Cardinal, who has gone on from this Oscar-worthy performance to the "fame" of generally ignominious supporting roles in a few Hollywood movies, including *Dances with Wolves*) is "part Indian" ("Which part?" one of Lily's children wants to know; "My left foot"), dark-skinned, dark-haired, physically robust.

*Class*. Lily is British upper-class, with "pots of money," and brings with her from England all her inherited class presumption. Roseanne is working-class, with no capital to fall back on when she loses her job. When she accepts Roseanne as "daily help," Lily, well-intentioned and "liberal," never lets her forget that she is "mistress" and Roseanne the "servant." As Lily takes her class status for granted, the film's treatment of class is articulated most explicitly through Roseanne's invariably shrewd comments. To her lover Eddy, in bed: "I know one thing for sure—the only difference between her and me is money. But one hell of a difference." Then, in their reconciliation in Roseanne's home after Lily dismisses her in a fit of rage/hysteria, in response to Lily's slightly gushing expression of pleasure: "Going to make a speech about the happy poor next?"

*Mistress/servant*. Lily, trying to "settle in" to an unfamiliar environment that is totally alien to her ("It's so forlorn," she says of her new home somewhere outside Lac LaBiche, a small town in Alberta) with the three youngest of her four children, repeatedly pleads with her husband David to hire someone to help her with the household chores. Circumstances throw Roseanne in their path and (partly from his own devious and only half-conscious motives) he offers her the job. Lily's use of her class status ("Lily of the gilded upbringing," as David refers to her later) as a means of insulation and protection is beautifully established in her insistence on the traditional, ritualistic "interview" ("Do you have references? . . . Have you done this kind of work before?"), the more inappropriate as we have already perceived Roseanne's strength and intelligence, know (as does Lily) that she is the mother of several children, and is aware of Lily's desperate need of assistance. Roseanne, on the other hand, while accepting the "servant" role, maintains her dignity and self-respect by means of a consistently ironic stance that just keeps on the tactful side of insolence.

*Marriage/nonmarriage*. Lily suggests to Roseanne (who, near the beginning of the film, has been physically assaulted by Eddy in the restaurant where she worked) that she see a marriage counselor. Roseanne looks at her incredulously: "We're not *married*!"—though previously Eddy, wanting to patch things up, has responded to Roseanne's succinct "Shit for brains" with

"Two of those kids are mine." Later, as the two women garden together and Roseanne begins to test how far she can go, she turns it back on Lily with good-humored irony (the ironic repetition of other people's phrases is a recurrent motif of her characterization): "Ever thought of seeing a marriage counselor?—You *are* married, aren't you?." To which Lily, after a moment's hesitation between resentment and acceptance, capitulates with a wry smile: "Oh yes. *Very.*"

*Entrapment/autonomy.* The film makes it clear that Lily's sense of being "very" married has little to do with love, nothing at all to do with sexual ful-fillment, and everything to do with social convention; she is trapped not merely in a legally binding relationship but in the whole network of assump-tions and expectations concerning conjugal and maternal dedication that validates it socially. Roseanne's rejection of marriage allows her a (relative) autonomy that includes, especially, the ability to stand up to a man who abuses her, but also a freedom from fixed social roles, a freedom to make her own decisions. Lily, out of "loyalty" as an upper-class British wife and mother, has *had* to come to Lac LaBiche, *has* to be supportive of David, despite everything (I shall return to the "everything" later), *has* to keep the family unit together; her husband (as patriarch and breadwinner, for all his wife's "pots of money") decides not only where she shall live but what friends she shall have and how she will relate to them.

*Mothers.* Lily tells Roseanne that her mother—who is in the film only by reference—was always distant, sent her away to school at the earliest oppor-tunity, and (apart from leaving her "pots of money") more or less broke off relations with her when she married David, regarding him as their social inferior (even though David is a doctor, she couldn't accept a son-in-law whose father "worked with his hands").

Set against this is the portrayal of Roseanne's native Canadian mother Beatrice, unobtrusive, seldom speaking, often critical of her daughter, but keenly observant and always "there" to the point of being taken for granted. There is no question here of sentimentality or condescension: the film is never tempted to "make a speech about the happy poor." It is in fact quite clear that the mother's supportiveness is to some degree a consequence of her doubly oppressed condition (as woman, as native); she is a person who asks for nothing and expects nothing. Yet her emancipated, self-assertive, and demanding daughter (who behaves in ways her mother would never have dreamed of) is strong because of her, and has inherited the mother's supportiveness, critical shrewdness, and generosity: Roseanne is raising not only her own children but an unwanted child of her sister's as if he were equally her own. The film also credits Beatrice with—besides stoical resignation—intelligence, and Roseanne's habitual barbed irony is another inherited trait. When Roseanne apologizes to Lily for her remark about the "happy poor," Beatrice moves quietly across the room (in the background of the image) to the wall calendar. Asked what she is doing, she replies, good-humoredly, "In thirty years I've never once heard you say you were sorry, so I'm marking that day." The mother-daughter relationship throughout the film amounts to a convincing embodiment of women's solidarity across a seemingly extreme generation gap, a solidarity built upon mutual understanding, sympathy, acceptance, and respect.

**Children**. Only one child (Lily's eldest, Robert) plays an independently significant role in the narrative (as at once witness and judge, the film beginning and effectively ending with him). Aside from him, what is most important is the two women's attitude to and treatment of their children. The contrast is established within minutes of Roseanne's beginning work as Lily's "hired help"—in Lily's panicked reaction when she finds Nicky (the second son) carving windows in a cardboard packing-box to make a house ("Didn't I tell you never to play with knives?"): the knife was given to him by Roseanne, as a matter of course, in the interests of creative play, the incident setting working-class tough-minded practicality against upper-class squeamish overprotectiveness. The protectiveness extends far beyond the fear of physical injury; no secrets are kept from Roseanne's children, while the Sutton family lives under the constant shadow of the unspoken and the unspeakable, the principle extending (by tacit agreement) to the husband-wife relationship, wherein problems known to exist can never be discussed. Robert becomes the crux of the opposition, the cause both of the breach between the two women and its resolution.

The film's presentation of Robert is one of its many triumphs. Throughout her work to date, Anne Wheeler has shown a sensitivity toward and concern for children, and particularly for their situation within family structures: *Cowboys Don't Cry*, *Angel Square*, *Bye,Bye Blues*, and *The War Between Us* (already a distinguished oeuvre, and apparently virtually unknown outside Canada) exemplify this to differing degrees. Especially, the concern is with the young male child whose "socialization" is incomplete, her young boys all retaining strong traces of "femininity." The archetypal instance is perhaps her fifteen-minute contribution to the television series *Ray Bradbury Theater*, the episode "The Martian," adapted from one of the stories in Bradbury's *Martian Chronicles* ("The Locusts," aka "The Silver Locusts"), in which the "Martian" of the title, manifested as a young human boy, is *literally* destroyed by the demands of hysterically possessive parents.

Wheeler treats Robert, the already deeply harmed son of *Loyalties*, without the least trace of "cuteness," condescension, or sentimentality, but with consistently sensitive insight into his vulnerability. Roseanne's unsolicited, and at the time unappreciated, advice to Lily to "leave him alone" (at breakfast, the morning after his arrival from his boys' boarding school in England, when Lily is telling him "how much you'll like it here" and trying to bribe him into acquiescence with promises of jeans and cowboy suits)—the advice that precipitates Roseanne's dismissal—has resonances far beyond the immediate situation. Robert (as firstborn, burdened from birth with the mantle of patriarchal tradition) has clearly never been "left alone," the impositions on him including the agony of life in a school where "everybody knows" of his father's disgrace (for an incident still withheld from the audience at this point in the narrative).

Sullen and withdrawn, Robert strikes us as being irreparably damaged when we first meet him. It is Lily's sensitivity to her son's needs (a sensitivity partially compromised by her "loyalty" to those class and gender assumptions that dictate how a male child should be raised and what he should be, a sensitivity emphatically not shared by his father) that eventually forces her to recognize that Roseanne's characteristically terse and tactless comment is absolutely on the mark and leads to her decisions to keep Robert at Lac LaBiche and to visit Roseanne to apologize and reconcile—crucial stages in her evolution.

*Families*. Enough has perhaps been said, or at least implied, to make the necessary point, but to sum up: The film presents us with two models of family, the nuclear family of the Suttons, the extended family of Roseanne, the latter flexible enough to include a grandparent and a nonbiological child, both of them valued and fully incorporated into the group.

There is of course no question as to which the film prefers. Yet the extended family is neither idealized nor presented as a viable alternative in today's civilization: its archaism is subtly underlined, most notably by its enclosure in a cramped modern bungalow clearly not designed for it. The grandmother's brief speech, in the sequence of the lakeside picnic, about the appropriation of their original land by white people, is by no means merely a well-meant sociological irrelevance. It speaks for a potential of family life now lost in all but remote rural areas—not a solution to all problems of course, but vastly superior to what has replaced it.

*Men*. The film's presentation of Eddy and David is built upon a basic premise that can sound, again, on paper simplistic and potentially sentimental: part-Native American / working-class / sexually healthy / redeemable versus white/professional class/sexually perverted/unredeemable. Again, it seems to me that the treatment of character and social context is so convincingly thought out and heartfelt that any apparent reductivism is transcended. Eddy's "healthy sexuality" is associated with a brutish "masculinity" that has to be rectified before a satisfactory relationship with Roseanne becomes feasible. The "masculinity," indeed, is connected not only with violence but with possessiveness, fear of women's autonomy, and a desire to define women solely as wife/mother/homemaker.

In the first scene in which he and Roseanne appear, we are kept in the dark about their relationship: she is a waitress in the drinking area of the hotel in which Lily spends her first evening; Eddy attempts to "feel her up," then assaults her when she indignantly resists, striking her across the mouth and inflicting the injury that will require stitches and leave a slight permanent scar. The incident is rich in those complex relevances (theorized by Roland Barthes in *S/Z*) upon and through which classical narrative is structured:

- Although Lily does not personally witness the assault (she is in the more formal and genteel restaurant area), it stands in for the crudity

First night in Lac LaBiche: David and Lily in the restaurant
with Audrey (extreme left).

and vulgarity of Lac LaBiche culture against which her upper-class refinement initially revolts but which the film reveals as having compensatory advantages (energy, camaraderie, directness, a sense of community, however debased its values) from which she is (again initially) excluded.

- It brings together Roseanne and David (who, as a doctor, volunteers to accompany her to the hospital to treat her wound).

- It develops doubts already implanted about the Suttons' marriage—David's readiness to leap to his professional duty appearing simultaneously as an eagerness to get away from his wife (during her first evening in her new environment, weary with travel fatigue and burdened with three young children); further, Roseanne's injury is not *that* serious, and there must surely be other doctors at the hospital capable of putting in a few stitches.

- In retrospect (when we learn that Eddy and Roseanne have been lovers for some years and that he is the father of two of her children), the incident appears somewhat different: it establishes the macho/patriarchal nature of their (initial) relationship, his assumption of proprietorship, his resentment of the fact that she has her own workplace independent of him, his sexual possessiveness (his "advances" are those of any drunken customer getting fresh, hence an expression of his awareness that this is the kind of thing she encounters—and perhaps responds to—every night).

The incident is answered by the bedroom scene much later in the film, where Eddy and Roseanne (whose mother, with her habitual sympathetic diplomacy, has taken the kids to the movies for the evening) discuss in bed their possible future and the conditions that would enable it. In the interim, the process whereby Roseanne reaches her decision to take Eddy back is beautifully charted: Eddy's revelation that he gave up drinking the day after he beat her up; his attempts at propitiation by loaning her his truck; Lily's (somewhat condescending) approval of him ("rather charming in his own way") when he deposits the truck at the house, after Roseanne has refused his offer; their son Jesse's confused needs and allegiances ("You still look beat up. . . . He *said* he was sorry"); Beatrice's typically tacit but nevertheless potent influence.

We register all of these narrative elements less as determining pressures than as contributing factors, the decision being very much Roseanne's own. The renegotiation of the relationship, as the couple lie in bed, is extremely tentative, with no guarantees. At dinner, Eddy has talked of his acceptance in a heavy-equipment operator's course that provides family housing, adding hopefully, "All you have to do is have a family" (the moment when Beatrice decides to take the kids to the movies!). Roseanne now opens with the suggestion that she might go back to school too (with Eddy wondering what for), and goes on to assert her intention of trying to get back her waitressing job. When Eddy tells her he'll be making enough money, she tells him it's because she *wants* to. He accepts, with obvious reluctance ("I'll give it a try, Rose"), and offers his own countercondition: "But you've got to stop telling me and everybody what an asshole I am." To which she replies, pointedly, "I'll give it a try, *Edward*."

Similarly, the presentation of David Sutton (Kenneth Welsh) is less simple than the white/professional/perverted formula suggests. For a start, he comes from a working-class background and, although he has cultivated an impeccable "British" accent, can still resume his (presumably native) Yorkshire dialect when it suits him. (It suits him, significantly, on occasions when he refers to his wife's class status—the "famous upper-crust resilience" with which he encourages her to adjust to the "forlorn" environment of Lac LaBiche.) He has not (as Roseanne assumes) married Lily for her "pots of money"; they live on his income, not her capital, and she even has to appeal to him on the issue of employing a servant. Nor—if one ponders the relationship retrospectively—has he married her solely because of her social status: he is clearly considerably older than she is, and they have been married at least twelve years (Robert is "nearly twelve"), so we must assume that Lily was very young at the time of the wedding—young enough to appear an attractive wife for a compulsive molester of teenage girls anxious for respectability and upward mobility; he may well have imagined that marriage to Lily would "cure" him. And though it seems at times tempted to do so, the film never quite makes David out to be a monster. (Our response to Roseanne's "I wouldn't touch that creep with a crowbar," when she thinks Lily suspects her of having designs on her husband, is not entirely unsympathetic, but we have been made too aware of the pressures of class and gender expectations on the individual to despise David completely.)

David's inability to function sexually with adult women is further exacerbated by his constant sense of Lily's class superiority—her status, her wealth, her education, her classical music, her proficiency at the piano, her refined "lilywhite" beauty. If the film certainly does not ask us to excuse his erotic obsession with the adolescent daughter of a working-class part-Indian woman (particularly as he allows himself to succumb to it with so little struggle), it at least permits us to understand something of its sources. One of the film's greatest strengths is its refusal to present its tensions and conflicts in *simply* individual terms: we are consistently referred to the social structures and social conventions. The use of the 1931 Tod Browning/Bela Lugosi *Dracula* (which the young girl Leona, babysitting for Lily while she and Roseanne go out for the evening to celebrate Lily's birthday, is watching on television when David arrives home unexpectedly from his fishing trip) provides a telling ironic contrast. The clip shows Dracula controlling a woman by a mere gesture of his hands: the patriarchal myth of irresistible male potency is immediately juxtaposed with the desperate, messy rape in the mud of a struggling adolescent. (All this said, it can still be argued that it is a pity that David's form of sexual deviancy is one unacceptable by *any* moral standards—the issues would have been somewhat more complex had he been presented as gay, for example, and attracted to adult males. But perhaps I am falling into the common trap of rewriting films to make them conform to my own experience, the Sutton marriage reminding me so much of my own.)

The question of identification—always a crucial issue in one's experience of a classical narrative film, and susceptible of infinite inflections and variations—becomes especially interesting in *Loyalties*, given that the potential audience for the film was presumably envisaged as *(a)* North American, *(b)* middle class, *(c)* urban, and *(d)* white. There isn't a single figure in the film who offers such an audience the possibility of an instant, uncomplicated identification. At the outset, the primary identification figure is Lily: not only is she the first major character to be introduced (though it is interesting that the first point of view, in the deliberately obscure precredit sequence that forms the beginning of the film's chain of hermeneutics, is Robert's, at this stage unidentified)—she represents our access to an "alien" culture, like, for example, Jean Arthur in *Only Angels Have Wings* or Eva Marie Saint in *Exodus*, the intermediary through whom we explore and become acclimatized to the culture's values. This identification, though functional and important in guiding our initial reading of the action, is qualified from the outset by two factors: Lily's upper-class British persona (as alien to the presumed audience as the society of Lac LaBiche), and the early introduction of sequences centered on Roseanne, from which Lily is absent. It has also to survive Roseanne's description of her as "a real airhead." The film's structuring strategy is progressively to transfer this *primary* identification from Lily to Roseanne, a figure multiply alien as nonwhite, nonurban, and nonmiddle-class. It would be unjust to say, in a film in which the acting—from lead roles to the most subordinate "support"—is uniformly excellent, that Tantoo Cardinal "steals" the picture; yet her remarkable presence, in the only major role our cinema has so far seen fit to offer her,* certainly gives substance to—"realizes"—the transference implicit in the movement of the scenario.

It is in relation to Lily, nonetheless, that the film's attitude to the culture of Lac LaBiche is defined. The note is struck at the beginning, when she is welcomed at the airport by the spontaneously but aggressively neighborly Audrey (invited, no doubt, by David, to minimize the potential awkwardness of the conjugal reunion), then subsequently in the restaurant, with Audrey's well-meaning, good-natured crassness ("I just *love* the way you people talk") and Lily's glance of gratitude at David when Audrey can't understand why he has booked his wife and children into a hotel for the few days before their house is ready, when they could have stayed with *her*. The film is far from endorsing Lily's well-bred superiority, but its grasp of the barrenness of a society without roots and without a sense of tradition, its inhabitants an easy prey to the values and indulgences of consumer-capitalism, is absolutely sure. Audrey's garden party, with its Quiche Lorraine, the straw-berry daiquiris that she discovered in Hawaii (and that Lily describes as "rather like pudding"), and the steady escalation into general drunkenness, is a marvelous example of the film's control of tone and attitude. The atti-tude is never derisive or unkind—quite the contrary. The concern is with cul-tural deprivation (Audrey, as suburban housewife, apparently spends most of her afternoons drinking herself to sleep), and the quiche and the daiquiris come across, not as instances of bourgeois pretentiousness, but as mis-guided attempts to fill an absence. It is the inherent good will that gets the emphasis. By the end of the evening Lily (who initially wished only to be taken home) is ready to admit that she rather enjoyed herself; indeed, at the moment when David removes her (having discovered that one of the guests with relatives in England might know or find out about his past), she is on the verge of accepting some "really good dope."

However, the level of Lac LaBiche culture into which Lily becomes (through Roseanne) most nearly integrated is not the bourgeois-professional but the proletarian: the garden party is balanced by the sequence in which Roseanne takes her out to celebrate her birthday (the birthday that David has forgotten in favor of a fishing trip), and Lily "lets her hair down" both lit-

---

*Since this was written, Tantoo Cardinal has appeared in *The Education of Little Tree*, a well-intentioned but thoroughly compromised and sentimentalized movie about the history of the American Indians, made primarily for children (who, now totally seduced by the spurious spectacles of the contemporary action movie, will keep away in droves). The vibrant, passionate, and sexual star of *Loyalties* is here rel-egated to the role of "Granma." As Little Tree's education is supervised largely by males, it is a thank-less role.

erally and metaphorically. Perhaps the moment that most decisively marks her liberation from her inherited value system is her delighted reaction when Roseanne, invited to perform with the band, publicly dedicates her first song to "that classy broad over there." The working-class culture is certainly not idealized (like Audrey's "garden party," it is characterized predominantly by heavy drinking, and it is a world in which women are "broads," classy or otherwise, who get slapped around by their husbands and lovers), but it *is* presented in terms of warmth, generosity, and a strong sense of community (even the entertainment is communal, Roseanne's public rendering of "Happy Birthday to You" being greeted by a spontaneous display of lighter flames held up around Lily).

The partial, qualified identification with Lily is never entirely lost: partly sharing, partly critical of, her attitudes, we learn with her throughout the film. But as the narrative progresses, Roseanne becomes its dominant presence, its moral center, the source of strength. Although we learn with Lily, it is important that we are never entirely certain how much *she* has learned— or, more precisely, how completely she has mastered and internalized her lessons. The effectiveness of the final scene depends upon this uncertainty, and its suspense is not achieved by withholding information so much as by

A mother's vengenance: Roseanne after her daughter's rape.

the maintenance of doubt as to whether Lily will still permit herself and her actions to be determined by her social conditioning. That we register the ending as the "right" one has less to do with a sense of inevitability (it has been convincingly enough prepared, but so has its opposite, the "pessimistic" ending that Roseanne herself actually anticipates) than with our sense that, given a reasonable choice, it is always better for an artist to opt for generosity toward his/her characters.

At the film's conclusion a new identification figure emerges—Robert, giving retrospective point to the fact that his was the first point of view we were invited to share. We register an important difference, I think, between Roseanne's hysterical denunciation of Lily ("Call yourself a woman? Bitch!") and Robert's denunciation of his father ("Bastard! Bastard! You did it again"). Both comments are (given the circumstances) fully understandable, and both are in a sense just. But the justice of Roseanne's is too absolute; we want to temper it with mercy, and of course she implicitly withdraws it in the reconciliation of the final moments. Robert's judgment, on the other hand, is definitive: if David is in some ways pathetic and a victim (of gender and class pressures and conditioning), this does not absolve him from personal responsibility for his monstrous actions. Throughout, Robert has shown marked "feminine" characteristics (in terms of our culture's definitions of gender), such as sensitivity and delicacy. We understand, from his clearly irreversible rejection of his father, that he will grow up woman-identified, perhaps gay, and this is touchingly confirmed by his immediate request to see Leona when Lily brings her children to Roseanne's home.

A friend has raised the objection that the film never really confronts the abysmal treatment of the native population in white Canadian culture or adequately expresses the anger that native Canadians feel. No Indian woman, he said, would ever make friends with an Englishwoman, whom she could regard only as an oppressor. I think, put like that, this is not only unduly harsh, but asking the film to take on issues it never in fact proposes—it would have to start from an entirely different premise. Roseanne is, after all, only *part*-Indian, and she has become largely (if uneasily) integrated into white culture.

The objection is, however, worth reformulating more generally, in relation to the film's overall stance: is it ultimately contained within a modified liberalism that can accommodate its race/gender insights? *Liberalism* and *radicalism* can never be entirely discrete conceptually; there will always be areas of overlap, and those areas will always be uneasy, ambiguous, without the satisfying demarcation of clarity that can make our lives and beliefs so simple (at great cost). To put it another way, one can never *successfully* equate radicalism with an uncompromising "return to zero." One could certainly describe the film's reinstatement of a modified concept of marriage and family (through Eddy and Roseanne, with the failure of the Sutton marriage attributed to one man's abnormality rather than to the institution itself) as a "liberal" project. At the same time, one must insist that the implications it generates push the "liberal" boundaries pretty near bursting-point, and that it is difficult to conceive of ways of human relating that would totally exclude *all* possible concepts of "marriage" (not necessarily permanent, heterosexual, or monogamous) and "family" (not necessarily biological or indissoluble, and certainly not "nuclear"). A "liberal" movie that pushes the boundaries this far lends itself very readily to "radical" appropriation.

# PART IV

# ROMANTIC
# LOVE

# CHAPTER 8

# The Two "Gaslights"

My purpose here is to develop the somewhat perfunctory remarks I threw out (related there to the evolution of Ingrid Bergman's screen persona) about George Cukor's *Gaslight* in *Hitchcock's Films Revisited*; the film offers certain profound insights into the nature and consequences of the phenomenon we call "romantic love." But I want first to dispose—hopefully once and for all—of a peculiarly persistent and unjustifiable myth: the myth that the 1939 British version (directed by Thorold Dickinson) of Patrick Hamilton's play is "obviously" superior to the thoroughly rethought Cukor version of five years later.

The myth arose, it seems to me, out of the thoroughly justified sense of outrage generated by the scandalous and counterproductive behavior of MGM at the time the film was made. Anxious, apparently, to avoid invidious comparisons, MGM attempted to buy up and destroy all prints of Dickinson's good little film. More than a half century later it is still very difficult to see it; the print I saw turned up some years ago on American television proudly (if, under the circumstances, somewhat brazenly) heralded as an MGM presentation. (As MGM presumably owns the rights, the studio might make some belated amends by releasing the earlier film on video and laserdisc; comparison with MGM's own product is quite fascinating, highlighting the qualities of both versions, but really the company has nothing to fear from the Dickinson version.) The initial prejudice against Cukor's film is, then, quite understandable, especially in Britain, yet there seems little reason behind its perpetuation: such a stance cannot survive any serious examination of the two.

The British version can be found superior from only one perspective—that derived from an aesthetic once taken for granted as an "absolute" but the dominance of which has been long challenged and (I thought) discredited: a certain notion of "realism" for which a more accurate term is "verisimilitude." Leonard Maltin's *Movie and Video Guide* predictably reaffirms the old consensus in terms of "wonderful atmosphere." Certainly, this indicates the film's strength; a real effort has been made to re-create Victorian England both in the lavishness of external detail and in the psychology and mores of the characters. Beside this, attempts at verisimilitude in the Cukor film (though it reveals everywhere his usual care over significant decor) amount to little more than a handful of what semioticians would call "signifiers of Victorianicity." Dickinson's film was made, after all, primarily for a British audience many of whose members would have grown up within the period the film depicts; Cukor's, aimed primarily at an American audience, is under much less an obligation to make the period convincing beyond a certain point. Both films "open out" the play in the interests of "the cinematic," but the ways in which it is opened out differ significantly. Compare the two sequences (at least after the opening) where the action moves furthest outside the confines of home/prison: the visit to the Tower of London in Cukor versus the visit to the music hall in Dickinson. The former is (as I shall show) central to the very different thematic of Cukor's film; the latter's only justification (beyond, presumably, the determination to be "cinematic" whilst giving the audience brief relief from the tension generated) is that it facilitates a further display of period "color." (I neither know nor care whether Victorian music halls could afford to import whole troupes of cancan dancers from Paris; "verisimilitude" doesn't necessarily imply a strict adherence to fact.)

The concern with period authenticity extends to the British film's essential theme—the study of Victorian social/sexual relations, and in particular the social conditioning of the submissive Victorian wife who must never allow herself to question the behavior and activities of her husband, about which she was supposed not even to have any curiosity. (Again, I am not concerned with whether Victorian wives actually behaved like that; there is sufficient documentation that such were the expectations of the culture.) This suggests, I think, how the film's greatest strength is also its chief limitation: it is strictly a "period piece" in a sense in which Cukor's film is not. The reaction it evokes is something like, "Yes, of course, that is the way people behaved back in those days. Aren't we lucky to know so much better?" I find the reactions of young female students to the two films especially interesting: they accept without question Diana Wynyard's behavior in the Dickinson film, and become absolutely furious with Ingrid Bergman in the Cukor, to the point of wanting to reject the entire film. This suggests to me that the fact that Cukor's film is "period" only in the conventional sense— the stylized Hollywood notion of Victorian England—may not necessarily be the weakness it at first appears, for it greatly diminishes our ability to distance ourselves from the characters and their psychological makeup. If "things are different now," we may nonetheless retain the uneasy feeling that they are not different enough, that the legacy of the past is still with us and not so easy to cast off.

An account of the most important ways in which Cukor's film (or C, below) parts company with Dickinson's (D, below) seems to me to establish definitively the former's greater richness and complexity, and to show why it is so very much more disturbing and so much more relevant to our own age, anticipating many of the insights into male sexual anxieties that have been developed since the advent of 1960s feminism. I shall cite the differences (in no particular order of importance) for the sake of clarity, using (in the interests of brevity)the above-indicated initials to distinguish between the two versions.

Cukor's *Gaslight:* romantic love and the devious beloved
(Charles Boyer, Ingrid Bergman).

*The murder victim*. In D she is a simple old woman, devoid of charisma or sexual attractiveness, seen working at her needlepoint. In C she becomes a prima donna, a great opera star whose most famous role was the Empress Theodora. On the one hand, a helpless old woman; on the other, a woman in her prime of great sexual charisma and associated with immense power. The other differences all follow on from this.

*The portrait*. In D, there is none. In C, the portrait of Alice Alquist in her magnificent jeweled costume as the Empress Theodora hangs over the mantelpiece, dominating the living room. One might digress here at length on the recurrence of portraits of women, especially dead (or supposedly dead) women in Hollywood melodramas: the portrait of Gene Tierney in *Laura* that similarly dominates the living room and is the source of Dana Andrews' obsession; the portrait of the de Winter ancestor that "stands in" for the dead Rebecca in Hitchcock's film insofar as Rebecca copied her dress for a ball. The motif can be interpreted in different ways, but the most obvious is that the image stands for the "strong" woman viewed, in patriarchal culture, as a challenge and a threat to men. In all three of the above examples, the woman is the (actual or desired) victim of the man who wants to murder her because he can't dominate her.

*The murderer's profession*. In D we never learn the profession (if any) of *Louis* Bauer (presumably, in the present, he lives on his wife's money, though it is not clear what he did in the past). In C, *Sergius* Bauer (Charles Boyer), prior to his marriage, is a professional accompanist—in the past, in Prague, but still no more than an accompanist many years later, now no longer accompanying great opera stars but the barely competent pupils of music teachers. Moreover, he was not merely Alice Alquist's accompanist but a spurned suitor: in D, we never learn the contents of Louis Bauer's incriminating letter, but Sergius's is a pleading letter, begging the diva to see him "one last time," eloquent in his sense of humiliation.

*Familial relations*. In D the murderer is the old woman's nephew; in C his wife Paula (Ingrid Bergman) is Alice Alquist's niece. The only point of the former seems to be plausibility—there has to be an explanation for his having access to her home. The point of the latter is crucial: Paula is not only related to the murdered woman (and has been brought up by her as if her own child); she also *looks* like her—so much so that, in adulthood, she can be mistaken (by Brian Cameron in the Tower of London sequence) for her "ghost." We must assume that for Sergius Bauer as for Detective Cameron (Joseph Cotten) she is a reincarnation of the great prima donna, the empowered woman, even if she can't sing very well.

*Stars*. The absence of vocal ability is more than compensated for by the casting of Ingrid Bergman, who (as discussed at length in *Hitchcock's Films Revisited*) throughout her Hollywood career was associated with various forms of strength, vitality, radiance, and empowerment. Compare Diana Wynyard, ideally cast for the very different requirements and thematic of the British version: from the outset frail, pallid, slightly anemic, the perfect embodiment of the submissive and powerless Victorian wife, a woman who seems to invite domination, intimidation, manipulation, and martyrdom. Compare also *Notorious*, ostensibly a spy/suspense thriller, but really about Bergman's vibrancy, energy, charisma, sexual power, and how men feel threatened by it and conspire to punish her for it. This is also the theme of Cukor's film, and has no equivalent in Dickinson's.

One may add here the reminder that D has no equivalent for the courtship segment, and shows us nothing of the couple before they move into the London house, the scene in which the husband accuses his wife (here Bella) of hiding the little picture being in fact the first time we see them alone together. The courtship sequences, in Italy, establish at once Paula's radiance and health, and the theme of romantic love, the perils of which are signaled to us from the outset: our introduction to the adult Paula has her practicing (to the accompaniment of her future husband) the love duet from *Lucia di Lammermoor*, an opera about a woman driven insane by the behavior of men.

*The murderer's motivation*. In D, Louis Bauer has married Bella only because she is rich and easily victimized; she has provided him with the money that makes possible the purchase of his aunt's house, with which his wife has no connection. In C, Sergius Bauer's motivation is far more complicated—and far more interesting. He sees Paula not merely as his means of possessing her aunt's house but as a reincarnation of the woman who used him as an accompanist and spurned him as a suitor. The sadism here, in other words, has a significance beyond a mere necessary plot device—beyond the intention of driving a woman insane in order to get her out of the way, gain final control over her money and possessions, and ensure his own safety. It becomes the vengeance of the humiliated male ego against the empowered woman.

*Romantic love*. As I have already suggested, the essential theme has shifted considerably. Where D was about the plight of the Victorian wife, regarded as her husband's possession and brought up to behave accordingly, with no desires beyond that of subordinating herself obediently to *his*, C is about another kind of entrapment altogether, the trap of romantic love, of which all that we know about Paula suggests that she is a predestined victim. Traumatized by childhood experience (we never know exactly how much she witnessed, but she was awakened by noises in the night and found her aunt's body), living always in the shadow of the distinguished, internationally renowned woman who brought her up (yet quite unequipped to emulate her achievement), she projects onto a man the ideal self-image that she has constructed but can never realize. For the romantic lover does not fall in love with a human being but with an ideal image that is at once narcissistic and compensatory; any disturbing personality traits or defects that appear to threaten the "reality" of this image must be blotted out, their existence rigorously denied, an explanation other than the obvious one found and obstinately believed. Bella, in D, is unable to believe what is from the beginning obvious to the audience, because the dutiful Victorian wife must not believe ill of her husband: we are given remarkably little indication that she is or ever was romantically in love with him, the marriage as depicted giving the impression rather of a social arrangement. Paula, on the other hand, cannot permit herself to believe ill of the man (or, more accurately, the ideal image) to whom she has committed herself emotionally, unreservedly and irrevocably.

This produces one of the film's most breathtaking and poignant moments (one must attribute its effect as much to Bergman as to the intelligence of the scenario—this is surely one of the great performances of the Hollywood, or any other, cinema). I refer to the moment when Cameron leads her to confront the buried knowledge that has always been there: that the noises in the attic above the conjugal bedroom are real and explicable, that they have an identifiable human origin. He says: "You know who it is, don't you?" Her response is: "No . . . no . . . it *couldn't* be him"—the most marvelously precise definition of the relationship between conscious and unconscious knowledge.

*The glove and the detective.* Alice Alquist's glove—Paula's discovery of which is immediately juxtaposed to her unveiling of the portrait, the Empress Theodora in her regal splendor—was worn by her in Gounod's *Romeo and Juliet*; its missing partner was given away to a secret admirer (who turns out to have been a ten-year-old boy). Bauer's obsession with the jewels is therefore connected to Cameron's possession of the glove: the latter another "fetish" perhaps, but in this case one that can be readily surrendered, returned to the giver (or to her reincarnation). The connotations of the two

*Gaslight:* betrayal and revenge.

roles (a young girl in a reciprocal love relationship, an all-powerful ruler) are also very different.

The transformation of the middle-aged, pudgy ex-policeman of D into a young and eligible romantic hero seems at first glance a weakness, a concession to what Hollywood believes to be "popular taste," and it is perfectly possible that such a condition was imposed by the studio. If so, Cukor and his screenwriters have made of him something more than a mere convention (even that "happy ending" scene at the conclusion offers no guarantee beyond that of convention that Paula and Cameron will become a couple), working him into the overall pattern of significance. By voluntarily returning the glove, Cameron demonstrates the readiness and ease with which he can accept the notion of female empowerment. What is significant is not the mere production of "Mr. Nice Guy" but the way in which, by the return of the glove, "Mr. Nice Guy" is defined in relation to Bauer. One should also point out that his relation to Paula is less that of potential lover than of analyst. Where his counterpart in D is a father figure and possessor of "the truth" which he then reveals to an astonished Bella, Cameron's function is to induce Paula to reveal it to herself, getting her to confront things that, deep down, she already knows.

*The jewels.* In a sense, all the above is mere preface to "the jewels." And this is the point at which to remind readers that Cukor's *Gaslight* was produced during the period when Hollywood's "discovery" of Freud was at its height, the point at which Freudian theory becomes a central animating presence of the melodrama and film noir. I have already touched upon the film's awareness of the relation of the "conscious" to the "unconscious" (or the "repressed"). In fact, the appropriation of Freudian theory is here far more subtle and sophisticated than in many explicitly "Freudian" movies of the 1940s (see, for example, the surface sense of Hitchcock's *Spellbound*). Was it "intentional"? I think this is one of those rare instances where we can answer with a decisive "Yes": every change made from the Dickinson original can be traced back to it.

In D the initial murder was committed simply out of greed. The elderly aunt's rubies are "famous" but not spectacular, and we are told that Bauer could have sold them for £20,000. In C it is made explicit that the royal jewels, gift of a king to an admired diva, are *too* famous—their market value is nil because they would be immediately identified. The key to the whole film is Bauer's final recognition that he *never understood* his obsession with them: the revelation clearly invites us to look for a psychoanalytic interpretation. But we scarcely need even Freud here; everyone is familiar with the colloquial expression for the male genitals, "the family jewels." Alice Alquist not only possessed the jewels, she even (as we learn at the denouement) flaunted them in public, stitched into the royal robe of "the Empress Theodora." Bauer associates the jewels with "royalty," i.e., supreme power: hence the Tower of London sequence (which has no equivalent in D and is far more than a "cinematic" opening-out), where, in an astonishingly apposite connection, the Crown Jewels are juxtaposed with the executioner's block on which Lady Jane Grey and Catherine Howard were decapitated.

We have, then, the twin (and continuously intertwined) concerns of Cukor's film: the examination of the perils—for the woman under patriarchy—of "romantic love"; and the study of the sexual pathology (still very much with us) of the male confronted by the empowered woman, the woman who owns or has appropriated "the jewels." Far from being a mere "period piece," the film actually *explains* the contemporary backlash against feminism.

*Sanity/insanity.* D delivers, at its conclusion, a simple irony—Louis Bauer, who has spent the whole film trying to drive his wife insane, goes insane himself. In C the irony is more subtle, and infinitely more poignant. Sergius Bauer's final moment is clearly privileged: it is the only time in the entire film when he isn't "acting," as he knows he can no longer deceive his susceptible wife and has abandoned all hope of obtaining "the jewels." The moment reverses the sense of D; here, for the first time in the film, Bauer becomes *sane.* He leaves the audience with the question he asks Paula, and asks himself: had it not been for his pathological obsession with possessing the jewels, could there have been something real between them? The moment, conceptually brilliant, is greatly intensified by the casting— Charles Boyer, "The Great Lover" and feminized male, Bergman the "masculine" woman, potentially the ideal couple. The question is one that many men are still asking themselves today—and if they're not they should be.

I claim Cukor's *Gaslight* as a feminist film, and an extremely strong one. I am aware that this places me in direct opposition to many feminists who see the film as reproducing and reinforcing the victimization of women for the pleasure of male spectators (the implication being, presumably, that the definition of a feminist film is one that presents role models for women today). A further implication, which is to me quite incomprehensible, is that male spectators identify with the Charles Boyer character: the film seems absolutely to preclude such a possibility. *Gaslight* does not merely reproduce, inertly, the victimization of women, and certainly not with any relish; what it does do is expose and subject to peculiarly astringent analysis the reasons for that victimization through the centuries. And although the film was made in 1944 and is set in a period much earlier, its analysis remains disturbingly relevant today.

# CHAPTER 9

# "Letter from an Unknown Woman": The Double Narrative

## Ophuls and the Critics

Until relatively recently, Max Ophuls' work was generally perceived as minor and marginal, treated with a condescension that verged at times on veiled contempt. (A closely parallel case is that of Josef von Sternberg.) The films were regarded as somewhat frivolous, lacking any serious concern with "social problems." The oppression of women under patriarchy—the central subject of all Ophuls' best work—was not perceived as a social problem; indeed, it was barely perceived at all. Not only were the films almost exclusively concerned with women's problems (such as love and marriage), which were by definition of minor importance; they were also marked by such "feminine" traits as, on the level of style, gracefulness and decorativeness, and, on the thematic level or the level of affect, tenderness and sensitivity. Ophuls' habitual gravitation toward an identification with the women's position—the trait that most obviously distinguishes his work from that of his fellow-émigré Douglas Sirk (with which it otherwise has so much in common, including their common association with Brecht)—was cause not for celebration but for uneasiness, even distaste. The general consensus (implicit or explicit) of a predominantly male critical establishment was that the films were neither serious nor "manly"—men having, prior to the 1960s, a monopoly on seriousness.

All this has changed (the change, like most matters cinematic, being initiated in France and especially in the pages of *Cahiers du Cinéma*). Yet I don't think the magnitude of Ophuls' achievement has even now been fully recognized, and there remains a widespread critical imbalance (with a very few exceptions, among which the work of V. F. Perkins is the most significant) in the valuation of the various "periods": specifically, an underestimation of the Hollywood movies in favor of the European periods between which they are sandwiched, and especially the four late French films. His last film, *Lola Montès* (1955), is still commonly regarded as his "masterpiece." It *should* have been: conceptually it is extraordinary. But for me it is disastrously flawed by the casting of Martine Carol, in a role that might have been written for the Dietrich of the von Sternberg films.

The imbalance is easily understandable: one might say that everything conspires to produce it, from casual but deep-rooted anti-Hollywood prejudice to the more recent fashionable academic wisdom. The former has been gradually eroded, yet it still continues to operate, often at unconscious levels. Three of Ophuls' American films (*The Exile*, *Caught*, and *The Reckless Moment*) fit without evident strain or discomfort within the Hollywood conventions (genre, narrative patterns, shooting/editing style); the late French films do not.

The late films also reveal an obvious "superiority" to those who hold a more romantic view of authorship and creativity than my own: they were made in conditions of "complete artistic freedom" (at least as that term is popularly understood). *Lola Montès* was of course savaged by its producers after shooting was completed—cut and reedited, the elaborate flashback structure rearranged chronologically. But the restored version, though allegedly not quite complete, contains nothing that was not shot by Ophuls, the flashback structure is reinstated, and the long takes appear to be unharmed. These films can therefore be read (as the Hollywood films cannot) as "pure self-expression," with the Ophuls signature legible in every shot. More interesting is their appeal to Formalist critics. Three of the four Hollywood films function comfortably with the "Hollywood codes" of shooting and editing: the camera moves more, and takes tend to be longer than, the average, but they do no more than push certain of the "codes" to permissible bounds. Ophuls celebrated his return to Europe by opening *La Ronde* with a six-minute take, unprecedented in Hollywood at that time outside Hitchcock's *Rope* and *Under Capricorn*, and still, more than forty years later, without equal in its foregrounding of the medium and the fabrication of illusion (I have not forgotten Robert Altman's *The Player*). The last four films are all characterized by an employment of the long-take-with-camera-movement that far transcends the Hollywood norms. There can be no doubt that Ophuls felt constrained and frustrated by the exigencies of working within the "Hollywood codes," and it is logical that Formalist critics, searching for alternatives to such constraints, would attach great importance to the French films and little or none to the American.

It is not my purpose to belittle the extraordinary achievements of Ophuls' final period, the precise nature of which depends upon the creative freedom he enjoyed. However, for me *Letter from an Unknown Woman* remains his finest work, and I cannot prefer any of the late French films (not even *The Earrings of Madame de . . .*) to *The Reckless Moment*. For me, the value of a film resides not in formal innovation or stylistic freedom *in themselves*, but in the density and complexity of meaning generated within it, to which style and form contribute. And "meaning" is, on the whole, less likely to be generated by the individual *auteur* in isolation than by the intricate interaction of many factors within which directorial creativity plays the decisive, vitalizing role. These factors include ideological assumption, generic convention, specific subject, and the contributions of numerous collaborators of whom screenwriter, star, cinematographer, and producer are likely to be the most important. Nor are these factors ever in practice clearly separable: all are interdependent, and ideology (with all its possible complexity, tension, and internal contradiction) pervades the ensemble. To say that *The Reckless Moment* is as much a Hollywood film as an Ophuls film is in no way to belittle or diminish it. That its extraordinary quality—its concentrated significance—derives to a great (but not precisely definable) extent from Ophuls' participation cannot be doubted. Anyone who *does* doubt might look again at, for example, the sequence that introduces Donnelly (James Mason)—his intrusion into the bourgeois home. All the Ophuls fingerprints are there, though contained within the Hollywood codes, and the scene is an unsurpassable example of cinematic *thinking*.

## "Letter from an Unknown Woman": Background

*Letter from an Unknown Woman* (1948) is a somewhat different case. Both thematically and stylistically it is the closest of Ophuls' Hollywood films to the European work before and after, its narrative bearing striking parallels to those of *Liebelei* (1933) and *Madame de . . .* (1953). Ophuls makes the subjects of *Caught* and *The Reckless Moment* his own through his creative intervention; the subject of *Letter* was his already.

There are, however, significant differences between *Letter* and the late French films, and they derive plainly from Hollywood practice. Despite the fact that the film is a "typical" Ophuls project, and set in a studio "Vienna, about 1900" (just such as we shall watch Anton Walbrook construct a few years later in the opening shot of *La Ronde*), the available evidence shows that he didn't initiate it, and the question of authorship is more problematic than it is in the French films. I have been unable to trace this to its source, but it seems widely accepted that the screenwriter Howard Koch laid claim to the film, on the familiar grounds that it was "all in the script." Well . . . it's a marvelous screenplay, and one certainly doesn't wish to denigrate Koch's contribution. On internal evidence—the evidence of the mise-en-scène—the *film* belongs to Ophuls: I doubt whether anyone familiar with his work before and after will wish to challenge that.

More interesting—from the viewpoint of Ophuls' relation to Hollywood—is the presence of Joan Fontaine as star and her (then) husband William Dozier as the originator of the project. It is clear that without them *Letter* would never have been set up: it was conceived from the start as a "star vehicle" for Fontaine, and various directors were considered including (incredibly, but according to Donald Spoto) Hitchcock. The subsequent French films are peopled with stars: indeed, the first two (*La Ronde* and *Le Plaisir*), productions of quite reckless extravagance, are populated by almost all the major French stars available. Yet neither would, I think, be regarded as a star vehicle in the Hollywood sense—a project deliberately designed from the beginning to showcase a star. A direct consequence of this was studio interference that clearly amounted to restrictions on Ophuls' freedom. I have been privileged to see unpublished transcripts that document the changes (in which Ophuls appears to have acquiesced, with varying degrees

*Letter from an Unknown Woman:* Lisa's mother tells her of the move to Linz (Mady Christian, Joan Fontaine).

of resistance). They all center on Fontaine-as-star, and most are motivated by the necessity for close-ups. Some of these were imposed on Ophuls during shooting, others cut in after shooting (whether "directed" by Ophuls or not isn't clear). I shall limit myself to the most obvious example, one that I had long suspected before the documentation confirmed it. The entire scene of the departure for Linz at the train station (when Lisa runs back to offer herself to Stefan/Louis Jourdan) was clearly designed by Ophuls as a single sequence-shot: after the inserted close-up of Fontaine as she hesitates, making her decision, the camera resumes its movement from the exact point it had reached before the cut. (Obviously, the close-ups demanded at script stage or during shooting are far better integrated.)

The one instance to which Ophuls seems to have objected quite strenuously has nothing whatever to do with the interruption of long takes: the moment at the end when Stefan, on his way to the duel, turns at the gate to see a ghostly Lisa in the doorway. Presumably, what he intended was for Stefan to turn, see the empty doorway where Lisa had stood, and smile; we know what he is remembering without having to be shown it. Here I am on Ophuls' side, though I don't think the superimposition of Fontaine (superfluous rather than, as Ophuls thought, "sentimental") does serious damage.

I used (under the influence of Bazinian theory) to make something of a fetish of long takes, especially with camera movement: the longer the take and the more elaborate the movement, the better. Recently, the opening shots of *The Player* and *Bonfire of the Vanities* have demonstrated eloquently that long-take-with-camera-movement has nothing necessarily to do with the production of meaning, and may have a lot to do with the self-serving egoism of the director ("Anything Welles could do, I can do longer"). The interference with Ophuls' long takes (which, had I been told of it twenty years ago, I would have regarded as a desecration) does not now particularly offend me. I think it may even work to the film's benefit, and the fact that the director's protests appear to have been somewhat less than impassioned may suggest that he half-realized this too. Compare the film with *Madame de . . .*, a film with clear narrative parallels (both culminate in a duel with pistols in which the husband kills his wife's lover as a matter of honor) but with a very different heroine: Louise (Danielle Darrieux) is from an entirely different class background and lacks Lisa's essential innocence and purity, her romantic idealism. The close-ups of *Letter* bring us into much closer, more intimate contact with Lisa than we are ever permitted with Louise. Perhaps more important, *Madame de . . .* lacks the particular narrative strategy that distinguishes *Letter*, not only from any of the late French films, not only from any other Hollywood movie, but from any other narrative film I have ever seen. Ophuls must have been well aware that here it is not merely the distance of the camera that defines the necessary detachment from our central identification figure, Lisa.

## Film and Novella

A few words need to be said of the film's relationship to the Stefan Zweig novella from which it was adapted. I recall that when the film came out there was a general agreement that Ophuls had "softened" the original (doubtless another of his "feminine" traits, and the charge was repeated with *La Ronde*). In fact, the novella strikes me as both cynical *and* sentimental (two supposedly opposite attitudes that frequently go in harness, the one often as cover for the other), and Ophuls' film is neither. It was of course the cynicism that confirmed the novella's superiority, cynicism being such a mature and sophisticated attitude to life.

The words can be few indeed, as the film's transformation of the novella depends essentially on Ophuls' systematic exploration of a potential of his medium which has no possible equivalent in literature. But it seems appropriate to catalogue the major deviations in the narrative content (the minor ones are innumerable).

1. The entire framework of the film (the duel with Lisa's husband, etc.) is completely absent from the original.

2. The Stefan of the novella is a writer, not a musician (an obvious enough change, given the different aptitudes of the two media, but one that leads to numerous felicitous details of invention).

3. Stefan, even at the end, never manages to remember Lisa, and her letter has no discernible effect on his life.

4. The novella is quite explicit about Lisa's resort to prostitution; the film reduces this discreetly to Lisa's remark in the letter that there are times she prefers to pass over. The change (the only one presumably dictated by the Hays code) is of little importance, the theme of prostitution being treated far more fully and subversively in the film.

5. Lisa does not marry, for security or any other reason; she is offered the opportunity but rejects it. Her wealthy suitor remains a shadowy, undeveloped figure, and cannot be compared to the film's von Stauffer.

It seems clear to me that Ophuls and his collaborators have transformed a slight, anecdotal tale of minor distinction into a film of a density and richness that continue to surrender fresh secrets on every viewing.

## Movement/Stasis

I have no great faith in statistics, especially when they are applied to complex and delicate works of art. Whether the number of shots in a given Hollywood film conforms to the average, exceeds it, or falls below it tells us nothing about its value. It does, however, tell us something about its particular nature, and thereby offers a useful starting point. *Letter from an Unknown Woman* is a film consisting of (not counting the credits) 366 shots, in 169 of which the camera moves. The number of shots is well below the Hollywood average, the number containing camera movement well above it, the proportion unusually high. As movement (and its close relative time, which we all know never stands still: Stefan's line, "For us, all the clocks in the world have stopped," is one of the most ironic in all cinema) is for Ophuls far more than a stylistic flourish but has a thematic/metaphysical dimension, it seems legitimate to add to this total the twenty-five shots (not strictly camera movements) inside a moving vehicle. There is also the significantly ambiguous scene (it unites the movement/stasis opposition and is placed at almost the exact midpoint of the film) in the "fake" railway train in the Prater, where the moving scenery gives the illusion of the movement of a train.

## The First Ten Shots

Of the film's first ten shots (up to the beginning of the visualization of Lisa's letter), seven contain camera movement and an eighth (shot 2) is set within a moving carriage. This throws into strong relief the moment when the constant motion is arrested (shots 7 and 8): shot 7 dramatizes very precisely the notion of "arrest," as Stefan, reading the letter's opening sentence ("By the time you receive this letter I may be dead"), freezes abruptly in mid-movement, in the act of raising his hands to his face from the water basin. The moment establishes a central structuring principle: the movement/stasis opposition will be developed throughout the film—Stefan's constant restless, dissatisfied movement (from country to country, city to city, woman to woman) countered by Lisa's stasis (her waiting, her unshakable commitment and constancy), the opposition finally resolved in the ultimate arrest of death. The letter itself signifies death, and Stefan will die (or so we assume), shortly after the film ends, as a direct result of reading it.

The opposition is enacted at many points in the film. Some of these follow simply from the characters' relative social positions/economic status: in "Vienna, about 1900" the man goes to pay (for a single white rose, or for another foreign country to be viewed from the Prater railway train) while the woman sits and waits. Most significantly, however, all three of Stefan's and Lisa's decisive encounters are dramatized in this way—Lisa holding the door when Stefan (on his way out) sees her for the first time; Lisa motionless in the street near his apartment when he passes, becomes aware of her, turns, comes back, initiating their one night of love; Lisa waiting by the piano in his apartment while Stefan moves about, checking his appearance, sending his servant out for food ("the usual things"), fetching champagne.

The relationship, however, is not presented simply in terms of opposites: they also complement each other. Our first view of Stefan, at the end of the film's first shot, has him framed in the open window of a carriage, leaning in to talk to his friends; our first view of Lisa (shot 11) will be of her framed in the open window of a removal van, peering in at Stefan's possessions. The parallel introductions establish a complex pattern of identity and difference to which I shall return later.

The movement/stasis opposition, finally, must not be seen in merely personal terms ("characterization"). One function of this opening sequence is to establish the context within which Lisa's letter is received and read: the "man's world," defined in terms of duels, debauchery, worldliness, and cynicism. The letter, with its religious insignia and intimations of mortality, not only interrupts the flow of camera movement, it intrudes into this world and its values, asserting their opposites (purity, innocence, spirituality) and identifying them with the "feminine." Stefan and Lisa are consistently presented as exceptional rather than ordinary, but their ways of expressing their exceptionality are presented as determined, ultimately, by the cultural construction of gender in terms of polarized opposites.

## What Happens in Shot 11?

In shot 10 Stefan begins to read the letter, and Lisa's verbal narration begins on the soundtrack, carrying over the dissolve into shot 11. Joan Fontaine's voice (immediately identifiable), refined, romantic, sincere, somewhat dreamy, asserts at once a narrative authority: the voice of the "star" is also the voice of "truth," our invitation to an unquestioning identification.

The possible relationships between verbal and visual narration have been very little explored in Hollywood cinema and only very occasionally outside it; usually, we are lulled into taking for granted an identity between what is said and what is shown. But the potentialities are extremely complicated and far-reaching; they arise from the basic and inalterable fact that the visual narration must always, and necessarily, convey far more information than the verbal. Consider an elementary example: the sentence, "There was a pencil on the table." If we read this sentence we assume we understand it perfectly, and each of us doubtless forms his/her immediate mental picture; yet it is certain that, to varying degrees, each of us will see a different table and a different pencil. So what of the filmmaker who must render it as a visual image? There is no way it can be realized without telling us a hundred other things: Is the table round, square, rectangular? What size? A coffee table, a dining table, a tripod table . . . ? Is it bare or covered with a cloth? If bare, what kind of wood (or metal, or plastic)? If covered, is the cloth plain or patterned? What color is the pencil? Is it sharpened? If so, with a sharpener or a penknife? Is there an eraser at its end? Is it cylindrical, triangular, polygonal? The filmmaker (or his set designer) would be forced to answer all these questions, and would in most cases answer them quite unconsciously, the one consideration being plausibility (the kind of table the house's inhabitants might be expected to choose, or be able to afford) and not in any way disruptive, drawing unwanted attention.

Another example: "I entered the room. She was seated on the sofa, reading a book." The filmmakers could show us just that, making the scene "realistic" with plausible and nondistracting decor. But what if, as the narrator's voice uttered the words, we were shown her sitting in an armchair, knitting, or peeling an orange? We would have to assume that the narrator was either insane, a liar, or had misremembered; whatever we deduced, the authority of the verbal narration would be very seriously undermined, we could no longer identify it with "the truth," and we would be ready to distrust the narrator also on less trivial matters. (Except in very rare instances—*Last Year at Marienbad* [*L'Année Dernière à Marienbad*] or *Puzzle of a Downfall Child*—we always trust the image over the word, which is why the "lying flashbacks" of Hitchcock in *Stage Fright* and Rudolph in *Mortal Thoughts* arouse so much resentment.) Ophuls—far more subtly—never contradicts Lisa. Her narration is allowed its own integrity, which he respects, even venerates; it is, as far as it goes, "the truth." But it is *her* truth, not his.

At the beginning of shot 11 Lisa is telling us that "I think everyone has two birthdays: the date of his [*sic*!] physical birth and the beginning of his conscious life." As she says this, in her dreamily romantic voice, the delivery men unloading the van into which she is peering knock a piece of furniture against Stefan's harp, producing an ugly discordant "twang." We must assume, obviously, that she did not notify Stefan of this in her letter, written as she was dying. But what we have here is something significantly more than the addition of "neutral" detail, it is a contradiction in *tone*: from the outset, Lisa's narration and Ophuls' narration are set in partial conflict, and that our first intimation of this is stirred by the notion of "discord" can hardly be accidental.

There can be no doubt of Ophuls' sympathetic commitment to Lisa and her romanticism, nor of the film's communication of that commitment to the spectator: Lisa, from the beginning of her narration, is and remains the film's dominant presence and our leading identification figure. Yet that identification is constantly qualified—or counterpointed—by an ironic detachment. We believe, accept, sympathize with, everything Lisa tells us, everything she experiences. But we are continuously aware of so much that she *doesn't* tell us, and often (we assume) is unaware of: everything, specifically, that might threaten the dominance of her romantic vision, opening it to question. I don't think the fineness of balance Ophuls achieves and sustains—it has the uniqueness of the greatest art, beyond theory, beyond successful imitation—has been fully appreciated (except by V. F. Perkins, to whom anyone who attempts to analyze this film must be deeply indebted): the balancing of two apparently incompatible modes, romanticism and irony, without ever permitting one to overwhelm or disqualify the other, without ever lapsing into sentimentality or cynicism.

## The Consequences

The strategy established in shot 11 is immediately developed in shots 12 and 13. Lisa's instant infatuation, not with Stefan whom she has not yet seen, but with his "beautiful things," is rudely interrupted by her mother, who summons her indoors from an upstairs window. As she moves through the hall, the janitor is complaining "Who is going to clean *that* up? Me I suppose"; as she mounts the stairs (accompanied, without a cut, by one of Ophuls' elegant crane movements, involving us in her ascent), the delivery men, precariously hauling Stefan's grand piano up on pulleys, are complaining about having to move a musician ("Why must he play the piano? Why not the piccolo?"). Lisa passes without comment or apparent awareness, lost in her dream, in the romantic aspirations the "beautiful things" arouse in her. As the letter has just announced this as the beginning of her "conscious life," we may be alerted to the things of which she is *not* conscious—here, most obviously, the extremely unromantic existence and labors of the working class.

The film develops this theme most elaborately in the Prater sequences. Lisa remains in the "train" while Stefan goes to pay for the next country they will visit, closing the door of the compartment. We see, as she does not, the mechanisms and toil by means of which the romantic fantasies of the bourgeoisie are constructed: the old woman, heavily muffled against the cold, who takes the fare; the old man, similarly muffled, who must laboriously pedal the machinery that produces "Venice" or "Switzerland" to order. And in the following sequence, on the dance floor of the café, we are privileged to overhear the comments exchanged by the sausage-chewing, beer-swilling members of the all-women's orchestra, kept long after hours as the lovers prolong their tryst: comments that neither Lisa nor Stefan hears.

Leaping to the end of the film, we may link this with the most telling point made *against* Lisa with any degree of explicitness: her jarring failure to acknowledge in any way whatever the mute manservant John (Art Smith), on her final visit to Stefan's apartment, a failure underlined when we discover than John remembers Lisa perfectly when Stefan, who has fathered her child, does not. John's awareness of, and kindness to, Lisa has been stressed earlier in the film; to Lisa, wholly absorbed in the possibly imminent fulfillment of her lifelong fantasy, he is simply a nonperson.

Two films later, *The Reckless Moment* provides a striking parallel. There, Ophuls transforms the stereotypical figure of the black maid into arguably the most intelligent, certainly the most *aware*, character in the film; but, because Sybil (Francis Williams) is black and a servant, Lucia Harper (Joan Bennett) is quite incapable of recognizing the solidarity and support she offers until it is too late. The superior awareness with which the films credit both Sybil and John is attributable precisely to the fact that they are outsiders: "mere" servants, and respectively black and handicapped, they remain spectators, distanced from the tragedies of the bourgeois protagonists they serve, at once the most qualified to intervene and the least likely to be invited to do so.

The film's treatment of class—never a conscious issue for Lisa, very much one for the viewer—is complex and comprehensive. Ophuls' semimythical Vienna is real enough to make possible a systematic analysis of the class structure, from the exploited workers up to the aristocracy represented especially by von Stauffer: a reminder that, in his early theatrical days, Ophuls was associated with Brecht, and that he made what is arguably the most rigorously and authentically Brechtian of all films (*Komedie om Geld*, 1936) is not out of place here. Lisa's aspirations are clearly in part a product of her uneasy class position. The apartments of Stefan and of Lisa's mother are in the same building, Stefan's luxuriously furnished and equipped with a live-in manservant, that of Frau Berndle (Mady Christians) shabbily furnished and servantless. Her late husband, superintendent of the municipal waterworks, has left her with nothing but his pension, and she is clearly living beyond her means; hence her marriage to Herr Kastner, the military tailor from Linz. Stefan, as artist-celebrity, has freedom of movement, including easy access to the aristocracy. Lisa falls in love before she has even seen him (moreover, she assumes him to be "quite old")—first with his possessions, then with his music. The film never allows us to think of her, of course, as a "social climber": what she is attracted to is not mere vulgar wealth or social position, but the fineness of the cultural artifacts wealth can buy and, more especially, the emotional, spiritual, and imaginative freedom of art and freedom of movement of the (male) artist, to whom the whole world is open. She marries von Stauffer for the security of her illegitimate child, not for any personal material motive.

Consideration of the film's presentation of class structure leads inevitably to its presentation of the position of women within it. I intend "presentation" to carry its Brechtian overtones: by heightening awareness without actually disrupting the "realist" mode, the double narration "presents" as much as it "represents." It is scarcely news that patriarchy has divided women into two basic categories, the wife/mother and the whore; where so many films reproduce this inertly, without apparent criticism, *Letter* through its stylization, its "presentational" manner, its *obtrusive* structuring of "twinned" scenes and shots—produces a critical awareness of it. It also subtly undermines the wife/whore opposition by collapsing the two categories. Prostitution, explicit in the Stefan Zweig novella that was the film's source, is repressed from the film's surface (though, as noted, Lisa does say in her letter that there were times—after the birth of the child, before her marriage—that she prefers not to think about), but returns to haunt it everywhere; the question of whether or not Lisa actually resorted to it becomes irrelevant. The notion of women as merchandise for purchase by the male pervades the film, from its early depiction of Stefan's nightly "conquests" to the ultimate horror of the old soldier's attempt to pick up Lisa as she flees from Stefan's apartment. The theme receives its fullest elaboration in the presentation of the dress shop of "Madame" Spitzer (Sonia Bryden), where the women come to purchase clothes and their husbands come to purchase the models.

It is crucial to the film's meaning that it presents marriage and the role of wife not in opposition to this but simply as an alternative form of the same thing. The three marriages (two actual, one projected) in the film are all based upon the woman-as-merchandise motif. There is the direct paralleling of Frau Berndle's marriage to Herr Kastner and Lisa's to von Stauffer: in both cases the woman sells herself for her own and her child's financial security, and both are essentially loveless, at least on the woman's side (given the portrayal of Herr Kastner, we are not encouraged to take seriously Frau Berndle's nervous and defensive assertion to Lisa that she can still "be in love with a man"). If the men—or at least von Stauffer—"love," it is the kind of love sanctioned and nurtured by patriarchy that is contaminated at its very roots by the principle of possession: the image that introduces (and defines) Lisa's marriage is of von Stauffer fastening a tight-fitting diamond necklace around her throat, a signifier at once of payment and ownership. The projected marriage—of Lisa in Linz to the young lieutenant (John Good) who confidently anticipates an "outstanding military career"—is presented similarly; she is dressed up as a "lady," instructed by mother and stepfather how to comport herself, offered up as an attractive object for purchase, an acquisition. The narrative moves directly, with flawless logic, from that to Lisa's employment in Madame Spitzer's establishment.

Ophuls' figure for the embodiment of patriarchal oppression (consistent not only throughout *Letter* but linking it to earlier and later films, notably *Liebelei* and *Madame de . . .*) is the military man—the higher the rank the greater the oppression. The figure, in its various forms and ranks, pervades the film: the elderly general who approaches Madame Spitzer to negotiate for Lisa (and is told, "She is not like that . . ."), and the young soldiers who tap on the window at night to attract her attention; the young lieutenant in Linz and his high-ranking father whose role he is destined to reproduce; von Stauffer himself (his exact position and function are not clear to me, but on formal occasions he wears a military uniform, and has crossed sabers on the wall behind his desk; the old soldier who accosts Lisa in the street. Even Herr Kastner is a "military tailor." Given this context, one of the film's most chilling moments—a tiny detail, almost thrown away—is the appearance during the famous long take (often held to be the "key" to the film) in the opera house lobby of a small boy dressed in military uniform, led by the hand by his military father. The moment permits one to construct a (chrono)logical chain of transmitted patriarchal deathliness: the child in the opera house—the young lieutenant in Linz—Johann von Stauffer.

As the privileged signifier of patriarchy the figure has complex connotations: that patriarchal prestige depends, not on personal distinction, but on externals like uniform and rank; that patriarchal authority, though powerful, is more shell than substance; that the notion of "domination" takes many forms—domination of the enemy, of women, but above all of the self, and of the "feminine" within the self. In the last resort, what the figure signifies for Ophuls is deathliness—the "triumph of the will" that stamps out life in the name of "order," "propriety," "morality," "honor," "tradition." Hence *Liebelei*, *Letter*, and *Madame de . . .* all progress inexorably toward the execution of the lover (in *Liebelei* only the *supposed* lover) at the hands of the wronged and righteous military husband. It should be added that Ophuls' vision darkens as his work progresses, the lover becoming progressively less innocent and less attractive. Stefan is less sympathetic, and infinitely more corrupt, than the young officer of *Liebelei*, and Donati in *Madame de . . .* (though far from "corrupt" as that term is generally understood) far less sympathetic than Stefan, securely inscribed (as diplomat) in the oppressive and discredited patriarchal order, from which even romantic passion cannot extricate him.

## "She Is Not Like That . . ."

Which brings us to the crux (and core) of the film, Lisa's romanticism and the complex, delicately balanced attitude (commitment to, detachment from) that is defined toward it. This cannot possibly be understood except in relation to the whole. A long time ago, F. R. Leavis coined the phrase, "The Novel as Dramatic Poem." It became the basis for his exploration of George Eliot, Conrad, James, Lawrence, and eventually Dickens: the proposition that a great novel can be distinguished from lesser works by the interrelatedness of all its parts and aspects—that it cannot be adequately read "just for the story," but must be seen as a complex organism in which everything is related to and dependent upon everything else. I see no problem in extending this concept to film, and I claim *Letter from an Unknown Woman* as one of the supreme examples of "the film as dramatic poem.'

Essentially, Lisa's romanticism represents an instinctive refusal to live within and be bound by the class and gender constraints of her culture; as such it is revolutionary. It achieves grandeur and nobility because it totally rejects the socially inscribed and sanctioned subordination of women to patriarchal privilege, and because in doing so it at once transcends and rejects the wife/whore opposition of patriarchal culture. Yet a condition of that transcendence is that the romantic fantasy is by definition incapable of fulfillment, and leads inevitably to destruction and self-destruction. It is its rigorous working-through of this quandary—unresolvable, within the social context described, except in death—that raises the film to the level of tragedy.

Consider, first, one of the finest and subtlest of the film's "twinned" shots, the two high-angle shots of Stefan's homecomings, with the camera positioned on a landing above the staircase. In the first, the teenage Lisa has fled from the threatened departure for Linz and has waited for hours to offer herself to Stefan. The camera is behind her and to her left, so that it has something of the effect of a point-of-view shot whilst keeping Lisa within the frame. Looking down, with her, we watch Stefan enter the lobby with his latest conquest, go through the customary exchange with the janitor ("Who is it?"/"Brandt"/"Good evening, Mr. Brandt") that echoes through the entire film, and escort the giggling woman into his apartment. Lisa leaves for Linz. In the second shot, the foreground is empty but the camera occupies the same position and executes the same movement. Stefan's companion of the night is now Lisa, totally immersed in the apparent miraculous realization of her lifelong dream.

It is an extraordinary moment. What we have here is clearly a further refinement of the "double narration": the examples I gave earlier were limited to the *content* of various images; the present instance is created essentially by Ophuls' use of the technical specificities of mise-en-scène—camera placement, camera movement, decoupage. It is by these means that we are allowed a position of ironic detachment that is not available to Lisa. The primary meaning might seem to be: Look, you fool, you're just one of a whole nocturnal procession . . . But Lisa is not a fool, and the effect is far more complex. Not only is she different from the other women (the "groupies" of "Vienna, about 1900") whom Stefan brings home; we have seen that he has registered this difference and is deeply impressed by it. To appreciate Lisa we must do justice to Stefan: to see him as merely worthless and contemptible is to miss much of the film's complexity, and the depth of its tragic sense. In fact, the film provides the means for us to understand him rather intimately.

Like Lisa, we are introduced to the young Stefan through his piano playing: he is practicing *Un Sospiro*, the popular virtuoso piece by Liszt that provides the film's main theme music, difficult but not among his all-but-impossible. At the work's most taxing moment Stefan falters, makes a mistake, breaks off abruptly—then, instead of repeating the passage, slams down the piano lid and leaves the apartment. In a later sequence Lisa steals from her mother's apartment at night to eavesdrop, through an open ventilator-window over the stairs, on Stefan playing. Again he is practicing *Un Sospiro*; this time he gets the passage right. Lisa smiles.

Taken in conjunction, the two scenes tell us a great deal about Stefan and about Lisa's fixation on him. The first reveals his insecurity. He is a "young prodigy," whom the artistic world, the public, the press, expect to have an outstanding musical career (the parallel/opposite of the "outstanding military career" anticipated by the young lieutenant). His reaction, in the first scene, to his momentary failure (giving up, going out, perhaps to the artists' café he frequents, instead of systematically analyzing and mastering the problem) speaks eloquently of his fear of not being able to meet those expectations (which are also his own, of himself). It is easy to grasp from this the compensatory role that sex and "conquests" play in his life—not just distraction, but reassurance: if he can never quite become the great pianist of his own and others' expectations, then he can always demonstrate his attractiveness to women, proving it over and over again, conquering with each, if only temporarily, his fears of inadequacy. The function of the second scene, on the other hand, is to establish the reality of Stefan's potential, though a potential that will never be realized. And, as Lisa listens outside, on the stairs, we know that she is identifying with him and willing him to "get it right," and that when he does, it is imaginatively *her* achievement as much as his. The whole basis of the relationship—her fantasy of vicarious empowerment—is there, in the moment of her smile.

Stefan's clearly genuine response to Lisa when they eventually meet is the reawakening of his sense of his own potential, of the possibility of overcoming his addiction (for the ignominious role of women in his life appears the equivalent of that of drugs or alcohol). He acknowledges Lisa's difference in many ways, all of them touched with ambivalence or precariously suppressed cynicism (see his remarks in the restaurant about the advantages of having a "sorceress" on hand to keep him steady): his purchase of a single white rose from the flower-seller who anticipates that he will buy the "usual" red ones; his decision not to have the carriage (driven by another worker familiar with his habits) closed; his response to Lisa's concern (in the open carriage) that he not catch cold, arranging the scarf around his neck ("It's a long time since anyone did *that* for me").

The "twinning" of the staircase shots is not, then, a matter of simple irony. We are aware of difference as well as similarity, and the emotional response evoked depends upon the tension between the two, the similarity suggesting already Stefan's inability to break from his habituation, the difference the potential that is lost. It is also reasonable to conjecture that Lisa,

The romantic fantasy comes true? Lisa and Stephan (Louis Jourdan)
at the beginning of their one-night tryst.

in reawakening his sense of his potential, also reawakens his sense of the enormous demands this makes on him, and his fears of inadequacy. If this is so, then she herself inadvertently negates the fulfillment of her own desires.

It is unfortunate that the film's adoption of *Un Sospiro* as its theme music connects Stefan superficially to Liszt, the epitome of musical machismo and flamboyant "show-off" virtuosity; one wonders how much (if any) control Ophuls had over this. The scenario (on which he collaborated) associates Stefan much more consistently with Mozart, whose music in its endless and inimitable flexibility of expression exemplifies a perfect fusion of "masculine" and "feminine," strength and tenderness, assertion and yielding, pathos and exuberance. It is a fusion signally appropriate to Ophuls, who used Mozart's music in two other films: *Liebelei* opens with a performance, at the opera, of *Die Entführung aus dem Serail*; and, as my friend and fellow critic Robert Lightning pointed out, the music in the church sequence of *Le Plaisir* is Mozart's setting of "Ave Verum Corpus."

*Letter* connects Stefan with Mozart on three occasions. First, when the teenage Lisa goes to the library to prepare herself for him by reading the lives of great composers, it is the volume on Mozart that she selects, and the scene is accompanied (on the soundtrack) by the slow movement of the E-flat symphony. One can see her choice as merely fortuitous, but she has already begun following Stefan's career, and it seems permissible to suppose that she has been guided by reviews (she can't afford to go to concerts). Then, in the restaurant to which Stefan takes her on their one night together, a countess sends the waiter over to ask him to sign her program of the concert he has just given, congratulating him on his performance of Mozart's D Minor concerto ("the young Mozart could not have played it better"), and Lisa recalls that when he performed the work on an earlier occasion a review also compared him to the young Mozart (Stefan: "I was *very* young, there was that much resemblance"). The work (regarded by many as the "deepest" of the piano concertos) was clearly in his regular repertoire. Finally, Lisa (after her marriage) sees him again at the opera house when *The Magic Flute* is being performed. Stefan is unaccompanied, and has apparently not gone to meet anyone; one assumes that he went purely to hear Mozart's opera. The point is by no means a trivial one for anyone interested (as Ophuls certainly was) in classical music: Stefan's association with Mozart underlines his human potential and helps justify Lisa's belief in him, against all odds.

## Narcissism

To understand Lisa further it is necessary to invoke psychoanalytic theory. As I watch *Letter from an Unknown Woman* at least once a year, it is no great coincidence that I had just seen it when I read Juliet Mitchell's seminal *Psychoanalysis and Feminism*. Mitchell's consideration of narcissism immediately struck a chord, permitting me fresh access to the nature of Lisa's romanticism. Mitchell writes of narcissism predominantly in male terms, with reference to the Romantic poets, such as Shelley, and I have taken little from her but the basic perception: that romantic love is, almost by definition, narcissistic.

In its popular usage, narcissism is always regarded as a "bad thing," equated with excessive vanity. In the sense in which it is to be understood here, it loses such negative connotations, becomes something more like "necessary self-esteem." Its positive connotations take on particular significance when the term is applied to women, those "waitresses at the banquet of life" (Bette Midler's felicitous phrase, which perfectly applies to Lisa), whose self-esteem is liable to be frequently at a low ebb. For a woman, "romantic love" is a somewhat different phenomenon than for a man, for whom it inevitably accrues ugly overtones of the desire to dominate and possess (as supremely realized in *Vertigo*, *Letter*'s ideal companion piece).

Romantic love is never love for a person but for an ideal, and this ideal can only originate within the psyche of the lover. The ideal (related to Freud's "ideal ego") is projected onto the chosen love object, and the lover then mistakes the object *for* the ideal. On whatever level of psychoanalytic awareness the filmmakers consciously worked, *Letter* is very precise about this: Lisa falls in love with Stefan before she even knows what he looks like. It is of course fortunate for the continuation and development of the fantasy that he looks like Louis Jourdan, but physical attraction is not its origin. Her desire is to construct him as her ideal self, the "self" that is denied expression by the conditions of her society. Far from being the sentimental and sexist story of a woman who nobly sacrifices herself for the redemption of an unworthy man, *Letter* is the story of a woman driven to the *vicarious* realization of her own frustrated creativity. Lisa, as I have said, is not stupid: Stefan's *potential* self, and the ideal self that Lisa projects onto it, make a plausible enough fit, which is why the film is a profoundly compassionate tragedy rather than a cruel farce. Why, then, can the fantasy never be realized?

Primarily, because the ideal self constructed by the psyche cannot, by definition, be permitted any flaws or weaknesses. Lisa is perfectly able to make compromises for herself—working in Madame Spitzer's shop, marrying von Stauffer for the protection and security of her child (Stefan's child, and Stefan reborn). The compromises, however, are external and practical, an adjustment to the social realities—her refusal, even under pressure, to tell her husband that she is "happy" registers as a heroic gesture, the preservation of her integrity and fidelity, the "self" she keeps for Stefan. But where Stefan is concerned no similar compromise is possible. She cannot confront him on his return from La Scala; *he* must come to *her*, and if he has forgotten he must not be reminded. She cannot tell him that she is pregnant, or that she has borne his child. The reason she gives for this in the letter—that she wished to be the one woman who never asked him for anything—is illuminating: as Stefan must be either perfect or nothing, she must be perfect to match. One of the film's most painful moments is when Stefan looks at the photographs of his son that Lisa has enclosed—the son he has never seen, or been allowed to know existed—his face registering a nostalgia for something he never had and that Lisa in effect (in the name of perfection and integrity) has denied him. Lisa can never really *see* Stefan, let alone accept his weaknesses. She can allow herself to be aware that he is always looking for something he hasn't found, because the "something" is herself; beyond that, she can see only the fantasy ideal that she has superimposed upon him.

Hence the ultimate painfulness of their final encounter. When Stefan—his career effectively over, his habits of debauchery thoroughly confirmed—sees Lisa at the opera and confronts her in the darkness outside, we see a haunted, ravaged human being. The old habits are still there, trying to reassert themselves ("You must know that, where there is a pursued, there must also be a pursuer"), but it is clear that this is not a casual pickup but an impulse of desperation, a plea for help: if he does not remember Lisa as a person, he certainly recognizes *something*. When she visits him in his apartment he has recovered his poise, and the habits have taken over completely; he treats her as just another *belle-de-nuit*, a resourceful woman who has managed to evade her husband for the thrill of a one-night stand. She leaves. Given the terms on which she has built her life, she is of course right to do so, she could scarcely do anything else: her humiliation is so complete and so cruel, her fantasy at last ruthlessly demolished. Yet—such is the film's complexity—she is also wrong. Stefan, fetching champagne from another room, has just told her that "there was something you said to me last night that's been on my mind all day. Do you believe that?" Lisa responds softly, out of earshot, to herself, "No, I don't believe you," and departs before he returns. The camera follows her, then, as she leaves the apartment, stops to frame the table on which lies the bunch of white roses she has brought (with their accumulated significance—the flower-seller, this time male, told her that there were "just a few flowers left") and a guttering candle. If she had waited, Stefan would have had to tell her what it was she said that had haunted him (it could only have been, "What *are* you waiting for?" to which he responded, "That's a very disturbing question"), and the whole issue of the relationship, the "few flowers" of possibility remaining, would have been reopened. It would have been, of course, a relationship impossible for Lisa to accept: Stefan is a mere human being, and a ruined one, perhaps irrecoverably sunk in his addictions, no longer a plausible incarnation of the Ideal Ego.

Lisa's inability to understand Stefan, and the impossibility that she could ever "help" him (as he had once suggested, and she had echoed, during their one night of intimacy), is confirmed by a final small, almost "throwaway," touch: when the old soldier accosts her, fleeing from Stefan's apartment, and propositions her ("Take you somewhere? Anywhere—it makes no difference"), she glances up from him to the lighted window of Stefan's apartment, identifying the two men. But for Ophuls and the spectator there remains, surely, in the context of the film and its system, *some* difference: Stefan, however debased, cannot be identified with a "military man."

But Lisa herself, at moments, comes close to grasping that her fantasy is just that, and that she prefers it to reality. As they walk through the snow-covered grounds of the Prater, she explains to Stefan why he prefers the winter—because he can then imagine what it would be like in spring, whereas in spring there'd be nothing to imagine. The remark is central to the film, and to Ophuls' awareness, consistent through his entire career, of the dis-

The single white rose.

empowerment of women in patriarchal society. One may link it to her remark, in the foyer of the Vienna Opera, so often taken for the "message" of the film, that "nothing happens by chance," that everything is predetermined and out of one's hands.

If it is appropriate to apply rigorously to the film that much-debased word *tragic*, it is because here so much is lost, and there was so much at stake.

## Oedipus Rears His Head Again

It may seem surprising that I have left consideration of the film's Oedipal patterning so long, and that I now, having arrived here at last, propose to play down its importance. Oedipus—at least in his Lacanian extensions—has, after all, dominated most film theory for several decades. It has been demonstrated many times over that every Hollywood film is really about him (and, it would seem at times, about nothing else): the "Oedipal trajectory," whereby the rebellious Son learns to accept his symbolic castration and to identify with the Father, assuming his position, and is rewarded with the necessary woman, replacement for the mother he has had to relinquish, has been traced through Hollywood movies ad infinitum and post nauseam, each film ending with the construction of the "good" heterosexual couple, the new Father and Mother, the woman subordinated to the man, her essential function being the restoration of his potency; or, if it can't be constructed (because of death or necessary separation), the reaffirmation of its supreme value via the sense of tragic loss. It is not entirely clear to me that this is much more interesting than having someone (who has just found it out) solemnly demonstrate that most of Mozart's and Haydn's first movements are in sonata form.

I am not going to contest its general validity: it would be surprising if it were *not* the case. The core of our cultural formation is the patriarchal nuclear family (though today the nucleus shows welcome signs of imminent dissolution, the attempts of right-wing politicians to reassert "family values" becoming increasingly desperate, extreme, and hysterical), and, on the level of the unconscious, the Oedipus complex and its resolution have been the means by which it is perpetuated. If such a structure is crucial to a given culture, we might logically expect it to play a defining and formative role in that culture's popular art. Two tendencies, however, strike me as singularly unfortunate. One is the tendency to *reduce* Hollywood films to the reproduction of the Oedipal trajectory, at the expense of all the other layers of meaning generated, and to assume that the reproduction is invariably inert and uncritical. The other is to repeat and reinforce Freud's error in assuming (as he does most of the time) that the Oedipal process is somehow necessary, innate, universal and unchangeable.

Of course, you can't change the unconscious by glaring at it sternly and shouting "Change!" However, there is every reason to believe that it is as subject to *social* change as our conscious beliefs and assumptions. It is perhaps more resistant, because it is largely inaccessible: it will not change overnight, as a false assumption can if it is rectified. The change will occur gradually, over the years, perhaps over several generations. As the position of women becomes stronger, as "family values" become increasingly besieged (it was never necessary, in the past, for politicians to scream about them from platforms), as the variety and complexity of human sexuality becomes ever more widely recognized and accepted, so the hold of Oedipus on our culture will be loosened. It would be absurd (absurdly premature) at this stage to abandon Freud, whose work still holds many of the keys to the future, if they are put to the right uses. Yet isn't it equally absurd to apply his ideas (developed, precisely, within the rigid cultural formations of "Vienna, about 1900") without the slightest modification, as if nothing had changed and as if the unconscious were not changing with it? But as my editor Roy Thomas commented, "One would think so—except for those who also have no problem imposing the cultural and social strictures of two thousand years ago (or a thousand years ago, or even *forty* years ago) onto contemporary society!"

This is why, although I continue to draw on psychoanalytic theory when it suits my purposes, I do so with increasing caution and decreasing confidence, preferring to concentrate my attention on *social* formations and to examine the psychic formations of the individual in their context—to place films within the currents of change rather than the stasis of Freudian (or any other) essentialism. Nonetheless, the Oedipal patterns of *Letter from an Unknown Woman* are certainly insistent enough to demand acknowledgment.

So insistent, indeed, that they can hardly be described as inertly reproduced within the film, any more than can gender roles and class positions. The function of the "presentational" manner is to make *all* the thematic material accessible to conscious analysis. Perhaps the clearest instance of this, as far as Oedipus is concerned, in all Ophuls' work is the last shot of *The Reckless Moment*: the supposed (re)construction of the "good couple" and the reconstitution of the united family. As Lucia (earlier described by Donnelly as a "prisoner" of her family), after weeping uncontrollably on the conjugal bed, descends the stairs to take her husband's transatlantic phone call, the "family group" forms in the background of the shot, each member regaining his/her prescribed role and position: useless, obsolete grandfather; undervalued and disempowered black maid; son (resistant throughout the film to formal attire), dressed in an adult-style suit; daughter, wearing her mother's fur coat—the bourgeois Oedipal family par excellence. As Lucia, in the false and gushing manner required by her position as mother and wife, mouths the inane reassuring platitudes that are expected of her, the camera cranes down to frame her behind the bars of the banisters. It is one of the most devastating and desolate "happy endings" in Hollywood cinema, the candor of its irony outdoing even Sirk, who was to work his own variation on it (with the conjugal positions reversed, but Joan Bennett again in the wife/mother role) six years later in *There's Always Tomorrow*.

Oedipal patternings crisscross throughout *Letter from an Unknown Woman*. In the sequences of their one night of love, Lisa is cast as both Stefan's mother (fixing the scarf around his throat in the carriage: "It's a long time since anyone did *that* for me") and his daughter ("Now I see you as a little girl"); her desire to be his mother (as well as his muse) is realized through her own child, also named Stefan (and Leo B. Pessin, besides being a remarkable child actor, is a remarkably plausible young Louis Jourdan), who is allowed to sleep in her bed (though only when she isn't in it). The film can be seen to move toward the "tragic" version of the Oedipal resolution—the "son" killed by the "father" for taking away the "mother." The "father" is in fact divided into two, both significantly given the same Christian name, though in different languages: the film's culmination has the benign father, the servant John, patting Stefan on the back (if he could speak he would be saying, "You're doing the right thing, my boy") as he leaves to receive his execution at the hands of the punishing father, Johann von Stauffer. Other critics may well wish to base an entire reading of the film on such patterns, or at least place far greater emphasis on them than I do. They are in no way incompatible with what I have written, but they do not enormously engage me.

More interesting to me (because more directly related to my concern with gender construction, resistance to it, and the consequences of that resistance) are the hints the film offers about Lisa's own Oedipal progress, which is to say the least idiosyncratic. That Lisa has rejected the "correct" female progression (accepting her own "castration" and learning to identify with the mother) is clear: her desire to be Stefan's "mother" is secondary to her desire to identify herself with him, to become his "better self" which is also her own ideal self; if she repeats her mother's pattern (marrying a man she does not love for security), this is because it is the "option" society forces upon her. The dialogue in the Prater "train" makes it clear that Lisa identified with her father, and acquired from him the tendency to escape into fantasy; he brought home travel brochures, and father and daughter (after he had put on his "traveling coat") toured the world in their imaginations. Lisa says, "He had the nicest eyes," and Stefan, gazing into her own, responds, "I can see them." Lisa's father, then, held the social position of the Symbolic Father (breadwinner of the patriarchal family), but was in himself essentially a passive, "feminized" figure. One might, if one wished, trace from this Lisa's rejection of the prescribed female role, her desire for identification with the male, but at the same time her constant passive "waiting," her stasis, her constant imaginative refusal of the social realities even when she accepts them as material necessities. The danger of such an interpretation is, not that it is "wrong," but that it tends to restrict everything to the psychology of the individual, without acknowledging that such psychology is determined by the social formations about which the film is so detailed and eloquent, and that it is the social formations that must be changed.

I cannot leave this without drawing attention to one marvelous throwaway moment in the film that enacts Lisa's commitment to (literally) the male position. After she first sets eyes on Stefan she determines, as the prospective object-for-the-gaze and female supporter of male enterprise, to improve herself for him—taking more trouble over her personal appearance, going to the library to read the lives of the great composers, etc. This is shown us in a series of very brief vignettes, one of which has Lisa attending dancing class. She arrives late, and watches, for a moment, through a glass partition, the two lines, male and female, practicing their steps. Then, still outside the partition, she joins in—on the male side.

## The Ending

As I began with the beginning I must end with the end, thereby reproducing in criticism that closure and symmetry so deplored by those critics who reject mainstream narrative cinema as inherently reactionary, totally enslaved by the "dominant ideology."

Closure there is, certainly. We can be sure, at the end, of a number of things: that Stefan goes voluntarily to meet his death at the hands of von Stauffer; that he has undergone some form of moral, or spiritual, redemption, by reading the letter and recovering the past; that Lisa has, after all, triumphed, although her victory has necessitated the deaths of herself, her lover, and their child. In the film's first shot, the clock strikes two, the carriage arrives, rain is falling; at the end the clock strikes five (it is near dawn), the carriage departs, the rain has stopped. Three hours (compressed to eighty-seven minutes of remarkably concentrated screen time) have elapsed, fifteen-plus years have been recaptured, the hermeneutics of the opening (Will Stefan fight the duel? Who is this lethal antagonist? Why is it being fought? etc.) have all been resolved. One can read (if one wishes) the reaffirmation of the value of the good heterosexual couple: Stefan understands that he should have married Lisa, reformed his ways, allowed her to fulfill her "ideal" Oedipal role as muse/wife/mother/daughter. Inspired by her, he could have been a great pianist, had a happy domestic life between concert engagements, and basked in Lisa's wifely (if somewhat demanding) admiration.

*Is* that what Stefan understands? Is it the meaning of his enigmatic, rueful smile, as he turns at the gate for the last time to see either Lisa-as-ghost or an empty doorway (depending on whether you respect the completed film or the wishes of its director)? Or is it the kind of closure that the semiotics/structuralist school has taught us to *impose* on Hollywood films at the expense of all other available meanings, overvaluing the purely conventional aspects of the narrative movement at the cost of all the authentically creative particularities of the actual work in front of us?

Before attempting to answer such questions (and my answer will of course already be obvious, at least in principle), I must consider briefly one further interpretation, somewhat alien to my own position, that carries considerable weight, supported by a number of concrete details: a Christian—and specifically Catholic—reading of the film.

Lisa's letter is surmounted by the insignia "St. Catherine's Hospital," and the sign of the cross. It ends with (replacing her signature, as she died before she could sign it) a message from "Sister Teresa" (who apparently makes a habit of reading people's private and very intimate correspondence): "May God have mercy on you both." When Lisa waits, watching for Stefan, on the night of their meeting, she is standing beside a niche in which is placed a statuette of the Holy Virgin. At the end of the film Stefan, the sinner, is redeemed by reading the letter; Lisa, who is also a sinner as well as a savior, is redeemed by redeeming him. Dawn; the rain has stopped.

It is easy, of course, to dovetail this reading with the banal "reaffirmation of the good couple" one—each supports the other. It is lent a particular plausibility by the fact that it is the *only* reading that really explains John, the mute servant: he is Stefan's guardian angel. John, clearly a privileged character, is permitted an apparently supernatural knowledge. It is not just that he remembers Lisa (who appears not to remember *him*) when Stefan doesn't. He seems to know the content of the letter (and we are certainly not to suppose that he has steamed it open!) and the effect it will have on Stefan; how else to account for the fact that he does *not* (contrary to his master's instructions) summon a cab for Stefan's "indefinite" stay abroad? And how, for that matter, does he know the letter is from Lisa (as she has died before completing it, there can scarcely have been a return address on the envelope)? I think this reading is available to anyone who wants it. Doubtless, just as Catholic dogma, in all its baffling convolutions, has an answer to everything in human existence, such a reading could account, if pursued far enough, for everything in the film. I would add only that Ophuls' attitude to Catholicism in the late French films (*Le Plaisir* and, especially, *Madame de . . .*) is distinctly more ambiguous and can be read ironically, as it cannot, I think, here.

## "If You Have a Message, Send It Western Union"

Samuel Goldwyn's famous remark—on a certain level characteristically crass—has quite profound reverberations when one is seriously discussing art and its function. We cannot possibly know what the precise intentions were when Max Ophuls, Howard Koch, William Dozier (the instigator, head of Rampart Productions at the time), Joan Fontaine, John Houseman (the producer), or Franz Planer (the cinematographer) all made *Letter from an Unknown Woman,* or even who *controlled* those intentions. Even if we hypothesized (what is clearly untrue) that it is purely and unproblematically "a film by Max Ophuls," and could go back into the past and ask him, we could not expect that the result (though it would undoubtedly be of great interest) would be a "definitive" statement. I have no desire to "fix" *Letter from an Unknown Woman* within one meaning. I offer only to define what seems important to *me, now,* as an individual very much involved in contemporary debates about, and attitudes toward, gender, sexuality, feminism, and I refuse to slip into the error (common to academic, or basically conservative, critics) of asserting or implying that my reading is "objective," "definitive," etc. On the other hand, I would passionately defend its validity, and have frequently done so against determinedly "modern" young students who wish to tell me how stupid Lisa is and how deplorable it was that Hollywood would produce films about so retrograde a female stereotype. ("Modern" is, as Peter Ustinov tells us at the beginning of the American release version of *Le Plaisir,* what we all like to call ourselves while we are still alive.)

So, how do I read the film's conclusion? For me, the crucial moment (which the mise-en-scène underlines) is where Stefan, leaving to face his death, plucks the single white rose from the bunch Lisa has brought him, and places it inside his coat over his heart (the point at which von Stauffer will of course aim). Stefan's enigmatic smile as he sees (or doesn't see—it really doesn't matter) Lisa for the last time, acknowledges less his moral redemption (though that is of course important) than his realization of everything, and the sadness of it, the loss.

I shall not attempt to answer the question, What does Stefan understand? He, like Lisa, is but a character (if a leading one) in a highly complex, intricately organized, "dramatic poem," and whatever *he* understands does not necessarily coincide with what the viewer understands. It was a single white rose that he chose for Lisa, at the outset of their night together, as his acknowledgment of her difference, her "specialness." In reciprocating the gift by accepting the rose and his own death, he not merely acknowledges her but identifies himself with her: he can become in death—and *only* in death—the ideal ego of Lisa's creation. In accepting death at the hands of von Stauffer (who is, in his well-meaning deathly way, merely fulfilling the requirements of patriarchal/masculinist "duty," the function of the "military man"), Stefan is not merely completing the (negative) Oedipal trajectory, he is refusing the accoutrements of masculine privilege, the illusory "power and freedom" (to quote *Vertigo*) that men have throughout history sought to appropriate. Is this not why, at the end of the film, one experiences such a sense of uplift? Not because Stefan has achieved some vaguely defined metaphysical "redemption," but because the terms of that redemption are in fact so precise, specific, and rooted in the social organization.

But this is still not sufficient. Closure or not, and despite the fact that Stefan dominates the framework, this is Lisa's film (is it not, after all, that intellectually despised commodity—a "star vehicle" for Joan Fontaine?). We never identify with Stefan as intimately as we do with Lisa; the main body of the film is far too powerful for the framework to close it off in any neat, conventional, schematic way. For the spectator, surely, Lisa survives Stefan's death: it is *her* film, absolutely. Implicitly, almost every major female Hollywood star (Garbo, Dietrich, Crawford, Davis, Hepburn, Stanwyck . . .), and the characters they embodied, seem to be calling out for the advent of the women's movement of the sixties and seventies. Lisa, in her apparent self-sacrifice and in the "self" that she obstinately refuses to sacrifice, is among the most eloquent.

# PART V

# WOMEN—OPPRESSION AND TRANSGRESSION

# CHAPTER 10

# Three Films of Mizoguchi: Questions of Style and Identification

The work of Yasujiro Ozu, from almost the beginning of his long career, shows a remarkable consistency both of form and subject matter (though a consistency that half-conceals quite subtle ideological shifts); Kenji Mizoguchi, on the other hand, the other generally acknowledged grand master of classical (pre-Kurosawa) Japanese cinema, was a chameleon, drastically transforming both style and ideological position with every major change in the social-political situation. Beside the obstinate integrity of Ozu, his career may appear superficially that of either a cynical opportunist or a vacillating weakling, a weathercock turning with every ideological breeze. It is the quality of his work, in every one of the major phases, the irresistible sense conveyed by his best films of a powerful creative involvement and commitment, that forbids so easy a judgment.

One may divide the career into five more or less sharply defined phases, each covering only a few years, each apparently determined by either a significant shift in the Japanese sociopolitical situation or (in the final phase) a personal conversion.

1. *The Early Years (1920s–early 1930s)*. There isn't very much I can say here: so little survives, even less is accessible in the West outside the occasional touring retrospective. But unlike the equivalent period in Ozu's work, it seems characterized by a striking uncertainty, as if Mizoguchi were casting around for a form, a style, a theme, an artistic commitment. The plot synopses in Dudley and Paul Andrew's invaluable reference book, *Kenji Mizoguchi: A Guide to References and Resources* (1981), suggest that Mizoguchi was already attracted to (or perhaps was merely assigned) melodramas centered on women, but these are interspersed with thrillers, comedies, action

films . . . the genre movies one might expect from a professional working within a large and constantly developing commercial industry in many respects comparable to Hollywood. Noel Burch (*To the Distant Observer*, 1979) offers the plausible suggestion (based on what little is available) that Mizoguchi in this period set himself to master completely the "Western codes," prior to his radical rejection of them in the 1930s (a rejection that lasted, however, only a decade).

2. *The "Radical" Period (1935–1939)*. There was a potent and widespread Leftist protest movement in Japan in the 1930s, ultimately suppressed by the Fascist government just before World War II. Mizoguchi for a time committed himself to this, proclaimed himself a Marxist, and made films that are "radical" both in form and content. They include *Osaka Elegy*, *Sisters of the Gion*, and *Story of the Last Chrysanthemums*.

3. *The War Years (1940–1945)*. The government demanded patriotic or nationalistic movies celebrating feudal values; certain films of the previous period were banned. Mizoguchi obliged with a brief series of samurai films (a genre he disliked—outside this period his *jidai-geki*, or "period" films, are never samurai movies), practicing his stylistics and playing down the jingoism as much as possible. Though it produced one of his generally acknowledged masterpieces, the nearly four-hour epic *The Loyal 47 Ronin* (aka *The 47 Ronin*), this seems (understandably) the thinnest of the four mature phases.

4. *The American Occupation (1945–1949)*. The American occupying authorities diametrically reversed the demands of the war years: filmmakers were to participate in the liberalization and democratization of Japan, and anything favoring traditional feudal values was forbidden. Mizoguchi responded with his most explicit and outspoken "feminist" films (*Victory of Women*, *My Love Has Been Burning*), ironically pushing feminist analysis and political demands further than any American commercial films before or since.

5. *International Celebrity/Conversion to Buddhism*. The films by which Mizoguchi is still best known in the West (despite Noel Burch's powerful championship of the "radical" works) all come from this late period (1950 to his death from leukemia in 1956): *Ugetsu Monogatari*, *Sansho Dayu* (*Sansho the Bailiff*), *The Life of Oharu*, *The Princess Yang Kwei-Fei* . . .

It must be said at once that, while I think it is accurate to claim that each of these periods (or at least the last four) has distinctive characteristics, both thematic and stylistic, none is perfectly discrete; there are anomalies within all of them: for example, *Story of the Last Chrysanthemums*, though "radical" in its own way, doesn't quite fit, thematically, with the Marxist rage and rigour of *Sisters of the Gion*; and Mizoguchi's last film, *Street of Shame*, is in many ways a throwback (in the midst of his "Buddhist contemplation" period) to the protest films of the 1930s or the explicitly feminist films of the late 1940s. And in every period there are films that I have not yet been able to see. The division, by and large, remains valid.

Two tendencies—one stylistic, one thematic—fragilely unify all five periods: stylistically, Mizoguchi's constant interest in and exploration of the possibilities inherent in the long take or sequence-shot; thematically, his constant magnetic attraction to women and their social position. In the latter case, period 3 (the war years) is an obvious exception, yet even here Mizoguchi contrived to center one of his samurai movies (*The Famous Sword*) on a female protagonist who becomes a warrior, with possession of the title weapon, in order to avenge the death of her father, thus conscripting feminism in the service of the patriarchy! The crucial point, however, is that the nature both of the long take and of the commitment to women varies radically from period to period, the change in one always paralleling the change in the other. The long takes of *Sisters of the Gion* are quite different in kind and expressive function from those of *My Love Has Been Burning*, which in turn are quite distinct from those of *Ugetsu*; in the late movies, the feminist rage and protest of earlier films gives way to portrayals of women as noble sacrificial victims (though still, very clearly, the victims of patriarchy), but nevertheless, the rage and protest return at the very end (qualified by an all-but-overwhelming despair and pessimism) in *Street of Shame*.

As with his closely parallel account of Ozu, Noel Burch's chapter on Mizoguchi in *To the Distant Observer* makes an invaluable starting point. As with Ozu, the criterion is the fundamentally negative one of the rejection of the "Western codes," those weapons of cultural imperialism; this leads logically (again, as with Ozu) to an extremely high valuation of the works of the 1930s and early 1940s, and the summary dismissal of virtually everything since (though *Chikamatsu Monogatari* is praised for its "radical" use of sound). While Ozu, however, merely lapsed into "academicism," Mizoguchi committed the far more heinous sin of capitulation to the "Western codes," the long-takes-with-camera-movement of the late films being mere extensions of the work of Welles and Wyler. The basic premise—that the systems of representation (or "realist" illusionism) developed during and since the Renaissance are somehow inherently harmful or reactionary and must be abandoned—seems to me simply unacceptable.

However, anyone today who chooses to write on *Sisters of the Gion* does so in Burch's shadow and owes a great debt. His formalist analysis of the film is meticulous and exemplary; for me it has performed one of the prime functions of criticism—to open my eyes. I shall use his analysis here for a purpose of which he may strongly disapprove: to demonstrate the film's perfect unity of style and meaning, a unity one could equally exemplify in films that lie outside the period that Burch singles out.

**I**

## *Sisters of the Gion* (1936)

What is *Sisters of the Gion* about? The answer is scarcely very obscure, as in this period of intense political commitment Mizoguchi is little interested in subtlety, ambiguity, ambivalence, contradiction—the shadowy borderlines of, for example, *Ugetsu*: the film builds logically to what amounts to a direct address-to-audience statement of its "message" which (although the film's very detailed analysis of the consequences of patriarchal-capitalist oppression cannot be reduced to it) is not, in context, in the least jarring. During the 1930s, Mizoguchi's predilection for exploring the social position and predicament of women fused with his brief (but apparently strongly committed) espousal of Marxism. Accordingly, the concern of *Sisters of the Gion* (and of its more tentative immediate predecessor *Osaka Elegy*) is, very explicitly, with patriarchal capitalism and the victimization of women within it. But the film goes further. It is about a socioeconomic system in which everyone—male, female, employer, employee—is ultimately a victim: a world in which there are no "villains" to use as scapegoats, and no uncontaminated heroes, because the system spreads its poison through every level and each individual.

A related question: with what character or characters in the film is it possible for us to identify? Those who believe that identification is constructed exclusively by style will immediately shout "No one!" And that is perhaps (with qualifications) the right answer for the wrong reason. The phenomenon of identification, and the construction of identification in a film, are far more complex than has generally been recognized, depending on a number of factors that include, but are by no means restricted to, such tangibles as the close-up versus the long shot, or the use of point-of-view shots. Take the case of Ozu: no one, I think, can doubt that in *Late Spring* we are gradually led to a fairly complete identification with Noriko (Setsuko Hara). Yet she is filmed throughout in exactly the same way as the other characters—same lighting, same angle, same distance, no POV.

Those, then, who, like myself, believe that—while stylistic devices can be (sometimes even crucially) important—identification has a great deal to do with the construction of the scenario, the position of characters within the narrative, and the general tendency of our culture (or of any culture) to find some modes of behavior more sympathetic than others, may answer, with equal conviction, "Omocha." They, too, seem to me correct, up to a point—but a point reached relatively early in the film. We identify, I assume, unambiguously (as surely did Mizoguchi) with Omocha's closing statement. But to identify with a statement is not at all the same as identifying with a character, especially when the statement is placed, as it were, in quotation marks (by an abrupt, shocking change of style), as "The Message of the Film." We can also identify with Omocha (Isuzu Yamada), without too many qualms, throughout the opening scenes of *Sisters of the Gion*, before the full import of her position has been enacted for us. We can feel a certain satisfaction in her manipulation of wealthy patriarchal capitalists. But her exploitation of a working-class man (Kimura, the kimono store clerk)? And her betrayal (it amounts to that) of her own sister, even if it is for the sister's assumed good? Omocha is clearly the film's "hero," insofar as it can be said to have one; but, as I said earlier, Mizoguchi's concern is with a system (at a certain stage of its evolution) within which there are no uncontaminated heroes, and in which "pure" actions are impossible.

I suppose other identification figures (partial, at least) are Omocha's sister Umekichi (Yoko Umemura) and the clerk Kimura (Toizo Fukami): they are both victims, and victims are the easiest characters with which to identify. Kimura's revenge on Omocha (extremely brutal, narrow-minded, without the least insight into her position) disqualifies him absolutely (though without at all justifying Omocha's treatment of *him*). As for Umekichi, in a conservative melodrama she might well have emerged as the heroine, endlessly oppressed, endlessly suffering, accepting her "destiny." Mizoguchi, doubtless aware of this possibility, takes great pains to make it difficult for us to identify with her at any point (compassion alone is insufficient grounds for identification): the film depicts a society to which the only valid response is revolution, and Umekichi's conformism, while understandable and pathetic, is also registered as deeply stupid and self-oppressive, even as we register the stupidity as socially conditioned. Her fate is scarcely better, though less spectacularly violent, than her sister's; the essence of the film is that this is a society in which no one—neither the conformist nor the nonconformist—can win, especially if they are women.

The film, centered on the predicament of the geisha, opens with a succinct and bitterly ironic presentation of the essentials of a culture within which geishas exist and struggle to survive, by "fair" means (Umekichi) or foul (Omocha). "Presentation" rather than "representation": I want to evoke (here, as with Ophuls) the Brechtian distinction, while insisting that there is no clearcut boundary. The dog-eat-dog world of business, its seesaw of success and failure, is epitomized in the opening bankruptcy auction, shown in a lengthy lateral track (Burch's "scroll-shot") along the side of the rows of vulture-bidders; the ensuing exchange between the ruined capitalist Furosawa and his clerk Sadakichi introduces the key theme of *giri* (obligation). *Giri* is the essential underpinning principle of traditional Japanese culture; it amounts to the assumption of unquestioning duty toward the figure of the patriarch (emperor, feudal lord, father, husband, employer, etc.). Here, Sadakichi is effusively but humbly offering the totally undistinguished Furosawa his continuing devotion. The camera, in the first of the abrupt and unsettling movements which partly characterize the film's style, turns right to reveal, beyond a sliding panel, a new space we hadn't known existed: Furosawa's wife is packing what little is left of her belongings and complaining angrily that her husband has lost not only all *his* money but all hers as well. The conditioned subservience of the clerk is juxtaposed with the humiliation of the wife, establishing another central theme, women's financial powerlessness in a society in which ownership is the prerogative of the male.

I want at this point briefly to consider *Osaka Elegy*, made earlier the same year. Oddly, it seems to have received more recognition than *Sisters of the Gion*, though the latter is by far the more assured work (it is also much tougher, more intransigent, which may account for the widespread preference for the earlier film). Burch describes it, very perceptively, as a point of hesitation in Mizoguchi's development: hesitation between acceptance and rejection of the "Western codes." Certain sequence-shots strikingly anticipate the style of its immediate successor; they stand out in the context of a film shot mainly in a style that would not have been unacceptable in the Hollywood of the 1930s. Especially, a number of shots, with their elaborate mise-en-scène of foreground decor at once distancing and decorative, testify to Mizoguchi's interest in von Sternberg, whom he greatly admired. The Sternberg influence is carried over thematically into *Sisters of the Gion* (think, for example, of the parallels between Omocha and Dietrich's Concha in *The Devil Is a Woman*, made about a year earlier). Thematically, indeed, *Osaka Elegy* is a perfect companion piece: it is as single-mindedly dedicated to the analysis of the oppression of women *within* the family as *Sisters of the Gion* is beyond it, to the extent that each film seems to necessitate the other. *Giri* (and its devastations) is once again a central concern. The West, of course, has its own concepts of *giri* (duty to one's country, to one's parents, to one's husband . . .), but they have never been quite as formalized and explicit as is the case in traditional Japanese culture. It is important to recognize this to appreciate the full audacity of these films, even more radical in a Japanese context than they appear to us. In *Osaka Elegy*, Ayako (played by Isuzu Yamada, who also plays Omocha, and was much later to be Kurosawa's unforgettable Lady Macbeth) is effectively destroyed by her reluctant dedication to the interests of the males (first father, later brother, both equally mean-minded and selfish) in her family, who repay her for her sacrifices by disowning her and casting her out for dishonoring them. The ending implies that she has only two remaining options, suicide (which she rejects) and prostitution.

Which might be said to lead directly into *Sisters of the Gion*. After the opening, a six-shot sequence develops the theme of *giri* and introduces the two sisters. The elder, Umekichi, brought up in geisha quarters and totally conditioned to traditional values, renews her commitment to the ruined Furosawa (paralleling the clerk Sadakichi) because, in his days of affluence, he helped her to attain her current enviable status, and undertakes to look after him in his new poverty. The younger, Omocha, who has gone to college, has acquired a certain critical awareness of the profession in which she nonetheless remains trapped, and expresses her anger at her sister's passivity and submissiveness, arguing that as men always exploit women it's time for women to use their intelligence and their sexuality to exploit men. The sisters' names (I am indebted for this information to a Japanese projectionist who worked on one of my film courses) reflect their respective positions in the geisha hierarchy: Umekichi ("Plum-blossom") is a name used by upper-class geishas; Omocha (literally, "piece of toy," i.e., plaything) establishes the character's lower-class status. Given her lowly position, her rebelliousness appears even more outspoken and audacious.

The film's intricate patterning of all the varieties of victimization—Furosawa a victim of the business world, his clerk a victim of *giri*, his wife a victim of the principle of male control of money, Umekichi a victim of her conditioning—is given a further dimension a few scenes later. Umekichi must have a new and expensive kimono if she is to be allowed to participate in the geisha dance-festival, which could be important to her career; to acquire one, Omocha manipulates Kimura, the young clerk of the cloth merchant Kudo, who she has learned is interested in her but for whom she earlier expressed a casual contempt. She seduces him into supplying the extravagant kimono material, fully aware that he will have to steal it and risk jeopardizing his employment. Hence the oppressed becomes also the oppressor. Previously, Omocha's explicit aim of exploiting men was assumed to refer to the powerful and wealthy exploiters; here, she extends the principle to the exploitation of a junior employee.

The central movement of the film is concerned with Omocha's determination to replace Furosawa with a wealthy patron for her sister, which involves not only the manipulation of dominant males (Furosawa and the scroll merchant Jurakudo, the chosen replacement) but also of Umekichi, who must not be allowed to grasp what is going on. In one of the film's longest (and static) sequence-shots, Omocha (claiming to speak for her sister as well) explains to Furosawa that his presence is now inconvenient. He leaves but, deprived of the opportunity to exploit the *giri* of a geisha, immediately seizes the opportunity to exploit that of his ex-employee Sadakichi, whom he meets, opportunely, in the street. Omocha goes to sleep until her sister gets home, and then, in another static long take in extreme long shot, tells her that Furosawa left without giving a reason. Kimura visits Omocha to propose marriage, then hides and sneaks out when his boss Kudo arrives to confront her with her role in Kimura's theft of the kimono material; she promptly sets about seducing him (in the film's longest take, over three minutes) with flattery, manipulating him into becoming her patron.

It is clearly not only to Western eyes that the three middle-aged businessmen (Furosawa, Kudo, Jurakudo) appear virtually indistinguishable: the actors were carefully cast for their close resemblance. Mizoguchi's point is that they are not merely indistinguishable but totally undistinguished, token figures lacking charisma and even individuality; success or ruin in the world of business is not determined by personal characteristics but simply by the movements of the capitalist seesaw, one going up as the other comes down.

The remainder of the film describes how Omocha's schemes backfire, the various threads of the net she has woven entangling and virtually destroying her as they fall apart. Umekichi discovers what has happened to Furosawa and how it came about; Kimura finds Kudo and Omocha together, denounces them, and, over the telephone, informs Kudo's wife of what is going on. Umekichi also denounces her sister and moves out to devote herself again to Furosawa; Kimura exacts a terrible revenge, having Omocha flung from a fast-moving car, severely injuring and perhaps crippling her for life. The closing sequences have the sisters reunited in despair. After visiting the hospital Umekichi returns home to get her things and learns that Furosawa has moved out during her absence, returning to his wife who is setting him up in a factory. In the last shot (another long take), Umekichi, at Omocha's bedside, attempts to console herself with the belief that she did her duty according to the demands of the culture; but Omocha, prone, almost immobilized, and in great pain, angrily upbraids her for her self-destructive conformity, moving to a passionate and despairing diatribe against the lot of the geisha, the camera (static until this point) tracking in to frame her in mid-close-up, in what must be seen as the film's single recourse to camera-rhetoric, so that her speech seems directed straight at the spectator.

We can now return to the question of style and its contribution to the film's total meaning. The structural patterning of different forms and strategies of exploitation/manipulation gradually embroils all the characters, defining them as at once exploiters and victims trapped within the structures of a culture founded upon principles of competition, domination, and greed. The formal and stylistic strategies Mizoguchi adopted (the term "Brechtian" inevitably springs to mind, whether or not there was any direct connection) appear not merely appropriate but essential, their rigorous distancing pulling us back from the characters as *individuals* to allow us to become aware of the oppressive and pervasively corrupting *structures* that determine their actions and their various defeats. In this it is an exemplary Marxist film (Marxist first, feminist second) and therefore unlike the films from Mizoguchi's other periods, where the emphasis is precisely reversed, especially in the films made during the American occupation (notably *My Love Has Been Burning*). The main features of the style can now be made explicit:

*The long take.* There are only 123 shots in a film lasting just under seventy minutes—twenty-six of them in the single brief sequence of Kimura's revenge (the car ride), in which Mizoguchi deliberately and drastically disrupts the film's dominant style. (As reference, one may point to a Hollywood film of similar length and comparable distinction: *I Walked with a Zombie*, which no one is likely to consider overedited, contains just over five hundred shots.)

*The static camera.* I have noted the long take as a stylistic preference crossing Mizoguchi's various periods; but the long takes of *Sisters of the Gion* are radically different from those of the films of the forties and the fifties. There, the camera moves in the great majority of shots, its movement involving the viewer in the action (though never in the kind of direct point-of-view identification associated with, for example, Hitchcock). Here, on the contrary, camera movements are sparse, the exception rather than the rule; we remain spectators, never participants.

*The long shot.* Mizoguchi's cinema generally favors the long shot, but never in the later films as rigorously as here. With few exceptions (an obvious one is the brief scene of Omocha preparing herself for what she believes to be a date with a wealthy patron but which is in fact the "date" with Kimura that leaves her crippled), we are denied the "personalizing" effect of being brought in close to the characters, watching their expressions, sharing their emotions. In the late films, the distance between camera and actors shifts continuously during a single take; in *Sisters of the Gion*, on the relatively rare occasions when the camera moves, it does so to *preserve* distance, receding slightly if the characters move forward.

*Flatness.* In the later films Mizoguchi is at great pains to communicate that sense of space associated with "Realist" cinema and extolled and theorized by André Bazin—the sense of a world continuing beyond the frame. Hence the preoccupation with foreground/background relationships, with depth of field, with characters entering and exiting the frame. This is perhaps especially striking in the creation of tiny detail irrelevant to the immediate action (though not to considerations of mood and atmosphere, which in the late films assume immense importance): as the four protagonists of *Ugetsu Monogatari* push off the boat for the celebrated sequence of the lake crossing, we see tiny figures scuttling through the mist in very distant long shot (and at the extreme top of the screen); in *Sansho Dayu*, as the mother and children move toward the water for a similar (and similarly disastrous) journey, a tiny figure, stooped and sinister, creeps across the image in the far background. Where space in these films is opened up, in *Sisters ofthe Gion* it is claustrophobic; characters are placed centrally in the image, the edge of the frame is crossed very rarely, background action is virtually eliminated.

**▌▐**

## *My Love Has Been Burning* (1949)

*My Love Has Been Burning*, made thirteen years later during the American occupation, offers a fascinating comparison, which will further demonstrate why I believe that style can never be usefully separated from substance. What is right for the earlier film would be absolutely wrong for the later. The comparison also gives me the opportunity to attract attention to a still little-known film that I would number (along with *Sisters of the Gion*) among Mizoguchi's dozen or so masterpieces (has any other filmmaker given us so many?).

In *Sisters of the Gion* Mizoguchi comes as close as is probably possible, within a narrative form, to denying the spectator the pleasures of identification altogether. *My Love Has been Burning* is another matter entirely: within the Mizoguchi oeuvre (or what of it I am familiar with), it occupies, with its close companion piece *Victory of Women*, the furthest opposite extreme. In the films of Mizoguchi's final period, although the women are consistently the chief objects of compassion (one might almost say, in certain cases, reverence), identification is typically divided among several characters. This is most obviously the case in *Street of Shame*, with its multiple plotlines, but it is also true of *Ugetsu* and *Sansho Dayu*, where the women share centrality with the male figures. *My Love Has Been Burning* offers its audience a single, central figure with whom—at least on the emotional level—we are encouraged to identify totally and unreservedly.

Was Mizoguchi's capitulation to the "Western codes" prompted by the problems of adapting to the imperatives of the American occupation? Perhaps. The capitulation is in any case highly selective, Mizoguchi seizing upon certain congenial aspects of the codes (he continues to reject, for example, the shot/reverse-shot figure that is such a staple of Hollywood editing) and pushing them to extremes, with the result that, while there is no single moment for which stylistic equivalents might not be found in Wyler or Welles, the film as a whole has no parallel in Hollywood production. Certainly one must admire the intransigence of an artist (Bresson, for example) who refuses all compromise, but such an artist will have difficulty flourishing within an overwhelmingly commercial industry (Ozu was fortunate in that the subject matter of his films secured him a sufficient popular following).

There is another type (more common, but perhaps no less admirable) who is able to make a virtue of necessity, accepting imposed restrictions but discovering ways of turning them to his/her advantage. All the major figures who have been able to sustain a career in Hollywood are of this kind. Take a simple and celebrated example: critics have often singled out the deep focus shots through open doorways or amid rock formations in *The Searchers* as instances of Ford's artistry and personal signature. Yet the film was prominent in Warners' brief venture into VistaVision, with its extreme clarity and quasi-three-dimensional depth of field, and it is at least plausible that the famous doorway shots (though not without precedent in Ford's work) were initially motivated by the studio's demands for the exploitation of the new medium—demands that Ford found compatible and on which he capitalized enthusiastically. Or consider the response of certain artists to censorship: Satyajit Ray, filming *The World of Apu* and, confronted with the necessity of expressing erotic tenderness within a cinema that forbade even kissing, communicating Apu's tenderness for his new wife by having him discover one of her hairpins on the pillow beside him, a moment one may find more authentically erotic, in the delicacy of its suggestion and the actor's smile, than any of the sequences of naked heaving bodies to which we are now accustomed; or Buñuel, prohibited from showing Viridiana moving in with her cousin at the close of the film that bears her name, having her instead sit down to a three-handed card game with the cousin and his housekeeper/mistress/victim.

I have no sense whatever, watching *My Love Has Been Burning*, of constriction or compromise, let alone of cynical opportunism—rather, of the delighted seizing of a marvelous opportunity. The film's stylistic choices are, as in *Sisters of the Gion*, perfectly congruent with the subject matter, just as systematic, just as rigorous; they happen to be—necessarily—different choices.

Omocha (the closest to an identification figure that *Sisters of the Gion* allows) is not an authentic feminist heroine: at no point does she *oppose* the socioeconomic system, she merely seeks to exploit its possibilities for women (never understanding that they don't exist), so ends up, as she began, trapped within it. Eiko Hirayama (Kinuyo Tanaka), on the other hand (the central character in *My Love Has Been Burning*), is above all a *politicized* figure; her stand against women's oppression is from the start fully conscious, although, at first, she is not fully aware of the odds. The film, essentially, is constructed as her and the audience's shared learning experience: if the audience did not identify with her, the film would fail. Hence its central stylistic strategy, a figure established near the beginning and repeated with variations at key moments throughout the film, which is also the film's means of building identification (never, in Mizoguchi, a simple matter of subjective camera or point-of-view editing). Mizoguchi retains the long take, adding camera movement and adapting it to the particular exigencies of his narrative (there are actually *fewer* shots—110, to *Sisters'* 123—although the film is about twenty-five minutes longer).

We watch the arrival by boat of a celebrated feminist leader and teacher (based, like Hirayama herself, on an actual historical figure). Hirayama, a simple schoolteacher, in long shot, her back to the camera, emerges from the crowd of welcomers and introduces herself; the leader responds cordially, inviting Hirayama to talk with her later, before she becomes swallowed up in the crowd; the camera (which moves freely in all the film's long takes) tracks in on Hirayama (now facing us), though never approaching closer than medium-long-shot (a distance maintained throughout the film), so that we see her expression of joy and inspiration. The film's subject is Hirayama's education in full feminist awareness, each sequence constituting a painful "lesson" which the spectator is invited to share: she must learn, especially, the dangers, within a culture built on structures of power and domination, of trusting too readily (especially men). We experience what she experiences (though never through her eyes, in any literal sense), the film's many sequence-shots-with-camera-movement analyzing the action and closing (in most cases) on Hirayama as she registers its significance. In the course of the film she must learn to reject, systematically, those variously trapped within the patriarchal mindset: first her parents, then her first lover Hayase (Eitaso Ozawa), finally her second lover Omoi (Ichiro Sugai), the supposedly enlightened and progressive leader of the "Liberal" party, all of whom in different ways and to differing degrees betray her trust. At the end of the film, disillusioned but determined to continue the struggle, she has only Chiyo (Mitsuko Mito), the servant girl victimized by both gender and class position. The film's final sequence-shot, in which Chiyo joins Hirayama on the train, ready to begin her own education, closes on the two women in medium shot, Hirayama holding Chiyo in her arms and wrapping her within her dazzlingly white shawl, which floods the screen with its radiance. If Omocha, in her lonely and unscrupulous rebellion, will always be defeated, we feel that Hirayama, armed with the understanding she has reached, will never be.

This figuration takes on additional meaning in the film's penultimate scene. Hirayama has discovered that her lover and colleague, Omoi, leader of the "progressive" party and just voted into office, has been using her protégée (and the couple's servant) Chiyo as his mistress: Chiyo is a "low" woman, and that's how "low" women are meant to be used. Hirayama leaves, to found a college for women where they will be taught to fight patriarchal oppression. But the camera remains, after she has gone, to move in to frame Omoi (and subsequently Chiyo, who moves into the frame), showing him (perhaps!) beginning to learn, as Hirayama has been learning throughout the film. There is nothing sentimental or indulgent in this moment, which strengthens rather than weakens the film's feminist statement by suggesting that men are capable of learning from women.

**III**

## Ugetsu Monogatari (1953)

Mizoguchi's final period seems to me more complicated and problematic than has commonly been acknowledged; certainly, it can no longer be taken as self-evident that it contains his greatest works. The rash assumption of its supremacy (dating from the 1950s) rested upon a number of factors: the early work was little known and largely inaccessible; the films on which the valuation was based were those that won prizes at international film festivals, specifically *Ugetsu Monogatari* (chosen to represent Mizoguchi in the *Cahiers du Cinéma*'s list of the "ten best films ever made," at a time when that magazine had the prestige of including among its critics most of the leading prospective filmmakers of the nouvelle vague—Godard, Truffaut, Chabrol, Rivette, Rohmer . . . ), *Sansho Dayu*, and (to a lesser extent) *Chikamatsu Monogatari* and *The Life of Oharu*—all, significantly, *jidai-geki*; the numerous other works from this prolific period were as little known as the earlier films. Personally, I think this very high valuation of these films (especially the first two) still stands, and is in fact unassailable: it has withstood the assaults of

Noel Burch (capitulation to the "Western codes") and certain feminist critics such as Frieda Freiberg (*Women in Mizoguchi Films* [Melbourne, 1981]) (Mizoguchi reneges on his earlier feminism and celebrates women as sacrificial victims). Among the late works they are stylistically the most adventurous, aesthetically the most beautiful, emotionally the deepest and most complex. The other films of the period (surely the most varied in subject matter since Mizoguchi's early days), while never undistinguished, cannot be numbered among his finest works.

What happened? The most respectable explanation (and clearly of great importance in understanding *Ugetsu* and *Sansho*) is his conversion to Buddhism, seemingly as abrupt as his conversion to Marxism in the 1930s, but also, on the evidence of the films, as genuine. (If he had lived another ten years, would it also have been as short-lived?) The least acceptable (though not necessarily without a grain of truth) is simply that he was growing old and losing something of his creative drive, settling back into an acquiescence in stylistic conformity (the "Western codes") and producing work that lacks the passion and rage of earlier periods. Supportive evidence for this might be found in, for example, *A Geisha* (aka *Gion Festival Music*), which was once erroneously regarded as a "remake" of *Sisters of the Gion*, but its subject matter offers enough parallels to invite comparison. Here, the submission to the "Western codes" becomes complete; stylistically, there is nothing in the film that could not be paralleled in the work of the finest mainstream Hollywood filmmakers (George Cukor, for example). Protest is still demonstrably present, but it is less naked, muted by the evident desire to produce "rounded" characters: the male exploiters, though portrayed unsympathetically, are far less dehumanized; where Omocha and Umekichi represented *positions* rather than the complex characters of "realist" fictions, the women of *A Geisha*, Miyoharu and Eiko, are presented as women trying to maintain a certain integrity in a male-dominated society that constantly threatens them, naively believing that you can become a geisha without being coerced into sex or (in Eiko's case) raped.

A third explanation, less honorable than these: After *Rashomon* (1951) won its European award and opened Japanese cinema to the West, Mizoguchi became obsessed with gaining international recognition (even, according to legend, going to the length of taking with him to Venice a miniature Buddhist shrine and praying that *Ugetsu* would get the prize). Cynics may argue that we owe *Ugetsu* and *Sansho* to Mizoguchi's shrewdly opportunist recognition that what Western audiences required of Japanese movies was a taste of the "exotic," especially "period" films with plenty of "atmosphere" and what semioticians would call "Japanese-icity."

Indeed, all three of these explanations may have been, to varying degrees, contributing factors; but anyone who thinks the last is sufficient in itself is incapable of recognizing authentic creativity. In these films Mizoguchi develops certain potentialities inherent in the "Western codes" to a peak of expressivity that is probably unsurpassable in the direction he has chosen—the potentialities of Renaissance painting (perspective, the illusion of three-dimensional space, foreground and distance, the placing and framing of people and objects) translated into the potentialities of mise-en-scène, which permit the addition of movement, both within the frame and of the camera.

It is true that we have come a long way, here, from the materialism (in both the capitalist and Marxist senses) of *Sisters of the Gion*, and also from the passionately feminist demand for social change of *My Love Has Been Burning*. The break with the former is absolute, with the latter perhaps not quite: the "love" of the title, which is essentially Hirayama's love for women and commitment to their liberation, already has strong spiritual associations. Today, arguably more than ever, we need a cinema of protest, and it is easy to see why the greatest works of Mizoguchi's last period are out of fashion. Their emphasis on the spiritual and mystical, on transcendence, on a withdrawal from the cruelties of the material world into a more private world of acceptance, implicit everywhere in the films' aesthetic beauty ("style" and "content," as always, being one), will inevitably be mistaken for a retreat into reaction and conservatism, the triumph not only of the "Western codes" but of "bourgeois ideology," by those committed to the denial that life *has* a spiritual dimension. But one must ask what, exactly, is being accepted in these films? Certainly not the cruelties of the world: rage and protest are still there in abundance, although they are no longer the films' be-all and end-all. The acceptance is not "acceptance *of*" but "acceptance *despite*": the horrors perpetrated by human beings cannot be accepted, but they can, with great pain and loss, be transcended.

The charge that the films represent a betrayal of Mizoguchi's earlier feminism can I think be easily discredited. For one thing, the late *jidai-geki* are all based on preexisting texts; for another, Mizoguchi is always scrupulously faithful to the realities of the precise period in which they are set, not merely the costumes and architecture but the mores, the social conventions, the gender positions available. Does anyone imagine that an Omocha or a Hirayama could have existed or survived in feudal Japan, where *giri* was the overriding principle in all relationships? (It is interesting in this connection that the subplot of *Ugetsu*, with its extremely assertive and angry wife, derives not from a source in Japanese literature but from a tale by Guy de Maupassant.) The films exist, in any case, beside the late *gendai-geki* (modern-dress films) in close juxtaposition: the "sacrificial victims" of *Sansho* and *Ugetsu* must be seen in relation to the fury and disgust with which Mizoguchi depicts the social situation of the prostitutes of *Street of Shame* (a political work if ever there was one), their degradation by men within a culture that is supposed to be leaving feudalism behind.

It might in fact be illuminating to reorganize Mizoguchi's films not in the chronological order of their production but in their historical chronology, from the eleventh-century *Sansho Dayu* to the contemporary (in 1956) *Street of Shame*: one would see, I think, that Mizoguchi was consistently sensitive to the *historical* positions of women in Japanese culture, the options open to them in every period. If he had lived another decade he might well have discovered a whole new thematic and manner of address in feminist activism.

*Ugetsu Monogatari* is a far harder film to describe (both thematically and stylistically) than *Sisters of the Gion* or *My Love Has Been Burning*. Twenty-five years ago I would have assumed that this automatically made it also, by definition, a greater one, as its difficulty is clearly one of complexity rather than confusion, and complexity seemed to me then the fundamental prerequisite of great art. I am no longer so convinced of this, yet the film continues to draw me to it like a magnet: few years go by without my watching it again. Its complexity (its problem?) lies in that its meaning is no longer (like that of the films discussed above) clearcut or single-minded. Is it a "Buddhist" meditation on the material world ("Vanity of vanities, saith the Preacher, All is vanity") and the possibility of transcendence, or a very earthly assault on "masculinity" and its cost for women? Certainly it seems to be both. Is it a denunciation of the aesthetic beauty which (via the Lady Wakasa) it also celebrates? Yes, confusing as that sounds. What exactly is the relationship between subplot and main plot? Do they simply coexist as parallels, or does one throw particular light on the other (Tobei's transgressions appearing so much coarser, so much more *obviously* foolish and destructive, than Genjuro's)? Is the Lady Wakasa evil, a fairly precise parallel to the City Woman of *Sunrise*? Or another victim? I sense that Mizoguchi's inability or refusal to supply pat answers to these questions is what the film is actually about. If this is "confusion," it is confusion very consciously orchestrated, and perhaps that is the point where confusion becomes complexity.

I am not, therefore, going to presume to "explain" *Ugetsu* (as I attempted to do, in my youthful forty-year-old arrogance, twenty-five years ago). I shall instead offer a number of "probes," a recourse that will seem cowardly to those who believe in pat answers, but which I increasingly recommend to anyone foolish enough to try to elucidate great works of art.

1. The title *Ugetsu Monogatari* is taken from a book of fantastic stories by Akinori. "Monogatari" means "tale" or "tales"; "Ugetsu" is a certain phase of the moon. An approximate translation of the title appears to be "Tales of the Rain-dimmed Moon," which beautifully evokes both the film's visual

poetry, its shadow worlds of light and shade, and also its elusiveness of meaning. It in fact uses three stories, two from Akinori's collection (the story about the ghost princess, the story about the ghost wife) fused to construct the main plot, with de Maupassant's "A Decoration" providing the barely recognizable subplot. One of the film's complications ensued from studio interference—in Mizoguchi's conception, the subplot was to culminate in Tobei and Ohama achieving worldly glory as samurai and courtesan respectively, but the producers found the irony either too harsh or liable to be misunderstood. The original scheme, then, proposed precisely balanced parallel opposites: Genjuro (Masayuki Mori) loses the world but saves his soul, Tobei (Sakae Ozawa) loses his soul but gains the world. In the film as we have it, Tobei, confronted by his responsibility for his wife's degradation, abandons his ambitions and returns to the dogged tilling of the land.

2. More interesting, however, is Mizoguchi's partial transformation of the "ghost princess" story. Akinori's original is called "Lure of the White Serpent," and Wakasa does indeed turn into just such a creature at its climax: she is quite simply a demon, a figure of supernatural evil and no more. By transforming her into the agonizingly human (if still supernatural) Lady Wakasa (Machiko Kyo), Mizoguchi both complicates and deepens the tale. By combining Akinori's two tales of the ghost princess and the ghost wife, and combining in Genjuro their male protagonists, Mizoguchi seems to invite us to draw parallels between the apparent opposites, Miyagi (Kinuyo Tanaka) and Wakasa. Both are the victims of patriarchal presumption, both die, and both are essentially Genjuro's victims.

3. With its archetypal good wife/errant husband/"bad" woman triangle, the main plot of Ugetsu invites comparison with Sunrise, which seems to me very illuminating. Some might regard the difference as essentially cultural, Murnau's film grounded in the oppressed and oppressive, airless atmosphere of German Expressionism, Mizoguchi's in the traditions of the Japanese visual arts, with their refinement, delicacy, sense of perennial freshness, every object and detail appearing to have breathing space. But with the cultural difference (and of course inseparably connected to it) is a personal one. Elsewhere in this book I have discussed Sunrise as Murnau's act of self-oppression; in contrast, I take from Mizoguchi's films a sense of personal freedom, of the free functioning of creativity, to which even his freedom to change and adapt from period to period might be felt to attest. The two films' lakeside sequences, in which the man surrenders himself to the Erotic, offer a particularly fascinating comparison. In Murnau the Erotic is associated with night, fog, and mud; in Mizoguchi with dawn, fresh air, sparkling water, openness, beauty, it becomes the realm of the Japanese Aesthetic. Murnau's City Woman (with strong connections to the hideous vampire of

*Nosferatu*) is allowed no sympathy or compassion, she is a purely destructive figure; Mizoguchi's ghost princess is a touching, vulnerable figure, associated with art and beauty, and ultimately as much a victim as Miyagi, Genjuro's betrayed and abandoned wife. She is thereby at the center of the film's problems of interpretation, rendering the simplistic moral code of *Sunrise* inoperable.

The realm of the erotic is also, in a quite literal sense, the realm of Art, the environment in which Genjuro is shown by Wakasa the exquisite art objects which he appears to recognize and accept as his own works but which we know he could not possibly have made in the "real" world, the world in which he lives with Miyagi and their child (apart from the question of his apparent abilities, where could he have got the materials?). We must take the objects as the works of another, possible Genjuro, a Genjuro who might-have-been. The crucial point is that this "possible" Genjuro corresponds to a "possible" Mizoguchi, a Mizoguchi who could, if it would have satisfied him, have contented himself with producing works of exquisite aestheticism and nothing else. That he was fully capable of this is amply demonstrated in this central segment of *Ugetsu*; witness its culminating sequence: Wakasa takes Genjuro to the little pool formed by a hot spring, in which we see him reclining as she tends him. Then she moves around to the far side and begins to disrobe, the camera remaining on Genjuro as he watches in delighted fascination. Then, when we hear (but do not see) her enter the pool, he lunges ecstatically across toward her, and the camera, instead of following him, moves away in the opposite direction, its delicacy and tact heightening the implication of eroticism by leaving what ensues to our imagination. There is then a rapid track with dissolves over grass, ending in what, from the viewpoint of "pure" aestheticism, must be the film's most beautiful composition—the lovers on a fine lawn by the lake, in the half-light of dawn, a single tree at the water's edge, the delicate tracery of its branches silhouetted against the shimmering lake, the square of fabric on which the lovers disport themselves placed obliquely both to the camera and to the lake's edge, creating an intricate pattern of intersecting sight lines. The moment (and the entire segment) is immediately "placed" by the sequence that follows, plunging us back into the horrors and terrors of the "real" world and reminding us that Mizoguchi never made "art for art's sake": his aesthetic sensibility is always subjected to the discipline of *meaning*.

4. The "placing" of the realm of the aesthetic/erotic is not, however, achieved exclusively by its context; the critique is implicit in the segment itself, in which "high" art is clearly associated with privilege and patriarchy. Wakasa herself is a work of art (whereas we are surely to view Miyagi as a work of "nature"), a patriarchal construction embodying the masculine con-

cept of an ideal feminine beauty. She tells Genjuro that everything she knows about art appreciation was taught her by her father; her clothes, her graceful movements, her delicate mincing steps, her dance gestures, her singing are all the product of that careful training that "perfects" the woman as object for the male gaze. The point reaches explicitness during her song (itself a celebration of "choicest silks" as much as of love), when the long-departed father suddenly joins in, the lights dim, and the camera tracks across the darkened room to show what is left of him: a grotesque skull-like mask with a gaping, devouring hole where the mouth should be, and from which the voice (admired by the aged nurse precisely for its "masculinity") appears to be issuing. (There is a parallel scene in *Sansho Dayu*, though without the supernatural element—the scene of the visit to Sansho's labor camp by the envoy from the Minister of the Right, for which occasion Sansho stages an elaborate dance performance which no one watches, the envoy being far more interested in the gold and jewels in the tribute chest. Here the display of aesthetic beauty, useless if prestigious, is placed in the context of the horrific conditions of life within the compound.)

5. Wakasa's father, a former great feudal warlord, can stand as a succinct embodiment, at its most grotesque extension, of "masculinity" as represented in the film. For, if *Ugetsu* can be claimed as a feminist film (and I think it can), it is not so much in its depiction of women's suffering as in its absolutely uncompromising analysis of masculinity and its devastating effects. All the film's disasters, from the cosmic to the individual, can be traced to the masculinist drive for power, domination, acquisition, in all its manifestations.

This is most explicit in the representation of war and the military in its various strata, from the warlords down through the samurai (to whose ranks Tobei aspires, abandoning Ohama [Mitsuko Mito] to rape and prostitution), to the starving soldiers who kill Miyagi; put crudely, it is men who make wars and it is women who are the prime sufferers. But male egoism assumes subtler forms in the leading protagonists: not merely Tobei's absurd ambition, "boundless as the ocean," to participate in the "glory" of battles and butchery, but Genjuro's money greed and, subsequently, under the influence of the ghost princess, his greed for fame as a great artist and his naive response to the flattering attentions of a beautiful, wealthy, and aristocratic woman.

What is one to make of the wandering Buddhist priest? I have always found him an arbitrary recourse, a mere deus ex machina necessary to bring Genjuro back to his senses. But if we see him (as I think the film invites us) from Wakasa's viewpoint, he becomes an extension of the theme of the patriarchal oppression of women into religion as a further male-dominated, male-constructed instrument of oppression and denier of the erotic. I leave the question open. But however ambivalently one views him (an agent of good? an agent of evil?), I still find his introduction into the film abrupt and unprepared.

6. The question of identification is especially interesting in *Ugetsu*, where we find neither the rigorous denial of *Sisters of the Gion* nor the single-minded endorsement of *My Love Has Been Burning*. The women remain the *emotional* center of the film: from the outset, Miyagi's gentle rebukes and Ohama's furious diatribes tell us quite unambiguously that the men are simply *wrong*. Yet it is the men who carry the action and determine the whole course of the narrative, it is the men whose exploits and experiences we follow throughout the film, with the brief exceptions of the sequences showing Ohama's rape and descent into prostitution and the mortal wounding of Miyagi. The men are our identification figures on one level, the women on another; to put it crudely, we *learn* with the men, we *suffer* with the women. The men never entirely forfeit our sympathy, simply because their behavior and their aims are so recognizably "human," not in the sense of some indelible "human nature" but in the sense in which gender roles have been largely taken for granted in our cultural past. Yet the women make so strong an impression in the vulnerability of their social situation that we never forget them even when they are absent for long stretches of screen time. The overall effect, consistently traceable in the film's stylistic choices, the camera in the great majority of shots moving freely with the characters but always maintaining a contemplative distance, is of simultaneous involvement and detachment: we are invited to "see things whole," the characters always placed within a world that is "real" even when fantastic, moving within landscapes and decor at once tangible and mysterious.

7. The film's final segment centers our attention on the child, who seemed hitherto little more than a "prop," at most a means of increasing the vulnerability and pathos of Miyagi's predicament. As Genjuro kneels at Miyagi's grave and we hear her voice telling him that she has not left, she is here beside him, the camera tracks slightly left to reveal the child kneeling beside his father; if Miyagi lives on (in a practical as well as metaphysical sense), it is in the form of the *male* child for whose life she gave hers. The sense of reconciliation that the film so powerfully conveys is not restricted to the Buddhist notion of transcendence (which I have no desire to downplay), not only mystical: it is also a reconciliation of traditional gender opposition, the child at once closely associated with the father and identified with the mother. Hence the film ends with the celebrated tracking/crane shot that echoes by inversion its opening: handed his bowl of rice, the child runs with it to the grave to share it with his mother as an offering and a symbol

of remembering and belonging; the camera cranes up to show, in the far distance, two other men working in a field, reminding us of a whole world in which the individual destiny is controlled by forces beyond its control, but which it can ultimately transcend.

# CHAPTER II

# "Persona" Revisited

What follows is part addendum to, part correction of, the account of *Persona* I offered in my book on Ingmar Bergman almost thirty years ago. That account was written after my first few viewings of this inexhaustibly fascinating, disturbing, and difficult work, and at the height of the widespread "Bergmania" in which I shared, leading me to gloss over aspects of the film (or, more precisely, its second half) which I believe I always found troubling. The tendency to repress one's own doubts about a film one admires and wishes to celebrate is not an uncommon critical failing (which does not of course excuse it). What was then, and perhaps remains today, the most influential account of *Persona*—Susan Sontag's in *Against Interpretation*—seems to me guilty of the same fault and for similar reasons: it was written in the heat of excited discovery, with insufficient exposure to the film, a state of mind that also accounts for its demonstrable errors (never corrected in its numerous reprints, and still reproduced by students in their essays), of which the most damaging is the assertion that it is Alma who sucks Elisabet's blood (rather than vice versa) in the hallucinatory later sequences. The mistake is damaging precisely because it violates the integrity of the women's very clearly defined characters, which never disintegrate or merge to *that* extent, and in doing so undermines Sontag's basic thesis, that the film resists all traditional methods of interpretation. To claim that a film not only cannot but *should not* be interpreted seems to me simply another form of evasion, allowing the critic to sweep aside all possible problems and deflecting any inconvenient questions of value.

I still stand by the main thrust of my previous account, the relevance of which has scarcely lessened in an age that has given us the Gulf War Massacre, the horrors of Bosnia-Herzogovina and Somalia, the rise to prominence of the serial killer, the daily revelations of the pervasiveness within our own culture of child abuse and violence against women. But I want to reopen the question of *Persona* (1966) from a somewhat different (but not incompatible) perspective, without repudiating my earlier testimony to the film's extraordinary first impact. I don't think I can say now what I said then any better: I simply want to say something else. And, by way of leading to the "something else," I want to fill in what now appears, inescapably, the gaping hole in my earlier analysis, an undertaking made possible by social developments of which I have only become aware since the early 1970s—feminism, the gay/lesbian movement, the interrogation of gender and sexuality. These have, it seems to me, *necessarily* changed our whole attitude to cinema, often revolutionizing the interpretation of specific movies, revealing what was always there but not acknowledged: it now seems, for example, that the von Sternberg/Dietrich films of the 1930s were previously incomprehensible.

The "gaping hole" can be defined simply by asking, Is it possible to imagine a version of *Persona* in which the two leading characters are men, an actor and a male nurse? (The reader is invited here to pause and make the attempt . . . )

The answer must I think be no, or, at most, "only with extreme difficulty, and it would be a different film." And it is worth considering that both Sontag and myself refer to the issue of lesbianism only casually, within a single sentence. She at least *used* the word; I acknowledged this (as I now see it) crucial aspect of the film only in a passing reference to Alma's wanting Elisabet as "combined elder-sister-and-lover." Again, as in the chapter on Ozu, I am employing the term *lesbian* here in its widest sense; patriarchy likes to have it as merely indicating something "kinky" and perhaps titillating. Here it implies: the bonding of women in mutual support against male dominance; the refusal to accept that a woman is defined by her relationships with men; the sufficiency of woman-to-woman relationships (which may include, but are not restricted to or necessarily defined by, sexuality).

Bergman has often been accused of opportunism in his use of political actualities lifted out of their context and reduced to signifiers of an inner, psychological turmoil: the Vietnam and Warsaw Ghetto images in *Persona*, the parallels between Vietnam and his imaginary, ideologically vague, civil war in *The Shame*. Such charges, which seemed valid at the time (and perhaps on a superficial level remain so), must also be looked at in their historical context: they belong to a period before the more profound and radical revelations of the women's movement had received any wide dissemination and acceptance. At its deepest levels, *Persona* has only gradually become readable over the past few decades; like *The Shame* (in many respects a more expository, more lucid, more *conscious* development of its essential themes), it exists at the confluence of "politics" and sexual politics. Hence it allows me to take up, and bring into sharper focus, the concerns of chapter 2 ("Fascism/Cinema").

"Natural causes," "acts of God" aside, it seems clear that the manifold horrors of our world, which it is imperative now that we face squarely if we are to survive, must be attributed overwhelmingly to men: to men as individuals (for the issues of personal responsibility and personal guilt must not be evaded), but more fundamentally to masculinity, as it has been socially constructed, and to its political extension "masculinism." Every political system in the world today (and as far back as history can take us) has been male-founded and continues to be male-dominated; the women who slot into these systems (as opposed to rejecting and opposing them) are able to do so only at the cost of repudiating their female specificity—their integrity as women—and denying the *fact* of women's oppression throughout history and continuing into the history that we are currently living. It is vitally important that "herstory" be written, but the achievements it celebrates will inevitably be, by and large, the achievements of resistance. The female guards we see emerging from the concentration camps at the end of *Night and Fog* (to whom the female psychiatrist of *Persona* bears a startling and significant resemblance) can stand as a grotesque but not inappropriate image of what women do to themselves when they lend themselves (for their own survival or for material betterment) to patriarchy and masculinism.

When Elisabet (Liv Ullmann) cowers, appalled, from the Vietnam newsreel, and stares in horrified fascination at the Warsaw Ghetto photograph, she is expressing the sense of powerlessness that women (and sensitive males) experience in the face of horrors wrought by masculinism: the horrors that reproduce themselves in generation after generation in the names of imperialism, nationalism, patriotism, organized religion, every existing system of which is at every level patriarchal—founded by men, sustained by men, promoted by men, for the validation and safeguarding of male privilege. What the first (and finest) movement of *Persona* so magnificently and subtly dramatizes is the gradual, tentative empowerment of women through female bonding—"lesbianism" in the wider sense. The bonding, fragile from the start, disintegrates, for reasons that are to some extent inherent from the outset, for Elisabet and Alma are incompatible not from mere differences of character but on the deepest levels, more cultural than personal.

The difference is sometimes seen in terms of innocence and experience, but that is too simple; it is more profitable to describe it in terms of conformity and nonconformity, acquiescence in and resistance to social conditioning, the woman who enters into and accepts her "correct" position in the

"Symbolic Order" of patriarchy and the woman who refuses. Bergman's choice of *Electra* as the play during which Elisabet (at first intuitively, later as a conscious decision) chooses not to speak gets great emphasis from the repeated images of the actress on stage and in costume. A puzzling choice at first sight: Bergman has shown little interest in Greek tragedy, either as a filmmaker or a theatrical producer. He has, however, from very early in his career shown a marked interest in Freud, and Freud's first term for what he subsequently chose to call the "female Oedipus complex" was the "Electra complex"—the process by which the female learns to accept her patriarchally prescribed role, relinquishing the father and her own innate masculinity, identifying with the symbolically castrated mother. (The inappropriateness of the Electra myth, in which Electra identifies with the father and assists in the mother's murder, to Freud's theory seems screamingly obvious, and one understands why he abandoned the term. Yet it lingers on in general parlance, and I am convinced that Bergman had it in mind here.) By refusing to continue with the play (she completes that performance, then withdraws into total silence), Elisabet is rejecting her "correct" positioning in the Symbolic Order.

As Elisabet is often perceived as a "monster," evil and sadistic (a view of the character which the film's second half regrettably makes partly tenable), it is important to emphasize that, initially at least, Bergman invests her with quasi-heroic qualities of intelligence, integrity, compassion, and even nobility. This is established in the privileged moment when we first see her alone, outside Alma's point of view. Alma (Bibi Andersson) visits her in her room, opening the curtains to let in the sunlight, chattering to her in her cheerful, banal way, the socially sanctioned stereotype of the "good little nurse" perfect in her training, switching on the radio beside Elisabet's bed. A play is in progress, perhaps a fragment of a soap opera, in which a woman is begging for forgiveness. After a few seconds Elisabet begins to laugh, silently, bitterly, scornfully. Alma interprets the reaction purely in terms of the play's "bad acting," not questioning its content, and when Elisabet (in one of her abrupt changes of mood) angrily switches off the radio, treats her patient to some trite, well-intentioned, condescending remarks about the importance of art. It is clear that Alma's interpretation of Elisabet's reaction is incorrect, or at least incomplete. What Elisabet finds, first funny, then infuriating, is not merely the stilted acting but the play's stereotypical reproduction of patriarchy's prescription for the cure and incorporation into "normality" of the transgressive woman: to ask forgiveness. Alma then finds some classical music (nice and soothing, to distract a difficult patient from her psychological problems) and leaves the room.

The music is the slow movement of Bach's E Major Violin Concerto, and its potential effect is quite beyond Alma's comprehension. I noted in my book on Bergman the importance for him of Bach: his music is already quoted in *Wild Strawberries*, but it takes on its full significance in the later films, from *Through a Glass Darkly* on. Three instances seem particularly apposite here: the moment in *The Silence* when Ester (Ingrid Thulin), in the desolation of her life and a stale foreign hotel room, listens briefly to the "Goldberg Variations" on a transistor radio; the moment in *Cries and Whispers* of passionate "lesbian" contact between the two sisters (Thulin and Liv Ullmann), celebrated by the sudden surging on the soundtrack of one of the suites for unaccompanied cello; and the performance of another of the suites in *Autumn Sonata* that marks the one moment of repose and togetherness, wrought by the music. On one level the use of Bach's music is consistent through all these films: it signifies for Bergman a possible transcendent wholeness which our civilization has lost, a spiritual potential yearned for but forever beyond the characters' reach, the music's formal conventions reflecting the sense of a confident social order within which sorrow and disturbance continue to exist but can be contained. Hence, as Tony French points out in his supple and sensitive analysis of *Through a Glass Darkly* in *CineAction* 34, the specific piece chosen is not necessarily consoling, certainly not "nice and soothing" to anyone sensitive to its nuances, and this is certainly the case in *Persona*. Bergman's sensitivity to Bach is eloquently embodied in the mise-en-scène, which subtly but precisely "echoes" the music's progression. The piece, in the minor, is among Bach's most somber and tragic utterances, but Alma switches it on and leaves the room just before the magical, poignant moment when the mood briefly lightens, the music trying to modulate into the major: the effect is like a glimpse of pale sunlight appearing from behind cloud. At this point Elisabet turns directly into camera and full light. The image begins to darken at the exact moment when the minor key (in the obstinately recurring bass figure) definitively reasserts itself. Then, as if in response to the music's shift, Elisabet (the screen now in heavy shadow) turns away from us on to her back and covers her face with her hand in a gesture of despair. Those familiar with the work will know that the movement is contained between two of Bach's most exuberant and celebratory, a mood and a containment for which there can be no possible equivalent in the film or the torn and strife-filled world it represents, on both the personal and cosmic levels.

The rich implications of this moment (I know of no artist who, working at the peak of his/her creativity, can pack more meaning into a simple, almost "empty" scene) are developed in the second moment of intimacy we are permitted with Elisabet, outside Alma's consciousness—the "Vietnam" scene, which immediately follows, as if in explanation, Alma's "I wonder what's actually wrong with her?" I cannot agree with Hubert I. Cohen (in his meticulously researched, detailed, and perceptive *Ingmar Bergman: The Art of Confession*) in confidently asserting that this is Elisabet's "nightmare": one has only to invoke the freedom from "realist" convention that modernism permits, and the high level of stylization Bergman has by this point established, to accept it as a representation of a waking experience. But "nightmarish" the scene certainly is.

Elisabet paces her room at night, sleepless, troubled, her hands clasped and pressed to her chin in a gesture of frustration, as if she doesn't know what to do, or whether the decision she has made is any sort of answer. She moves to the door as if to open it—deciding, perhaps, to abandon her stance and make contact. Then she turns to the images on the television screen: a newsreel showing the self-immolation of a Buddhist monk, his will and his belief so strong that he can maintain the gesture of an arm raised in protest even as he burns agonizingly to death. Does she empathize with his agony, even as we (surely) empathize with her appalled recoil? Or does she see him as carrying her own protest to its logical conclusion, a conclusion that obviously terrifies her? It is evident, in any case, that on some level she identifies with him—with his agony, his desperation, his protest, his readiness to go all the way—in his acknowledgment of the masculinist horrors of a world characterized overall by aggression, domination, mindless cruelty, and helpless suffering, and in the possibility of passive protest and the awareness of its probable uselessness.

There follows immediately (the sequence of scenes is not arbitrary, one must search out its inner logic) the scene of the husband's letter, read aloud to her by Alma, confronting her with her "correct" but rejected role of wife and mother, increasing at once her rage and her guilt. The husband is sympathetic but quite uncomprehending, quoting a remark of Elisabet's made shortly before her withdrawal as if it were entirely devoid of irony or ambiguity: "Only now I understand what marriage is about." What he has learned from her is that they should look at each other as if they were two anxious children, full of kindness and good resolutions—including, presumably, the resolution to "be a good little girl"—his inability to comprehend his wife equalled by his sentimentalization of childhood. He then asks if she "remembers saying all that," suggesting at least the possibility that she didn't, that he is imposing on her his own interpretation: it must strike us as somewhat incongruous that she would follow such remarks by immediately "grabbing at his belt," presumably in a gesture of aggressive sexual desire or desperation. She crumples the letter and tears in two the enclosed photograph of their sickly-looking son.

Bergman moves from this at once to the scene with the psychiatrist, the most obvious logic of which is to follow Elisabet's decisive rejection of the traditional female roles with its contemporary alternative, the "strong" woman who has made her way in the man's world, on its terms, within yet another overwhelmingly patriarchal institution whose main function has become that of restoring its patients (victims?) to "normality" rather than to health. (The former would lead to conformity, the latter the impulse toward revolution.) She understands Elisabet about as thoroughly as the psychiatrist at the end of *Psycho* understands Norman Bates, with exactly the same motive of establishing her "knowledge" and "authority," and much the same aim, that of explaining her away as an unfortunate inconvenience. At least she seems somewhat less complacent, as if the struggle to keep at bay all the human realities that lie beyond and constantly threaten the ideological concept of "normality" were a terrific strain, won only at great human cost. To understand Elisabet would be to see that concept shattered irreparably, and her whole position threatened; she therefore resorts to a brutal, bitter sarcasm, cruel, insensitive, and repressive, if necessary for her own self-defense. (The character, who appears in the film less than five minutes, is surely among the most brilliant "cameos" in the cinema, a whole life, and the necessary judgment on it, suggested with extraordinary economy and precision.)

Alma, the good little girl who clasps her hands behind her back as she attends to the instructions of her "headmistress" in a classic stance of obedience, accepts her conditioning without question. She has chosen one of the professions considered appropriate for members of the "weaker sex," whose duty it is to serve; she identifies both with her own mother ("My mother was a nurse until she got married") in the "correct" Oedipal fashion, and with her mother figures, the retired nurses in the home she describes to Elisabet; she automatically assumes (it scarcely seems a choice) that she will marry Karl-Henrik and bear his children ("It's nothing to worry about. It's so safe"). The contact with Elisabet at once rescues her from this fate and condemns her to the desperation and torment which, at the end of the film, she may or may not be ready to transcend. The film (and Bibi Andersson) is quite extraordinary, I think, in suggesting that, while on the surface Alma is fully acquiescent in the patriarchal order and the woman's ignominious role within it, deep down she has always been aware of this falseness: Elisabet disturbs and frightens her from their first moments of contact.

Elisabet is a deeply disturbed woman, hence a potentially dangerous one. It is greatly to the film's credit that it fails to "explain" her in terms of personal psychology: her resistance to patriarchy, her refusal of "the dominant ideology," is sufficient. Those who remain comfortably within it cannot understand this. I have been during my life both "Alma" and "Elisabet," and I understand it very well. I also understand that "Alma" will always be a part of "Elisabet," just as "Elisabet" has always been a part of "Alma." The ideology is our home—the home in which we grew up. While we remain within it, however constricted and frustrated we may feel, we have "nothing to worry about. It's so safe": we know the rules. As soon as we step outside, renouncing it, we are alone, we have no bearings, there are no rules any more, we must discover new ones or construct our own. Though less abrupt, it is as frightening and disorienting as the experience of birth must be, when the infant leaves the security and warmth of the womb (even if it felt a bit uncomfortable at times) for a strange new world in which its first experience is usually to get slapped and made to scream. Like birth, it is also a necessary one, if our civilization is to progress and redeem itself. Hence the ambivalence of our feelings toward Elisabet: she is dangerous, frightening, "other," yet admirable and necessary. (It is usually those who refuse to see the two women as more than "characters," to be judged on the level of personal psychology and behavior, who find her a "monster.") What Bergman cannot do (because he is a man? because he is an inhabitant of a country where all the social problems are believed to have been solved by many years of quasi-socialist government, but where patriarchy and capitalism remain the dominant forces? or only because he is Bergman?) is dramatize the possibility of constructing a new "home" of solidarity and mutual supportiveness. It could never be as secure as the home we have relinquished, since it lacks the sanction of tradition, yet it makes life and further development possible, it enables us to develop our creativity, not negate it in impotent rage. It is surprising, however, how far the film goes—at least through its first half—in *suggesting* the possibility.

Elisabet's rejection of her role in the patriarchal order is remarkably complete, refusing all compromises; one might see her rigor as the positive aspect of her ruthlessness, or see the ruthlessness (which all but destroys Alma) as its unfortunate consequence. Before her silence, she has rejected both marriage and motherhood, and not merely as abstract ideas. The moment when she tears the photograph of her child is deeply shocking, registering the brutality, the stifling of "natural" feeling, the psychic cost, which the rigor enforces: she cannot allow herself to get sucked back into the life she has rejected, and the emotions that belong to it. (I shall return to Bergman's attitude to motherhood later, as it becomes a crux of the film's later episodes.) Her silence is the logical culmination of this process, at once the most rigorous statement of her refusal to participate in a system she repudiates and a retreat—the silence becoming as much a protective barrier as an assertion of defiance. It also strikingly anticipates the position that certain feminists have developed out of Lacan: language itself is patriarchal, the acquisition of language being a decisive step in entry into the Symbolic Order. The quandary this produces (if language is patriarchal, how can a feminist speak?) is not only Elisabet's.

## The Beach Orgy

The chink in Alma's armor is her memory, half shameful, half nostalgic, of the so-called "orgy" on the beach in which she and her friend Katerina had sex with two young boys, her one subversive and potentially liberating experience, though she cannot afford to let herself recognize it in those terms. Its significance lies in the thoroughness with which it breaks almost every traditional rule of sanctioned sexual contact, in which it is remarkably systematic.

- *Monogamy.* Not only is Alma "unfaithful" to Karl-Henrik, there are *two* boys involved in the encounter; although she only has intercourse with one of them (twice in fairly quick succession), the other, Katerina's partner, is in close proximity throughout.

- *Privacy.* There appear to be no spectators, but the activity takes place on a beach, not in the seclusion of a bedroom.

- *Children's sexuality.* We are not told the ages of the two boys, but it is clear (from the word *pojkar* and the fact that they need encouragement and guidance) that they are "boys" in the literal sense, presumably in their early teens, just pubescent, inexperienced.

- *Active female sexuality.* The women throughout take the active role, encouraging the boys for their own pleasure and reveling in their own sexuality outside the bounds of patriarchal containment.

- *Group sex.* It is clear from Alma's narration that much of the excitement and pleasure of the encounter come from sharing, watching each other, participating emotionally and sensually in each other's enjoyment. Hence,

- *Lesbianism.* The women do not have actual sexual contact with each other, but much of the stimulus arises from their close physical proximity.

The "orgy" bursts all the bonds of social convention that restrict the free expression of human (and especially women's) sexuality. But more important still are the two ways in which Bergman caps Alma's narrative. She tells Elisabet that after she got home the same night, she and Karl-Henrik made love, and it was better than it had ever been before. Alma finds this surprising but it is perfectly logical: far from damaging the couple's relationship, the encounter on the beach improved it by freeing the woman's desire, releasing previously unknown sexual energies. Inevitably, social convention was restored: the fact of the encounter couldn't be shared with her lover, and Alma, finding herself pregnant, had an abortion. It may seem incongruous to describe an abortion as the restoration of social convention, but it is clear here that the motivation was less Alma's reluctance to have a child than the inevitable uncertainty as to the child's parentage—the "correct" male line must be preserved.

The other way in which Bergman caps the narration is by concluding it with the two women in bed together, and with the first intimations of lesbian physical contact. Alma relives her experience by recounting it to Elisabet, and it is the act of *sharing* that makes this contact possible: Elisabet, touched by Alma's shame and confusion, comforts her by stroking her face and taking her in her arms. It is, on one level, a maternal gesture, a reminder that the source of lesbianism is in the intimate contact of mother and female child.

## The Lesbian "Fantasy"

The scene in which Alma, waking in the night, sees Elisabet coming into her room and they caress in front of a mirror is marked as a privileged moment in the film. It is the first sequence (if we leave aside the precredit and credit sequences) whose status in relation to the narrative's "reality" is uncertain, and this uncertainty is underlined by a stylistic break: instead of the clear high-definition images that have characterized the visual style up to that point, it has a misty, hallucinatory, dreamlike quality. But its status as dream or hallucination is not clear either: Alma first gets up for nothing more unusual than to get herself a drink of water, and the mistiness is rationally accounted for by the sound of a distant foghorn. It anticipates the notion of fusion that will become so prominent later (and to which it seems to me undue significance has been attached, by critics and by Bergman himself); but it does so in a strongly positive way, the intermingling of the two women in a gesture of great tenderness and intimacy suggesting the mutual identification from which Alma will later recoil violently in rage and horror, yet remaining here less a matter of "fusion" than of intimate togetherness. Most important, it represents the one *positive* memory that Alma retains at the end of the film, reliving it as she looks for the last time in a mirror before leaving the beach house, and reacting with an expression of regret and loss. If the film leaves us with any hope for Alma's future, it is surely in this retained image of female togetherness.

Is it offered as a "real" experience or as Alma's fantasy? We cannot, I think, be sure. If we incline to the latter it is largely because, when Alma asks her if she visited her in the night, Elisabet shakes her head and looks puzzled, and she has no immediately apparent reason to lie. And it is Alma who has so much to gain from achieving identity with a strong, independent, emancipated woman. Yet the film implies, through the specifics of cinematic progression from image to image, that Elisabet has also benefited from an experience that may have been another woman's fantasy. The shot that immediately follows the nocturnal lesbian encounter shows her in close-up, on the rocks by the sea the next morning, taking a photograph directly into camera: photographing the spectator, perhaps, but also, more immediately, the cameraman and, by implication, the director-screenwriter, the males who presume to control her both as the character Elisabet Vogler and as the actress Liv Ullmann. Never has the male gaze been returned more pointedly, empowered directly (if we respect the progress of the editing) by lesbian togetherness.

Given the radical breach of that moment—the look straight into camera at the persons controlling and viewing the film—it seems possible to question the authority of Elisabet's subsequent denial of the nocturnal encounter. I have tried (with the help of videotape) the experiment of watching twice in quick succession the moment of denial (Elisabet/Ullmann shaking her head), the first time assuming that she is telling the truth, the second assuming that she is lying because she can't cope with the implications—the responsibilities—of a close relationship with Alma. The image works perfectly both ways (a perfect validation of the "Kuleshov" experiment?). One has to ask, then, whether the ambiguity of the nocturnal union represents a fully achieved artistic effect (that is to say, of realized significance in the film's total context) or a hesitation, perhaps a fear, on the part of Bergman. For the ambiguity makes possible the film's subsequent perverse choice of narrative route, its descent into types of material that are disturbing in the wrong way—disturbing, that is, not because they confront us with an awareness of the horrors of our civilization but because they draw us into unproductive and essentially morbid personal obsessions, at the same time—and as necessary corollary—rejecting any possible alternative movement toward health. If Bergman's "breakdown" enabled him, in the first part of *Persona*, to move into completely new, potentially both rich and radical, areas, the reminder of the film can be read as a hysterical retreat back into the ambiguous comfort of neurosis.

When I wrote the book containing the earlier account of *Persona*, I failed sufficiently to acknowledge the ways in which Bergman's astonishing creativity
is repeatedly thwarted in the later films by neurotic blockage. In certain
films this takes a very precise form: the blockage is literally enacted in the
film's structure. There is a strong positive movement toward health,
abruptly halted by either a hiatus (*The Shame, A Passion*) or by the unprepared and arbitrary introduction of a new plot development (*The Touch*), followed in turn by the revelation that "everything has gone wrong"—the
"going wrong" produced not by any sort of narrative logic but by the arbitrary intervention of the author (literally, in *A Passion*, where Bergman's own
voice tells us that "six months have gone by and . . .").

*Persona* is a slightly different case because here the shift in tone is not
entirely unmotivated: whether the nocturnal visit took place or not, Alma
has clearly misread the *degree* of Elisabet's involvement with her; and the
fateful letter (especially if we take Elisabet's failure to seal it as an unconscious wish that Alma read it) is Elisabet's way of distancing herself from a
relationship that is getting out of hand and beginning to threaten her. All
this, and Alma's response to her illicit reading of the letter, is plausible
enough. One may ask, however, whether it is not altogether too flimsy a pretext to bear the symbolic and emotional weight of all that follows. Elisabet's
self-imposed silence may be theoretically admirable and heroic (though useless) as a response to the horrors of a masculinist-dominated world, but
when it prohibits all explanation and discussion with another equally distressed woman it becomes perverse cruelty, its original motivation pointless
in such a context. And one is forced to ask whether Bergman himself is not
unhealthily complicit in the cruelties and the anguish that overwhelm the
film's last third—whether the combination of sadism and masochism
belongs less to the fictional characters than to their (male) creator. Repeated
viewings (I have found) do nothing to clarify the obscurity of the "five
episodes" where the film moves into a dimension of psychic fantasy. My own
experience has been that the film's first half retains its fascination and its resonance, while the sections following Elisabet's perusal of the Warsaw
Ghetto photograph become increasingly difficult to sit through, not because
they are disturbing but because they yield so little, are merely unpleasant in
the worst sense, as representations not of the horrors of contemporary
human existence but of the artist's own sickness, in which he permits his
authentic creativity to drown.

Particularly obtrusive and (in the bad sense) disturbing—and, I might add,
on repetition *boring*—is the episode of the twice-told story. It is surely the
passage in the film that most taxes the viewer's patience, its insistent and

reiterated morbidity far exceeding any meaning one may legitimately extract from it. The meaning, however, such as it is, constitutes a significant part of the problem: the horror of Elisabet that the film communicates here (negating all the character's positive and heroic aspects) is motivated solely by the accusation that she was a bad mother, and the sequence culminates in Alma's appalled awareness (and hysterical rejection) of the notion that she and Elisabet have somehow merged, become identical, the only possible basis for which is that she, Alma, had an abortion. Worse, one cannot help wondering whether, on some (perhaps unconscious) level, Bergman equates what Elisabet is alleged to have done with the fate of the young boy in the Warsaw Ghetto. All sense of the admirable aspects of Elisabet and her protest is here submerged in Bergman's animus against a woman who rejected the role of nurturer.

That something damagingly personal (in the narrow sense) here throws the film askew seems confirmed some years later by one of the worst films of Bergman's maturity, *Autumn Sonata* (1978). Bergman's initial project seems to have been to balance, while pitting against each other, two embittered women (mother and daughter) and two great actresses (Ingrid Bergman and Liv Ullmann); and for its first half the film seems to be attempting to maintain a corresponding balance of sympathies (which it also makes a feeble attempt to restore in the cross-cutting of its conclusion). Progressively, the balance collapses, and the film degenerates into what amounts to a hysterical diatribe against a woman who neglected her children for her career as a great concert pianist. The parallel with Elisabet is obvious—the Charlotte of *Autumn Sonata* is virtually an elaboration of the "twice-told story." The worst that one can reasonably say of Charlotte is that she should never have married and had children in the first place: presumably, like Elisabet, she allowed herself to be propelled into an inappropriate role by conventional societal expectations of the "womanly." Yet by the film's climax every evil has been heaped upon her, culminating in the ludicrously irrational charge (which she, equally irrationally, is made to accept) that she was solely responsible for her younger daughter's incurable, and surely physiological, degenerative disease. Ullmann's summation of her mother's evil (which the film doesn't explicitly endorse but certainly doesn't contradict) has to be heard to be believed: "People like you are a menace. You should be locked away so you can't do any harm." It is common knowledge that Ingrid Bergman tried to rebel against the burdens of guilt and wickedness heaped upon her character; her own personal history might suggest that on some level (conscious or unconscious) Bergman was using the actress herself in a particularly cruel and malicious way. (One might compare—very favorably—Rossellini's complex and sympathetic ways of building on that same personal history, especially in *Europa 51.*)

With a naïveté quite astounding for an artist of such proven intelligence, Bergman insisted in an interview that he does not have an ideology (one might as well say, "I don't have a nervous system"). One must assume that he mistakes the ideology that has consistently circumscribed his achievement throughout his career—what one might define as "the ideology of the Human Condition"—for "truth": human relations are simply *like that*, it has little (if anything) to do with social organization (let alone the "economic base"), or with the construction of the individual psyche within a specific and analyzable cultural formation, and there is really nothing much anyone can do about it. Such a position was established very early in his career, and fully elaborated in the first film he both wrote and directed, *Fängelse* ("Prison," though released in the United States as *The Devil's Wanton*). In the first half of *Persona* (a film conceived, significantly, in the immediate wake of a severe illness and breakdown), he comes perilously close to challenging this ideological position; the last third (formally the most "progressive" work he has ever done, if one equates progressiveness with avant-gardism) mercilessly reimposes it.

*Note:* Readers wishing for an antidote to the above account of *Persona* might find it in the article by the distinguished Swedish psychiatrist Göran Persson, published in *CineAction* 40. The article was written as a direct response to my own account of the film and differs from it in almost every detail. Written from a strictly psychoanalytic (and not at all political) viewpoint, it offers probably the fullest and most convincing account of what were probably Bergman's intentions when he made the film. While I admire it, I don't feel that my own reading, coming from so fundamentally different a perspective, is threatened by it.

# PART VI

# RACE AND GENDER

# CHAPTER 12

# "Mandingo":
# The Vindication of an Abused Masterpiece

It is virtually impossible to talk about race without talking about sex.
—Mitchell Shore on Spike Lee (*CineAction 40*)

"There are times when even you white men speak the truth."
—Aissa, in Joseph Conrad's *An Outcast of the Islands*

No film is more urgently in need of revaluation than *Mandingo*. On its release in 1975, it was rejected out of hand by the critical establishment (all white, and predominantly male) as "exploitation" and "trash," and no one seems interested today in reexamining the assumption that it is indefensible. In my opinion it is the greatest film about race ever made in Hollywood, certainly prior to Spike Lee and in certain respects still. Despite the abuse heaped upon it by critics, it did not go totally unrecognized, however: in America it received an award (for its screenplay) from the NAACP; in England (where I was living at the time of its release) there were reports that in districts of London with large black populations it was being greeted with standing ovations. In the eyes of the white intelligentsia this made it, no doubt, even more deplorable: "those people" should not be incited to revolution. I saw it then, and was bowled over; repeated viewings over many years have only increased my admiration.

The accepted wisdom on *Mandingo* can be found concisely summed up in the entry in Leonard Maltin's *Movie and Video Guide*, that indispensable barometer of contemporary liberal-bourgeois "taste," which is also probably the most *widely* influential book on film currently available. After assigning it a "Bomb" the writer (whom I shall assume for reasons that will become obvious was male) goes on to describe it thus: "Trashy potboiler will appeal only to the s & m crowd. [James] Mason is a bigoted plantation patriarch, [Susan] George his oversexed daughter, [Ken] Norton—what else?—a fighter. Stinko!"

One may reasonably begin by questioning whether the writer had even *seen Mandingo*; one would assume it to be impossible to sit through the film (however inattentively) and emerge with the impression that Susan George plays James Mason's daughter (she does, after all, with his full encouragement, marry his son). That "oversexed" is wonderful, a sociological testament in itself: rejected by her husband after their wedding night when he discovers that she isn't a virgin (she has been involved—reluctantly, the film suggests—in an incestuous relationship with her obnoxious elder brother, which is one of her chief motives for wanting to escape from her home), Blanche is forced into a life of total abstinence, and experiences what one would assume to be the perfectly natural need of an adult woman for sexual satisfaction. This, in the writer's eyes, makes her "oversexed"—apparently the Victorian belief that women should merely "lie on their backs and think of England" still thrives. His verdict, in fact, precisely echoes that of Blanche's husband (that she "sure behaves strangely for a white lady") when she caresses him and begs him to make love to her.

The writer's other objections to the film, being vaguer, are more difficult to refute. Mede (Norton) is *forced* into becoming a "fighter" against his will. And I find it difficult to see in what ways the "s & m crowd" (a group worthy only of the writer's blanket contempt) would obtain pleasure or gratification from the film's catalogue of horrors unless one assumes that this "crowd" consists exclusively of psychopathic sadists (who presumably also egg themselves and each other on by readings from Toni Morrison's *Beloved*). Nor do I see why anyone would lavish such demonstrable care over mise-en-scène on a "trashy potboiler."

In fact, *Mandingo*, today, should need no vindication: it was done very thoroughly some twenty years ago by Andrew Britton (*Movie* 22) accompanied by a fascinating interview with its director, in what surely deserves classical status as one of the finest examples of analysis in the history of film criticism—as deserving as, for example, the *Cahiers* reading of *Young Mr. Lincoln* (available in translation in *Movies and Methods*, 1976) or Stephen Heath's of *Touch of Evil* (*Screen* 16, no. 1 [1975]). I write very much in Andrew's shadow: I have wanted to write on *Mandingo* for many years, but have felt deterred by the sense of having little to add. Yet the weight of "accepted wisdom" is so strong. Andrew's article has never been answered, the analysis never refuted—it can't be. Therefore it has been ignored and conveniently forgotten, and the accepted wisdom, although effectively discredited, still reigns. I have no confidence whatever that my own efforts will elicit any different response (no one, as far as I know, has answered my vindication of *Heaven's Gate*, which continues to be treated as a fiasco), yet I feel compelled to make the attempt. I am encouraged by the experience of showing the film to large classes of students, by the generally powerful impression it makes, and, especially, by the enthusiasm of black students, who find at last a pre-Lee Hollywood film about race to which they can relate unconditionally.

The absence of any reasoned opposition raises a wider issue, and again one that today is consistently evaded: the issue of evaluation. The notion that a work of art can have a profound effect on the individual sensibility—can change one's life, one's way of looking and seeing—is treated as either without importance or merely false, a delusion. This leaves art without any discernible function other than that of filling up the dance cards of aspiring academics attending conferences, but that function has now achieved such prominence that all else dwindles into insignificance. I shall, however, insist, in my incorrigibly naive way, that evaluation is the true and inevitable goal of any criticism that aspires to real intelligence (as opposed to the latest cleverness): in Leavis's terminology, intelligence about "life," which is not necessarily the intelligence that can manifest itself on a résumé and acquire for its possessor a tenured position at a university.

## "Miscegenation"

If *Mandingo* is the greatest Hollywood film about race, it is because it is also about sex and gender (for precisely the same reason, the finest Hollywood film about race from the "classical" period is *I Walked with a Zombie*, a far more interesting and suggestive movie than the various well-intentioned "liberal" social problem films about race produced in the 1950s). Like *promiscuity*, *miscegenation* is one of those words that appears, in our culture, to have almost exclusively ugly, negative connotations of which it is unlikely that it can ever be completely purged. The power of the connotative level of language in its social consequences can scarcely be overestimated, though it is difficult to estimate accurately (to what extent, for example, can we attribute the increasing acceptance of homosexuality to the simple fact that people stopped thinking in terms of "homosexual" and began thinking in terms of "gay"?—was this a cause or an effect of the acceptance?).

An issue I raised earlier in discussing "promiscuity" is also relevant here: the enormous and unwarranted importance our culture has continued (as part of the legacy of the past) to attribute to the sexual act. While a likely consequence was an unwanted child, it was logical that this simple and natural means of communication had to be mystified with such terms as "sacred," "keeping oneself pure," "saving oneself for the one right person," etc. It would be logical that, in cultures where simple means of birth control are readily accessible, such formulations would be seen as mere superstition, but this has not, by and large, so far been the case. To some extent the old mystique of sex lingers on, but it has largely been replaced by a new one, the mystique of "permissiveness" or pseudo-liberation, the pursuit of sexual experience as thrilling in ways only circumstantially connected with sexual pleasure: the thrill of "cheating," the thrill of doing things one's parents (officially at least) disapproved of, the thrill of conquest (the "Don Giovanni syndrome," the notion of "scoring" implying at least the keeping of a *mental* catalogue). For some, no doubt, there is a very special thrill in having sex with someone of a different skin color, the breaking of another taboo.

If we genuinely wish to end racism we must attack it at its sources, of which the irrational dread of miscegenation is perhaps the most fundamental, just as the irrational horror at actual sexual activity between men (lesbian sex, as we know, has its place in heterosexual pornography, gay male sex emphatically does not) is fundamental to homophobia. In mainstream cinema, miscegenation has, like homosexual love, barely been allowed to exist unless it is presented as degrading. How many Hollywood films can you think of in which an interracial couple are not only treated positively but allowed to continue *as* a couple beyond the narrative's conclusion? Offhand, I can think of only two in the classical period (*The Big Sky* and *Guess Who's Coming to Dinner?*) and two in the postclassical (*Love Field* and *Strange Days*).* Of the four, *The Big Sky* seems to me the most interesting precisely because no one ever mentions it in this context: of the major Hollywood directors, perhaps only Hawks could have treated the theme with such a total lack of fuss or self-consciousness, never presenting it as an "issue." Of the other three, *Guess Who's Coming to Dinner?* was generally felt to be compromised by the fact that, skin color aside, Sidney Poitier's character was so obviously a highly desirable son-in-law, essentially an upper-middle-class, upwardly mobile, cultivated white man in a black man's skin; though it might equally be argued that this draws attention to the absurdity of *color* prejudice by making color the only possible objection to the union. *Love Field* and *Strange Days* are both recent films, coinciding with the appearance of positively viewed gay male relationships (*Philadelphia*, *Frankie and Johnny*). Neither was

---

*This book was completed early in 1997; since then there have been other instances, of which the strongest and most remarkable is Mike Figgis's splendid (and grotesquely underrated) *One Night Stand*, a film which, for its intricate interweaving of gay and racial issues, would certainly have earned a chapter in the final section. See also my article, "The Spectres Emerge in Daylight," in *CineAction* 43.

given credit for its audacity in any reviews I read, presumably because of a vague "liberal" sense that even to express surprise at the depiction of a successful interracial relationship was somehow politically incorrect. *Love Field*, undervalued by the critics and a box office failure, was boldly centered on the developing black man/white woman relationship (though even here sexual intercourse had to be discreetly implied rather than shown). (A few other recent films have managed to project liberating images of interracial sex—the steamy sex scenes between Laurence Fishburne and Ellen Barkin in *Bad Company*, the highly erotic French-kissing of *Freeway*—but the narratives allow the relationships no future.) In *Strange Days* sex is more tangential, but I found it very moving that (albeit in a seriously flawed film that literally "cops" out of the black revolution the first part seems to promise) the beginning of the New Millennium was celebrated by the union of black and white. The corollary of this may be found in *The Pelican Brief*, in which the generically guaranteed final union of hero and heroine never transpires, not because of any discernible aspiration to originality, but simply because he is black and she is white. Or how many of those advertisements in which a happy heterosexual couple laugh together over an alcoholic beverage have you seen in which the man is black, the woman white (or vice versa, which appears to be slightly less unacceptable)?—after all, we whites have to "protect" our womenfolk, don't we? Didn't Mr. Hatfield teach us that when he saved his last bullet for Lucy Mallory?

What is the rationalization of what today surely seems a very strange and antiquated prohibition? Presumably that the children of any resulting marriage will be of "mixed blood" and will have difficulty in "belonging," in being accepted. But belonging to what, accepted by whom? The answers must be, respectively, "To nothing worth belonging to" and "By people one wouldn't wish to know anyway." A child's basic need is to be loved and respected, respect involving the recognition of his/her existence as an autonomous human being with individual desires and interests. A child who is listened to will in turn listen—to parents or parent figures who can explain ridiculous and long discredited prejudices and bigotry and demonstrate by example the way to react to "what the neighbors say." My point is that such irrational rationalizations are mere cover-ups for a more profoundly irrational distaste for close intimate contact with a skin of a different color, a distaste to which it is difficult to admit precisely because one *knows* it to be irrational.

The intellectual argument against miscegenation is that it dilutes cultural traditions and identities—a line of argument which, pursued to its logical conclusion, could only reach total separatism, since *any* contact between different cultures will inevitably result in mutual modifications (to whatever degree). The argument seems premised on the assumption that a culture is a unified and unchangeable entity which must be accepted in toto, and which at the same time must insulate itself against outside influences. To me this is a foolish and dangerous position: it implies, for instance, that we must not be critical of cultures that oppress women and gays even more than they are oppressed in our own (though it must be added that the other side of this is equally foolish and dangerous—the use of other cultures to pat ourselves on the back and tell ourselves how progressive we are in comparison, so that we can sit on our asses, twiddle our thumbs, and look smug). It also implies that we shouldn't support progressive movements in other cultures, and ultimately that all cultural traditions are by definition good, and exempt from criticism, except our own—surely the epitome of white guilt which, while fully understandable and thoroughly justified, is quite unprofitable.

A coherent and integrated cultural identity is indispensable to oppressed peoples struggling to establish themselves against their oppressors: it acts as a unifying agent, gives them an alternative to set against the culture that oppresses them, a flag around which to rally, and by extension a practical agenda of goals. But it is simultaneously, by its very nature, divisive and eventually obstructive to development; the problem is to know when to begin to relinquish it. If we really believe in multiculturalism we should be thinking beyond all the sources of division, beyond all forms of nationalism that promote separatism. Racism, like homophobia and sexism, is all around us, it is in the air we breathe, but there is at least, today, a steadily growing *awareness* of it which barely existed when I was young. It should become possible at such a time to begin examining one's own cultural tradition critically, discarding what seems obsolete, retrograde, and harmful, admitting influences from other cultural traditions. Such at least has been my own experience as an Englishman. It was around the age of seventeen, for example, that I began refusing to stand for "God Save the King/Queen," having become aware by then of the manifest futility of petitioning a nonexistent deity to save a superfluous monarch: my first hesitant step in discarding British nationalism which (very far back in the distant reaches of history) had bound us together as a race and supported us in our struggles, but had long since degenerated (as nationalism always does) into imperialism, domination, the subjugation of "the Other" to its power and will. What I have retained is embodied mainly in the work of great artists, especially in this case poets and novelists, and my sense of a cultural tradition to which I can feel I belong now embraces the work of, for example, Toni Morrison, Spike Lee, Ozu, Tanizaki, Hou Hsiao-Hsien. The ideal multicultural society must also be, by definition, one moving steadily and by general consent toward liberation, the casting-off of the shackles of the past by which the development of every cultural tradition is impeded, accompanied by the careful, responsible, and respectful reassessment of everything in that past that is still alive and worth retaining.

## Generic Affinities, Thematic Trajectory

If *Mandingo* is not a "trashy potboiler," what is it? Most obviously (but least interestingly), it has its place in a heterogeneous cycle of "black"-centered movies produced in Hollywood in the 1970s and ranging in "respectability" from Wyler's *The Liberation of L. B. Jones* to the "blaxploitation" films. It towers above all of them, its themes embracing issues that go far beyond race, its deeper resonances having little to do with "trends" or topicality. Three generic forms seem to me clearly relevant:

1. *Gothic melodrama.* The fundamental ingredients are there: the "terrible house," now in a state of decay, with its unspoken past history; the imprisoned and persecuted woman; the dark, powerful, sinister patriarch.

2. *Shakespearean/Jacobean tragedy:* the hero with a tragic flaw; the "revenge" theme; overt, extreme emotions; violent, "excessive," apocalyptic conclusion.

3. *Greek tragedy:* a legacy of guilt that must be expiated, a "curse" that can be purged only through the catharsis of catastrophe—the "curse" here being the history of slavery and its appalling effects, not only on the black slaves but on the white "masters"; relentless logic rigorously pursued to a devastating conclusion perceived as inevitable from the outset.

The curse on the House of Atreus has its roots in a monstrous past quite beyond the *personal* guilt of its eventual victims; similarly with the curse on the House of Maxwell. Just as the working through of the curse to resolution and catharsis begins effectively with Agamemnon (his sacrifice of Iphigenia, itself commanded by the gods), so the curse on the House of Maxwell effectively begins with James Mason's patriarch, although it is clear that he is himself a tool of a preestablished Higher Order: in place of the "gods" the film defines a monstrous, irrational, inhuman but omnipresent ideology. (Without suggesting conscious intention, one may note the interesting "coincidence" that a number of the slaves have names taken from Greek or Roman history/mythology: Cicero, Agamemnon, Ganymede.)

Its generic affinities help toward a definition of the film's guiding theme, which can be stated abstractly without reference to racial questions: the entrapment of all the characters within an ideology against which their bet-ter instincts rebel but which proves so powerful and so indoctrinated as finally to overwhelm every positive impulse.

The entrapment is all-pervasive: no leading character acts freely, none can break out of the ideological system the film defines, no one (with one excep-tion) is capable of a "pure" action. The one exception, the only character whose behavior the film clearly endorses, plays only a very small role and is killed halfway through—Cicero, the revolutionary slave, hanged for his pre-sumption. The film is perfectly (if by necessity circumspectly) clear on this point: only black revolution could overthrow the system, which is beyond redemption, yet a successful and unaided black revolution is impossible within the conditions depicted, in which the power of the whites (however fallen into decay the symbolic mansion) is absolute. The blacks, on the other hand, are never depicted as stupid or unaware; if they are "helpless" it is purely because of social circumstance. And "social circumstance" here is very different from that of, say, the unpardonable *Mississippi Burning*, in which the civil rights movement of recent decades is depicted as entirely dependent upon the intervention of "liberal" whites from the North. Aside from Cicero's defiance, the film communicates the terrifying sense that every character ultimately does what he or she "has" to do, their actions determined in the last resort by ideological mechanisms whose functioning can lead to nothing short of cataclysm (which the film's climax unflinchingly provides—there is no more authentically "terrible" resolution anywhere in cinema).

## Cicero and Mem

The original posters for *Mandingo* aptly and brilliantly parodied those for *Gone with the Wind*—instead of Scarlett in the arms of Rhett, the film's two interracial couples (Hammond/Ellen, Mede/Blanche). For many years, *Gone with the Wind*, with its overwhelming prestige and popularity (rein-forced and perpetuated by its various revivals), had offered general audi-ences a sentimental travesty of white/black relations and the "realities" of slavery in the Deep South: the proposition that some Southern families were kind to "their" blacks (the truth of which one doesn't have to doubt) not only distracted attention from the many that weren't but obliterated the fun-damental humiliation, the fact of slavery itself. Whether the horrors depicted in *Mandingo* are in their detail any more historically correct than the reassuring platitudes of its predecessor is beside the point (they are some-what different from, though no more nor less appalling than, those cata-logued by Toni Morrison in *Beloved*, which has not as far as I know been accused of cheap sensationalism). The film's exposition, defining the attitudes of the white masters to their slaves, is firmly, single-mindedly grounded in this fundamental reality, the humiliation of being owned: it is there already in the blues that accompanies the credits, sung by Muddy Waters ("I was born in this time / To never be free"). The exposition parallels the humiliation of the male slaves (treated *literally* as cattle or dogs—their examination by the trader before purchase, Cicero made to fetch a stick—or forced like Mem the house slave to agree that blacks have no souls) as well as the female slaves (the denial of sexual choice, the "Mandingo wench" Big Pearl enduring her "pleasurin' " by the young white master who has first go at the virgins, instructed by her mother to thank him "whether he gives you nothin' or not"). The scenes, eloquent in themselves, also prepare later "key" events: Mede (the Mandingo of the title) will be brought in for purposes of

*Mandingo:* inspection and purchase.

*Mandingo:* the cure for rheumatism (James Mason).

breeding with Big Pearl, not knowing that she is in fact his sister. Cicero (sold, hence chained for the night so that he can't escape) speaks the thoughts and feelings that arise naturally from what we have been shown ("How y'all feel layin' here chained while white men walk about, do his pleasure with a black girl?"), which prefigure his subsequent overt rebellion and inevitable death. Mem's (Agamemnon's) subservience and self-abnegation are revealed as mere expediency: guided by Cicero, he is breaking the ultimate law by learning to read—the blacks (as Cicero says) kept from learning because the whites know deep down that they are just as human. When Mem, in the film's finale, at last "does the right thing" (by killing the right person), he takes on Cicero's role as revolutionary.

The remarkably rich and concise exposition—culminating in Mem's terrible punishment—effectively defines the "curse": the crime of slavery, the all-pervasive corruption and dehumanization that results from the absolute power of one race of human beings over another. The Falconhurst plantation grows only slaves (we see no crops of any kind), breeding them and selling them. At its head is Maxwell (James Mason) the monstrous patriarch who believes that blacks have no souls and can therefore quite appropriately be treated like animals. The film supplies one unforgettable image of him, sitting with his feet upon a small black boy in the belief that this will drain out his rheumatism, an image dramatically powerful in itself but having a clear symbolic extension (the all-powerful master literally setting his feet upon the next generation of slaves), and suggesting an ignorance and superstition equal to anything voodoo could offer. The blacks, consistently presented as intelligent, aware, and potentially revolutionary, cling to whatever dignity is permitted them; it is the white masters, who treat them as animals and deny them the possession of souls, who are depicted as something less than fully human. In the midst of all this is Hammond (Perry King) and his "wound"—"symbolic castration" if you like, or simply the imperfection that sets him apart (physically and psychologically) from the all-powerful Great White Male. The physical imperfection is the source of both his worst aspects (the fear of impotence, of "femininity," and his attempts to compensate) and his best (his vulnerability, which makes it possible for him to empathize with the oppressed, so long as his fears are not awakened). One may note here that *Mandingo* was one of the first commercial movies ever to show full-frontal male nudity. The point is less trivial than it sounds: if male power is "possession of the phallus," then it is important to the film's project that it show, in its male protagonist, that the Phallus is, after all, only a penis.

## Hammond's Mission

Maxwell despatches his son on a mission with two objectives: Hammond is to acquire *(a)* a Mandingo slave, and *(b)* a wife, both essential for purposes of breeding. The parallel, central to the film, between blacks and women as the victims of white male power, is established immediately—women, like slaves, are to be inspected, traded, and owned ("Go take a look at Cousin Blanche. If she ain't to your taste there are other white ladies . . ."). The film does not, of course, suggest that the parallel is exact; white women live in material comfort, are pampered and held up for admiration. But it makes quite clear that the ignominy of their situation is comparable, if not in degree, then in kind, the result being that they, like the blacks in the presence of their masters, have to act all the time: Blanche's grotesque performance for Hammond as virginal Southern coquette closely parallels Mem's equally grotesque subservience within the Maxwell household.

Ham accomplishes both objectives (one might say) successfully—the "success" setting the mechanisms whose working-out will bring about the final complex catastrophe, the deaths of three main characters, the spiritual and psychological destruction of Hammond himself. First, however, he acquires a third, unauthorized, possession, the most sympathetically viewed of the five leading figures, also indispensable to the narrative's inexorable progress: Ellen, the black slave with whom he falls in love. The sequence is notable for the delicacy which is just as much a presence in this "trashy pot-boiler" as its uncompromising brutality. It also vividly dramatizes Ham's "tragic flaw," on which we are given a double perspective—from the view-point of the ideology presented *in* the film, and from that of the ideology implied *by* the film. The former can be put succinctly: Hammond can never become his father (the dehumanized figure who is at once the product of the ideology and its monstrous exponent). The latter involves the recognition that Ham, indoctrinated from birth, can never clearly detach himself from the former.

The two-part sequence is built, in fact, upon the opposition brutality/tenderness. In the first part Ham and his prospective brother-in-law Charles are brought "gifts" for the white masters—female slaves ("wenches") for their use, inspected by Charles in the approved manner before acceptance. Ellen having been passed on to Ham (she is a virgin, which Charles considers involves too much work), Charles proceeds to brutalize Katie, humiliating and beating her, forcing her to concur in his "She likes it too" when Ham tries to intervene, then kissing her violently on the mouth. Ham is shocked, and not only by the brutality: white morality decrees that a "wench" must never be kissed on the mouth, betokening intimacy rather than treating her as an object for use. The second part (Ham and Ellen alone together in another room) is initiated by Ham's "It makes me sick," taken by Ellen as referring to the cruelty; Ham is "strange for a white man" because he "cares what a white man do to a wench." She then asks about his leg, how he got the wound; instead of reacting with anger, he admires her honesty, understanding that she asks out of concern, without malicious intent. It is a succinct and unostentatious depiction of the beginning of a mutual attraction: she is attracted by his difference from other white men (which she immediately links to his "wound"); he begins to feel tenderness for a black woman (in reaction against Charles' brutality?—or because he responds to her awareness of his difference?). Barriers begin to crumble, a development beautifully and subtly suggested in Ham's self-correction when Ellen can't look into his eyes (which is forbidden to blacks): "If you're *told* to do it . . . if you're *asked* to do it . . ." They are separated in the frame by the foreground vertical of the bedpost; Ham draws her toward him, the camera moving with her so that the "obstacle" passes from the image; she looks up at last, meets his eyes. There follows one of those moments that defy verbal description, which can stand as well as any as exemplifying the delicacy of Perry King's performance: Ham's repeated hesitations before he is able to kiss her on the mouth, as he clearly desires. The scene will be echoed, answered, balanced, much later by the climactic scene between Blanche and Mede which begins, as here, with the black character forced to obey, then develops before our eyes into an exchange of tenderness.

The two official objectives of Ham's mission—the acquisition of Mandingo slave and white wife—are connected by immediate juxtaposition. This establishes the film's fundamental principle of construction: the paralleling of the oppression of blacks with the oppression of women, the structure culminating in the brutal destruction of the evidence of miscegenation between a white woman and a black man in the murder of Blanche's and Mede's black child.

Hammond is clearly the film's central character, and the closest it offers to an identification figure. As his actions are directly responsible for all the film's disasters, and as he is the perpetrator of the two climactic murders of characters we certainly find sympathetic (if flawed), identification is, to put it mildly, problematic; yet his predicament should be easy enough to identify with for anyone (including the author of this book) sufficiently aware of the difficulties of extricating oneself from the ideological conditioning that begins at birth and continues throughout one's formative years, the influence of which, with all its protean transformations and subterfuges, is almost impossible to eliminate completely. (The more perceptive and incisive critics of this book will doubtless be able to trace its unconscious workings.) Hammond's treatment of Blanche (source of most of the subsequent catastrophes) is only partly determined by ideological assumption—that a white "lady" is *supposed* to be a virgin on marriage and sexually passive after it. His revulsion is powerfully compounded by psychological factors, the feelings of vulnerability/inferiority derived from his physical impediment (though his sense of that as somehow disabling, a mark of specifically sexual inferiority, is itself ideological). For him, a woman *must* be a virgin because the idea of comparison with other males of possibly greater potency/prowess is unendurable. He can function sexually with Big Pearl or Ellen because both are not only virgins but his social inferiors, his slaves. He can function with Blanche on their wedding night because her virginity, as white lady, is a given, until he realizes the truth. As for the prostitute whose advances he rejects in the brothel, not only is she white and obviously *not* a virgin, she also strongly resembles Blanche. The genuineness of his love for Ellen (what *is* love, anyway?), while not in question, is qualified by the fact of her complete sexual submissiveness, the submissiveness she has been taught from infancy as her means of survival. We see, then, that Blanche's desperate sexual advances, far from seducing him, make voluntary intercourse more impossible than ever; and he has ready to hand, as excuse, the standard ideological reaction—that her behavior is "mighty strange for a white lady."

The scenario's juxtapositions of scenes are consistently intelligent and meaningful. The scene in which Hammond rejects Blanche is followed immediately by the tender (but troubled) scene between Hammond and Ellen, in bed, when she tells him that she is pregnant—a scene subsequently "answered" by Blanche's pregnancy by Mede, in this intricately and densely structured film. The Hammond/Blanche scene was characterized by the stark, bare decor of the room (in Falconhurst—the South in decay—there is minimal furniture and a conspicuous absence of carpets), a room whose chief defining feature is a mirror on every wall. The Hammond/Ellen scene narrows the visuals to the bed, surrounded by gauze curtains that suffuse the lovers in a soft, warm light. Hammond reacts with delight to the news that Ellen is to provide the plantation with another "sucker," the confirmation of his manhood. But the realities of the relationship are immediately foregrounded when Ellen asks him, hesitantly, to give the child his (the assumption seems to be that it will be a boy) freedom when he comes of age. We see, perhaps more clearly here than anywhere else in the film, the coexistence of the two Hammonds: his first reaction is shock that anyone would suggest such a thing (the child will be, after all, not his son but another slave for the Maxwell slave industry); then, in response to Ellen's tears, he agrees. The subtleties of this "trashy potboiler" are nowhere more in evidence than in this scene. Aside from the precise analysis of Hammond's confusions of allegiance, it also gives Ellen the one moment where her motivation in accepting the sexual relationship with Hammond is allowed to be more complex than simply "falling in love." His initial response (the response of a vulnerable man scared about his potency) to Ellen's request is instantly to ask her whether *she* wants to be free (i.e., to have a choice in relating to him). She is allowed by the film to hesitate a significantly long time before she reassures him.

In the overall structure, however, the point that emerges, by implication, is even more fundamental, connecting race politics and sexual politics. With the product of the union of a white man and a black woman, there is at least a choice (though one in which the black mother has no say): the child can either be sold into further slavery or given his liberty, at the whim of the white owner. But with the product of the union of a black man and a white woman, there is no choice: the child must be instantly put to death, the terrible secret buried with it.

It is the juxtaposition of the two scenes (Hammond/Blanche, Hammond /Ellen) that (in terms of the film's thematic progress) determines the hideous scene in which Blanche whips Ellen, causing her to fall down the stairs and lose her baby. But here there is an even more interesting juxtaposition—the Blanche/Ellen scene is contained within two others, the departure of Hammond and Mede for the fight that will prove Mede's potency, and the fight itself, perhaps the ugliest and most difficult to watch prior to *Raging Bull.* The point of the juxtaposition should be clear: two women set against each other in brutal enmity, two blacks forced to fight to the death, both instances either directly provoked or actually supervised by the Great White Male.

Hammond's relation to Mede is more difficult to define (and this relates to a weakness of the film that I will deal with later). Hammond buys Mede because that is what he has been sent, by his father, to do; but there is obviously more to it than that. Hammond's obsession with Mede's prowess as a fighter goes quite beyond any of Maxwell's demands: Mede becomes Hammond's potency, the extension of the phallic power in possession of which he feels so insecure. Is he also in love with Mede? The film gives us no clear indication of any sexual ambiguity there, yet his fear of sexually active women makes it psychologically plausible. More suggestive is Mede's name, an abridgment of "Ganymede" (as "Mem" is an abridgment of "Agamemnon"). Ganymede was the beautiful youth with whom Jupiter fell in love, the god carrying him off to be his "cupbearer," very much as Hammond carries off Mede to be his slave. Without wishing to press the point, it seems clear that Hammond is in some sense emotionally involved with Mede, and this adds a further complexity to his actions when he discovers that Mede has had intercourse with his wife and fathered her child.

The film develops a situation in which Hammond is at once agent and victim of the consequences, in which even his most positive impulses accelerate the movement toward disaster. Take, for example, the gift of the necklace and earrings, chosen by Maxwell for Hammond to give to Blanche on his return from town. Initially, the gift is merely another move in the father's determination that they produce an heir for Falconhurst, guaranteeing the patriarchal lineage (a move he follows up by locking the couple in the bedroom together: Blanche was, after all, brought to Falconhurst for breeding purposes). Hammond gives the necklace to Blanche, who greets it with the delight of a young girl (perhaps the closest we ever come to seeing the *real* Blanche), spontaneously embracing Hammond who in turn is touched by her simple sincerity and is able to respond. But he has already given the matching earrings to Ellen, who then wears them ("innocently"—

she doesn't know they were not intended for her—but perhaps not entirely so: black slaves should not receive valuable love-gifts from white masters and flaunt them in public) when serving dinner in Blanche's presence. The divided gift establishes a new stage in his commitment to Ellen, but it simultaneously underlines the unthinking and brutal cruelty with which he treats Blanche. It is the latter's recognition of the earrings that motivates her revenge on Hammond, which in turn leads to her own death. Her immediate response, however, fatal in view of his personal psychology, is to taunt him with sexual inadequacy—whereupon he demands to know who her previous lover was, and she blurts out the truth, that it was her brother, Charles.

Hammond's simultaneous concern for Ellen and provocation of Blanche is (movingly, disturbingly) developed in the sequence that follows, one of the film's finest, marked by its two most elaborate and expressive tracking shots. The first, and longer, leads us down the procession of slaves who have been sold, whom it is now Hammond's task to deliver to their new owners, the men lined up on foot, the women and children in a cart at the rear. Earlier, when Ellen asked Hammond to grant their child his freedom, she mentioned the distress of another female slave, Didy, whose infant had been sold; Hammond now—inspired, we assume, both by his love for Ellen and his final rejection of and disgust with Blanche—saves Didy's infant from the cart and returns him to her. It is the first and only moment in the film where Hammond openly and publicly stands up to his father, directly disobeying his orders: the point, then, where he is closest to extricating himself from his past conditioning and obeying his own human impulses. Empowered by this, he then invites Ellen to sit with him in the front cart, at the head of the procession (though the limitations of his rebellion are made equally clear—Ellen sits behind, not beside, him). The film's emotional complexity is epitomized in the second tracking shot, that follows shortly after: from an upstairs balcony, we look down at the procession of slaves led by Hammond, Ellen close behind him; the camera tracks with it, then turns to show Blanche watching, abruptly moving swiftly toward her so that we see her reaction to an action that amounts to her public humiliation; with her, we see Hammond looking up, apparently unperturbed, even pleased, by the realization that she has witnessed his public acknowledgment of Ellen.

What exactly do we mean when we talk about "tragic inevitability"? Perhaps "plausibility" would be better: in theory, Hammond *could* discover that racial prejudice is an evil, Blanche *could* just leave. But in the context the film defines, neither of these is even remotely plausible. Blanche's reaction is to send for Mede to "service" her (not only, surely, because he is extremely attractive, but because he essentially belongs to, and is loved by, Hammond).

Hammond's subsequent reaction, when he discovers what has taken place, is to murder them both. We have the sense that both reactions are "inevitable," but perhaps "likely" would be better. I submit that for anyone who rejects the "trashy potboiler" view of the film (and has there ever been a more blatant defense against emotional involvement?) the last ten minutes remain, after multiple viewings, very hard to watch, precisely because we have been led to sympathize so intensely with all the four characters involved.

The Hollywood cinema has still not produced, even today, a "miscegenation" scene that comes even close, in explicitness and intimacy, to the Blanche/Mede scene of intercourse (our "enlightened" cinema of the 1990s comes no closer than the Bokeem Woodbine/Reese Witherspoon French-kissing of *Freeway*). But what exactly transpires in this scene? Blanche's immediate motivation is revenge; Mede initially pleads to be excused. But the development clearly suggests that they begin to respond to each other, at the very least on the erotic level. More than that, we learn subsequently that she has sent for Mede four times—three times beyond simple revenge. Even *Mandingo*—one of the most audacious films ever to come out of Hollywood—can only go so far; after the first encounter, we never see them together again. Yet we are free (I think) to infer much more. What, after all, is heterosexual erotic response? The response of any cock to any vagina? The sequence suggests much more, but exactly what is not clear: a coming together of two people aware of their mutual (if distinct) oppression? What *is* clear is that the lovemaking (and the scene's explicitness is crucial here) develops into something quite beyond the enforced "duty" of a black slave to a white mistress.

Both Hammonds (the ideological, the psychological) are involved in the final catastrophe: the former because white wives and black slaves must never be sexual partners; the latter because *(a)* Blanche (as his wife) has betrayed him; *(b)* Mede (as his slave) has betrayed him; *(c)* Mede (as his "surrogate phallus") has done what he has failed to do—satisfied Blanche sexually, and impregnated her; *(d)* although he doesn't know that Blanche was responsible for the death of the child conceived with the woman he loved, the loss of that child of permitted miscegenation must be felt as an unconscious motive for the murder of the wife and slave who produced a child by "illicit" miscegenation. The horrific, and very messy, murder of Mede is the logical outcome of this tangle of motivations. So is Hammond's brutal rejection of Ellen (perhaps the film's most emotionally painful moment) as she tries to prevent it: the woman who elicited Hammond's finest feelings is suddenly just another "nigger." But it is very striking that the only two halfway decent sexual relationships depicted in the film are both interracial.

I think, implicitly, I have already made clear the film's weak spot: the product of whites, it appears unable to cross racial boundaries to the extent of developing a corresponding empathy with its black characters, and it is easy to see how this could be used against it. Ellen's attraction to Hammond remains a "given" and is never analyzed, beyond the elementary point that he is "strange for a white man." Her moment of hesitation as to whether she wants to be free (in the bedroom scene when Hammond agrees to give her "sucker" his freedom), potentially expressive, has no context or development. And Mede's feelings for Blanche are left to the audience's conjecture. At the same time, the film's refusal to fall into the trap of idealizing its black characters should be respected: Mede, the obviously "heroic" black character, is clearly contained within the film's complex of oppression and self-oppression: he is ready, for his own survival (or advancement?), to kill a fellow black in a fight organized by his oppressors.

Within a film industry still dominated by the "Great White Male," it remains an extraordinary achievement, still unrecognized as such. *Mandingo*'s hour has come: it was vastly ahead of its time. I write in 1997, only three years before the film's twenty-fifth anniversary. In this age of celebratory reissues, among the childish regression of the *Star Wars* trilogy, *The Godfather*'s uneasy complicity with its obviously monstrous Mafia family, *The Graduate*'s unpardonable contempt for mature women, *Mandingo*—if its current distributors had the least intelligence, awareness, integrity, or sheer guts—would have a place of honor.

# TOWARD LIBERATION

# CHAPTER 13

# Narrative Pleasure:
# Two Films by Jacques Rivette

It has come to seem increasingly unlikely that Rivette will ever take the place one had once anticipated for him, among the central figures of modernist cinema. His oeuvre has proved extremely uneven, the length of some of the films (not necessarily the longest) seeming disproportionate to their rewards. I speak, of course, as one for whom formal experimentation and play with narrative are not in themselves—initially beguiling as they may be—of great lasting interest when divorced from any demonstrable richness and density of significance. The enormous potential one saw opening up in *Céline and Julie Go Boating* (*Céline et Julie Vont en Bateau*, 1974) has had little by way of sequel.

The achievement of that film remains what it was—one of the peaks of modern cinema. But it was not done justice to by Rivette's Anglo-Saxon champions (to whom one nevertheless owes a great debt of gratitude, to Jonathan Rosenbaum particularly); the effect of their constant (and almost exclusive) emphasis on narrative freedom and formal innovativeness was to create a somewhat abstract impression of the films, stressing the central importance of the play with narrative (which is undoubted), but leaving the reader with the feeling that it didn't much matter what the narratives were *about*. An interview with Rivette published in *Film Comment* (by Rosenbaum, Lauren Sedofsky, and Gilbert Adair, Sept.-Oct. 1974) managed to discuss *Céline and Julie* at some length without at any point engaging with it as, centrally and predominantly, a film about women and one of the most radical and positive feminist statements the cinema has so far achieved. (Adair went so far as to inform us that the film is "open to as many interpretations as there are spectators," a not unfamiliar form of critical abdication, given spurious credibility by the then-fashionable myth of the "open text"; in this case, demonstrable nonsense.)

My aim here, then, is not merely to keep alive the battle for the wider recognition of Rivette's best work, but also to restore to it the social-political significance and force its champions have tended to obscure. Besides *Céline and Julie*, that "best work" seems to me most convincingly exemplified by *L'Amour Fou* (1968).

As a preliminary, one must briefly confront the films' most obvious eccentricity and commercial stumbling-block, their inordinate and inconsiderate length: *L'Amour Fou* (256 min.), *Céline and Julie* (a more modest 192 min.). Why must the films be so long? The simplest—and perhaps most important—answer is that there *is* no socially acceptable reason. None of the usual pretexts that justify the length of, say, *Gone with the Wind* (222 min.), *1900* (243 min.), or *The Deer Hunter* (183 min.) operates here. The length of our cinema programs is closely bound up with the more obvious conditions of contemporary consumer-capitalism: alienated labor, the five-day week, the nine-to-five job, the nuclear family, a norm common to all levels from manual workers to executives, necessitating that—weekends apart—"leisure" be packed into a two-to-three-hour time slot between the time the kids are put to bed and the "early night" required for the next day's toil. Otherwise, in one of those brutal but revealing popular phrases in which our culture is rich, "Time is money"; and if we are going to surrender up to four hours of our "money" to watching a spectacle, we must be repeatedly assured that the spectacle we are buying is extremely expensive and that we are purchasing a visibly valuable commodity, whether in the major stars and "cast of thousands" of the past or the "special effects" and explosions of the present. Rivette's films, on the contrary, are visibly and unashamedly cheap—despite their length, they are transparently "low budget" (*Céline and Julie* was even shot on 16mm film). Nor is the length validated by complexities of plot, large numbers of characters, "epic" events. What is the plot of *L'Amour Fou*? Sébastien tries (and fails) to produce Racine's *Andromaque*; Claire goes mad. Rivette could easily have told it to us in fifteen minutes and spared us the superfluous four hours.

The very format of the films, then, represents an act of cultural transgression; if we felt that the length was "necessary" it would no longer be transgressive. The question "Why this length?" provokes a reciprocal one: Why the standard length? Why should we automatically expect our movies to last between ninety minutes and two hours, feel cheated if they are less, and demand particular justification if they are more? Rivette not only demands our time, he demands our patience; we have to sit through long stretches of film in which nothing much (in terms of the conventional narrative expectations to which mainstream cinema has conditioned us, leading us point by logical point through the traditional process of order-disturbance-crisis-restoration/replacement) seems to be happening, or much the same thing seems to go on happening or to happen all over again. Yet few people who have sat through the films wish them shorter (some, of course, reject them altogether). The apparent longueurs (the films seem shorter every time one sees them) are the most effective means of forcing us to question the experience mainstream cinema offers us, the positions in which it places us. As with the question "Why this length?"—the question "Why are we being asked to watch *this*?" raises a reciprocal one: Why are we normally asked to watch the particular patterns that "this" transgresses? Further questions then rush in: What makes a narrative "interesting?" Are we conditioned to apply only very restricted criteria of "interestingness"? Can we learn to be interested by other narrative procedures? The issues are radical, and as political as you want to make them.

Thus far I have not said more than Jonathan Rosenbaum has said many times over. But once this much is established one must go beyond, to ask, with such prolonged *doing*, What actually is *done*?

The overthrow (or voluntary abdication) of the male author-director is at once the subject of *L'Amour Fou*'s narrative and enacted in its formal strategies; this abdication then becomes, not the subject, but the conceptual basis of *Céline and Julie Go Boating*. Crucial to this is *L'Amour Fou*'s systematic foregrounding of the processes of representation. Its structure resembles a Chinese box, or one of those nested babushka dolls that Claire (Bulle Ogier) purchases and dismantles in increasingly desperate frustration; at the same time, the business of representation is no longer the prerogative of a single omnipotent patriarchal figure but divided among a number of representers operating in different media and on different levels. Rivette persuaded Jean-Pierre Kalfon to conceive and rehearse a production of *Andromaque*; he then invited André Labarthe (at that time a leading critic on *Cahiers du Cinéma*) to make a TV documentary (16mm) on the rehearsals, interviewing the actors about their roles and experiences. Both Kalfon and Labarthe were allowed complete autonomy in producing and directing, while their endeavours remained within the bounds of fiction: that is to say, there was never any serious question of the play's actually being staged or of the documentary's being shown on television. We have, then, Rivette making a film of Labarthe shooting a documentary of Kalfon producing a play by Racine reinterpreting a Greek myth. It is true that the top level of representation—Rivette's 35mm film—is not called into question, i.e., its mechanics are not foregrounded in the Godardian manner (the showing of cameras, clapperboards, etc., the acknowledgment of the actors as actors), the other levels (where the mechanics *are* foregrounded) being contained within a form of "realist" fiction. But the film consistently promotes such awareness of the presence of representational media that awareness of the film as itself a construct becomes inescapable, simply the outward covering of the Chinese box. The problem of representation (how does one produce Racine? how does one direct actors? how does one film a rehearsal?) is an important and explicit component of the film's thematic; on the formal level, the frequent cutting between visibly distinct 35mm and 16mm footage ensures that the spectator's awareness of filmic means is never allowed to lapse for long.

Central to the film is the analogy implied between Sébastien (Kalfon) as producer and Rivette as filmmaker. Sébastien's crisis of confidence in himself—his increasing uncertainty as to what he is doing and his right to do it—is precipitated by Claire's refusal of direction and her withdrawal from the play: each stage in his progressive abdication as controller of the performance is counterpointed with the deterioration of their relationship and Claire's retreat into insanity. Sébastien, throughout the film, vacillates between a desire to surrender authority (over the production, over the text, over Claire) and a fear of surrendering it; one might cite his ambivalent attitude to the pop-up toy with which he and Claire play in bed, where he both resents the fact that the toy refuses to pop up and contemplates (positively) the possibility of a female pop-up toy. His own descent into madness (or a state resembling it) is left ambiguous in its motivation: on one level he voluntarily enters insanity to join Claire, as his only means of retaining contact and helping her; on another, the descent appears a logical consequence of his abdication, a personal necessity, partly a self-punishment (expressed most clearly in the scene where he slashes his clothes and lacerates himself with a razor blade). I know of no other film, except *Persona*, that so powerfully communicates the terror of moving out of one's ideologically constructed, socially conditioned and ratified, hence *secure*, position and identity, into . . . what? Which is precisely the question with which the film leaves one: a *political* question if ever there was one.

For a moment, it looks as if both the Claire-plot and the *Andromaque*-plot are going to be resolved. Insofar as his sharing of her madness is an act of therapy, it is successful, but in an unpredictable and ironic way: when she emerges from her insanity it is to the realization that she must leave him. Whereupon he phones his assistant and calls a rehearsal. We are reminded that, whereas *he* abdicated from a clearly defined position as patriarchal organizer, *she* had nothing much to abdicate *from*. But, just as Claire's train journey (with which the film begins and ends) has no defined goal, so the first performance never happens. Sébastien (actor as well as producer, hence indispensable to the production) lies slumped on the floor of the apartment, listening to fragments of the record of disintegration on Claire's tape recorder, while the theater audience waits.

In a scene that asks to be read as confessional, on the part of Rivette as well as Sébastien, the latter talks of the intention and status of the production of *Andromaque*. He has reached the conclusion that Racine should be spoken as "conversation," and this emerges in the context as not only a perception about the text but a perception about actors—that each should speak as him/herself, instead of having a uniform style of delivery imposed by the producer. In the event, the production that finally evolves becomes a striking equivalent for the overall method of the film, its idiosyncratic balance and tension between naturalism and formalism: the actors' "conversation," without forfeiting its naturalness, becomes ritualized by the use of a battery of percussion instruments to punctuate the statements.

Sébastien's second conclusion, connected to the first, is that the purpose of the production should be the satisfaction of the participants rather than of the audience. This is clearly central to Rivette's cinema, and appears a direct affront to many traditional "democratic" assumptions about art and entertainment—that the prime function of art is communication, that the artist should "respect" her/his audience, that the first consideration should be to give the audience what it wants. But Rivette would, I think, reject only the last of these (which marks, in any case, the point where "democratic principle" merges into capitalist exploitation, what today's audiences appear readiest to pay their money for being precisely the reiteration of ideological banalities dressed up in the most expensive trimmings possible). Indeed, his respect for his audience is continuously demonstrated in the way they are left free to accept or reject what is communicated.

Much film theory of the past decades has been posited, implicitly or explicitly, on the assumption that the position defined for the spectator of mainstream cinema is one of absolute passivity: she/he is simply moved along, a helpless pawn, from cut to cut and suture to suture, every response predetermined. Well, perhaps, as Renoir said, there is *some* truth in every theory and it depends upon the application. I don't believe *this* theory applies to any of the films, mainstream or otherwise, dealt with in this book. It is difficult to imagine a truly nonmanipulative art: what could it possibly be like? Take, as a possible instance, Andy Warhol's *The Chelsea Girls*, in which we sit before the unedited takes of a static camera watching people do little of any consequence ("behave," I suppose). This may appear at first completely nonmanipulative, but isn't its point the pointlessness of the "life" (if it can be called that) we are shown, and haven't we been, by the end, manipulated into sharing in this sense of pointlessness? We are free, certainly, to move around, leave the theater, go out for more popcorn, fall asleep for a while, but, short of rejecting the film and its position (as we can with *any* film), we are not free to adopt a different attitude from that implicitly conveyed.

Yet, if no film can be either totally manipulative or totally nonmanipulative, there are clearly degrees: *Triumph of the Will*, for example, is about as manipulative as the cinema can get (so is much of Hitchcock—this is not in itself a value judgment); *The Rules of the Game* (*La Régle du Jeu*) and *Before Sunrise* might stand as two of the *least* manipulative of mainstream films, but *L'Amour Fou* is arguably less manipulative than either. Its length and longueurs are one aspect of this. A central principle of mainstream cinema has been economy: the assumption that the "meaning" of the work becomes clear in certain climactic or integrative moments of particular richness and complexity, which the rest moves up to and away from, but to which everything in the work must be felt to be relevant or necessary. (The moment in *The Deer Hunter* where the "one shot" of Robert de Niro's charismatic mastery becomes the bullet Christopher Walken fires into his own brain might stand as a superb example.) This principle is not lacking in *L'Amour Fou* (one could clearly point to certain scenes, certain events, certain phases in the narrative, which are of obvious structural/thematic significance, where "things come together"), yet its dominance is significantly challenged. The structuring "moments" are not signaled in the ways to which we are accustomed, and there might be more than usual disagreement as to precisely which moments they are. We are allowed an unwonted degree of freedom in terms of where we find significance, what weight we give to various actions, speeches, gestures, how we distinguish between the more and less important. The one exception, Sébastien's walk through the streets toward the end of the film, marked by subjective shots and overwrought music, culminating in his self-confrontation in a mirror-window, strikingly highlights by disruption the film's overall method and mode of address.

*L'Amour Fou*, despite the fact that Sébastien and Claire are given roughly equal screen time, remains essentially centered on the male. Throughout, it is the male who acts, the woman either being passive and helpless or acting ineffectually and futilely (e.g., her attempts to buy or steal a basset). This inequality is supported by the formal procedures, the "producers" (of the film, of the documentary, of the production, of the play) all being men; the sequences involving Claire are necessarily 35mm footage directed by Rivette (however much interpretative freedom was permitted Bulle Ogier), with no equivalent for the foregrounding of representation in the rehearsal scenes. The pattern of male action/female passivity is broken only by Claire's two *negative* decisions—to leave the play at the beginning of the film, and to leave

Sébastien at the end. (The decisions can be seen as positive in that they are necessary steps toward Claire's liberation, but both take the form of rejection rather than affirmation.)

*L'Amour Fou* is structured on the Claire/Sébastien opposition: the two central characters are opposed throughout, the central conflict is between *them*. *Céline and Julie Go Boating* is structured on a very different set of oppositions which unite the two central characters and pit them against the weight of the past, the weight of ideology. It is not coincidental that the central characters of *L'Amour Fou* are male and female, while those of *Céline and Julie* are both women; here, women become fully autonomous, and it is they who decide and determine the action and its outcome, both as characters and as actors.

The credits attribute the scenario to Juliet Berto (Céline), Dominique Labourier (Julie), Bulle Ogier, Marie-France Pisier and, finally, Rivette, "dialoguing with" Eduardo di Gregorio; the women worked out their own roles and determined the whole progress of the film, Rivette providing only a suggested starting point. With Berto and Labourier particularly, the distinction between actor and character is continuously blurred: we often have the sense that Céline and Julie are constructing the film out of their imaginations, as it goes along. In place of the traditional reading progress whereby we decipher a previously constructed work in order to arrive at and share the author's privileged position of knowledge, we share here, to an unwonted degree, in the process of construction, the division between that and the process of reading becoming narrower than in any earlier fiction film I can think of. At the same time, the traditional reading process is foregrounded in Céline and Julie's attempts to decipher the story within "the House of Fiction," experienced initially in tantalizing fragments: they become the readers of a novel, spectators at a play, the audience in a movie theater (debating, at one point, whether or not there should be an intermission, and deciding against it)—but reader/spectators miraculously given the power to enter the fiction, intervene in the action, and change its predetermined outcome.

The endlessly replayed events in the "House of Fiction" are derived from a very early short story and a much later novella by Henry James—respectively, "A Romance of Certain Old Clothes" and *The Other House*. A brief synopsis will clarify much of the action and the issues. The two works are connected by their premises: an oath sworn by a husband to a wife on her deathbed, and its ultimately fatal consequences. In the early work, the oath is that the husband will never allow his wife's fine clothes—stored in a locked trunk in the attic—to be worn by anyone but their very young child, when

*Céline and Julie Go Boating:* Juliet Berto as Céline.

she grows up; the "terrible vow" of *The Other House* is more drastic: the husband solemnly promises never to remarry while their small daughter remains alive (his dying wife, having had dreadful experiences with her stepmother, wishes to spare the child a repeat). In the short story, the husband marries his late wife's elder sister who, always consumed with jealousy of her sibling, becomes obsessed with the possession of the clothes; in the novella, the husband is the object of the intense and obsessive passion of a woman who eventually drowns the four-year-old girl, attempting to frame the sweet young woman with whom the husband is in love.

The film is structured on a systematic series of oppositions between the Céline/Julie story and the story within the house; to trace these oppositions is to make explicit the film's radical significance.

**"Reality" versus fiction.** The film creates its own "reality," which is more fantastic than the events in the "House of Fiction," easily accommodating the supernatural, the fanciful, the inconsequential; its fiction, though presented in fragments, is governed otherwise by the laws of classical realist narrative (plausibility, character consistency, etc.) and has no room for the illogical or for magic (except insofar as the characters in the house are ghosts from the distant past). The fragmentation (we, along with Céline and Julie, at first receive only flashes of the story, which we have to piece together like a jigsaw) effectively destroys the illusionist power of realist fiction, while the magical nature of the film's "reality" undermines the dominance of ideological norms based on assumptions, common sense, and the "normal." The events within the house are not merely fictitious but literary, adapted from works by an illustrious male author noted for formal perfection, conscious artistry, and the systematic suppression of an authorial viewpoint; Céline and Julie (or Berto and Labourier) invent their own fiction/reality, foregrounding the process of construction.

*Present versus past.* The characters in the house—apart from the child Madlyn—are the "living dead" (the parallels with George A. Romero's zombies, in *Dawn of the Dead*, may not be immediately obvious but, once noted, are extremely suggestive). They represent the past that hangs over the present (its structure of values, as recorded in its literature): the legacy of an obsolete but still potent ideology. Céline and Julie create their present *against* this past, in the process destroying its power. The characters in the house (all of whom wish the child dead and are its potential murderers) are governed entirely by the inherited assumptions of patriarchy; Céline and Julie (whose single-minded endeavor is to *save* the child) reject these assumptions and look toward a future of liberated, autonomous beings—necessarily much less clearly defined.

*Spontaneous versus staged.* Rivette has made it clear that, by the time shooting began, the film was thoroughly scripted. Nonetheless, it sets up a clear distinction between the free, impulsive, spontaneous behavior of Céline and Julie (whose scenes consistently have the feel of improvisation), and the extremely stylized, "acted" behavior (literary dialogue, theatrical movements and delivery) of the people in the house. Céline and Julie are marked as "free," able to invent their own lives; the "house" characters are imprisoned in a predetermined performance, their lines given them by an author, their attitudes and actions determined by the dominant ideological assumptions (about money, marriage, romantic love, gender . . .). This is underlined by the incessant repetition of lines, scenes, gestures: they are actors trapped in a perpetually repeated play, ghosts doomed forever to reiterate their life's misdeeds, puppets of ideology.

*Freedom versus entrapment.* Céline and Julie have free movement: they come and go as they please, wander at will; the apartment is simply a place to eat, sleep, and be together. Sophie, Camille, and Olivier, on the other hand, never go outside the walls of the house (until the film's penultimate scene, where they are *literally* immobilized): their lives are circumscribed by its walls. The house, all the inhabitants of which plot against, manipulate, compete, essentially hate each other, recalls Sartre's *No Exit* (*Huis Clos*); it might be seen as itself a symbol of the dominant ideology, "the house we live in" or wish to move out of and see demolished.

*Autonomy versus marriage.* Céline and Julie reject marriage, and with it the assumption that a woman is defined, given her meaning, through her relationship with a man. In one scene, Céline takes Julie's place when Julie's childhood sweetheart Guilou returns to resume their "ideal" relationship. Guilou wants everything a man is supposed to want of a woman: a wife/mother (they are both dressed in virginal white) and a whore (their exchange of obscene dialogue). Céline (as Julie) leaves him literally with his pants down. In the house, on the other hand, marriage is the supreme aim: the entire "house of fiction" plot is centered on the two women's efforts to capture Olivier (to which end the murder of Madlyn is the necessary means), their only way of securing an identity for themselves.

*Female-oriented, male-oriented.* Céline and Julie control their own lives, driving out all the manifestations of male domination. The scene in which Céline takes Julie's place to annihilate Guilou is balanced/answered by the scene in which Julie takes Céline's place in the nightclub and denounces—in a moment perhaps derived from *Dance, Girl, Dance* (Dorothy Arzner, 1940) but carried much further—the managers and customers who want to objectify women as sexual images for the male gaze. In the house, although the actions are mostly initiated by the women, it is the apparently passive male who determines them and gives them their aim. Olivier dominates everything not through any force of personality but simply by his position as patriarch (father of Madlyn, owner of the house, controller of money), the women's motivation residing solely in their competition to become his next wife. Camille and Sophie habitually construct themselves as objects for his gaze, in their modes of dress and makeup, their calculated poses, their facial expressions; their activeness is repressed and perverted into intrigue and manipulation. The Céline-Julie relationship. on the contrary, represents a celebration of women's activity, of unrepressed, open, and positively directed energy. Their beauty—marked as natural, nonconstructed—the beauty of women being themselves, for themselves—is of quite another order from that of Camille and Sophie. The formal, calculated dress of Camille and Sophie—and the former's obsession with the trunk of clothes in the attic—is contrasted with Céline and Julie's comfortable, informal, careless attire.

***Telepathic communication versus suspicion and distrust.*** If Céline takes Julie's place to "ruin" her chances of marriage, and Julie Céline's in order to lose her the chance of a job (and a possible future in white slavery), we are not invited to read these actions in terms of underhandedness or betrayal. Rather, we are led to believe that each is simply executing the other's real wishes because she knows what those wishes are and is better able to fulfil them: each frees the other from a role in the dominant patriarchal order in which she might, alone, have become trapped. Repeatedly in the film the existence of a magical, telepathic communication is confirmed (see, for example, the moment when Céline brings Julie a bloody Mary at the precise moment when Julie decides to ask for it).

In the house (the imaginary "real" world of bourgeois ideology), on the other hand, there is no direct communication at all, only subterfuge, deception, manipulation, paranoia. Everyone plots against everyone, all interpersonal communication (which requires, as its basis, the *desire* to communicate) is blocked. By juxtaposing the action in the house with the Céline-Julie relationship, Rivette realizes the potential of James's fiction to be read as a devastating critique of heterosexual relations under patriarchy.

The characters of "the House of Fiction" (Bulle Ogier, Marie-France Pisier, Barbet Schroeder).

*Friendship versus enmity.* Céline and Julie, not without initial hesitation and difficulty, establish as close a togetherness as is compatible with the preservation of personal autonomy. In the house, the women can never be friends: they are divided forever by their competition for the male, their only access to power. Although history (or, more particularly, "herstory") is not lacking in accounts of women's friendships, it also contains more than ample evidence of the ways in which women have been divided by the ideological dominance of the male; even a film like Cukor's *Rich and Famous,* whose theme is the celebration of a friendship between two women, celebrates it because its victory is achieved at great cost and against almost overwhelming odds.

*Childishness versus "maturity."* This is an aspect of the film that has been found problematic. Throughout, Céline and Julie behave like children; how, then, do we, as adults, accept them as embodying a new (if tentative) ideal? But the house represents the alternative: "maturity" is an ideological concept, built upon the norms of patriarchy. According to the ideal these norms are meant to embody, the "mature" man takes possession of the woman, becomes in turn the father; the "mature" woman acquiesces in the patriarchal structure, accepts the role of wise, kind mother. The very concept of "maturity," that is to say, is an aspect of the oppression of women (and gays) in our culture: "maturity" as we know it is heterosexual-male-defined. Olivier, the patriarch, complacently passive in his power at the center of things, is mature; Camille and Sophie, desperately competing for his favors, ready to murder a child to achieve their glorious end, hating each other (and really themselves) while pretending affection, are not immature, they are simply maturity gone wrong. On the other hand, Céline and Julie, not needing men for their definition, loving and accepting, the rescuers of the child the mature people wish to kill, are themselves children. Both sets of characters play games, but in somewhat different senses: Céline and Julie play for fun and intercommunication, from a delight in life and togetherness; the "games" of Camille and Sophie are surreptitious (emblematized by the traditional game of "Grandmother's footsteps" at the party).

*Céline and Julie Go Boating* raises a number of challenging questions, not the least of which is how we can continue (or whether we *should* continue) to relate to the past. We need, today, films like *Gaslight* and *Letter from an Unknown Woman* precisely because they help us to understand where we have come from, or, more precisely, what some of us are trying to escape. But suppose—and, in the context of the 1990s the supposition has become extremely difficult—the liberated civilization (socialist, feminist, freed of all gender, sexual, and racial prejudice) actually came into being, would these works (and most works that we have considered masterpieces) lose their relevance, slip back into the status of museum pieces? It's very difficult for me to say this, loving these films as I do, but I think the answer must be yes. I cannot see, in a society in which all problems of class, gender, sexuality, and race had been thoroughly and harmoniously resolved, how people of either sex could continue to relate to *Letter from an Unknown Woman* except as a historical exhibit. And although this film has been so central to my life, I cannot honestly see that this would be a bad thing.

In the present state of our civilization, however, such concerns are purely hypothetical: liberation, as I have tried to envision it, has never seemed further away, in a world where even life itself is under threat. Meanwhile, for those of us (a minority, it seems, when one looks about one) who are on the side of "life," *Céline and Julie* at least suggests one way in which the works of the past can still be of use—for their exposure of the impossible tensions, the impossible strain on human relations, that the patriarchal-capitalist system (which the Right is determined to reimpose, and in the conspicuous absence of any unified Left) continuously reinforces.

One traditional figure of long standing is at once recuperated into the film and partially rethought: the Romantic image of the Child as symbol of the future, of hope, of new life, of possible transformation—a figure whose long literary history has been cogently documented by Peter Coveney in his book *Image of Childhood*. Madlyn acquires complex connotations in the course of the film. She is, first and foremost, a real child, treated by her "loving" relatives as a disposable pawn in their power game, treated by Céline and Julie as a person, without condescension or sentimentality. But she is also linked to the childhood of both. In physical appearance she strikingly resembles Céline and could easily be taken for Céline-as-child; Julie's conversation with her old nurse reveals that the child in the house next door who became sick and disappeared (Madlyn in the past, the Madlyn who died in the "House of Fiction") was just the same age as Julie. Madlyn, then, is the child in the two women—the healthy, growing part of themselves which they rescue from entrapment and destruction within patriarchal ideology.

I want finally to consider certain possible objections to the film, and to define the nature of its achievement. One objection I have encountered (interestingly, from men), that the depiction of Céline and Julie draws lavishly on thoroughly traditional myths of "the feminine" (the association of women with cats, witches, and children), can be turned to the film's advantage. The argument of, at least, certain branches of feminism is not that "feminine" characteristics do not exist, but that *(a)* under patriarchy they have been misrecognized and undervalued and *(b)* they should not be regarded as the exclusive property of women (any more than "masculine" traits should be exclusively male), but as potentially common to both sexes. The aim would be, then, not to reject the myths but to cleanse them of their pejorative connotations and challenge the use to which they have been put— the construction of Woman as "the Other." Men, for example, have traditionally laid claim to "reason" for themselves, established it as the superior quality, and compensated women, condescendingly, by allowing them "intuition." One may certainly argue that men lose at least as much as women from such a dichotomy. The answer would be, not to deny the existence of "intuition" altogether, but to revalue it. In the film, Céline and Julie consistently use their intelligence, but never at the expense of "magic." The film's supreme moment triumphantly affirms magic over the "moronic logic" of the laws of narrative, by finally breaking down the boundaries between "reality" and "fantasy": the moment when, after their last "dream" of rescuing Madlyn from the house, Céline and Julie awaken to discover that the child is indeed there with them in the apartment. It is one of the great liberating moments of cinema—the moment, in fact, that allows Céline and Julie to "go boating," and to pass the ghosts, now stiffened into total paralysis, drifting downstream (back to the past, where they belong) as the women row Madlyn upstream toward the future.

Two other objections I have heard raised may be allowed a little more legitimacy, especially when they are placed in close juxtaposition; taken together, they perhaps point to an area of equivocation in the film. On the one hand, its treatment of men, and of the possibility of heterosexual relations, is entirely negative: the male characters (both within and outside the house) exist solely on the level of parody and are denied even a rare moment of grace. On the other, the treatment of Lesbianism (in its sexual aspect) is curiously shifty and ambiguous. With her friends (male and female) in the bar, Céline explicitly rejects any suggestion that she and Julie have a sexual relationship ("She's not a dyke"); yet it is unmistakably implied that the two women share the same bed. We seem to have a choice between interpreting Céline's remarks as just her way of dealing with casual acquaintances who "wouldn't understand," and seeing the women's relationship as presexual, the affectionate romping and cuddling of schoolgirls (which of course has strong sexual connotations, the question becoming the extent to which they are acted upon). Having dared so much, the film might have dared further: to give us the first positive images of sexual Lesbianism in the history of narrative cinema. As it stands, sexuality itself seems unfortunately restricted to the maneuverings of the characters in the house or the obviously undesirable effusions of Guilou and the oglings of the customers in Céline's boîte.

The film's achievement remains extraordinary. It was made precisely at the time when it was fashionable, at least within academic film theory, to insist that radical feminism was incompatible with pleasure (or "entertainment"), which was strictly controlled by the male gaze: one thinks especially of Laura Mulvey's seminal article "Narrative Form and Visual Pleasure," and the practice of the Mulvey/Wollen collaboration *Riddles of the Sphinx*. This film—and especially its sustained centerpiece, "Louise's story told in thirteen shots"—still remains challenging and theoretically interesting (though does anyone still see it?), but our notions of "pleasure" would have to be redefined beyond recognition before it could be claimed as entertainment. The impression one took from the Mulvey/Wollen intervention was of a clearcut choice between mindless surrender to the addictive and reprehensible seductions of mainstream cinema on the one hand, and sheer cerebral hard work on the other. *Céline and Julie* at the very least suggests ways of breaking this impasse. This is not, unfortunately, to assert that the film is accessible within the bounds of mainstream culture—it is probable that audiences for it have not significantly exceeded in numbers those for *Riddles of the Sphinx*, which, though never achieving commercial release, had frequent exposure on the campus circuit. Yet, while never pandering to ingrained viewing habits, while systematically exposing the dominant codes of narrative, characterization, and representation, *Céline and Julie* engages its viewers in a narrative play that permits identification, fun, suspense, emotional involvement; it allows, indeed encourages, pleasure; one can describe it as immensely entertaining, without stretching the customary meaning of the word to the breaking point.

To consolidate this hope for the future of narrative, I want to return briefly to the comparison I threw out earlier with *Dawn of the Dead* (1979). Romero's film is formally more conservative, more traditional, than Rivette's, containable (just) within a familiar Hollywood genre; though extremely audacious, it cannot commit the narrative transgressions of Rivette. Nonetheless, it stands as a further reminder of how traditional narrative can be stretched and bent into progressive forms.

The parallels between the two films are very striking. Like the inhabitants of the "House of Fiction"—though in a less elaborated and complex way—Romero's zombies, mindlessly gravitating to the shopping mall, represent the habits of the past from which the living characters must strive to extricate themselves (the makeup of Rivette's ghosts, in the last part of *Céline and Julie*, is almost identical). The film never reaches anything quite comparable to the positive image of women in Rivette's film, but it follows Fran's development as she progressively casts off the entrapments of patriarchy: notions of the woman as inferior, as helpless, as irrational, as passive; the acceptance of herself as an image for the male gaze; the notion of marriage as a norm (the moment where she rejects the engagement ring offered by her lover is crucial). At the end of the film the emblems of male power are either transferred to the woman or surrendered (Fran flies the helicopter, the one surviving male relinquishes the rifle to the zombies). The film even offers an equivalent for the rescue of Madlyn in Fran's unborn child, carried out of the clutches of the past toward a precarious and uncertain future. There is also, throughout the film, a strong element of play, in the stylized comic-strip violence, in the film's awareness of itself as a genre movie, as fantasy: the audience is invited to participate in a macabre and bloody game that manages to remain, by virtue of the stylization, simultaneously serious and good-humored.

It is clear that the most audacious and radical films will continue to be made outside the commercial mainstream; but it is equally clear that this in no way precludes the continued use of narrative. The copresence in 1970s cinema of *Céline and Julie Go Boating* and *Dawn of the Dead* offers a timely reminder of the possibilities of significant parallel developments in different spheres of independent filmmaking, at different degrees of remove from the mainstream. Our delight in storytelling and story-hearing, while it needs to be carefully scrutinized, does not have to be abandoned.

# CHAPTER 14

# Drawing Earl:
# The Lessons of "Life Classes"

That I am devoting two chapters of a book mainly concerned with rereadings of generally recognized "classics" to studies of two Canadian films, both obscure and one (*Life Classes*, 1988) virtually unknown outside Canada and barely known within it, will appear to some merely quixotic, to others perhaps no more than a token gesture of gratitude to the country that has been my home for the past twenty years. Nothing could be further from the truth. Within Canadian film culture I have made myself thoroughly unpopular for my alleged lack of interest in Canadian cinema, and, worse, for my openly expressed dislike of certain films that have received far greater national acclaim and international recognition than the two I have singled out. To yet others, it may appear both pointless and frustrating to write at length on films they may never have a chance of seeing—but if nobody draws attention to them, what hope have they of *ever* gaining recognition? So let me make this clear: I write about *Loyalties* and *Life Classes* because I love them; I went so far as to include the latter in my list for the last *Sight and Sound* international critics poll to choose the ten best films ever made. With *Life Classes* especially, I am aware of no incongruity in giving it a place beside the works of Ozu, Renoir, Ophuls, etc.

The titles *Loyalties* and *Life Classes* (both wonderfully apt and precise in relation to the films) are not exactly "box office." Would the films have received more distribution if they had been called , respectively (and plausibly), *Psycho Rapist* and *Take Off Your Clothes*? But then, the patrons of *Life Classes*, especially, would have been as audibly disappointed as those who attended screenings of Godard's 1964 *A Married Woman* (*Une Femme Mariée*) when it played briefly at a soft-core porn theater in London, advertised as "Twenty-four hours in the Life of an Adulteress!!!."

The phrase "conceptual underpinnings" occurs twice in *Life Classes*. The first time, it is used by the pretentious woman who interviews Mary Cameron (Jacinta Cormier) for employment shortly after she arrives in Halifax from the remote seaboard of Nova Scotia, to express her superiority to a young woman who enjoys "painting by numbers." The second time, it is used by the art historian whose lecture Mary attends, with reference to De Kooning, Kandinsky, etc., to describe the concerns of various modern artists: that it is not the outward appearance but the inner energies and tensions that structure an art work. The theme, if not the phrase, is further developed in the instructions of the teacher of the life classes for which Mary becomes a model, a woman presented as intelligent and sympathetic, and who influences Mary's development. I deduce from this *(a)* that director William MacGillivray would like to point our attention to the "conceptual underpinnings" of his film, beyond the "realist" level of character, action, and behavior, but *(b)* that he has a dread of appearing pretentious. Diffidence seems to me an important component of the authorial personality that gives *Life Classes* its particular distinctness and distinction (it is the least arrogant,

*Life Classes:* director William MacGillivray on the set of the opening scene.

rhetorical, or ostentatious of films); intelligence is another. Taking the hint, I shall concentrate on the film's thematic level, examining five concerns which continuously interpenetrate: feminism; the relation of present and future to the past; the country/city opposition; the different artistic modes available in contemporary culture; attitudes to the media and technology. If "diffident," the film is certainly not unambitious.

Mary Cameron never becomes fully aware that she is part of an international political movement (though her friend and workmate Gloria is, asking during a seminar about "the politics of being a woman artist in Germany today"), and the word *feminist* does not occur in the film. Yet the most obvious and dominant level of its discourse—the "evolution of a woman's consciousness"—is unmistakably feminist, every lesson that Mary learns being both personal and more-than-personal. I might justly have described the film as being about "the evolution of a *feminist* consciousness." It is (for better or for worse—I don't mean this as a value judgment) more explicit about this than the earlier film with which it most invites comparison, Bertrand Tavernier's *A Week's Vacation* (*Une Semaine de Vacances*, 1980). It is a comparison to which *Life Classes* stands up remarkably well (no small tribute, as *Une Semaine . . .* remains among the best work of one of the contemporary cinema's most distinguished figures), considering Tavernier's enormous advantages—long experience of feature filmmaking, working within a long-established and vital artistic (and critical) tradition, with incomparably superior financial resources and technical facilities. In fact, I am never aware, in watching *Life Classes*, of any technical shortcomings: MacGillivray has the true artist's ability to find the means fully to realize his concerns within the available resources, and there is never any sense of a discrepancy between ambition and technique. I have heard the term *minimalist* applied to the film, presumably as a means of describing the strict economy of MacGillivray's style: it is a film entirely devoid of frills and flourishes, there is no attempt to woo the audience with a seductive charm (which is one of the things about it I find so captivating), and, aside from the use of slow motion in the credit sequences, there is a total rejection of cinematic rhetoric (the 360-degree tracking shots, which I shall discuss later, are strictly functional, not decorative or "show-off").

Against the complete confidence and authority of the Tavernier film, one must acknowledge a certain hesitancy and reticence, the "diffidence" I spoke of earlier: it is what gives the film its engaging freshness, with its suggestion that this filmmaker from Nova Scotia and Newfoundland, lacking the long cinematic tradition that nurtures a Tavernier, was having to reinvent cinema all over again for himself. These are qualities that have been theorized by Canadian critics, preoccupied with defining an indigenous national culture, where none exists, as peculiarly Canadian. *A Week's Vacation* is every bit as "French" as *Life Classes* is "Canadian" (or "provincial Nova Scotian"), but no one as far as I know has found it necessary to apply that term to pigeonhole it and, in doing so, by implication drastically circumscribe its significance. MacGillivray's film belongs to the world (or at least deserves to). The hesitancy and reticence can be equally attributed to the supposition that MacGillivray is a profoundly honest person tackling issues of immense international cultural significance gently and unpretentiously, feeling his way rather than making assertive statements.

If I had been shown *Loyalties* and *Life Classes* unprepared, and asked to guess which was made by a woman, I would unhesitatingly have chosen *Life Classes*. This is partly because *Loyalties* adopts unquestioningly the mode and norms of the dominant (hence patriarchal) tradition—in my opinion a perfectly defensible strategy, but one to which many feminist writers on film have expressed strenuous opposition. The style and enunciation of *Life Classes*, on the other hand, consistently suggest a search for an alternative mode of expression subtly deviating from the norms by a process of selection and emphasis (we are not talking *Riddles of the Sphinx* here). Further, the enunciation is characterized by qualities our culture tends to regard as feminine (sensitive and reticent, as against the forceful and direct "masculine" address of *Loyalties*). Even the treatment of David Sutton in Anne Wheeler's film might be read as a not uncommon form of male masochism and guilt, as against the feminist firmness with which Earl (Leon Dubinsky) is treated in *Life Classes*.

More important, however, is the extraordinary intimacy and inwardness of MacGillivray's relationship to his central figure, both actress and character. This impression is by no means contradicted—rather the contrary—by the fact that we feel we "know" Mary Cameron rather less completely than we "know" the women of *Loyalties*. The latter have the life of fully realized fictional characters, fully known by their authors who created them. The "life" of Mary Cameron is something more than that: she is allowed to retain something of her mystery, the not-quite-knowability of a human being. In other words, the relationship of filmmaker / actress / character is rather more complex here. Though I shall postpone discussion of the opening and ending credit sequences—the framing prologue and epilogue—one aspect is relevant here. In a shopping mall, we are led to watch a supposed television interview with Jacinta Cormier, supposedly attending the premiere of *Life Classes* in Halifax and questioned about the character she plays. Her genuine response expresses a complex combination of empathy and uncertainty, with "I guess" a key phrase: "She's a product of the culture . . . and a victim, I guess . . . and the changes that it's going through." She is both like and unlike Mary: "I grew up in a small town too, and like her . . . I was (pause) *forced* (sounds uncertain of the word's appropriateness), I guess, to leave home . . . Mary eventually becomes more . . . " (sentence left incomplete). Was the role difficult for her? "Yes . . . No, not really. I came to know her. Not that it was easy. She's a very complex character. I'm still not sure I fully understand her or her motives." Mary Cameron is, of course, a fictional character who does not exist outside the film. But Jacinta Cormier does, and she both is and is not Mary Cameron. There is then the relationship of MacGillivray to Cameron/Cormier, which seems at once symbiotic and distanced, and which determines the viewer's relationship: we both identify with Cameron/Cormier and study her.

Mary's development, while in some ways dependent upon her family and environmental background, which she never entirely abandons, is accelerated by the move from Cape Breton to Halifax. The small town/country community is never sentimentalized, either past or present. The film's view is that, if there ever was once a form of "organic culture" there of any character or distinction, it is now irretrievably lost, and nostalgic laments for its passing would be a waste of time; if it ever existed, its traces have been thoroughly obliterated by the irresistible flood of consumer capitalism, technology, and the media. The predicament of Mary's grandmother, drifting into senility in almost total isolation ("No one has any time for old ladies") eloquently sums up the sense of cultural deprivation which the film shares with the Alberta of *Loyalties*: on the one hand she clings to otherwise long-abandoned straws from the past (memories, snatches of Gaelic), on the other her days are passed propped in front of a TV screen watching the "stories" (as she calls indiscriminately whatever drifts before her consciousness—soaps, sitcoms, newsreels, commercials . . . ). Neither is the city in any way glamorized; but it is presented as offering Mary opportunities for self-realization, for reaching an awareness (of herself, her potential, her social position) that she could never have reached in the country.

Central to this process of self-realization is Mary's discovery of herself as an artist, the various stages of which coincide with MacGillivray's inquiry into the modes of contemporary art and his defense of a qualified representationalism, leading to an implied congruity between Mary's paintings and his film (hence further confirming his identification with his leading character). Before I examine those stages (which are essential to the film's structure, both narrative and conceptual), I must confront one possible objection, the question of plausibility. Mary's somewhat abrupt discovery of authentic creative gifts (it is not clear exactly how much time passes between her first attempts at "personal" expression and her solo exhibition, but it appears to be a matter of months rather than years) imposes some strain on credulity.

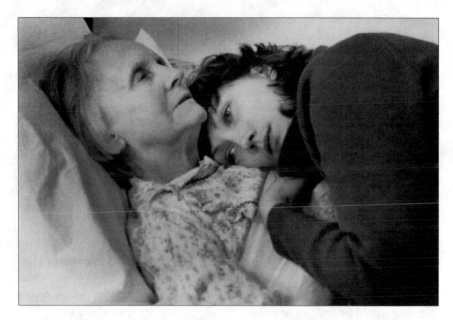

*Life Classes:* Mary Cameron (Jacinta Cormier) with her grandmother
(Evelyn Garbary).

The point I want to make is that, while arguably *improbable*, it is not *impossible*. Many of the attacks on Realism have centered on the assumption that it can only endlessly reproduce what is already there (external appearances, social structures) and is powerless to change it. But why should Realism be tied to probability? Why not a Realism of the *possible*, allowing for greater freedom, the potential for leaps of the imagination (both the filmmakers' and the characters')? Mary's progress (essentially a "leap of the imagination") is validated by the spirit and progress of the film itself, its commitment to change, to the *making possible*, to increased awareness, experimentation, audacity. The stages of Mary's self-discovery are sufficiently complex and suggestive to provide a basis for this leap into the possible.

*Painting by numbers.* It is greatly to MacGillivray's credit that he never invites the viewer to feel superior to, or find ridiculous, Mary's painting-by-numbers, the first of her attempts to find an outlet for her creativity. Within the context of an impoverished rural culture—the obliteration of its past compensated for by nothing more fulfilling than supermarkets and television—Mary's loving care is felt as bringing a certain validity to an essentially noncreative medium, and is respected as such. We are aware from the outset of Mary's native intelligence, her capacity for reflection, criticism, discrimination, autonomous judgment; at this stage her creativity lacks any awakening in the form of a model or an external stimulus, any sense that more ambitious work is possible.

*The interview.* At the employment agency in Halifax, Mary's attention is drawn to an abstract, minimalist painting on the wall. The woman interviewer asks what she thinks of it, referring pretentiously to her own interest in "conceptual underpinnings." We register Mary's response ("Mine are better") as funny, certainly, but not stupid: its naïveté is set against the other woman's condescension and assumption of superiority, and Mary's confidence in the value of her own work—a confidence that does not strike us as arrogant—is an important pointer to the speed with which she develops her talent.

*The lecture on Modernism.* Mary accompanies her friend Gloria (her fellow-assistant in the department store where she gets a job, and part-time art student) to an art history lecture (the scene in which the term "conceptual underpinnings" recurs). Back in Gloria's room she expresses bafflement and hostility ("pictures you can't even make sense of"). We need not take this as MacGillivray's attitude to all abstract art (to identify with someone does not involve necessarily sharing all his/her opinions, and the film in no way satirizes the lecture); both Mary's exposure to modern art and her (initial) rejection of it mark an important stage in her critical evolution—her artist's sense of what interests *her*, rather than the critic's sense of what is of value. It is at the end of this scene that Gloria suggests that Mary supplement her income by "sitting" for $12 an hour.

*The life classes.* Mary's exposure of herself as nude model, itself an important step in her evolution as a person, is accompanied by her exposure *to* certain concepts of figure drawing that are crucial to her artistic development: both aspects of the experience teach her the lesson of freedom, the casting off of constraints imposed by her earlier environment. The teacher (a woman this time) instructs the students to make quick sketches ("gesture drawings") catching the body's action as Mary adopts different poses. The sketches are "not supposed to look like anything," the positive response to Mary's negative "pictures you can't even make sense of"; the aim is to capture the "inner core," not to produce outlines. At home afterwards with her child Marie, Mary attempts her first autonomous sketches, trying to capture the "inner core" of the small girl's body.

If I remember correctly, Julia Lesage once remarked at a conference that men should be banned from photographing women for at least ten years. I hope she would allow an exception in the case of MacGillivray. The way in which Jacinta Cormier is shot in the nude scenes (it might be taken as exemplifying the distinctions made in John Berger's thesis on the nude in the seminal *Ways of Seeing*, a work I have found much more helpful than Laura Mulvey's celebrated "Visual Pleasure" article) implies a distinction between two terms that are frequently confused—being looked at and being objectified. We are invited to *look at* Mary, as at once a beautiful woman and a person, the two being inseparable (nowhere in the film is she treated as merely *physically* beautiful). At no point is she objectified; we are always in intimate contact with her feelings, she is consistently a person rather than a body. The first scene in which she appears nude is eloquent on this point: we share her embarrassment and intense unease as she poses within a circle of students for the first time, even as the camera compels us to watch her, as if our presence were adding to her discomfiture. This is the least pornographic of films: the human body is progressively demystified, its anatomical detail no longer a dirty secret, source of sniggers and titillation, but mature, matter-of-fact reality. Hence nudity in the film, instead of being an act of oppression, becomes a liberating experience for both Mary and the movie's audience. It is important that Mary's nudity is balanced later by full-frontal male nudity: the young men participating in the avant-garde television "happen-

Director Bill MacGillivray considers how he will realize the drawing sequences in *Life Classes*. (Photo: David Middleton)

ing," and more especially Earl (the father of her child), the scene in which Mary persuades him to pose naked for her answering the three "life classes" sequences, the demystification of the body capped by the demystification of the phallus.

Crucial to the presentation of nudity and the nonobjectifying look at the female body is the set of three life-classes sequences, which constitute a formal progression in which similarity and difference are marked by the mise-en-scène. Each consists mainly (though not exclusively) of a 360-degree tracking shot around the studio, as Mary poses naked for the students, yet each offers a different perspective, the three taken together adding up to a three-dimensional description of the experience of the life class. In the first, Mary is the center of attention and empathy (shrinking, embarrassed, wondering if she should feel humiliated), the students kept in the background, anonymous and undifferentiated. The second focuses on the students, absorbed in the work, the teacher moving around to inspect their efforts, Mary entering the frame only later in the shot, the camera stopping when she is central to the image. The third shot concentrates on the students' drawings, the various (and markedly diverse) representations of Mary's body (or its "inner core"): while Mary is kept frame center throughout, her body is repeatedly concealed by the sketches as the camera circles.

*The German artist.* Gloria takes Mary to a special seminar celebrating the visit of a German sculptress, illustrated by slides of her recent work—a series of smooth bone- or horn-shaped abstract objects. The lecture, read in translation by another woman as the artist presides in silence, is verbose and obscure, an outpouring of pretentious jargon delivered reverentially. Question time follows, but the audience has by now been intimidated into total silence. At last Mary raises a series of simple practical questions ("What are these things made of? . . . How big are they? . . . How does she carve them so perfectly?") which are then relayed in translation to the artist, her answers paraphrased by the translator: "She has carpenters do it . . . She doesn't paint them herself, she has someone else do it . . ." "How come they don't tip over?" Mary asks. "She has a computer design them." Mary is driven to the ultimate question: "What does *she* do?" (The artist is becoming increasingly defensive/aggressive.) "She just *thinks* of these things." The sequence takes up again the notion of "conceptual underpinnings," carrying it to its parodic extreme: the totally alienated art of a "sculptress" who has no physical contact whatever with her materials. (At the same time, it is important that the objects are beautiful rather than grotesque or merely absurd, and Mary's questions—"How does she carve them so perfectly?"— implicitly acknowledge this. Nothing in this film is simple except its enunciation.) Although Mary is too diffident to be aggressive, the scene reminds me strongly of the Ursula/Loerke confrontation toward the end of Lawrence's *Women in Love*: the naïveté, which can easily be made to look like stupidity when faced by arrogant pretentiousness, comes across as a healthy and fundamentally intelligent response. In relation to MacGillivray, the scene is a reminder that, if our attention is being drawn to "conceptual underpinnings," this is not to negate our sense of the filmmaker's art as a fully human engagement, nor to invite us to neglect the film's flesh and muscle in favor of its skeleton.

*Children's drawings.* Exploring the country home she has inherited from her grandmother, Mary finds some of her own childhood drawings, from before she learned to "paint by numbers." The film does not explicitly connect this to her artistic development, yet it links Mary's adult art to another of the crucial issues, the sense of the past and its relation to the future: a so far unproduced screenplay of MacGillivray's which I have been privileged to read contains the line "If we lose the past, we lose the future." We may also recall the importance of child art in the work of certain key modern artists (Klee, Miro).

*The television "event."* This sequence draws together so many of the conceptual/thematic threads that I shall have to return to it. The film's ambivalent attitude to the event itself (a semiorganized "happening" in which the participants, male and female, naked, encased in cylindrical plastic curtains, perform songs associated with some important period of their lives in order to release memories and emotions in a stream-of-consciousness monologue) is epitomized in the presentation of the organizer, intelligent and efficient but bossy and inconsiderate (she also refers to women as "girls"). If the event is *almost* ridiculous, it is saved by its aim and function (realized especially through Mary herself, singled out by the television camera for the unconstraint with which she gives herself): the cathartic significance of self-discovery and self-revelation, the exposure without shame of the whole human being, of which the physical nudity is but the outward sign. Mary uses an avant-garde "happening" for the expression of, simultaneously, her commitment to the past and her sense of the need for change. The predominantly positive nature of the scene should effectively counter any suspicion that MacGillivray is hostile to Modernism or to experimental art. His film is itself Modernist in its audacities.

*Drawing Earl.* The film's presentation of Earl in many ways parallels that of Eddy in *Loyalties*. Both are working-class men of limited education who

Mary during the television "event": the butterfly breaking out of her chrysalis.

develop a sensitivity and a kind of rough grace through their ability to love, and more importantly learn to respect, a woman. It is their ability to learn and to adapt that makes possible the generosity with which the films treat them. Earl consistently recognizes Mary's superiority—not in class or education, but in intelligence, awareness, and sensibility: her superiority both to him and to their small-town environment, the superiority that leads Mary's peers to see her, quite unjustly, as a "snob." Mary is quite clear on the subject of Earl's limitations, refusing to tie herself to him in marriage, her affection for him having its source in sexual pleasure. Early in the film, when, confronted with the fact of Mary's pregnancy, Earl asks her what she's going to do (adding "I wouldn't make much of a . . ."), she promptly responds with "I know what I'm *not* going to do. I'm *not* marrying *you* . . . We both know what you do best, Earl. That's why we're where we are." Yet, while still at the end of the film refusing marriage (which he now wants), she never rejects Earl either, developing a certain respect for him because of his capacity to learn. There are three crucial steps in the progress of the relationship: *(a)* Earl, by chance, and thanks to his satellite dish, watches Mary's television appearance; in the course of the monologue she refers—with irony and affection— to his "great family jewels," linking this to her mother's and her own pursuit of the "family jewels," the women's quest for potency. It is this that provokes Earl's departure for Halifax in a spirit that combines pique with admiration; *(b)* Mary persuades Earl to pose for her in the nude. The film's theme of the liberating effect of nakedness is thus extended to the male, Earl gradually overcoming his extreme uneasiness at having "the family jewels" exposed to objective female scrutiny; *(c)* Earl attends Mary's art exhibition, discovering—with initial horror but swift acceptance—her revelation of his nudity to the public gaze. In the film's overall schema, *b* corresponds to Mary's first engagement at the life classes as a nude model, and *c* to her naked television appearance.

**The art exhibition.** Clearly, Mary's art exhibition, consisting exclusively of nude studies of Earl and delightfully billed as a "One Man Show," is the culmination of the process I have traced, the film's trajectory. We are not asked to view Mary as a great artist, and the show is not a particular success; the emphasis is on her own personal development, her realization of her talent combined with a feminist deployment of it, the returning of the gaze on to the naked male body. The sketches ("gesture drawings," as in the life classes) are at once representational and distinctively modern (like MacGillivray's film).

One of the film's major concerns (which also happens to be one of mine) is the tension between the need to acknowledge and respect the past and the need to distance oneself from it, the need for a sense of tradition and the need for radical change. One may begin a discussion of MacGillivray's characteristically intelligent exploration of this tension with the song that runs through the film as leitmotiv, and its precise function:

> My child is my mother returning,
> My mother, my daughter, the same.
> She carries us all in her yearning,
> Our sorrow, our peace, and our pain.

In itself, the song can be read as a succinct summation of the response of women to oppression throughout the history of patriarchy. Its function in the film is somewhat more complex. Mary and her mother, Mary and her daughter, both are and are not "the same": the same as the victims of oppression, quite distinct in their responses to it, the responses that their changing cultural situations make possible—the song's essentialism and resignation are powerfully countered by the film's progression. Mary's sense of the importance of preserving a continuity with the past is at all points accompanied by her need to break with it; it is not a paradox that her commitment to the past gives her the strength to take control and determine her own future. The commitment is of course highly selective: Mary identifies (through the song learned from her grandmother, which she sings interchangeably in English and Gaelic, the "second language" she claims in her employment interview) with the women's line, both the transgressive mother who left and the nontransgressive grandmother who stayed (but who tells Mary, in one of her moments of perfect lucidity, "You should have left long ago"). The father, unable to forget the affront to his male ego ("She made a fool of me, Mary, in front of everyone") has tried to obliterate the mother altogether, burning her letters and all photographs of her. Despite his efforts, the generations all come together in the scene after the grandmother's death when Mary and Earl explore the house she has bequeathed: Mary finds photographs of her mother and grandmother, and Marie, though left behind in Halifax, is "present" on the T-shirt Mary gives to Earl ("You can wear it in the tavern and brag to the boys"). It is important that she chooses, for the print, a photograph in which Marie appears to be crying: Earl will not be allowed the comforting illusion that everything's just fine.

This commitment to the women's line, the identification with oppressed women through the centuries, is accompanied (logically enough) by a firm rejection of the patriarchal nuclear family and the institution of marriage that is its foundation and sanction (if *Loyalties* is equivocal on this issue, *Life Classes* is not). Mary implicitly endorses her mother's abdication (despite the fact that the mother abandoned her as well as her husband) and reconfirms her independence by rejecting marriage to her child's biological father (as delivered by Jacinta Cormier, the last line of the film, the two simple words, "No, Earl," become one of the film's great lines, caustic, affectionate, and rock-firm all at the same time). It is characteristic of the film's (and Mary's) generosity that this rejection of patriarchal authority does not necessitate a rejection of *people*: Earl and the father are both present and acknowledged in the final scene.

The treatment of technology and the media, like every other aspect of the film, is highly intelligent. It is also consistent with the city / country opposition and the film's firm rejection of "Canadian pastoral" and all that goes with it: Mary, to retain her links with everything in the past that matters to her, will return to her grandmother's house every summer, but her future is in the city. The film opens (after the credits) with the installation of Earl's satellite dish, and it is partly through this that the attitude is defined. The dish accrues strong positive connotations: it is Earl's means to self-respect and dignity (his "phallus," if you will, despite its inappropriate shape, but a strictly nonoppressive one) in an environment that clearly does not encourage a sense of self-worth. It becomes the community's access to a wider world—picking up the program in which Mary participates and broadcasting it to both Earl and her father, forcing the latter to confront at last the negativity and self-insulation of his own attitude ("He said my mother was a whore," broadcast to the world in Mary's monologue) while initiating an entire new development in the former. More important, it becomes the individual's means of serving the community of which he is a member, in defiance of capitalist interests and authority: Earl is facing prosecution for using his dish to service more than one house. His friend has built a descrambler, but the American channels "went crazy," changing their codes every few seconds. In case we mistake this for simple nationalist anti-American diatribe, Earl is made to add that "the worst is the RCMP": it's the system and its minions that constitute the enemy. While it is never spelled out, the film's commitment to a form of socialism seems as clear as its commitment to feminism.

On the one hand, the dominance of the media, the capitalist function of television to fill up leisure and inhibit thought, is presented firmly: the grandmother sitting passively in front of "the stories," Earl and his friends boozing it up while watching sports programs. On the other, the film never shows the least inclination to indulge in nostalgic wish-fulfillments of a return to the simple life in a technology-free "natural" environment. MacGillivray's point is clear: it is not technology that is the enemy but the people who control it; more precisely, the socioeconomic system which it is made to serve and sustain.

I want, in conclusion, to return briefly (at the risk of some repetition) to the pivotal sequence of this perfectly constructed film, the avant-garde television performance. It is one of those marvelous sequences that guarantee the authenticity of works of art—the place where "it all comes together," where all the disparate themes, as in a piece of complex contrapuntal music, are suddenly caught up, revealed as the interlocking parts of a whole. The concept of the sequence is extremely audacious, the action arguably implausible and potentially risible: another triumph, in fact, of a "realism of the possible.'

All the themes I have explored are simultaneously present, their essential unity made manifest so that a summation of the sequence can stand also as a summation of this chapter. Mary, naked, sings her song (both in Gaelic and English); her monologue definitively "places" the men in her life (father, lover) and defines her relationship to them; it also establishes her commitment to her errant mother, the other links in the female line (daughter, grandmother) being "present" in the song itself. The celebration of continuity is contained within a celebration of innovation (the avant-garde "happening," which also defines artistic creation in terms of the human and the personal, in terms of "nudity" and the refusal of shame, in terms of rootedness in lived experience). The show itself is independent, broadcast via satellite, using advanced technology but outside the control of the dominant ideology or corporate capitalism. Finally, it is important that the woman artist who conceived and organizes it is *from* New York, and the transmission is intended primarily *for* New York. The film takes in its stride this extreme instance of "cultural imperialism": if "the enemy" is not technology, it is also not simply the United States, but the system that controls both (and Canada).

After eight years, *Life Classes* remains the finest Canadian film I have seen, but it doesn't require the qualification. In terms of the richness and density of meaning, it can stand beside any of the films discussed in this book, and deserves to be widely known and generally accessible.

## A Note on "Antonia's Line"

*Antonia's Line* (Marleen Gorris, 1995) would have earned a chapter to itself if (slightly to adapt Andrew Marvell) there were space enough and time; but it offers itself too appositely for comparison with *Life Classes* to be omitted entirely.

The grounds for comparison are clear enough: the two films' common concerns with *(a)* the development and celebration of a female autonomy no longer bounded and defined by men; *(b)* the expression of this through art (in Gorris's film, Danielle's drawings, Thérése's music); *(c)* the possibility that men could learn to adjust to this and accept it; *(d)* the crucial importance of preserving links through the female line of descent. One may ask how two films that have so much in common thematically can be so different in effect.

In one respect they exist in a precisely inverse relation: a film everyone has heard of and many have seen, a certified "crowd pleaser" (*Antonia's Line* received standing ovations at the Toronto Film Festival and won the 1995 Oscar for Best Foreign Film), versus a film almost no one has heard of that has pleased only a few individuals like myself. The opposition defines, up to a point, the very different *personalities* of the two films: *Life Classes* never *asks* to be loved; *Antonia's Line* does, insistently.

To understand *Antonia's Line* fully one must look back at Gorris's past work, *A Question of Silence* (1982) and its seldom shown and now apparently inaccessible successor *Broken Mirrors* (1984). *Antonia's Line* has been, in some quarters, misguidedly seen as Gorris's retraction of the stance of the earlier films; it seems to me to stand not so much in opposition to them than as their complement. They were about women under patriarchy and expressed an unrelentingly hostile attitude to men, logically and devastatingly argued in *A Question of Silence*, degenerating into hysterical hatred in *Broken Mirrors*;

*Antonia's Line* is a utopian fantasy about what a matriarchal community might be, with men (or at least a few of them) suddenly redeemable.

"Fantasy" is I think the necessary word, the film's "fantasy" characteristics by no means restricted to the occasional visions of Antonia's daughter Danielle and granddaughter Thèrése. It is a condition for the ideal matriarchal community that develops around Antonia (its growth determined partly by her actions, but more by the magnetism of personal charisma) that it exist quite apart from the movement of mainstream civilization, in an apparently isolated village that remains miraculously exempt from the incursions of corporate capitalism with its movie theaters, television, and supermarkets.

But Gorris cheats: We suddenly discover later that it lies within easy reach of a large modern university (necessary for the education of the intellectually gifted Thèrése), from which Thèrése rushes to reach the house of her mentor Crooked Finger, on the occasion of his suicide, arriving at the same moment as the villagers.

The film also betrays a disturbing essentialism. The characters of *A Question of Silence* (both male and female) were firmly placed within the social realities of our culture, their attitudes and actions influenced by their class and gender positions. The characters of *Antonia's Line* simply are what they are: the good Farmer Bas and his good sons, the bad Farmer Dan and his bad sons, have developed within exactly the same environment, and we are given no explanation for their difference beyond heredity. Unlike MacGillivray's precisely defined, logically developed Earl, the men of Gorris's film either can't learn or don't need to. Thèrése's husband Simon seems a particular weakness: the "ideal" male is conceived as the meek, submissive, nurturing figure that women were brought up to be in the past.

Antonia's "line" is clearly a very different affair from Mary Cameron's. If Mary draws sustenance from the examples of her mother and grandmother, it is in far more complex and ambivalent ways than the relatively simple relationship of Danielle and Thèrése to Antonia. As for Antonia herself, she comes across as some kind of miraculous "happening," an inexplicable force of nature; the only attitude to men, to relationships, and to life that she could have learned from *her* mother is entirely negative.

I don't want this to be taken as a rejection of *Antonia's Line*; I have emphasized those aspects of it that relate to *Life Classes*. A complete reading would find much more to discuss, especially the presentation of Crooked Finger, a character portrayed sympathetically whose view of existence offers the only formidable opposition Gorris permits to the film's utopianism. *Antonia's Line* has continued to move and excite me on many re-viewings: we need empowering utopian fantasies. I feel, however, that they must take into account the conditions within which we actually, today, exist and struggle, for how can we strive to reach a utopia in which it is impossible to believe? The sense of empowerment and uplift fades; the qualified, exploratory optimism of *Life Classes* survives. For me, Gorris's finest achievement to date remains *A Question of Silence*.

# CHAPTER 15

# Rethinking Romantic Love: "Before Sunrise"

> "You know, if there's any kind of god, it wouldn't be in any of us, not you, or me, but just . . . this little space in between. If there's any kind of magic in this world, it must be in the attempt of understanding someone, sharing something. I know, it's almost impossible to succeed, but who cares really? The answer must be in the attempt . . ."
>
> —CÉLINE (JULIE DELPY) IN *Before Sunrise*

I knew, the first time I saw *Before Sunrise* (1995), that here was a film for which I felt not only interest or admiration but love; a film I would want to revisit repeatedly over the years; one that would join the short list of films that remain constant favorites; and one that I would ultimately want to write about, as a means at once of exploring it more systematically and of sharing my delight in it with others—of finding that "magic" in the "attempt." I believe in the possibility of a "definitive" reading of a work only in the sense that it is definitive for myself at a certain stage of my evolution, that it "defines" not the work but my own temporary sense of it, the degree of contact I have been able to achieve, as clearly and completely as I can; but I do not feel ready, with *Before Sunrise*, for even that limited and provisional undertaking. What follows, then, should be read as a series of loosely interconnected and often tentative probes, the beginning of a "work in progress": a preliminary attempt to define why, for me personally, this film belongs among the dozen or so that exemplify "cinema" at its finest.

## Style

*Style* is a necessary word whose meaning we all think we understand until we try to give it a precise definition; indeed, like many necessary words, it may be useful only so long as its meaning remains somewhat vague. If we restrict it to camera style we can handle it fairly confidently, talking about long shots or close-ups, static or moving camera, high angle or low angle, long takes or rapid editing. Yet this is never sufficient, and such an analysis, however meticulous, may become actually misleading, as well as a way of privileging some styles of filmmaking over others. It might, for example, lead one to the conclusion that the films of Leo McCarey had no style at all, or at best a style lacking all distinctiveness and distinction, whereas its great distinctiveness (McCarey at his best is always instantly recognizable) arises not from the use of the camera but from the relationship between the director and his actors.

With director Richard Linklater one can indicate certain specific stylistic preferences—the fondness, for example, for long takes, both with and without camera movement—but this will not take one very far in defining the *feel* of the films, one's experience in watching them, to which "style" is obviously crucial. In this wider sense (ultimately the only valid one), style will always elude precise definition. Nor is the old style / content dichotomy very helpful. It works only if one reduces "content" to something like a plot synopsis or the "action" as one might narrate it to a friend: the "content" of a film is images and sounds, and the specific nature of those images and sounds is "style." To talk of the two as somehow distinct and separable is impossible, and the moment one begins to talk about "style" as something with an autonomous existence one also begins to misrepresent the film. This is true even of the work of directors who developed an instantly recognizable visual style, who are commonly seen as "great stylists." To take two obvious extremes (both of whom might, I think, have had an indirect influence on *Before Sunrise*), the visual styles of Ozu and Ophuls are inextricably a part of the meaning of their films; and—unless, again, we define "content" as plot synopsis—the content of a film is its total meaning, which can never be finally fixed (it will change subtly for each generation, as cultural change brings new perceptions). This is not to assert that style must "express" content in the sense familiar from traditional aesthetics. It would be more accurate to say that style is the artist's means of defining the relationship of the spectator to the film. Aside from the "realist" (i.e., illusionist) styles of most mainstream cinema (and those already embrace a very wide range of possibilities), there are the "Brechtian" styles (another wide range, as the term has been applied to everything from Sirk to Godard) and the various styles of melodrama. But they too are inextricable components of a film's meaning, its content in the wider sense.

Richard Linklater directing *Before Sunrise*.

## Levels of Meaning

The cover of the laserdisc of *Before Sunrise* gives (somewhat unusually) fascinating and useful information about the film's conception and creation. One can distinguish various stages in its progress from idea to realization:

1. Richard Linklater, in New York for a work-in-progress screening of *Slacker*, decides to visit relatives in Philadelphia; he meets a woman in a toy store, and they spend the night wandering the streets, talking.

2. Some years later (after completing *Slacker* and shooting *Dazed and Confused*) he sees this experience as the possible basis for a film.

3. Feeling the need of a woman's input ("I didn't want the woman in the film to be a projection of myself"), he enlists Kim Krizan (whom he had met when she auditioned for *Slacker*) as fellow screenwriter; together they compose scenes in which he provides the man's dialogue, she the woman's, but with some interchange (he wrote some of "her" dialogue, she some of "his").

4. Ethan Hawke and Julie Delpy are cast as the two leads, and there follows a series of consultations in which they also contribute ideas, often drawing on personal experience (*Hawke:* "It was like mutual group therapy, a

great way to begin"; and *Linklater:* "The fake phone call scene came from something Julie did with her girlfriends as a teenager . . . I thought it was brilliant, so we just worked out the scene from there . . .")

**5.** Filming begins, but the screenplay still leaves space for interpretation, improvisation, accident—e.g., the two actors in the "play about a cow" really *were* two actors in a play about a cow . . . (*Hawke:* " 'There were a lot of scenes like that.")

The laserdisc cover fails to maintain this level of interest and intelligence to the end (quoting *Glamour* magazine to inform us that *Before Sunrise* is "the most winning romance since *Four Weddings and a Funeral*," and apparently not grasping that this is an insult). But such firsthand documentation of a film's creation is all too rare; so often, we critics have to rely on interviews with directors discussing films they made ten or twenty years earlier, memories of which are inevitably partial, and colored by distance, bias, and exaggeration. Just one crucial step is missing: Why Ethan Hawke and Julie Delpy? How were they cast? Were other actors considered, approached, rejected? I ask because, given the result, it is absolutely impossible to imagine the film without Hawke and Delpy. (Tom Cruise and Nicole Kidman? Or, really to scrape the bottom of the barrel, Rob Lowe and Demi Moore?) It is clear, not merely from the account of its making but from the result, that Hawke and Delpy made themselves integral to the collaborative creative act: have any two actors ever given themselves more completely, more generously, more *nakedly*, to a film? The usual distinction between "being" and "acting" is totally collapsed. *Before Sunrise* is both, and indissolubly, "a Richard Linklater Film" (no one else could have made it) and a densely collaborative one. It would be an ideal subject for one of those "Special Edition" laserdiscs where, on an alternative audio track, the filmmakers and actors give a running commentary on the film as we watch. One hopes that some enterprising executive will organize this before the film recedes too far into the past.

This gives us three levels of reading: is this a film about Jesse and Céline (characters), Hawke and Delpy (actors), or Linklater and Krizan (filmmakers)? The levels are there, but they merge into each other to the extent of being ultimately undistinguishable from one another. The "style" (and also the meaning) of the film is not merely Linklater's decisions as to where to place and when to move the camera; it is also Hawke's precise gestures, Delpy's precise expressions, their intimate interaction—hence, ultimately unanalyzable on paper.

+ + +

Although it is not very useful, it seems necessary to say that the "meaning" of a great film is ultimately itself: the movement from shot to shot, the precise sequence of sounds and images. V. F. Perkins has demonstrated that the "meaning" of *The Wizard of Oz* is *not* reducible to " 'There is no place like home"; on a higher level of achievement, one must not reduce *Tokyo Story* to "Life is disappointing, isn't it?," or that favorite refuge of Western critics *mono no aware*, the Japanese expression of "the sadness of things"; and "For me, life is movement" does *not* sum up *Lola Montes*, let alone Ophuls in toto. Such explicit statements have their place in the fabric of a film's total meaning, but only as a contributing factor within a context that may qualify or even contradict them. I shall not, therefore, attempt to find a phrase to sum up the meaning of *Before Sunrise*, but I shall venture to suggest that its meaning develops simultaneously on three continuously interactive levels:

1. *Personal:* the detailed description of a highly specific relationship between two complexly characterized individuals.

2. *Social:* the exploration of contemporary (post-1960s/1970s feminism) attitudes to love, relationships, and romanticism.

3. *Metaphysical:* the pervasive preoccupation with death, time and transience, chance and arbitrariness—a world without any sense of certitude or confidence in the future.

## After the End

We know of course (having been told so many times) that characters in a fiction have no existence beyond it, and it is therefore improper to speculate about their lives outside it. But *Before Sunrise* seems to defy such a prohibition: everyone with whom I have watched it immediately raises the question of whether or not Jesse and Céline will keep their six-months-ahead date. The general consensus is that they probably won't, a conclusion one might find supported by both the melancholy *andante* of Bach's first viola da gamba sonata that accompanies the penultimate sequence, and the song that accompanies the end credits, with its refrain, "Hold me like a lover should/Although tomorrow don't look so good," and its celebration of "living light": there are simply too many of those mundane obstacles, too many highly unromantic practical questions (about money, work, travel, distance, where to live . . .) that seem trivial "before sunrise" but will begin to loom very large after it, as time passes. (So far I have found only one dissenter, but a very intelligent one—Lori Spring, filmmaker, teacher of screenwriting, and member of the original *CineAction* collective, who told me that she never had the least doubt that the date would be kept.) That the six-months date inevitably evokes *An Affair to Remember* doesn't really help, beyond reminding us that "happy endings" are no longer as generically guaranteed as they used to be. But the verdict is always reached with great reluctance, testifying to the continuing pull, despite all the battering it has received, of the romantic ideal as a powerful and seductive component of our ideology of love and sexuality. I think this response—the "realistic" acknowledgment of uncertainty, precariousness, the transience of feelings, the recognition that *amor* doesn't always *vincit omnia*, qualified by a "romantic" yearning for commitment, stability, permanence—corresponds very closely to the film's overall tone or "feel," accounting for the resonance it has for contemporary audiences (with more confident marketing, it could have been a runaway "hit").

There is a third alternative: that one will and the other won't. My initial reaction was that, if that were the case, the one who did would be Jesse. I thought this might be the product of some lingering trace of sexist prejudice—the "fickleness" of women and all that—but its tenability was subsequently confirmed by one of my female students, who came up, quite unprompted, with the same conclusion and offered the same justification—that he is the more "romantic," she the more "realistic." And indeed, if such idle speculation has any interest, it resides in the possibility that it throws some light on the film's "personal" level, the level of individual character. I found myself commenting earlier on Ethan Hawke's *gestures* and Julie Delpy's *expressions*. Obviously, the distinction isn't absolute; but Jesse habitually acts things out, as if constantly anxious to convey what he means—or thinks he means, or wants to mean—he can't simply "be" sincere but must continually demonstrate his sincerity. Of the two characters he seems the more insecure, the more vulnerable, the less mature. Céline—more educated, more aware, more intellectual, though not necessarily more intelligent—is far more at ease with herself, more stable, hence less demonstrative. There is no absolute opposition: the more times one sees the film the more complex the characters appear, both revealing certain basic uncertainties, anxieties about life and death, and by the end of the film she has shown a vulnerability that corresponds to his. But the initial impression, though much less confident, lingers. The intensity with which she clings to him in their final embrace before she boards her train, the expression of near-desperation on her face which he can't see but we can, suggest both that initially she will be the one who suffers the more and that she already has no real hope of a future with him; her intellectual awareness will help her to cope. One imagines him, back in America, obsessively developing (and insulating himself within) a romantic fantasy which he half knows to be unrealistic, while she continues to meet people, look outside herself, form other relations. (On the other hand he has his buddies, not to mention his dog!) And if he is at the station on the appointed date, a part of him will even take a certain masochistic satisfaction in his disappointment; she, meanwhile, will be smiling quietly to herself at the memory of a magical night, with pleasure, tenderness, and a passing regret, and will wonder where he is and what has happened to him before going on with her own life.

I have changed my mind many times as to whether to include the above conjectures or cut them, partly because I am uncertain as to whether they have any critical validity, partly because every time I see the film I become less confident of their validity even as interpretation. If I finally decide to leave them, it will be because the very fact that I surrender to such temptations indicates something very specific and very important about the way the film works. It is characterized by a complete openness within a closed and perfect classical form (an unquestioned diegetic world, the unities preserved, the end symmetrically answering the beginning). The relationship shifts and fluctuates, every viewing revealing new aspects, further nuances, like turning a kaleidoscope, so the meaning shifts and fluctuates also. No two individuals will respond in quite the same way, or in the same different ways on a second, third, or fourth viewing. Ethan Hawke's reference to "group therapy" has implications far beyond the first stages of discussion among filmmakers and actors; it extends to the audience and involves each individual spectator in a complex dialogue: Do you feel this, do you agree with that, how exactly does this affect *you*, your attitude to life, your ideas about relationships, the relationship you are in, the relationship you want; or do you really want a relationship at all? The questions the film raises are never answered, the uncertainties it expresses are never closed off. But in any case, the tug of the longing for permanence is so powerful that one would love to see a sequel (*Céline and Jesse Go Boating*, perhaps) in which they *did* keep the appointment, returned together to . . . France? America? . . . and tried to work out ways in which "commitment" is still feasible.

However, the question of "Will they or won't they?" may be a simple (and sentimental) evasion of the real question posed by the film's ending, which is far more radical and disturbing: Would it be better if they did or if they didn't?

*Postscript:* Richard Linklater told me, in a letter responding to this essay, that neither he nor the two actors ever doubted that the date would be kept, and they have even met to discuss the possibility of a sequel, "Six Months Later . . ." But "Never trust the artist(s)—trust the tale"!

## Points of Reference

Through its intimate and detailed treatment of its central couple, the film explores the possibility of "meaningful" or "successful" relationships today (in the aftermath of 1960s/1970s feminism, with its profound effect on male-female relations which the 1980s/1990s backlash has been unable to eradicate): a possibility at once longed for and called into question. The film provides three reference points or touchstones, constructing a backdrop against which the problematic of contemporary relating can stand illuminated. One is dramatized within the fiction, the other two are extradiegetic.

*The quarreling German couple on the train.* I take it that, like Céline and Jesse, we are not expected to understand what the argument is about (money is mentioned), but we get the impression that the mutual and bitter animosity is habitual, perhaps that it is one of those petty squabbles that often substitute for discussions of the *real* marital tensions that cannot be spoken. The couple are directly linked to Céline and Jesse, as the fight is inadvertently responsible for their first meeting: Céline changes her seat to get further away from their noise (she is trying to read), taking a seat across the aisle from Jesse; she and Jesse first make eye contact as the couple stride angrily past them down the aisle, and exchange deprecating smiles to acknowledge their shared awareness; they first make verbal contact when he asks her if she "has any idea what they were arguing about"; and their relationship may be said properly to begin with Céline's "Have you heard that as couples get older, they lose their ability to hear each other?." We are also shown, in a brief single shot, an elderly couple, silent, who perhaps have reached a stage of resignation and stagnation beyond bitchy arguments and who might be taken as representing what the fighting couple will become if they remain together. This is the immediate context within which the beginning at a new attempt of relating is placed—a marvelously succinct and unobtrusive statement of the film's thematic starting point.

*Dido and Aeneas, Lisa and Stefan.* The overture to Purcell's mini-opera *Dido and Aeneas* accompanies the opening credits, the tragedy-laden introduction over the white-on-black main titles, the *allegro* neatly synchronized with the first images, shot from the rapidly moving train, its final chord coinciding with the appearance of the director's credit. And, for any film-lover in the audience, the Viennese setting, the visit to the Prater, the complex examination (however different in spirit and conclusion) of romantic love, cannot fail to evoke *Letter from an Unknown Woman*. Both these reference points view romantic love as variously doomed and tragic, and in both the woman is at once the emotional center/identification figure and the prime sufferer, but there the parallel ends: the Queen of Carthage, abandoned by Aeneas, dying apparently of a broken heart (though possibly, following tradition and anticipating Berlioz, she commits suicide, the stage direction offering only the sparse and enigmatic *"Dies"*); the woman who has grown up, starved of power and the experience of beauty, in a petit bourgeois milieu in late nineteenth-century Vienna, and wastes her life in selfless (or selfish?) commitment to the potentially great concert pianist whose life is wasted already, in the impossible quest for vicarious fulfillment. These were surely intended (and if they weren't they should have been) as indicators of past attitudes to romantic love, and as such they cover, altogether, a remarkable time span: Virgil, Troy, Carthage, and "Italy" (to found which is Aeneas's divinely ordained destiny and his reason or pretext for abandoning Dido); Purcell's late seventeenth-century England; "Vienna, about 1900"; Hollywood, about 1947; and Vienna, 1995. (This is the first time a Linklater movie has evoked a past more distant than that of his "horror" film *Dazed and Confused*, and these are not the only references to it. There is the pervasive presence of Vienna, its architecture, its history; Céline's mini-lecture on Seurat ["I love the way the people seem to

Arrival in Vienna: Céline (Julie Delpy) and Jesse (Ethan Hawke).

be dissolving into the background," a description that might apply, less literally, to *Before Sunrise*, with its consistent concern with time and place and its repeated reminders of other human lives being lived—the actors, the fortune-teller, the poet, the people in the restaurant]; and the film's most purely magical moment where the couple, at dawn, on their way for Céline to catch her train and, they believe, about to say their last farewell, become suddenly aware of the sound of a harpsichord emerging from a basement apartment, where a very early riser is playing Bach's "Goldberg Variations.")

It is these reference points that imply the question I raised, implying (one might say) a signpost to an unknown destination. If a relationship must lead either to the tragic waste and desolation offered by past concepts of romantic love or to the stagnation and bitterness into which so many contemporary marriages seem to degenerate, would it not be better if Jesse and Céline were left at least with indelible memories of one magical night? The film's challenge is to define the unknown destination: if we *want* them to form a relationship (as surely we do), then it must be of a quite different order from anything offered by the familiar models. This is surely why the outcome becomes so important to us—not although but *because* it is so concretely realized and particularized (and certainly because the film convinces us so thoroughly of its potential value) it raises very acutely and precisely the fundamental questions for every spectator today: how *do* we relate? how *should* we relate? how *might* we relate?

In this context, comparison with *Letter from an Unknown Woman* seems especially suggestive, the films' extreme stylistic differences corresponding to an equally extreme difference in the depiction of romantic love. Both directors are obviously fond of long takes, but of a diametrically opposed nature: Ophuls' long-takes-with-camera-movement are meticulously choreographed trajectories guiding the characters from *here* to *here*, suggesting some form of predestination or entrapment (whether we interpret it in metaphysical or social terms seems a matter of personal bias, as both can find support within the film). Linklater's long takes—typically with a static camera, or with movement that is clearly determined by the movement of the actors rather than vice versa—leave the actors free, permitting spontaneity. That romantic love in Ophuls is viewed as inevitably tragic is always traceable to the subordinate position of women (with whom he plainly identifies) in patriarchal culture; in *Letter*, romantic fantasy is Lisa's only escape route from the ignominy and constriction of her social position. The lovers of *Before Sunrise*, on the contrary, meet and negotiate on a level of equality: it is difficult to see that Jesse enjoys privileges that are closed to Céline.

That the film, however one reads the ending, always seems so inspirational and life-giving is surely because, within a cultural situation that often seems incorrigibly and fathomlessly discouraging, it reminds us that there *have* been advances, and important ones, however minor they may appear amid the current right-wing devastation.

*Postscript:* In the letter referred to above, Linklater told me that he showed *Letter from an Unknown Woman* (along with Minnelli's *The Clock*) to Ethan Hawke and Julie Delpy a fortnight before shooting began; they found both films "inspirational."

## A Note on the Metaphysical Level

It may at first seem paradoxical (but is in fact absolutely logical) that a film so committed to life should be so pervaded by references to death. Death is, after all, the supreme test of one's sense of meaning. The couple's intimacy begins to blossom under death's shadow, when (in the lounge car of the train) Jesse describes his childhood experience of seeing his great-grandmother, just deceased, in the rainbow formed in the spray of a garden sprinkler, concludes by deciding that "death is just as ambiguous as everything else," and Céline confides that she is afraid of death twenty-four hours of every day.

Throughout the film, references to death counterpoint the continuous awareness of the passing of time (the few hours before they have to separate, the past centuries the film evokes). Jesse's sudden recognition, at dawn, that they are "back in real time" is immediately juxtaposed with their awareness of the sound of the harpsichord, and shortly followed by his imitation of Dylan Thomas's recording of an Auden poem about the impossibility of evading the passing of time, which leads in turn to their abrupt and frantic decision to meet again, just as Céline's train is about to leave. These intimations of mortality confer upon the relationship—however it is resolved—its beauty and importance.

## Identification

Like "style," *identification* is a necessary word whose usefulness diminishes in direct ratio to the rigidity of its definition; when it is reduced to counting POV shots (or simply to "the male gaze") the usefulness is somewhere around point zero. I have tried to address at some length the complex possibilities of identification (degrees of sympathy, "split" identification, conflicts of identification at different levels simultaneously, etc.) in the Ingrid Bergman chapter of *Hitchcock's Films Revisited*, and shall not repeat the full argument here (it has not, so far as I know, been refuted, just ignored, as is usually the case with arguments the current critical hegemony finds inconvenient). It will suffice to say that I use the term to cover the entire spectrum, from our sharing the experience of the entire action with a single character (who would have to be the audience's magnet of sympathy and present in every scene, a possibility that remains in the realm of the hypothetical), to the flickering and fleeting play of sympathetic attraction shifting from character to character. With the former extreme one thinks of Hitchcock, but in his films such "total" identification is invariably either brutally shattered or subtly undermined—by the abrupt demise of our identification figure (*Psycho*), by his sudden withdrawal from a crucial scene that reveals what he doesn't yet know (*Vertigo*), or by the systematic erosion of confidence in the acceptability of his behaviour (*Rear Window*). The latter extreme is also uncommon, but Renoir is its most obvious practitioner in, for example, *La Grande Illusion* and *Rules of the Game* (*La Régle du Jeu*).*

From first scene to last, *Before Sunrise* systematically and rigorously resists encouraging identification with one character above or against the other (and it's difficult to think of any other film that achieves quite this feat). Do men automatically identify with the male, women with the female? I doubt it, although our gender may of course entail a certain bias which the film goes out of its way to undermine: *some* men, *some* women, perhaps, but only those so fanatically devoted to the rights of their own sex that they are insensitive to the film's "style," the structure of its shots and its scenario, the marvelously achieved equality of its two central performances.

## Watching and Listening

When we talk casually of "reading" a film, most of us usually mean reading between the lines or below the surface, in order to extricate and explicate its "meaning," or at least its thematic complex. One does this, of course, with *Before Sunrise*, but the film demands more, a "reading" in a more literal sense:

---

*There may be a direct connection between Renoir and Linklater—there is certainly common ground, in the emotional generosity, the range of sympathy, the attitude that manages the difficult feat of being critical without being judgmental. I think particularly of *Slacker*: Renoir once said that the film he's always wanted to make but could never set up was one in which we would follow one set of characters for a little while, then others would walk by or appear in the background and we would leave the first set and follow the newcomers, who would shortly give way to yet others, and so on throughout the film. *Slacker* may be Linklater's realization (though very much on his own terms) of the film Renoir never made.

*Postscript:* Linklater has since confirmed that Renoir is among his favorite filmmakers, though he was not aware of the particular project cited here.

we must *watch* and *listen* simultaneously, with the most careful attention to every gesture, expression, and word, because "meaning," here, refuses reduction to "theme."

I have to confess, at this point, to a failure. Even on first viewing I told myself that I would "one day" analyze in detail the scene in the listening booth of the record store, in which nothing happens except that Ethan Hawke and Julie Delpy either do or don't look at each other, their eyes never quite meeting. After a dozen viewings I abandoned the project. I suppose one might try an elaborate system of charts and timings, annotating "direction of the gaze," when and how long each looks (or doesn't) . . . which would demonstrate nothing of the least importance. With no camera movement, no editing, no movement within the frame except for the slight movements of the actors' heads, nothing on the soundtrack but a not-very-distinguished song that may vaguely suggest what is going on in the characters' minds and seems sometimes to motivate their "looks" ("Though I'm not impossible to touch/I have never wanted you so much/Come here"), the shot seems to me a model of "pure cinema" in ways Hitchcock never dreamed of (not merely "photographs of people talking," but photographs of them *not* talking), precisely because it completely resists analysis, defies verbal description. All one can say is that it is the cinema's most perfect

*Before Sunrise:* the streetcar.

depiction, in just over one minute of "real" time, at once concrete and intangible, of two people beginning to realize that they are falling in love.

I shall content myself, then, with two scenes that, without at all lacking the essentials of "pure cinema," or the obligation of the spectator to watch and listen, offer themselves for some kind of clumsy verbalizing: the "Question and Answer" game on the streetcar, the imaginary telephone conversations in the restaurant. The scenes "answer" each other (within this meticulously structured film which manages to look as if "they made it up as they went along") in a complex pattern of similarity and difference. Both are games, played by the two characters as a means toward mutual understanding through play, occurring at different stages in the relationship's development—the first essentially a mapping-out of differences, the second a means of discovering each other's feelings and confessing their own, implicitly with a view to a possible future ("Are you going to see him again?"/"I don't know. We haven't talked about that yet"—followed by a silence). Jesse initiates, and partly controls, the first game, Céline the second. And the scenes are paired formally by a strict stylistic opposition: the film's longest single take (just over five minutes) answered by its most heavily edited sequence (forty-three shots in just over five minutes).

*Q&A.* The interplay of gesture and expression throughout the long uninterrupted two-shot is so dense and intricate that one really needs to watch it three times (as one can do without difficulty on the laserdisc as it is contained within a single "chapter"): once watching Hawke, a second time watching Delpy, a third time trying to "see" them both together. Otherwise, one's eyes dart constantly from one side of the frame to the other and one misses many of the nuances.

Gesture and expression are of course meaningless unless one is listening simultaneously and with equal attention to the dialogue, which defines certain important differences that in turn contribute to defining "this little space in between." Céline describes her "first sexual feelings" in terms of a romantic crush on a famous swimmer she actually met, Jesse his (after evading her real question, "Have you ever been in love?"—we learn later that he came to Europe to meet a woman and they have just broken up) in relation to "Miss July, 1978," in *Playboy*. The answers to, respectively, Jesse's "What pisses you off?" and Céline's "What's *your* problem?" are even more revealing. Her answers show a wide-ranging and enquiring (if embryonic) awareness of practical realities: social ("I hate being told by strange men in the street to smile, to make them feel better about their boring lives"); political (a war going on "300 kilometers from here" and "nobody knows what to do or gives a shit"); sociopolitical (the media are "trying to control minds" and

". . . it's very subtle but it's a new form of fascism really"); sexual-political ("I hate being told, especially in America, 'Oh, you're so French, you're so cute,' each time I wear black, or lose my temper, or say anything about anything"). His answer, on the other hand, while it also reveals an enquiring, thinking mind, is more abstract, philosophical-metaphysical: he speaks of reincarnation and eternal souls, and the ensuing conundrum of the increase in world population: "Fifty thousand years ago not even one million, ten thousand years ago two million. Now five to six billion. Where do the souls all come from—a 5,000-to-one split. So is this why we're so scattered, so specialized?" (While marginally more rational—if one accepts its premise—this recalls Linklater's own hilarious monologue in the taxi at the beginning of *Slacker*.)

*The imaginary phone calls.* The forty-three-shot sequence perfectly exemplifies that fundamental principle of Western (and other?) art, almost (but not quite) perfect symmetry. It is introduced, punctuated around the midpoint, and closed, by three identical two-shots of the couple opposite each other at the restaurant table; Céline's imaginary call has twenty-eight shots, filmed in strict shot/reverse-shot form; Jesse's has twenty-two, filmed similarly. To clarify:

The early hours of the morning.

Toward dawn.

| | |
|---|---|
| Shot 1: | Two-shot (the couple) |
| Shots 2–29: | Shot/reverse-shot (Céline's call) |
| Shot 30: | Two-shot (the couple) |
| Shots 31–42: | Shot/reverse-shot (Jesse's call) |
| Shot 43: | Two-shot (the couple) |

The restaurant scene follows the scene in the street at night that concludes with Céline's speech quoted at the head of this essay, the last words provoking a lengthy silence and a cut to long shot as they continue sitting on the bench; it is introduced (before the imaginary phone calls) by a series of shots of other customers: a mixed group at one table, two men playing cards, two bearded men conversing, a woman alone reading a book, an American couple (the man grumbling about the service), two men and one woman, laughing at a joke . . . other lives, other relationships, other problems. Céline's speech, and the other customers, create a context (both of lives and of ideas) for the couple's exploration (through the game) of each other's feelings and expectations, testing the possibility of a continuing relationship. I feel disinclined to dissect this wonderful sequence in detail. I would describe it as one of the film's high points, were it not for the fact that

Almost departure time.

it doesn't have any low ones. The use of play as a medium for revealing truths and emotions that one can't quite dare speak "seriously" is touching in itself, in its implications of vulnerability, the desire to speak out inhibited by the fear of being hurt, the suspension at the end—Jesse's question (in the role of Céline's confidante) "Are you going to see him again?" remains unanswered—anticipating the similar suspension in which the spectator is left at the end of the film.

## Final

Perhaps the film's moment of greatest tenderness occurs *after* the lovers have separated: the sequence of shots (accompanied on the soundtrack by Yo-Yo Ma playing Bach) re-viewing the places they visited as the new day begins, some with the first stirrings of activity, some still deserted, an old woman glancing disapprovingly at the empty wine bottle they discarded in the park where they made love. The sequence evokes the ending of Antonioni's *L'Eclisse* (*The Eclipse*), but without its sense of desolation and finality; rather, the feeling is of sadness and happiness inextricably intermingled, regret for the separation and the uncertainty but a deep satisfaction in the degree of mutual understanding and intimacy two human beings have achieved in a few hours, how nearly successful the attempt to bridge "this little space in between." And, as Céline says, the "answer," the "magic," must be in the attempt. The same might be said of the critic's relationship to the films she/he loves.

# CHAPTER 16

# Finale: "The Doom Generation"

The end answers the beginning: one of the fundamental principles of classical narrative. So be it, then, with a work of criticism dedicated to its defense, and to the celebration of its radical potential. *The Doom Generation* (Gregg Araki, 1995) might have been made to supply me with a fitting conclusion; it might also have been made after a reading of *Life Against Death*, the book by Norman O. Brown cited in my introduction. No film more precisely captures my own sense of where we are and where we are going. (*Nowhere*, 1997, the completion of his "teen trilogy" begun in 1993 with *Totally F***ed Up*, has proved, despite its suggestive title, a disappointment.) But the "nowhere" of *The Doom Generation* is given another, explicit, definition: as the sign with which the film opens says, "Welcome to Hell." Paradoxically, however, it is a hell in the midst of which his marvelously healthy and resilient young characters can still search for, and almost find, the "life" that opposes "death."

It is perhaps surprising, superficially, that I would feel so strong an identification with Araki's film and with its characters. I am at least forty-five years older than they are, and my aesthetic ideal might be best represented by the music of Mozart. But my sympathies are very much with today's young people, habitually separated off from "mature" humans (i.e., those apparently bent upon bringing about the end of our civilization, and perhaps of life on this planet) by the condescending term "kids." The most interesting among our young men and women are those who, in various ways, set up varying degrees of resistance to their incorporation into the contemporary norms of capitalist culture, the world of alienated labor and the nuclear family; they seem to *know*, instinctively, the cost of such incorporation. Their situation is appalling, and every allowance should be made for their antisocial behavior,

Flight to nowhere: Xavier Red (Johnathon Schaech), Amy Blue (Rose McGowan), and Jordan White (James Duval).

even though it can only prove, in the long run, both destructive and self-destructive.

Since Western culture has, in its current state of "progress," found ways, through the all-pervasive power of its media, effectively to bar young people from any hope of radical social change, or even of the least flicker of an authentic political idealism from any of the parties available to vote for, where are they supposed to go, what *constructive* alternatives are open to them, what are they supposed to *do*? Their own traditional answer (promoted and encouraged by the capitalist media, since it's far safer than any dangerous political ideas) has been "Sex, drugs, and rock 'n' roll." As Araki is explicitly and uncompromisingly anti-drugs (foregrounded in his recent films by actual printed slogans—here, DOWN WITH DOPE, UP WITH HOPE), he will never make a *Trainspotting*; and as he understands perfectly that rock 'n' roll by itself will not take you very far, the all-pervasive emphasis on sex in *The Doom Generation* is completely logical. Yet it is very different from the emphasis on sex in *Kids* (with which Araki himself has compared his work favorably, with complete justification). The two films have in common the awareness that, for today's disaffected and alienated young, the pursuit of sexual experience has become the dominant aim; but whereas Larry Clark's treatment of teen sex reduces it to the merely cynical, predatory, and self-serving, Araki's is passionate and positive, deeply romantic, seeing sex as a liberating force. Desire, thoroughly debased in *Kids*, is here cleansed, purged of all meanness, and reaffirmed. Clark's "kids" are treated as passive objects for his gaze, the gaze expressing both desire and repugnance; Araki identifies with *his* young people to the hilt, without ever glamorizing or idealizing them. He knows and they know that they are living near the endpoint of the decline of Western civilization, that they have no viable future and nowhere to go, but he loves them, believes in their impulses, and allows them authentically to find each other, while Clark's "kids" just meanly manipulate.

As I left the theater on the first day of the film's commercial run, a middle-aged couple were huffing and puffing their way out just ahead of me. "Films like that should never be shown outside of film school," the husband was proclaiming indignantly (and in tones clearly intended for the public at large), his wife dutifully and vigorously nodding in agreement. "That sort of thing is all the fault of Quentin Tarantino." Unable to restrain myself (given the extreme emotional state into which the film had thrown me), I informed him equally loudly that *(a)* Araki was already making movies before Tarantino began, and *(b)* Tarantino has shown himself obviously incapable of making a film as intelligent and beautiful. The man was either suitably chastened or merely taken aback, having assumed general agreement. The comparison, however, offers a useful starting point.

Presumably the film he had in mind was *Pulp Fiction*. *Reservoir Dogs* maintained a precarious promise of intelligence and can I think be defended, but since then Tarantino and *Pulp Fiction* have become more or less synonymous, thanks partly to its inherent smug smart-ass knowingness and partly to all the hype from our would-be-with-it reviewers. *Pulp Fiction* is an entirely spurious work, the product of a mind/sensibility that will probably now (thanks to the premature adulation) never transcend its adolescent immaturity, seeking at all points to involve the audience in its complacent sense of its own cleverness, its own emptiness and cynicism.* Cleverness—a cerebral activity governed by a concern with what is currently "hip"—must never be confused with intelligence.

Reviewers—mostly middle-aged and middle-class—have done their best to show their readers that they do not lag behind the "hipness" of *The Doom*

---

*Jackie Brown* can be seen as, at least, an attempt to break out of this impasse.

*Generation* either: of course, they know all about that. Understandably disturbed (no one is disturbed by *Pulp Fiction*), and needing a straw to grasp, they make supercilious remarks about the film's pervasive references to apocalypse, seeing these not as a passionate expression of desperation but as mere pretentiousness, or worse, clichés. Oh yes, the tone suggests, with a yawn of mature boredom, *of course* we know our civilization is coming to an end, so why does this young upstart have to burden us with all that stuff all over again? The fact is, reviewers today can't recognize passion when it confronts them, and wouldn't like it if they did, interpreting it as an embarrassment that shouldn't be permitted: far better celebrate the safe hipness of Tarantino. Why, after all, *should* we listen to prophets of doom? Life is a cabaret, isn't it, at least if you're healthy, wealthy, middle-aged, white, and male.

Unlike *Pulp Fiction*, *The Doom Generation* is a powerfully political film, although it never insists upon this, its politics being fully enacted in the narrative. We are not told the year in which the action is set, so are free to choose: either a heightened, surreal vision of the present, or a time in the near future when the already precipitous degeneration of the culture has progressed but one stage further—the year 2000 would be appropriate. Apocalypse is expressed not only in the "Welcome to Hell" of the opening or in the running gag of every storekeeper charging "6.66." It is there in the fleeting landscapes through which the characters pass: the clouds of gray smoke, the graveyard of wrecked cars—the pollution and detritus of capitalism. The film's culmination (to which I shall return) represents one of the most radical political statements in American cinema.

Probably what most upset the gentleman in the theater was the film's extreme and pervasive violence, the last few minutes being, admittedly, very difficult to sit through. In my view, the acceptability or otherwise of cinematic depictions of violence is dependent entirely upon the director's intelligence, his/her control over effect and meaning, the definition of the spectator's attitude to what is shown. The treatment of violence in *The Doom Generation* might justly be termed virtuosic: within a single film, Araki defines three distinct attitudes by means of three distinct, precisely controlled effects—comic, pathetic, horrific.

The comic violence is associated exclusively with the actions of Xavier (Johnathon Schaech), invariably performed in defense of the two innocent and nonviolent people to whom he has attached himself, against murderous aggressors: the Korean storeowner who clearly intends his sign "Shoplifters Will Be Executed" to be understood literally; the various people (male and female) who attempt to claim Amy (Rose McGowan) as their long-lost lover whom they will kill if they can't possess her. The pathetic violence has only a single instance, its effect being to heighten our sense of the three young protagonists' essential goodness—the incident in which Amy accidentally runs over a dog, which then has to be put out of its pain by Xavier, a moment of genuine grief at the death of a completely innocent and harmless victim, the three pausing in their wild flight to nowhere to bury it and stand in ceremonial silence over its grave. The horrific violence is reserved for the film's climactic bloodbath.

The absurdist treatment of possessiveness—the two men and one woman (in the bar/pool hall the dominant sign of which is OBEY) who lay exclusive claim to Amy and would rather have her dead than not at all—is central to the film's sexual politics. Araki has insisted (quite correctly—this is an artist who knows what he's doing) that the film is not nihilistic. Nihilism means belief in nothing: the truly nihilistic films (prominent today among many others) are *Blue Velvet* and *Pulp Fiction*. Nihilism is what capitalism has brought us to, and a stand against it is becoming increasingly difficult, but Araki (the true rebel, unlike Lynch and Tarantino, whose alleged "audacities" merely reinforce contemporary alienation) is exempt from it. *The Doom Generation* actually achieves, immediately before the climactic bloodbath, the realization of a utopian sexuality: the three characters, having progressively cast off all the bourgeois constraints and inhibitions (including, importantly, squeamishness about bodily functions), not only have by the film's end all fallen in love with each other but are able to accept it, without jealousy or possessiveness. As Xavier tells Amy earlier, "Guilt is for old, married, people." The absurd and essentially obsolete patriarchal notion that fidelity can or should be measured in terms of sex finally disintegrates. In the course of the film the three learn to become progressively in touch with their own and each other's bodies, with Xavier always the necessary initiator.

At the outset Amy is the lover of the timid, childlike, and virginal Jordan (James Duval). Subsequently, after pissing in front of her as she bathes, Jordan is able to overcome his inhibitions and make love with her in the bathtub, while Xavier (who is already attracted to both) masturbates outside the door. Later Xavier has sex with Amy, first in the bed next to the sleeping Jordan, completing the act in the car outside. To Amy's horror, Xavier casually reveals to Jordan what has happened, and Jordan accepts it. Then the earlier scene is reversed: Xavier and Amy make love while Jordan masturbates outside the motel window, watching them. In the final sequences, in the vast barn with its apparently miraculous double mattress and covers, after the tossing of a coin, Xavier and Amy make love and Xavier asks her to stick her finger up his asshole; she tells him it's disgusting then does as he asks, afterwards licking her finger. Then she and Jordan make love; to his horror, she sticks her finger up *his* asshole, and he finds he enjoys it. The sequence culminates in the three in the bed together, their bodies entangled, sharing each other, though Jordan has yet to accept his attraction to Xavier.

This progression through the film irresistibly evokes Norman O. Brown and his thesis that true liberation must involve the "resurrection of the body," the rediscovery of what Freud (with his own inimitable perversity) grotesquely termed "polymorphous perversity": the delight of the presocialized, uncorrupted infant in every facet of his/her own body and its functions. (How the natural condition of the infant can be described as "perverse" is not clear.) To be complete, "polymorphous perversity" must necessarily incorporate another fundamental Freudian concept—constitutional bisexuality.

The culminating bloodbath (the most terrifying I have ever seen in a fiction film, perhaps deriving from, but outdoing, the murder at the end of *Looking for Mr. Goodbar*) is precipitated directly by the moment when Amy goes outside to relieve herself and Jordan begins to respond to Xavier's desire for him: the image of the not-to-be-tolerated. Xavier is the film's most remarkable, fascinating, and challenging character (has anyone ever expressed erotic desire on screen more irresistibly than Johnathon Schaech?). Amy calls him, at one point, a "support system for a cock," and at another a

Xavier's omnisexual desire arouses Jordan's anxiety.

"demon from hell." His sexual insatiability is stressed repeatedly (when he claims that he's "good for seven times a night," we believe him). He is omni-sexual, his attraction to Jordan as well as to Amy clear from the start; he also admits to having had sex with a golden retriever (but the dog was a "con-senting adult"); when he masturbates he licks his own cum off his hand and savors it. If he is primarily motivated by his own drives, he also saves the lives of Jordan and Amy on three occasions. His final line, in the car as he and Amy drive away ("Have a Dorito?"), is not, I think, to be taken as cynical: he is above all a survivor, the *only* character equipped for survival in the world the film presents, ready for any contingency, able to take in stride even the horrific death of the man for whom he showed so much tenderness. He is, above all, the great liberator—if indeed a "demon," then one of the positive demons of William Blake's inverted Christian cosmology.

The bloodbath itself juxtaposes two images of "America." As a prelude to the castration and murder of Jordan, the gang of healthy all-American boys displays the American flag (immediately juxtaposed, as its necessary complement, with the swastika painted on the leader's chest) and plays the "Stars and Stripes Forever" ("Our favorite song . . . I pledge allegiance to the flag . . .") on a ghetto-blaster; these are presented as mere empty signifiers, drained long ago of all substance and meaning, relics of an always dubious patriotism that has lost whatever meaning it once had, reduced to a pretext for malicious and repressive violence, the mindless crushing out of any sense of new life, of the possible "life against death" toward which the film has moved. Against it is set Araki's America, exemplified by the essential purity of its three main characters: Xavier Red, Jordan White, Amy Blue—a possi-ble future the past is committed to stamping out. Jordan—the focal point of the film's "unholy triangle"—is murdered at the exact moment to which the whole film logically moves, the moment when the triangle's full meaning and potential is about to be realized.

> I think that of the movies I've made it's the most subversive. At the same time it's another road movie about teenagers, it has this bisexual edge: two beautiful boys, and the girlfriend of one of the guys. Very violent and intense: I call it "Last Tango for Teenagers." What I would like to accomplish with it, if it works on the level I want, is that it will be a film on the film fes-tival circuit, but at the same time I'd like it to appeal in a schizophrenic way to Friday night shopping mall teenagers because the concept of being able to do that really fascinates me.
>
> —GREGG ARAKI (Interview in *CineAction 35*)

Araki's work is, in spirit and nature, authentically subversive. Yet whether a film is or is not *effectively* subversive depends very much on who is watching it. A film made for art-house audiences, or for the audiences of avant-garde movies, however bold and shocking, is unlikely to achieve genuine subversion: its intended audience is already "there," so who or what is being subverted? Araki is attempting something extremely difficult—to make authentically subversive movies that will reach today's youth audience.

It is to be hoped that *The Doom Generation* is currently reaching its intended audience—the contemporaries of Amy, Xavier, and Jordan—on video. It is sadly ironic that, theatrically, it appears to have been carefully kept from contaminating them, sealed away in art houses and festivals. At the end of a course on Hollywood, I screened it for a class of about ninety, mainly first-year, students. A few walked out at various points during the screening, but those who stayed greeted it with tremendous enthusiasm, and many chose it as the topic for their essays in the final exam. It might well have drawn crowds at a "mainstream" theater—the same crowds of teenagers who have made of *Trainspotting* (with its ambiguous treatment of heroin addiction but very few ambiguities about gender and sexuality) a major "cult" success. Certainly *The Doom Generation* could be considered "dangerous": in the famous words of D. H. Lawrence such work "leads the sympathetic consciousness into new places, and away in recoil from things gone dead," always a grave danger in itself, and it encourages a sense of desperation. But desperation breeds anger, and anger, with only a little help, can be directed toward radical change.

# Index of Names and Titles

Note: Film titles are in italics; book, play, opera, magazine and article titles are in quotation marks, names in normal print; actors are indexed only when they are discussed *as actors*, not when they are merely listed as appearing in a given film.